Application of Gaming in New Media Marketing

Pratika Mishra
Presidency University Bangalore, India

Swati Oberoi Dham
New Delhi Institute of Management, India

A volume in the Advances in Marketing, Customer Relationship Management, and E-Services (AMCRMES) Book Series

IGI Global
DISSEMINATOR OF KNOWLEDGE

Published in the United States of America by
IGI Global
Business Science Reference (an imprint of IGI Global)
701 E. Chocolate Avenue
Hershey PA, USA 17033
Tel: 717-533-8845
Fax: 717-533-8661
E-mail: cust@igi-global.com
Web site: http://www.igi-global.com

Library of Congress Cataloging-in-Publication Data

Names: Mishra, Pratika, 1981- editor. | Dham, Swati Oberoi, 1983- editor.
Title: Application of gaming in new media marketing / Pratika Mishra and Swati Oberoi Dham, editors.
Description: Hershey, PA : Business Science Reference, [2019]
Identifiers: LCCN 2017061798| ISBN 9781522560647 (hardcover) | ISBN 9781522560654 (ebook)
Subjects: LCSH: Internet marketing. | Internet games.
Classification: LCC HF5415.1265 .A67 2019 | DDC 658.8/72015193--dc23 LC record available at https://lccn.loc.gov/2017061798

This book is published in the IGI Global book series Advances in Marketing, Customer Relationship Management, and E-Services (AMCRMES) (ISSN: 2327-5502; eISSN: 2327-5529)

British Cataloguing in Publication Data
A Cataloguing in Publication record for this book is available from the British Library.

Advances in Marketing, Customer Relationship Management, and E-Services (AMCRMES) Book Series

ISSN:2327-5502
EISSN:2327-5529

Editor-in-Chief: Eldon Y. Li, National Chengchi University, Taiwan & California Polytechnic State University, USA

MISSION

Business processes, services, and communications are important factors in the management of good customer relationship, which is the foundation of any well organized business. Technology continues to play a vital role in the organization and automation of business processes for marketing, sales, and customer service. These features aid in the attraction of new clients and maintaining existing relationships.

The Advances in Marketing, Customer Relationship Management, and E-Services (AMCRMES) Book Series

addresses success factors for customer relationship management, marketing, and electronic services and its performance outcomes. This collection of reference source covers aspects of consumer behavior and marketing business strategies aiming towards researchers, scholars, and practitioners in the fields of marketing management.

COVERAGE

- Cases on CRM Implementation
- CRM and customer trust
- Web Mining and Marketing
- Relationship marketing
- CRM strategies
- Online Community Management and Behavior
- Telemarketing
- Customer Retention
- E-Service Innovation
- B2B marketing

IGI Global is currently accepting manuscripts for publication within this series. To submit a proposal for a volume in this series, please contact our Acquisition Editors at Acquisitions@igi-global.com or visit: http://www.igi-global.com/publish/.

The Advances in Marketing, Customer Relationship Management, and E-Services (AMCRMES) Book Series (ISSN 2327-5502) is published by IGI Global, 701 E. Chocolate Avenue, Hershey, PA 17033-1240, USA, www.igi-global.com. This series is composed of titles available for purchase individually; each title is edited to be contextually exclusive from any other title within the series. For pricing and ordering information please visit http://www.igi-global.com/book-series/advances-marketing-customer-relationship-management/37150. Postmaster: Send all address changes to above address.

Titles in this Series

For a list of additional titles in this series, please visit:
https://www.igi-global.com/book-series/advances-marketing-customer-relationship-management/37150

Marketing Techniques for Financial Inclusion and Development
Dhiraj Jain (Symbiosis International University (Deemed), India) and Adya Sharma (Symbiosis International University (Deemed), India)
Business Science Reference • ©2018 • 311pp • H/C (ISBN: 9781522540359) • US $215.00

Diverse Methods in Customer Relationship Marketing and Management
In Lee (Western Illinois University, USA)
Business Science Reference • ©2018 • 333pp • H/C (ISBN: 9781522556190) • US $215.00

Handbook of Research on Social Marketing and Its Influence on Animal Origin Food ...
Diana Bogueva (Curtin University, Australia) Dora Marinova (Curtin University, Australia) and Talia Raphaely (Curtin University, Australia)
Business Science Reference • ©2018 • 453pp • H/C (ISBN: 9781522547570) • US $325.00

Analyzing Attachment and Consumers' Emotions Emerging Research and Opportunities
Giuseppe Pedeliento (University of Bergamo, Italy)
Business Science Reference • ©2018 • 308pp • H/C (ISBN: 9781522549840) • US $185.00

Building Brand Identity in the Age of Social Media Emerging Research and Opportunities
Amir Ekhlassi (University of Tehran, Iran) Mahdi Niknejhad Moghadam (Sharif University of Technology, Iran) and Amir Mohammad Adibi (University of Tehran, Iran)
Business Science Reference • ©2018 • 189pp • H/C (ISBN: 9781522551430) • US $145.00

Neuromarketing and Big Data Analytics for Strategic Consumer Engagement Emerging ...
Joana Coutinho de Sousa (Unlimited-Hashtag, Portugal)
Business Science Reference • ©2018 • 200pp • H/C (ISBN: 9781522548348) • US $165.00

Holistic Approaches to Brand Culture and Communication Across Industries
Sabyasachi Dasgupta (O.P. Jindal Global University, India) Santosh Kumar Biswal (Symbiosis International University, India) and M. Anil Ramesh (Siva Sivani Institute of Management, India)
Business Science Reference • ©2018 • 281pp • H/C (ISBN: 9781522531500) • US $225.00

For an entire list of titles in this series, please visit:
https://www.igi-global.com/book-series/advances-marketing-customer-relationship-management/37150

IGI Global
DISSEMINATOR OF KNOWLEDGE

701 East Chocolate Avenue, Hershey, PA 17033, USA
Tel: 717-533-8845 x100 • Fax: 717-533-8661
E-Mail: cust@igi-global.com • www.igi-global.com

List of Reviewers

Atul Kumar Agarwal, *Ansal University, India*
Arabinda Bhandari, *Presidency University Bangalore, India*
Jitender Bhandari, *Asia Pacific Institute of Management, India*
Tanusree Chakraborty, *Presidency University Bangalore, India*
Vijay Kumar Chaurasiya, *Indian Institute of Information Technology Allahabad, India*
D. P. Goyal, *Management Development Institute Gurugram, India*
Subodh Kesarwani, *Indira Gandhi National Open University, India*
Surendra Prasad Mishra, *Dr. Ram Manohar Lohia Institute of Medical Sciences, India*
N. K. Painuly, *King's George Medical University, India*
Pramod Pathak, *Indian Institute of Technology (ISM) Dhanbad, India*
K. Rajeshwari, *Great Lakes Institute of Management, India*
Aparna Sethi, *Pace Career Academy, India*
Gajendra Sharma, *New Delhi Institute of Management, India*
Savita Sharma, *Ansal University, India*
Saumya Singh, *Indian Institute of Technology (ISM) Dhanbad, India*
Sumant Tewari, *Babu Banarasi Das University, India*

Table of Contents

Detailed Table of Contents

The ever-changing marketing landscape has been upfront in adapting to innovations. People are getting attuned to tons of advancements concerning new media technologies over the past decade. For example, we now have different apps that are more mobile-friendly than inclined towards desktops. Such technological advancements have led to huge information generation every second. Today, information is best conceived when it is in form of attractive content. Content in this era majorly constitutes of audio-visual effects, also there is a gamut of interesting applications which has taken media to an inexplicable height. In such a dynamic environment, it is important to channelize one's efforts and resources towards profitable marketing. This is a period of disruption and whoever makes that first move to adopt it will have a greater hold on its customer base. The chapter guides the reader through the emerging new media marketing tools that can bring in the inevitable disruption.

This chapter will expound on the concept of gamification and its adoption by various brands. It will be focusing on advergaming, which is one of the very famous applications of gamification. The chapter will elucidate the various launch details of advergaming applications by various firms and brand websites including online games, social network sites, and interactive digital television. It will also discuss the techniques underlying gamification, which include game mechanics and game dynamics, which will also reveal the impact of advergaming on consumer engagement and decision making to buy a product or not and also the benefits to the brand site. The chapter will also explain the techniques and strategies of advergaming used by various product websites nationally and internationally and their effect on consumers and the product or brand websites.

Advergames bring newness and engage better with customers. However, there is debate among marketers and communication experts as to how this tool could be exploited in the field of advertising and positioning of brands to the best of their advantage. The chapter thus aims to present arresting qualities of advergames under the rubric of rhetoric and claims that a deeper and meaningful understanding of multimodal rhetoric is needed to design and create these games. Further, to understand the working of these games and how they engage with the users, two advergames have been analyzed using multimodal analysis method, and a multimodal rhetorical framework (MRF) has been proposed for the perusal of marketers and communication experts to use as per their need and discretion.

Online gaming has become a popular form of entertainment which has shifted children's playgrounds to computers, laptops, mobiles, tablets, etc. Children spend their time surfing, playing, and downloading games from the internet. Advergaming is one of the latest digital advertising techniques used by marketers to interact with the children for longer hours by embedding the brand messages in the game action. Advergaming is a blend of fun and promotion to capture the attention of children towards the advertising message associated with the branded product. The objective of this chapter is to determine how children pay attention and absorb the message given by the companies by considering hierarchy of effects models such as AIDA model and DAGMAR model. The purpose of this work as a whole is to bring more understanding of this innovative technique of promoting by detailing the elements, characteristics, advantages, and disadvantages of advergames to achieve communication goals.

As the present consumer market is no longer bound to traditional forms of advertising, it has led to several advancements including marketing through online platforms like digital and social media. One such advertising format that appeals most to the youth is advergames. The younger generation spends lot of time on the internet, giving an opportunity to the marketers to make the best use of this medium. Advergames, which consist of online gaming and advertising, are considered a promising form of reaching the youth market. Therefore, this chapter attempts to deal with the concepts related to advergames and a small empirical study showing the impact of advergames on children. The results of the study showed that there existed a relationship between attitude towards advergames and several variables involved. The relationship was most significant between entertainment and attitude towards advergames. The study of demographic variables showed no significant impact of gender, but there was a significant correlation of age with the persuasion knowledge, escape, and attitude towards advergames.

Advergames are a very dynamic marketing tool for companies coupled with being interactive, fulfilled, networked, creating positive connection with consumers, provides pleasurable environment marked by two-way communication. Food advergames target children population who without knowing the persuasive content of the games engage in the play. The purpose of this chapter is to highlight the psychodynamics of food advergames, how advergames influences children's eating attitude and behavior, and also discusses about the health hazards that food advergames bring in with itself. Finally, the chapter throws light on the impact and concerns of food advergames on children's eating behavior.

Utilizing internet, particularly social networking websites, for marketing is called social media marketing. It comprises designing a well-structured content that consumers can share with each other to help a company broaden its customer base and increase its brand visibility. However different social media platforms have different target audiences, and therefore, in order to succeed, it is indispensable for marketers to have a thorough understanding of tools and techniques required to attract different clusters of customers.

Technological changes led to the rise of digital advertising, advertising using internet and other technologies. In India, digital advertising is in the nascent stage with most of the transactions taking place in cash. After demonetization, the surge in the digital advertising was seen. This chapter reviews articles, news reports, journals, and books, and discusses the aftermath of the process on retail and online shopping, how it paves the way for a new trend of digital marketing, and the implications of the same on online shopping and digital payments and implications on the rural consumer. The way we communicate has changed in the past 5 years. A few years back, people were skeptical to buy online, and we never thought we would buy groceries, furniture, cloths online, but now we book our shows, tickets, everything is online and in mobile.

Gamification is a tool used for brand awareness to attract new customers and to make the present customers more loyal towards the product by making them engaged in an enjoyable manner. It has become one of the prominent topics of interest for many academicians and marketing professionals because of the simple reason that it is considered to be the one of effective ways to promote various services and products for many brands and other companies. This chapter explores gamification in the Indian film industry.

Foreword

It is with great pleasure that I have been asked to review the edited volume on a topic that is one of my great passions, that of Advergames. What started in the 1990s as quirky CD ROM based one-off media experiments in non-linear electronic marketing has matured into a fundamental global force that persists at the intersection of two of the most important industries, those of interactive games and digital advertising.

The advergames industry has grown dramatically in the past two decades. In that time there have been several parallel transformations that have collectively contributed to the important rise in this form of sponsored consumer engagement. These include the advent of software development companies that learned to shed outdated modalities of advertisement in favor of bringing advergames to massive audiences, by harnessing advances in a host of digital technologies and new levels of creativity.

As the popularity of video games grew, a greater representation of brand companies and other key organizations were attracted to the more positive aspects of advergaming. Budgets for advergames development and seeding increased dramatically, with many top tier campaigns crossing into levels of funding previously reserved for more traditional advertising methods.

As the audience for video games expanded from a highly segmented, typically teen male participant demographic, into a broad spectrum that balanced gender and age groups far more evenly, the potential for company sponsorship of advergames followed suit.

This wonderful book takes each reader deep into the exciting world of advergaming by delving into the relevant key advances in technology and how the Internet, browser capabilities, bandwidth improvements, increases in processing power, and other macro changes have created an almost perfect delivery mechanism for advergames to take hold and flourish. It smartly focuses on the explosion in mobile technologies such as smart phones, and carefully demonstrates how these devices allow for even greater penetration of the advergaming phenomenon as a more competitive form of advertising.

Practitioners and researchers in academia will appreciate this book's inclusion of topics such as social media and how marketers navigate platforms like Facebook to better target and seed sponsored advergames by leveraging greater reach and personalization. It brilliantly covers industry specific advergames techniques and shares with the reader many of those differences.

Most important to me, the Editors Dr. Pratika Mishra and Dr. Swatti Dham, along with the support of their publisher IGI Publication, should be congratulated for sparing no effort to recognize that the global audience for which electric media advertising is intended is growing increasingly weary of being targeted with intrusive and disruptive forms. Their wonderful book exemplifies the collective case for the greater adoption of advergames as a more consumer friendly vehicle, one that harnesses the thoughtfulness of invitation to replace interruption, and in doing so creates a more balanced exchange of values between advertisers and their intended audiences.

Regards and best wishes,

Anthony M. Giallourakis
Advergames.com

Preface

Games have always fascinated and entertained the human mind. While it does bring out the giggles of child in a person, designing and implementing a game is no child's play. Superficially a game seems fascinating, but it is the most applied form of strategies and simulating the mind in decision making (Chikhani, 2015) and redirecting without being noticed. Gaming is a phenomenon which is characterized by a competitive spirit in the participant along with a very high level of engagement (Reeves & Read, 2009). Games are classified into various sub groups (Deterding, Dixon, Khaled, & Nacke, 2011) on the basis of the seriousness and involvement of the participant in the game. Gaming includes Toys, Playful Design, Serious Games and a gameful design or the process of gamification. Gamification has been understood as the process of adding game design elements into non-playful contexts (McGonigal, 2012). The high level of engagement provided by the game is the advantage that people want to tap into by the process of gamification (Hendricks, 2013). The magnitude of this engagement can be estimated by the simple fact that gaming is the tool which led students away from their studies; it is the instrument that made children indifferent towards the parents. It was seen as a disruptive technology which reduced concentration and was a sheer source of distraction (Morris & Shin, 2003). Children were reprimanded from being overly involved in online games as it also reduced their physical activity and outdoor sports. But the same disruption is now being utilized for various innovative, creative and useful methods.

GAMING AND NEW MEDIA MARKETING

Marketers have always been on a look out for new and innovative methods to reach and connect with their audiences, and through online games they were able to do just the same in a highly interactive, measurable and focused way. With the onset of new media in late 1990s there was a sudden surge in attempts to use this media as a vehicle to carry the marketer's message. Unfortunately, this media type suffered at the hand of exclusivity. The number of audience that were actually fluent and conversant with using this tool was limited. But with time, and upgrade of technology in terms of high speed internet broadband, 4G services on mobiles, number of people which are now online has grown exponentially. This has led to the rise of the popularity of new media amongst marketers as well. Several tools such as social media, search engine optimization, blogging, are all quite prominent and well used. The gaming application which is heavily used for new media marketing is known as Advergaming – a combination of Advertising and Gaming. This technique uses online games on new media for the purpose of engaging customers and communicating regarding the brand, the product, its uses and benefits. Over the years there has been a strong invasion of Advergames as a tool to build customer engagement. The target demographic group which used Advergames started with children, but with time, this has progressed to adults as well. With changes in lifestyle, increase in leisure time and unlimited access to internet at finger tips, Advergames are no more limited to children. In fact, several studies show that the inclination of adults towards online games is much higher than children. This phenomenon has brought about a major shift in the type of industries which use Advergames as a tool too. Thus, this book compiles views of various authors from diverse streams to merge their knowledge pool and give a perspective to the idea of applications of gaming in the arena of new media marketing.

ORGANIZATION OF THE BOOK

The gaming industry has flourished and has harnessed the smart phones, social networking, standalone tools and has silently engrossed the entertainment industry, medical interventions, marketing's, behavioral modulations and every other facet of endeavour.

This book tries to bring out the application of games in new media marketing by exploring the various functions where the games are already being used. The chapters are carefully arranged which highlights the strengths of online games in various functional applications for an easy engrossment of readers.

The book builds the entire theme of gaming, its original applications in the food industry and children adulations of characters identifications, subsequent chapters bring out the ingrained of more contemporary areas of gaming applications like entertainment industry, therapeutic care, behavioural alterations, and exploring newer possibilities in research and businesses. The content of the book is not just limited to applications of gaming but also tries to understand the psychological perspective behind it. Chapters have been included which try to focus on the consumer's psychology as well as behavior towards the games. The book will-provide delight to readers and an engaging reading experience through its 15 chapters which are crafted-as follows:

Chapter 1: Advent of New Media Marketing Techniques – The Inevitable Disruption

This chapter discusses the evolution of New Media and the disruptive techniques now available to the marketers to reach out to their customers. It brings to light various interactive tools which give an edge over existing traditional media.

Chapter 2: Gamification and Advergaming – An Overview of the Innovative Brain Tool in the Field of Advertising

This chapter takes up one of the most common new media marketing tool; Advergames and elucidates the various launch details of advergaming applications by various firms and brand websites including online games, social network sites, and interactive digital television.

Chapter 3: Rhetoric of Advergames

This chapter explores the rhetoric which has been presented by the use of Advergames. Here the debate among marketers and communication experts as to how this tool could be exploited in the field of advertising and positioning of brands to the best of their advantage has been discussed.

Chapter 4: Advergames and Children

This chapter highlights how Advergames are voraciously used for creating connect with the children. It further explores whether the use of Advergames is actually able to create a valid intellectual connect with the children in the audience.

Chapter 5: Persuasive Advergames – Boon or Bane for Children

This chapter again picks up the challenges faced while using Advergames for attempting to connect with children. Here we also see a detailed discussion regarding the negative effects of use of Advergames for that demographic.

Chapter 6: Food Advergames and Children – The Psychodynamics

This chapter focusses on a niche style of advergaming that focusses on only food related products that are targeted for the children. This chapter focusses on the psychodynamics of the children that select to play food related Advergames and further influence the purchase.

Chapter 7: Understanding the Psychology of New Media Audiences From a Marketing Perspective

This chapter evaluates how the psychology of audiences changes while they are evaluating products under the influence of traditional media versus their response to the marketers on new media. Here the under lying consumer behavior is analyzed as a response to the marketers stimulus.

Chapter 8: Gap Between Mobile and Online Advergames – The Possible Effects of the Optimal Gaming Experience-Flow

This chapter explores the differences in response of the audiences when they are exposed to online mobile Advergames as compared to when they are exposed to Non-mobile based online Advergames. This chapter also enlists the advantages of each technique and the areas where these techniques should be applicable.

Chapter 9: Nuances of Media Planning in New Media Age

This chapter explains and explores the tools and techniques which need to be kept in mind while planning the media for any communication campaign and how to select a particular new media tool over another.

Chapter 10: Click to Brick – Case Study of a Virtual Reality Company

This chapter consists of success stories of gaming as a tool to reach out to the audiences of the millennial. It highlights the success of Virtual Reality and Augmented Reality in an attempt to bring about a personalized shopping experience.

Chapter 11: Social Media as a Marketing Tool

This chapter elucidates on the advent of social media and its use in the area of marketing. While social media was started as a tool to connect different people socially, it is now extensively used for the communicating marketers message a well as analyze the social trends of people from different demographics.

Chapter 12: Social Media Marketing – Tools and Techniques

This chapter illustrates the various tools and techniques of Social Media marketing and elaborates on the principles which need to be kept in mind while using the same in an attempt to make a campaign successful. It's one of the chapters that has immense scope of further research and explorations.

Chapter 13: Impact of Digital Advertising Post-Demonetization in India

India underwent a huge change after the economic reform of demonetization in the year 2016 which further led to increase in digital literacy and hence digital advertising. This chapter explores the overall impact which was brought about by this socio-economic change on the new media marketing tool: Digital Advertising.

Chapter 14: Gamification in Entertainment Industry – Glimpses From Indian Film Industry

This chapter examines the success stories of Advergaming as a new media marketing tool while trying to focus on the Entertainment industry specifically. Under this purview it specifically looks at the success stories.

Chapter 15: Gamification to Promote the Engagement in Healthcare and Wellness of Patients Under Therapeutic Care – Gamification and Healthcare

This chapter explores the use of Advergames and online games in providing virtual reality of hospital ambience in reaching out to patients and providing therapeutic care with positive vibes towards passage to full recovery. It has the ability to be in virtual indoor and could both monitor the progression and suggest immediate interventions. This is one area where there is immense scope of reach and implementation in developed and developing economies.

The chapters in this compendium has been selected from reputed authors and researchers across all disciplines where Advergames could have an impact and are in embryonic phase and would be replacing the practices with input from advancement in subjects. The selected practical case studies, crucibles of evolutions based on medical ethics and augmentations based on interventions are some of the unique features of this effort, the distinctive features in oncology, neurology, cardiology which have formed the cutting edge in this arena have been harnessed and this would stimulate the internalizations by young researchers and practitioners. In developing economies like India and other Asian countries the readers would find a gripping reality and deep penetrations attained by the advent of Advergames which has percolated every facet of healthcare and entertainment Industry. The advantages of this may be harnessed to spread awareness from communicable and non-communicable diseases. These tools have vital and lifesaving roles and can be adopted for other medical conditions like AIDS awareness campaign, Diabetes, stokes, physiotherapy and cardiac ailments. The initiative of Shri Narendra Modi, Prime Minister of India under the tutelage UN on yoga for global health care has a very positive reverberation across the spectrum of all age, sex and races and gaming could be a possible virtual 3D tutor to animate postures and practices both far awareness and preventive care.

The innovative gaming tools would further be explored by Industries at large which has grown in geometric proportion in fast few years and newer vistas of virtual 3D communication would be explored at the Silicon Valley and this will reach every house hold through social media tools. We invite comments, reviews and suggestions from the readers are welcome and may resonate in second volume which may soon be in offering with further advance features.

Best,

Pratika Mishra
Presidency University Bangalore, India

Swati Oberoi Dham
New Delhi Institute of Management, India

REFERENCES

Chikhani, R. (2015, Oct 31). *The History of Gaming: An evolving Community*. Retrieved from techcrunch: https://techcrunch.com/2015/10/31/the-history-of-gaming-an-evolving-community/

Deterding, S., Dixon, D., Khaled, R., & Nacke, L. (2011). From Game Design Elements to Gamefulness:Defining "Gamification". In *Proceedings of the 15th International Academic MindTrek Conference: Envisioning Future Media Environments* (pp. 9-15). New York: ACM.

Hendricks, D. (2013, May 8). *Complete History of Social Media: Then And Now*. Retrieved Oct 5, 2018, from smallbiztrends.com

McGonigal, J. (2012). *Reality is Broken: Why Games Make Us Better and How They Can Change the World*. Penguin Group.

Morris, S., & Shin, H. (2003). Global Games: Theory and Applications. In *Advances in Economics and Econometrics: Theory and Applications* (pp. 56–114). Cambridge, UK: Cambridge University Press. doi:10.1017/CBO9780511610240.004

Reeves, B., & Read, L. (2009). *Total Engagement: Using Games and Virtual Worlds to Change the Way People Work and Businesses Compete*. Boston: Harvard Business School Press.

Acknowledgement

We bow in reverence to the Almighty for bestowing upon us the opportunity and determination to embark on this edited book titled *Application of Gaming in New Media Marketing*. Learning is an active process hence perseverance to complete this task has been a fulfilling memoir. The book is a confluence of hard work and best wishes of many people and we extend our heartfelt thanks to all of them for their fulfilling and desirable efforts.

We are grateful to IGI Global for giving us this opportunity to edit the book on Application of Gaming in New Media Marketing. The team members from IGI Global, Ms. Maria Gilbert and Ms. Jan Travers has been extremely cooperative right from the inception of the idea of this book.

With earnest gratitude and profound thanks, we would like to acknowledge the continuous guidance of Dr. Vijayan Immanuel, Pro Chancellor, Presidency University and Mr. V.M. Bansal, Chairman, New Delhi Institute of Management.

We are indebted to Mr. Anthony M. Giallourakis who has coined the term Advergames and is also founder of the Original Advergames.com for consenting to review and write the foreword. His association has authenticated the efforts and intent.

Our sincere thanks to Professor Pramod Pathak and Dr. Saumya Singh, Indian Institute of Technology (ISM) Dhanbad for their continued faith and motivation. We are indebted to Professor D.P. Goral, Management Development Institute, Gurgaon, India and Dr. Kamal Kishore Sharma, StartUp Consultant, Ahemdabad, India for bestowing their best wishes and thoughtful guidance.

Dr. Mrinmoy Biswas, Registrar, Presidency University and Professor Teena Singh, Registrar NDIM has been a relentless support throughout the endeavor.

We are truly moved by the gesture and constant support shown by all the members of Editorial Advisory Board since the beginning of the idea of the edited book.

Our most honest thanks to all the authors for having faith in us and bearing with the time frame at each phase of the submissions. We acknowledge the contributions and their cooperation.

Last but not the least, cheers to friends and family for their love and support.

Pratika Mishra
Swati Oberoi Dham

Chapter 1
Advent of New Media Marketing Techniques:
The Inevitable Disruption

Harshita Gupta
Indian Institute of Technology (ISM) Dhanbad, India

Saumya Singh
Indian Institute of Technology (ISM) Dhanbad, India

ABSTRACT

The ever-changing marketing landscape has been upfront in adapting to innovations. People are getting attuned to tons of advancements concerning new media technologies over the past decade. For example, we now have different apps that are more mobile-friendly than inclined towards desktops. Such technological advancements have led to huge information generation every second. Today, information is best conceived when it is in form of attractive content. Content in this era majorly constitutes of audio-visual effects, also there is a gamut of interesting applications which has taken media to an inexplicable height. In such a dynamic environment, it is important to channelize one's efforts and resources towards profitable marketing. This is a period of disruption and whoever makes that first move to adopt it will have a greater hold on its customer base. The chapter guides the reader through the emerging new media marketing tools that can bring in the inevitable disruption.

DOI: 10.4018/978-1-5225-6064-7.ch001

INTRODUCTION

The constant lookout for the 'next big thing' by consumers, producers, marketers and other stakeholders has given the roots to disruption. "Disruption" is one amongst the much-adored jargons used in marketing industry now-a-day. It denotes an innovative idea which may change the way people think about something. This idea may take any form, for instance, an App that changes the way how everyone commutes on a daily basis or a service which changes the internet usage patterns of the masses overnight or it can be a gaming App that becomes a cult worldwide. Today, booking an Uber or an Ola for commuting purpose seems hassle free unlike five years back when it appeared to be a costly affair and a trustful ride was also a question. With the everyday evolving technology and sciences, a new product is launched frequently. This in turn calls for smart marketing techniques which are capable of delivering uniqueness when it comes to attracting consumers. Disruption in this industry is evident and marketing plays a great role in simplifying the use of a new concept introduced through disruption in the market. With the right marketing strategy, these companies are able to attract the maximum end users. Therefore, with the rise of disruptive innovations, it is essential to come up with disruptive marketing practices as well.

According to Christensen, Aaron and Clark (2002), disruption is an influential tool that is known to transform numerous industries like retailing to computers, and even to the education industry. Hence, "Disruption is how industries achieve the seemingly incompatible goals of increased access, higher quality, and lower prices" (Christensen, Aaron & Clark, 2002). Thereby, it brings in a new wave of innovation adoption. The marketing industry too is on a search of new tools which may result in huge impact and techniques which are not mundane. This search has given pedigrees to disruptive marketing practices.

Today, the competition is so immense that clearing the bottle neck is an uphill battle. The consumers have increased and so have the producers. Just making a product sound useful will not make it sell in the market place. Innovative products are no assurance to success if the marketing part is neglected (Nayak & Ketteringham, 1986). Therefore, the role of strong media usage for promotions comes into picture so that the product is not left un-noticed. The new age media is a strong platform to achieve exposure in the clutter. The new age media combined with disruptive methods can be a powerful tool.

There are several means of marketing that have arisen over the past few years. New media marketing methods being one of them. It comprises multimedia, social media and use of other online media technologies to promote one's product at a new level all together. The chapter focuses on the rise of different media techniques by discussing some of these in the light of the usage pattern to benefit the producers to market their product effectively. It serves as a reference to market researchers, practitioners, industrialists and journalists who are building their base to delve into new marketing tools. Also, the chapter serves as a reference for small business houses that wishes to grow their activities in the future.

OBJECTIVE

With disruptive innovation expanding its territory each day, it is imperative to come up with disruptive marketing tools to promote them. The chapter aims to review various new media marketing practices that are experiencing a rise in today's business world. The bottom line of these methods is targeted towards bringing disruption in the market place. Be it a gimmicky app meant to attract the eye balls of the consumers or a series of suspense creating advertisement on a social media, today companies are trying their level best to accommodate every possible attention from the buyers. Therefore, an insight into some of these tools namely Advergames, Video marketing, Guerrilla marketing, Social Media marketing, and Infographic marketing are covered in this chapter. Also, the chapter discusses the shift from desktops to mobile phones used for browsing and even for entertainment purposes. And how this shift has proven a boon for the marketers.

Disruptive Innovation, Disruptive Marketing, and the Associated Risk

Innovation is ladder to a successful society. It facilitates a progressive environment thrusting the power to 'create' in hands of as many individuals as possible. Kumar, et. al. (2000) defined innovation as "something that is invented for the first time and is a commercial success". Commercial success of an innovation describes its degree of usefulness to the society. When the usefulness of an innovative idea is huge by affecting a large part of the community and involves a considerable change in usage and consumption patterns, it is considered 'disruptive'. According to Cumming (1998), "Disruptive innovations are innovations that involve significant new technologies, require considerable change in consumption patterns and are perceived as offering substantially enhanced benefits". Disruption comes along with challenges of development and commercialization as uncertainty in terms of technology viability is high (Veryzer, 1998). Due to this, its dissemination amongst the people becomes difficult and needs to be taken care of. Generally, people are unaware of the potential enhanced benefits coming through a disruptive idea. Initial stages of introducing such an idea involves hesitation from the people for whom it has been designed for. As they cannot identify strongly with the needs which the disruption would cater to, it becomes hard and expensive initially to find itself a market that assists the new technology to translate smoothly in form of products for consumers to use (Mullins & Sutherland, 1998).

Any innovation taking place in an already existing industry is comparatively easy to understand and use than responding to a disruptive innovation. Such innovation does not create a new platform, instead add value to the existing one. This is unlike a disruptive idea which requires to build its own niche and attract new users. According to Rajagopal (2014), "In contrast to disruptive innovation, a sustaining innovation does not create new markets or value networks but only evolves existing ones with better value, allowing firms within to compete against each other's sustaining improvements". Now a day, companies try to keep themselves updated with the new technologies emerging on day to day basis. Reason being that if a company fails to be up to date to these advances, then it misses the opportunity which could have brought in disruption.

Although, disruption brings in the 'first move advantage' to the company which puts its faith and resources in the idea, but alongside the burden of huge risk and low initial profit comes attached (Rajagopal, 2014). The uncertainty of the technological feasibility of a disruptive idea results in not allowing the good companies to make their first move towards it. As every disruptive idea needs to enter the market structure and make its place there, it is necessary to strengthen its co-survival so as to avoid getting swiped away from the existing market (Christensen, 1997). A robust marketing campaign with new tools is one of the ways to stop the existing market forces restricting a disruptive idea to take its roots. Building a strong marketing strategy helps new ideas to sink in more comfortably amongst the masses. The recent times have given rise to new marketing tools which are in synchronization with the fast-moving technological advances. As these are apt to reflect the best possible image of a new product in the market to the consumers, they have gained the much-deserved popularity amongst the academicians, marketers and researchers. Some of these are Advergames, Video marketing, Social Media marketing, Guerrilla marketing, Infographic marketing, etc. The essence of these modern marketing tools is that they try to provide least hindrance to the exposed audience, unlike the traditional marketing tools which appeared everywhere to make an impression but resulted in being avoided.

The marketing strategies used in the past attempted to design the promotions after a product is developed and is ready to be marketed. The traditional tools catered to the products that has been produced. Today, the times have evolved, and companies thrive on the needs of consumers which even they are not aware of but they definitely need it to bring in some extra profits. They realize it only when they come across a product which offer benefits that facilitates more efficiency to the consumers. This has become possible due to disruption. Due to this reason, in current scenario, market looks for more robust and user-friendly marketing strategies. In order to come up with such strategies, a company must pay attention to changes in the patterns of the way consumers perceive a message. Consumers of 21st century appreciates 'information' which is not merely an advertisement to increase the sales. They are interested in the content which challenges their conventional thinking in some way or the other. This is where disruptive marketing strategies play their role and eventually leads to a better consumer-marketer environment. According to Thomas et.al. (2017), "understanding market-based value creation in the field of marketing has centered, to a large degree, on market orientation studies via field-based, discovery-oriented research. In some ways, market orientation – while viewed as the implementation of the marketing concept– became a disruptive marketing strategy for many organizations". A healthy relationship between the consumers and the marketers is considered as a key to a progressive market place.

New Media Marketing Techniques

To encounter the growing competition, it necessary to adopt to new marketing trends. Companies that fail to acclimate to novel ideas tend to perish in the bottle neck race. Following are some of the latest effective techniques used in the market place:

Advergames

Digitalization has given birth to many effective marketing tools. The digital marketing, just like marketing in general, is constantly evolving as the companies that use it strive to address more customers by introducing cleverer, original, surprising or enjoyable forms of advertisement (Bosák, 2016). Digital gaming is one of them. Lenhart, Jones and Macgill (2008) emphasizes that Digital games have become a mass phenomenon today. And social gaming as a part of digital gaming is an engaging platform for most digital game users (Lenhart et al., 2007). People tend to build and maintain social relations like friendship when they indulge in leisure time activities, social gaming being one of them (Feld & Carter, 1998). Kowert and Oldmeadow (2014) also commented on how internet connectivity has changed the way video games are played today, allowing people to connect worldwide in shared gaming spaces, helping players not only connect and interact but also to learn from each other. This sort interaction leads to development of a social system on one place and on other may also act as an interface for product advertisements and promotions. Since these transactions and interactions take place over digital media, these platforms present great opportunities to analyze user behavior (Balci & Salah, 2014). This valuable information on user behavior, in turn can help in developing marketing strategies. Social media has provided a dais to social gaming, which can be used for the concept of adver-gaming too.

Advergame is a novel concept of an emerging tool of Digital marketing used to attract adults and children to play in brand-oriented environments. Advergames are the electronic games which helps in promoting a product or a brand available on the website of companies and on other social media platforms which presents commercial messages in the form of online games Moore (2006). Therefore, Advergames can be defined as "an immersive mix of advertising and entertainment that takes the form of video games" (Obringer, 2007). Coined in 2000, the term 'advergames' was named after a company founded by Anthony Giallourakis. Though, the first advergames already made its appearance in the 1980s (Aarnoutse, Peursum & Dalpiaz, 2014). The blend of information with entertainment has made this concept popular over the time. According to Winkler and Buckner (2006), advergaming can both entertain the customers as well as induce consumers to develop positive attitudes toward the brands. This is possible due to the integration and interactivity that Advergames establish (Dobrow, 2004). According to Medium (2016), "an example of Advergaming is Get the Glass: an online 3D flash game which was launched in 2007 to encourage the consumption of cow's milk in the United States. The game is about the adventures of a family who is suddenly facing the situation of living without milk, and the only way to survive is to steal huge vessels of it". These games tend to educate consumers about benefits, specialties and key features of the product. Companies have resorted to these games for developing brand recognition too. For example, post the success of Angry Bird game, the brand Rio associated themselves with this game. The name of the game changed from "Angry Bird" to "Angry Bird Rio". Another example of Advergames can be observed in Figure 1 which shows the brand logo in the game. It helps in brand recognition.

Advergames can be bifurcated on the basis of *Mode of Advertising* and *Placement of Advertising*. On the basis of Mode of Advertising, Advergames can be either online or offline and on the basis of Placement of Advertising, it can be further divided into Traffic Engagement, Inside gaming, Around Product (Sharma, 2014). Based on this, marketers develop games to attract maximum attention from its users, lending an assertive impact of the brand. "Producers of advergames emphasize that the positive gaming experience transfers positive emotions to the brand", stated by Waiguny and Terlutter (2010). Today, many sectors like Retail sector, Travel and Tourism, entertainment and media, FMCG sector, Telecom, Education and Lifestyle, Food and Beverage brands are employing advergaming as a tool for advertisement purposes (Sharma, 2014).

The acceptability of product placement in Advergames has been studied to know if it is correlated with attitude of consumers towards advertisement in a broad-spectrum (Buckner and Winkler, 2006). Mackay (2015), in their paper on effect

Figure 1. Example of advergames used for brand recognition

of product placement in computer games on brand attitude and recall concluded that, "product placement within computer games is an effective means of fostering high spontaneous brand recall and even of influencing consumers less positively predisposed towards a brand (analogous to non-users)". As Advergames as genre of marketing is comparatively a new concept, more studies can be taken to consolidate the topic.

Video Marketing

With the advent of YouTube, video marketing has become a buzz term amongst the marketers. YouTube has evolved over a time to provide not only entertainment but also a stage for product promotion. The efficacy of this budding marketing tool has not been studied rigorously in Indian context. YouTube being one of the largest search engine after Google provides immense potential for advertising and promotions (Gupta and Singh, 2017). It accounts for a rich repository of information and insights regarding plethora of topics including that of markets and consumption (Dehghani, 2016). Hundreds of thousands of videos are uploaded every day on this popular platform (YouTube, 2008). YouTube, since its launch in December 2005, has been a leader in providing a major platform to all those who wants to watch, upload or share videos globally through websites, blogs, mobile phones, etc. (YouTube, 2008) As a result, it is one of the popular social media websites amongst various others. All one needs to do is to search for the related query and the site returns many options in form videos within a fraction of second. It offers features such as liking, sharing, commenting and subscribing making people put forward their views; which makes this website a popular hub for communication of any form for both consumers and marketers (Gupta and Singh, 2017). YouTube was sold for $1.65 million to the giant which is Google, making YouTube a multi-billion-dollar business (Sorkin, 2006). It generated massive advertising revenues for Google since then (Tan, 2009).

According to a report by Pixability (2013), YouTube has emerged as a highly influential market space where various brands engage with their audiences. Some of the positive drivers of YouTube advertising includes entertainment, informativeness, and customization (Dehghani, 2016). It has been successful in presenting information in a fascinating manner with help of audio and visual effects. This in turn attracts marketers to use this stage for product promotion and brand building. With YouTube, the brand also gets a chance to customize and modify the message to be conveyed to the customers. Customization according to the preferences of its viewers adds to the likeability of the platform by the marketers. This results in successful delivery of high-quality service options, making the consumption experience even better (Rao & Minakakis, 2003). YouTube with abundance of information provides consumers with a number of alternatives available in the market facilitating ease of making choices and decision. The two-way communication provided by this platform makes it more versatile.

Apart from the above mentioned three features of YouTube, a major attribute contributing towards the usefulness of this dais is Share-ability and Advocacy. YouTube sanctions the viewers to not only acquire information and network with each other but also to appreciate the videos by liking, sharing, commenting on and subscribing it. The feature helps any kind of promotional video to go viral amongst the consumer if it is alluring enough. Soon, in many cases, it becomes popular and everyone starts talking about it. Figure 2 summarizes some of the important dimensions of YouTube. The same features have resulted in popularity of video marketing amongst marketers. Therefore, considering the benefits of video marketing, it be considered as an effective tool while designing the marketing strategy.

Guerrilla Marketing

Achieving conventional aims with unconventional methods linking less of capital and more of creativity is Guerrilla Marketing (Kaden, 2006). The psychological and social perception of the society is changing, giving rise judicious buying and therefore, gaining a competitive edge in the market place has become a prime aim (Shakeel & Khan, 2011). Companies keep their best foot front to grab attention from

Figure 2. Dimensions of YouTube
Source: Gupta and Singh, (2017)

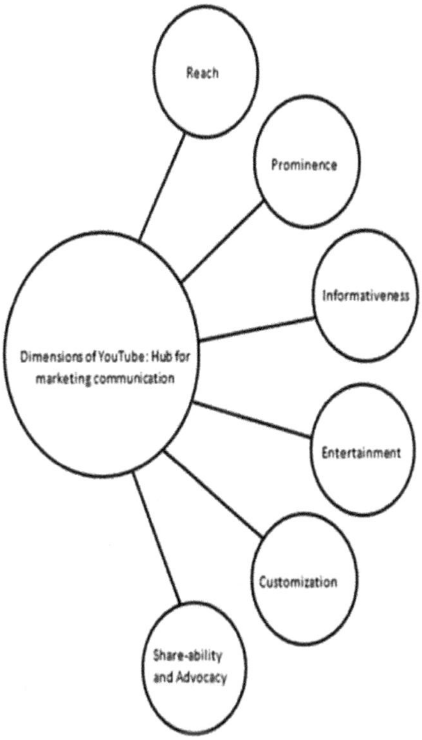

the consumers but sometimes it becomes too much for them to remain attentive to each and every message, resulting in avoiding the communication from these companies. Today, consumers attempt to block the Ads and other promotional messages as they are already surrounded with the same mundane advertisement all around which leaves them annoyed. Thus, it is essential for the companies to differentiate their marketing activities (Sharma & Sharma, 2014).

As now a day, it is difficult to reach consumers using the traditional marketing practices, guerrilla marketing is a tool which help brands to make the required impact. Creativity and the power of imagination are the strengths of Guerrilla marketing. So as to achieve maximum for a goal, it bundles different marketing strategies utilizing a number of practices which differ from traditional advertising. And with the hybrid of various innovative materials and methods it makes it possible to obtain maximum levels of turnover for the lowest cost (Bigat, 2012). Gaining competitive edge amidst the changing psychological and social perception of the society is a prime aim of the marketers. Guerrilla marketing with its innovative approach helps in bringing about the similar change. It strikes the consumers' mind in the most surprising way helping the advertisement to get retained in people's mind for a longer duration of time, hence leading to creation of customer base (Gupta and Singh, 2016). Further, Guerrilla marketing as a disruptive practice, if combined with the modern media technologies result in to a great platform to surface promotions. According to Isotraite (2010), the tactics used in Guerrilla marketing include Extreme Specialization, Aiming every effort at favorably impressing the customers, Providing service that goes beyond the customers' expectations, Fast response time, Quick turnaround of jobs, and Working hours that match the customer's requirements.

The history of Guerrilla Marketing revolves around 'guerrilla warfare', during which the Vietnamese made use of unique tools and tactics of surprise attack during Vietnam War in 1960s (Yüksel, 2010). Guerrilla Marketing works on the similar techniques which is to achieve conventional goals with unconventional approaches involving less of funds and more of creativity (Kaden, 2007). Conrad Jay Levinson is known as "father of Guerrilla Marketing" as he is the one who created this concept in his book Guerrilla Marketing (1984). Since then the concept has evolved further and is subsequently being used by various companies whether small or big. A perfect example of this practice is one carried by McDonalds shown in Figure 3.

The picture depicts a different sought of zebra crossing. It is an attractive way to promote one of the "top of the line products" of the company. McDonalds used its creativity to came up with a zebra crossing which indeed resembles the French Fries which is one of the top selling product of the company. No other product or brand can be displayed in this manner which makes it all the more eye-catching and anybody who sees it would be able to recall it easily. This captures the attention of

Figure 3. An example of guerrilla marketing by McDonalds

the consumers and hence contributing to the sales. Therefore, not only small and medium sized companies but even the big ones are using it to maintain their brand recognition.

So it is evident that the times have changed and no longer merely talking about one's product resulted in actual buying. Today, the arrangement of thoughts and ideas in most effective and creative manner has taken an upper hand. Successful companies have been known to use Guerrilla marketing in some form or the other to achieve great results.

Social Media Marketing

Advertising is an important 360-degree communication tool for the purpose of creating brand awareness (Krishnan & Sachdeva, 2011). It plays an inevitable role in the marketing industry. Multimedia graced this marketing industry with a scope to innovate with new ways of advertising. Amongst the most recent advancements in this digital age, Social Media is one of them where the social networking sites such as Facebook, LinkedIn, Instagram, Myspace, Twitter, Snapchat, etc. have progressively become a platform for sharing content amongst people from different walks of life and networking amongst themselves (Asem, 2013). Berthon et al. (2012) defined Social media as "a series of technological innovations in terms of both hardware and software that facilitate inexpensive content creation, interaction, and interoperability by online users". In the world of social media where content is the king, it has opened new avenues for the marketers to easily create eye-catching content which could reach to a phenomenal number of consumers. Such is the spread of social media usage. Social media websites are strong platforms for the marketers to promote their products and to create a long-lasting impression on the minds of the users. According to Gupta, Singh and Sinha (2016), Social media is considered as a fast-growing tool for enabling meaningful participation from the side of the consumers so that better services can be provided in return. Today, social media has emerged as a technology that has changed the configuration of the modern-day society by changing the way people lived and worked (Krishan, 2015).

Social media comprises of many websites, each of them specializes to provide users with a specific kind of focus. Like Instagram is a medium which is dedicated towards sharing content through pictures only. Similarly, Twitter is known for providing a platform to post one's views effectively in 140 characters. An example of the Social Media marketing can be seen in Figure 4 where Starbucks is using Twitter and Facebook platform for advertising their seasonal offers. Be it an introduction of new product to the brand or some new offers, company can post it immediately on their respective social media handle. The ease of presenting thoughts in varied formats like pictures, messages, music, vines, etc. has provided people with a common stage of knowledge sharing and knowledge building.

Figure 4. An example of social media marketing done by Starbucks using Twitter and Facebook

These websites are user-driven platform for focusing on one or different features supplied by the different social media websites. For a progressive insight building, it is necessary to have thoughts and views flowing in from different corners of the world resulting in valuable content creation. With the emergence of social media, content creation has achieved a boost. It has relocated people from being passive content readers into active content publishers involved in decision making process (Neti, 2011). Erragcha and Romdhane (2014) provided a classification of social media into the categories like based on its applications and uses; sites for online publication of opinions and information like blogs and wikis, content sharing sites like YouTube, sites allowing real time discussions like Facebook, tools for micro-blogging and publishing like Twitter, tools for social networking like personal 'livecast' platform, virtual networking platforms, and networked games sites.

When it comes to application of social media in marketing activities, advertising companies are considering it as a profitable tool. Social media promotional happenings revolve around making people easily and strongly connect with the brand. It helps in knowing the new technology which facilitates in building this connection and thereby using that technology for the benefit of the business and making profits (Chaturvedi & Gupta, 2014). With new innovations coming up each day, a company needs to get itself updated so as to design the promotional plans accordingly. Advertising activities not covering new innovative dimensions result in capturing less public attention. Social media helps both the marketers and consumers to interact in a better manner to exchange information. However, when it comes to choosing one marketing tool over other, researchers support the viewpoint that alone social media platform cannot result in a successful campaign, therefore, it should be coupled with other tools as well. According to Miller and Lammas (2010), some studies have that 70% consumers visit social websites for information seeking while other studies suggest that 90% word of mouth still happens face to face or by phones. Measuring the success of social media marketing is important before choosing it for promoting ones' product and this highly depends on qualitative metrics more than quantitative metrics. "These qualitative metrics include unique visitors, interaction rates, conversation size, conversation density, content freshness, author credibility, audience profiles and many others. While website traffic, hit rates, time spent online, and postings are considered as examples of quantitative metrics", as pointed by Miller and Lammas (2010). Therefore, there should be a conscious attempt in choosing a right marketing tool for a particular product and not blindly putting one promotional media to all the brands.

However, Social Media is a constantly sprouting universe where many services are created, disappeared and transformed and as mentioned in Nouala, et.al. (2016), "these spaces are evolving rapidly adapting one hand the needs of users through the creation of new functions and partly because technological development enlarges the range of possibilities". Marketers are looking forward to reaping maximum benefit from this platform.

Infographic Marketing

Information in form of graphics and pictures is easy to understand as it takes lesser time to infer from these as compared to going through big paragraphs of content. Cleveland (1994) pointed, "The human brain is able to identify and comprehend relationships and patterns more if data is encoded into visual forms". People go through headings and graphics which are more attractive to eyes. Infographics has the similar agenda. In this age of internet, a huge amount of content is already occupying the space, this calls for differentiating features in terms of data representation. Infographics is the response to the said need of the hour. Infographics are visual representation which is more engaging than the usual written format (Brafton, 2017). As explained by Scaife and Rogers (1996), "Virtual reality and visualization as means of representing and interacting with information are very much at the forefront of technological development". Earlier back in 1980s infographics supported the work of journalism and used to include magazines, newsletters, newspapers and reports but today it is recycled as a medium of storytelling (Siricharoen & Waralak, 2013). Specially in the digital age where the data needs to be quickly processed, it is necessary to attract people who only go through headlines and graphics to stop by something worth further reading (Siricharoen & Waralak, 2013). Infographics gained popularity in web 2.0 because of the inclusion of graphic illustrative data making it easier for readers to look at and digest (Byrne, 2011). According to Siricharoen and Waralak (2013), infographics display information in a limited space and an artistic format which helps in quickly passing on the facts and engage the readers to continue reading it. It facilitates essential data in an enjoyable to read and comprehend format. It consists of visual depiction with the help of diagrams, pictures, graphs, figures, etc. and summarizes the content of the subject to a visually appealing format making it quick to understand without going through the described word by word format.

Figure 5 shows the usage of Infographics to present data in a picture form to the consumers for a better understanding. The makers of Listerine Mouthwash visually represented a new survey data in a creative manner using graphics which revealed what Canadians put in their mouths and brushing's limited effect on cleaning mouths. Though it is quite a challenge to retain the amount of depth of the information as in the text format but a good quality infographic can bring in more attention of the readers as compared to a written piece of work. A bunch of graphics representing the whole set of information in a form which is easy and quick to comprehend is the crux of infographics. The salient features of this marketing strategy has led to a rise in demand of infographic marketing. But in order to successfully market the products with infographic marketing, it is essential to construct quality infographics which requires a high level of editorial research combined with fitting, thought-provoking and reasonable designs (Brafton, 2017). A conscious selection of graphics and designs matching the brand image is another imperative factor in this style of modern day marketing. A good infographic comes along with an article or a blog post so that is easy to make it to the search engines, hence boosting the SEO. This format of information display also generates its sharing on other social media platforms making it gain a wider spread. Buying ads on other search mediums for better promotion of infographics adds to the reach. Marketers are looking at infographics as a tool which will help their customers in building a better connection with their brand.

The Shift From Desktops to Mobile Phone: A Boon for Marketers

Modernism has introduced us to a more information-based society as compared to the earlier days. With internet coming into par, creation of information is huge. Social media has added to this state, resulting here is a constant flow of information in enormous amount. According to Pertierra (2005), "A major consequence of late modernity is the increasing intercalation and accumulation of information". Mobile phones have taken shape of a strong medium that allows a free flow of this humongous data in the universe. There are about 3.3 billion mobile phone users when compared to 500 million in the year 2000 (George S et al., 2017). Mobile Internet usage is growing

Figure 5. An example of infographic marketing used by LISTERINE mouthwash

at the rate of nearly 85% per annum (Chandra, 2012). With numerous technological advancements, the usage of mobile phones has evolved. In the past 4-5 years when mobile phone usage patterns have taken a drastic change. As per George S et al. (2017), “Indians are increasingly using the mobile phones rather than the land line telephones and Indian market has emerged as the second-largest market for mobile phone handsets next to China. In India, use of internet is enormous, especially in the young population”. Earlier used only for calling and texting purposes, now it is being used even for functions like managing ones’ bank accounts. This is made possible as the security provided by this interface has increased to a level where people find it trustable to pay online for their purchases of different sought. They find it easier to make a transaction on their phones rather than switching on their laptops or the desktops for the same. Pertierra (2005), commented, “Unlike desktops and other immobile technologies, mobile phones more closely resemble tools or prosthetic devices as extensions of the body”. With social media also leaning towards mobile phones, the ground in traditional time-location restrictions has also been broken (Okazaki & Taylor, 2013). Therefore, the ease of handling it and the versatility in the ways it can be used for a gamut of functions has made it prominent amongst people of all income groups.

Marketers, over the time, have realized that mobile phones have impacted life of the people not only locally but on a global level. As the time users spend using their smartphones has increased tremendously, it has opened a perfect field for marketing (Medium, 2016). It is pointed by Pertierra (2005), “the cell phone encourages an exploration of the world beyond its local boundaries”. Owing to the fact that mobile phones have become a part and parcel of ones’ life, marketers are focusing to tap this opportunity to their benefit. Advertising with the help of different mobile based application and games are the example of this. For example, Saavn is a mobile based application for streaming songs of different genres, companies are using it for advertisement purposes too. After few songs there would be an Ad playing which catches the attention the listener.

Figure 6 shows another example of mobile phone marketing where IDEA Cellular Ltd. started a campaign named ‘Use Mobile, Save Paper’ in partner with two of the leading coffee chains – Barista and Café Coffee Day. Under the campaign, visitors of these coffee shop could browse the menu and get the bill for their order on their mobile phones, saving the use of paper for the same. The campaign was a “green initiative” on one hand and a great marketing strategy on other. Advertisements like these through mobile phones result in a greater impact on the consumers, helping them to recall while making purchase decisions. Hence, over the time mobile phones are proved to be a successful disruptive tool, which marketers are using for promotion and advertisement. And there still lies a huge potential for this platform to grow further.

Figure 6. An example of mobile phone marketing

DISCUSSION

Innovations and new technologies have made the marketing environment more robust than ever. Disruptive innovation needs disruptive marketing tools to spread its usability. Where the traditional tools take time to provide a larger coverage in terms of their advertising impact, new age media is faster in attracting the consumers' eye balls. As these tools are new, marketers are reluctant to use them at first. But by taking a calculated risk of using them in the marketing mix may result in clearing some of the bottle neck. It is necessary that marketers get themselves updated with the new tools of promotion so that they are able to stand out in the crowd. The new tools like Social Media, Infographics, Advergames, etc. are based on the concept of disruption, which means using an innovative concept for enhanced benefits. Websites like Facebook, Twitter, YouTube shares valuable data on consumers' likes, preferences and behavior. This data can be used to interpret the latest trend in consumption patterns and can help marketers and industrialists in market analysis. The chapter focuses on some the new media marketing tools which will not only help the current marketers to build their promotion matrix judicially but at the same time will serve as a base for future research in this area. The chapter serves as a reference for small business houses that wishes to grow their activities in the future or aspires to market some disruptive innovation to the consumers. It will help these business houses to get themselves acquainted with what's new in the market. Also, the chapter serves as a guide for the Industry practitioners, academicians, journalists and researchers to build a base for further research in this area.

REFERENCES

Aarnoutse, F., Peursum, L., & Dalpiaz, F. (2014). The evolution of advergames development: A study in the Netherlands. In *Games Media Entertainment (GEM), 2014* (pp. 1–8). IEEE. doi:10.1109/GEM.2014.7048097

Asem, B. (2013). Networked Publics and Identity Construction: Towards an Era of Virtual Socialization. *Media Watch*, *4*(2), 161–174.

Balci, K & Salah, A. A. (2014). Automatic analysis and identification of verbal aggression and abusive behaviors for online social games, *Computers in Human Behavior, 53*(2015), 517–526.

Berthon, P. R., Pitt, L. F., Plangger, K., & Shapiro, D. (2012). Marketing meets Web 2.0, social media, and creative consumers: Implications for International marketing strategy. *Business Horizons*, *55*(3), 261–271. doi:10.1016/j.bushor.2012.01.007

Bigat, E. C. (2012). Guerrilla advertisement and marketing. *Procedia: Social and Behavioral Sciences*, *51*, 1022–1029. doi:10.1016/j.sbspro.2012.08.281

Bosák, P. (2016). *Utilization of advergames in marketing strategies*. Bachelor's Thesis.

Brafton. (2017). *Infographic Marketing*. Retrieved from http://www.brafton.com/glossary/infographics

Chandra, G., Anu, M., Noshir, K., & James, M. (2012). *Online and upcoming: The Internet's impact on India*. Bangalore: McKinsey and Company.

Chaturvedi, S. & Gupta, S. (2014). Social Media Promotions –Can We Restrict It Under Laws? *International Journal of Research –GRANTHAALAYAH*, *1*(1), 43-50.

Christensen, C., Aaron, S., & Clark, W. (2002). Disruption in education. In M. Devlin, R. Larson, & J. Meyerson (Eds.), The internet and the university: forum 2001. Academic Press.

Christensen, C. M. (1997). *The Innovator's Dilemma: When New Technologies Cause Great Firms to Fail*. Boston, MA: Harvard Business School Press.

Cleveland, W. S. (1994). *The Elements of Graphing Data* (Revised Edition). Hobart Press.

Cumming, B. S. (1998). Innovation overview and future challenges. *European Journal of Innovation Management*, *1*(1), 21–29. doi:10.1108/14601069810368485

Dehghani, M., Niaki, M. K., Ramezani, I., & Sali, R. (2016). Evaluating the influence of YouTube advertising for attraction of young customers. *Computers in Human Behavior, 59*, 165–172. doi:10.1016/j.chb.2016.01.037

Dobrow, L. (2004, January 15). How to Play Games and Influence People: Advergaming Emerges as New Ad Option. *Media Daily News.*

Erragcha, N., & Romdhane, R. (2014). Social networks as marketing tools. *Journal of Internet Banking and Commerce, 19*(1), 1–12.

Feld, S., & Carter, W. C. (1998). Foci of activity in changing contexts for friendship. In R. G. Adams & G. Allan (Eds.), *Placing friendship in context* (pp. 136–152). Cambridge, UK: Cambridge University Press.

George, S., Saif, N., & Joseph, B. B. (2017). A study on the mobile phone usage pattern and its dependence among medical students of a college in Kerala, India. *International Journal of Research in Medical Sciences, 5*(8), 3615–3619. doi:10.18203/2320-6012.ijrms20173573

Gupta, H. & Singh, S. (2016). Guerrilla Marketing: An innovative stride. *SMS Journal of Entrepreneurship and Innovation, 3*(1).

Gupta, H., & Singh, S. (2017). Social Media in Contemporary Marketing: YouTube Advertising for the Guerrillas. *Media Watch, 8*(3), 413–422. doi:10.15655/mw/2017/v8i3/49145

Gupta, H., Singh, S., & Sinha, P. (2016). Multimedia tool as a predictor for social media advertising-A YouTube way. *Multimedia Tools and Applications, 76*(18), 1–12.

Hanse'n, S. O., & Wakonen, J. (1997). Innovation, a winning solution? *International Journal of Technology Management, 13*(4), 345–358. doi:10.1504/IJTM.1997.001668

Isoraite, M. (2010). Guerilla Marketing Strategy Realization Assumptions. *6th International Scientific Conference.*

Kaden, R. J. (2006). *Guerrilla marketing research: Marketing research techniques that can help any business make more money.* Kogan Page Publishers.

Kowert, R. & Oldmeadow, J. A. (2014). Playing for social comfort: Online video game play as a social accommodator for the insecurely attached. *Computers in Human Behavior, 53*(2015), 556–566.

Krishan, R. (2015). Social Media Challenges and Adoption Patterns among Public Relations Practitioners. *Media Watch, 6*(1), 73–81. doi:10.15655/mw/2015/v6i1/55390

Krishnan, S. G., & Sachdeva, P. (2011). Brand promotion through internet advertising. *Media Watch, 2*(2), 28–30.

Kumar, N., Scheer, L., & Kotler, P. (2000). From market driven to market driving. *European Management Journal, 18*(2), 129–142. doi:10.1016/S0263-2373(99)00084-5

Lenhart, A., Jones, S., & Macgill, A. R. (2008). *Adults and video games* (Pew Internet project data memo). Retrieved from http://www.pewinternet.org/Reports/2008/Adults-and-Video-Games.aspx

Lenhart, A., Kahne, J., Middaugh, E., Macgill, A., Evans, C., & Vitak, J. (2007). *Teens, video games and civics* (Pew Internet project data memo). Retrieved from http://www.pewinternet.org/Reports/2008/Teens-Video-Games-and-Civics.aspx

Mackaya, T., Ewinga, M., Newtona, F., & Windischa, L. (2015). The effect of product placement in computer games on brand attitude and recall. International Journal of Advertising. *The Review of Marketing Communications, 28*(3), 423–438.

Medium. (2016a). *Advergaming and Gamification: Funny and Effective Digital Marketing Trends.* Retrieved from: https://medium.com/@ReputationDefender/advergaming-and-gamification-funny-and-effective-digital-marketing-trends-70b0a5b78617

Medium. (2016b). *Mobile Marketing: Why is it important for you?* Retrieved from https://medium.com/@ReputationDefender/mobile-marketing-why-is-it-important-for-you-f085b1c93a62

Miller, R., & Lammas, N. (2010). Social media and its implications for viral marketing. *Asia Pacific Public Relations Journal, 11*, 1–9.

Moore, E. (2006, July). *It's Child's Play: Advergaming and the Online Marketing of Food to Children.* Kaiser Family Foundation Report.

Mullins, J. W., & Sutherland, D. J. (1998). New product development in rapidly changing markets: An exploratory study. *Journal of Product Innovation Management, 15*(3), 224–236. doi:10.1016/S0737-6782(97)00081-7

Nayak, P. R., & Ketteringham, J. M. (1986). *Breakthroughs.* London: Mercury Books.

Neti, S. (2011). Social Media and its Role in Marketing. *International Journal of Enterprise Computing and Business Systems, 1*(2), 1–15.

Nouala, M., El Kebir, N. D., & Maitre, I. K. (2016). Social Media as A New Emerging Tool of Marketing: Effect of E-Reputation in Algerian Market. *Maghreb Review of Economic and Management*, *8*(2), 81–95.

Obringer, L. A. (2007). *How Advergaming works*. Retrieved from http://money.howstuffworks.com/advergaming.htm/printable

Okazaki, S., & Taylor, C. R. (2013). Social media and international advertising: Theoretical challenges and future directions. *International Marketing Review*, *30*(1), 56–71. doi:10.1108/02651331311298573

Pertierra, R. (2005). Mobile Phones, Identity and Discursive Intimacy. *An Interdisciplinary Journal on Humans in ICT Environments*, *1*(1), 23–44. doi:10.17011/ht/urn.2005124

Pixability. (2013). *The Top 100 Global Brands: Key Lessons for Success on YouTube: The Massive YouTube Ecosystem*. Retrieved from http://concept5.com/how-the-top-100-brands-use-youtube-for-marketing/

Rajagopal. (2014). *Disruptive Innovations and Technologies. In: Architecting Enterprise*. Palgrave Macmillan.

Rao, B., & Minakakis, L. (2003). Evolution of Mobile Location Based Services. *Communications of the ACM*, *46*(12), 61–65. doi:10.1145/953460.953490

Scaife, M., & Rogers, Y. (1996). External cognition: How do graphical representations work? *International Journal of Human-Computer Studies*, *45*(2), 185–213. doi:10.1006/ijhc.1996.0048

Shakeel, M., & Khan, M. M. (2011). Impact of Guerrilla Marketing on Consumer Perception. *Global Journal of Management and Business Research*, *11*(7).

Sharma, M. (2014). Advergaming – The Novel Instrument in the Advertising. *Procedia Economics and Finance*, *11*, 247–254. doi:10.1016/S2212-5671(14)00193-2

Sharma, R., & Sharma, S. (2014). *A Review of Guerrilla Marketing & Its Weapons. The international journal Research Publications*. Research Journal of Social Science and Management.

Siricharoen, W. V. (2013). Infographics: The New Communication Tools in Digital Age. *The International Conference on E-Technologies and Business on the Web (EBW2013),* 169-174. 10.4018/ijeei.2013040104

Sorkin, A. R. (2006). Dot-Com Boom Echoed in Deal to Buy YouTube. *The New York Times*.

Tan, S. (2009). *Predicting the determinants of users' intention in using YouTube to share video*. Institute of Information Management, National Chiao Tung University.

Tomas, G., Hult, M., & Ketchen, D. J. Jr. (2017). Disruptive marketing strategy. *Academy of Marketing Science*, *7*, 20–25.

Veryzer, R. W. (1998). Key factors affecting customer evaluation of discontinuous new products. *Journal of Product Innovation Management*, *15*(2), 136–150. doi:10.1016/S0737-6782(97)00075-1

Waiguny, M., & Terlutter, R. (2010). Entertainment in Advergames and its Influence on Brand-Related Outcomes for Children. In R. Terlutter, S. Diehl, & S. Okazaki (Eds.), *Advances in Advertising Research* (Vol. 1). Gabler. doi:10.1007/978-3-8349-6006-1_12

Winkler, T., & Buckner, K. (2006). Receptiveness of Gamers to Embedded Brand Messages in Advergames: Attitudes Towards Product Placement. *Journal of Interactive Advertising*, *7*(1), 37–46.

YouTube. (2008). *YouTube Fact Sheet*. Retrieved from http://youtube.com/t/fact_sheet)

Yüksel, A. B. (2010). Gerilla Sanatı ve Gerilla Reklamcılığı, Marmara Üniversitesi, Güzel Sanatlar Enstitüsü Resim Anasanat Dalı, Yüksek Lisans Tezi, İstanbul, s. 74, 75.

Chapter 2
Gamification and Advergaming:
An Overview of the Innovative Brain Tool in the Field of Advertising

Aanchal Aggarwal
Vivekananda Institute of Professional Studies, India

Nupur Arora
Vivekananda Institute of Professional Studies, India

ABSTRACT

This chapter will expound on the concept of gamification and its adoption by various brands. It will be focusing on advergaming, which is one of the very famous applications of gamification. The chapter will elucidate the various launch details of advergaming applications by various firms and brand websites including online games, social network sites, and interactive digital television. It will also discuss the techniques underlying gamification, which include game mechanics and game dynamics, which will also reveal the impact of advergaming on consumer engagement and decision making to buy a product or not and also the benefits to the brand site. The chapter will also explain the techniques and strategies of advergaming used by various product websites nationally and internationally and their effect on consumers and the product or brand websites.

DOI: 10.4018/978-1-5225-6064-7.ch002

INTRODUCTION

The past 15 years has visibly shown the rise of the virtual game medium in entertainment, culture, and as an academic field of study. The success of virtual games within the commercial entertainment industry is visible in file-breaking console income and hugely occupied online multiplayer environments – has spurred studies into their outcomes and relevance in the virtual age. The belief of the solitary teenaged white male gamer is not relevant: the common gamer is 30 years antique, is 45% likely to be female, and tends to play puzzle, board games. Although virtual games are a relatively new development, games have existed in human cultures for the reason that sunrise of recorded lifestyle as tools for amusement, relationship-constructing, education, and arguably survival. Games are firmly entrenched in human culture persevering with to steer our social and leisure lives on a scale unprecedented and yet historically anticipated.

The impact of traditional advertising is reducing, making conventional mass media channels less appealing for advertisers to spend money on. The 30-second advert is more and more changed by way of options which might be less in all likelihood to be skipped via customers, which include product placement and Advergames, or via formats that permit clients to control which persuasive statistics they would love to look, such as web sites, social community sites, interactive virtual television. As the media and marketing format landscape keeps to trade, entrepreneurs and advertisers need to advantage insights into what types of advertising paintings great in such new environments. Notwithstanding the growing significance of latest marketing formats, research in this location remains underdeveloped. This unique difficulty contributes to a better knowledge of ways these new persuasive industrial strategies have an effect on purchasers.

One of the predominant commonplace traits of lots of these new codecs is that they are attempting to hide the persuasive purpose of the industrial messages embedded in them. Indeed, logo placement in movies, television programmes and games try and combine brands into the content in this type of manner that their integration looks natural and 'innocent' and does now not cause persuasion understanding (Van Reijmersdal, Neijens & Smit, 2009; Wouters & de Pelsmacker 2011). Website customization and other online advertising formats including Advergames try and conceal their persuasive intent by using growing pleasurable, waft-inducing and less intrusive formats (Cauberghe & de Pelsmacker 2010). Social network sites use the web dating among their participants to unfold viral advertising messages and to circumvent the suspicion of persuasive intentions. The preference to hide commercial intentions from consumers has also lead to ethically arguable strategies together with stealth and buzz marketing and extra efficaciously influencing vulnerable target organizations which includes teenagers.

GAMIFICATION EXPLAINED

The term gamification first used in 2008, in a blog published by Brett Terrill (2008). He describes the phrase as taking game mechanics and applying them to different internet properties to grow engagement of users. In 2010, the term entered wider spread in the industry (Deterding et al. 2011) and in academia (Hamari et al. 2014).

It's difficult to find out an exact date on when the time period when the term appeared first however using a high rate research skills (and a google seek engine) famous that the time period was coined in 2003 by using Nick Pelling while describing his paintings as a representative for making hardware more fun. It wasn't until later in the 2000s even though whilst the phrase started out to gain greater attention. Sources have indicated that one of the first documented uses of the term turned into in 2008 when "gamification" changed into used in a weblog submit by way of Bret Terrill, who came out with overlaying discussions within the foyer on the Social Gaming Summit. He heard the term use in regards to "taking recreation mechanics and applying to other web properties to boom engagement". The time period become picked up by other blogs and slimmed down via losing the 'e', becoming "gamification".

Conceptually, Gamification is a way which applies the mechanics of gaming to non-gaming games. In enterprise Context it integrates game dynamics and game mechanics right into a website, on-line network, enterprise offerings and the like for engagement and participation. Gamification is the process of the usage of game mechanics and game questioning in nongaming groups to interact users and to clear up issues. (The Gamification Summit, 2012). Gamification normally entails applying game design thinking to non-recreation packages to lead them to more fun and attractive. It can doubtlessly be implemented to any industry and almost something to create amusing and attractive reviews, converting users into players (Nicholson,2012). The term gamification turned into coined by using Nick Pelling in 2002 however it did not benefit a great deal recognition till 2010. In 2010 this time period won full-size utilization regarding incorporation of social/praise aspect of games into software (Ong,2013). One of the venture capitalist identified the ability of the term and taken into consideration it the maximum promising vicinity in gaming (Marczewski, 2012).

Gamification approach exploits the inherent human dreams for competition, success, popularity, self-expression, altruism and closure. The technique objectives to interact with the clients and get them to take part, percentage and have interaction through an activity/ network. The middle tactic of gamification lies in providing rewards for the gamers to accomplish their dreams. The exclusive varieties of rewards that are used are factors, badges or levels, digital currency supplied to the user. A specific method is likewise applied wherein the present responsibilities are made to experience more like video games the techniques used in this method are adding significant alternatives, on boarding with a tutorial, growing assignment and adding narrative

Techniques Underlying Gamification

Game Mechanics

Mechanics are the dealers, objects, elements and their relationships in the game. They define the sport most of the time-based totally gadget, specifying what there's, how the whole lot behaves, and how the participant can engage with the sport international. (Nicholson,2012)

Game Dynamics

Dynamics are the emergent behavior that arises from gameplay, while the Mechanics are placed into use. Take Snakes and ladders, for instance. Everything you want to play, and the guidelines specifying the way you play is recreation mechanics. The dynamics are the procedures and behaviors that get up while you truly play the sport. (Bunchball,2010)

GAMIFICATION IN ADVERTISING

The effect of conventional advertising and marketing is decreasing, making traditional mass media channels less appealing for advertisers to invest in. The 30-2d ad is increasingly replaced via options which can be much less probable to be skipped by consumers, which include product placement and Advergames, or by codes that permit customers to control which persuasive statistics they would love to peer, consisting of websites, social community sites and interactive virtual television. As the media and advertising layout landscape continues to trade, marketers and advertisers have to benefit insights into what varieties of marketing work pleasant in such new environments. Notwithstanding the growing importance of new advertising codecs, research on this region remains underdeveloped. This unique trouble contributes to a higher know-how of the way those new persuasive business strategies affect customers.

Table 1. Game mechanics

Achievements	"a virtual or physical representation of having accomplished something"
Appointments	"game dynamics in which at a predetermined times/place a user must log-in or participate in game, for positive effect"
Bonuses	"a reward after having completed a series of challenges or core functions"
Cascading Information Theory	"information should be released in the minimum possible Snippets"
Community Collaboration	"a dynamic wherein an entire community is rallied to work together to solve a riddle, a problem or a challenge"
Countdown	"a dynamic wherein an entire community is rallied to work together to solve a riddle, a problem or a challenge"
Epic Meaning	"a sense of discovering something great or working towards achieving something bigger than the players themselves"
Levels	"a system by which players are rewarded an increasing value for accumulation of points"
Points	"a running numerical value given for any single action or combination of actions"
Status	"A rank or level of a player. Players are often motivated by trying to reach a higher level or status"

List of Game Mechanics as Adopted from Gamification.org 2012

Table 2. Game dynamics

Rewards Schedules	"The timeframe and delivery mechanisms through which rewards (points, prizes, level ups) are delivered. Three main parts exist in a reward schedule; contingency, response and reinforcer."
Status	"The rank or level of a player. Players are often motivated by trying to reach a higher level or status. Also relates to envy."
Achievement	"Achievements are a virtual or physical representation of having accomplished something. Achievements can be easy, difficult, surprising, funny, accomplished alone or as a group. Achievements are a way to give players a way to brag about what they've done indirectly as well as add challenge and character to a game."
Self Expression	"Self-Expression if properly done leads to a feeling of accomplishment and ownership which can result in loyalty".
Competition	"Competitive computer and video gaming is the act of playing a computer or video game in a competitive sense."

One of the predominant commonplace traits of a lot of those new formats is that they are trying to conceal the persuasive intent of the industrial messages embedded in them. Indeed, brand placement in films, television programmes and games try to combine manufacturers into the content material in this type of manner that their integration appears herbal and 'harmless' and does now not trigger persuasion information (Van Reijmersdal, Neijens & Smit 2009; Wouters & de Pelsmacker 2011). Website customization and other online advertising codecs which include Advergames try to hide their persuasive cause by means of growing gratifying, drift-inducing and less intrusive formats (Cauberghe & de Pelsmacker 2010). Social network sites use the net courting among their members to unfold viral marketing messages and to bypass the suspicion of persuasive intentions. The preference to hide business intentions from customers has also cause ethically arguable techniques consisting of stealth and buzz advertising and more successfully influencing inclined goal companies including youngsters. (De Pelsmacker & Neijens, 2012).

In-game advertising (IGA) is the inclusion of merchandise or brands inside a digital game. The important goal of such games is to entertain the participant. Similar to product placements in films, recreation providers offer slots to advertisers who can include their brand or product in the sport (Yang et al. 2006). These video games, but, aren't depending on ad placements for a cohesive playing enjoy. IGA can be included into the game play, both in a subtle or in a prominent manner, or it can be supplied during loading instances of the game. Static IGA is a fixed placement in the game whilst the game is released, and it can't be modified after release of the game. The advantage is that static marketing does not want online get right of entry to broadcast the snap shots into the game. The disadvantage is that no changes may be made after the sport has been released. In dynamic IGA, advertising and marketing slots are protected in the sport, which may be stuffed flexibly and by using exclusive advertisers. For dynamic IGA to work, the player ought to have a reliable Internet connection.

Advergames are awesome from IGA, as they are in particular designed and created to promote a brand, product, carrier, or concept. The principal goals of Advergames are to deliver a powerful message for the advertised brand and to gain higher traffic on emblem websites. Advergames are usually free of rate, downloadable from or playable at the emblem's website, easy and amusing to play, and offer brief rewards. They are primarily informal video games (Redondo 2012). Advergames commonly allow for brief playing time as well as for longer play time and can be easily played in the course of brief breaks within the day, inclusive of waiting instances, on capsules, or smartphones. Advergames have turn out to be fairly ubiquitous, and many Advergames characteristic food products, a number of an bad nature (Lee et al. 2009; Moore & Rideout 2007; Quilliam et al. 2011)

Advergames

In-Game Advertising (IGA) is the inclusion of products or brands within a digital game. The main goal of such video games is to entertain the participant. Similar to product placements in movies, sport companies provide slots to advertisers who can consist of their logo or product in the game. These games, but, aren't dependent on advert placements for a cohesive gambling enjoyment. IGA can be included into the sport play, either in a subtle or in a distinguished way, or it is able to be presented all through loading times of the sport. Static IGA is a fixed placement in the sport when the game is launched, and it can't be modified after release of the game. The gain is that static advertising does now not need on line get entry to broadcast the images into the game. The disadvantage is that no adjustments can be made after the sport has been released. In dynamic IGA, marketing slots are blanketed in the game, which can be stuffed flexibly and with the aid of distinctive advertisers. For dynamic IGA to paintings, the participant ought to have a reliable Internet connection.

Advergames are distinct from IGA, as they are in particular designed and created to promote a brand, product, service, or concept. The most important pursuits of Advergames are to supply a powerful message for the marketed logo and to gain higher traffic on brand websites. Advergames are commonly freed from price, downloadable from or playable on the brands internet site, easy and a laugh to play, and provide short rewards. They are more often than not informal video games. Advergames usually allow for brief playing time in addition to for longer play time and can be easily performed during short breaks in the day, which includes waiting times, on capsules, or smartphones. Advergames have turn out to be pretty ubiquitous, and many Advergames feature food merchandise, a number of an dangerous nature

How Brands Are Using Gamification to Boost Engagement

Dominos has incorporated gamification in to their mobile pizza ordering app. Users can shake their Droid or iPhone if they don't know what they want to order and the app with pick the toppings

Banner Ads

When Mazda launched three new models in 2015, they knew getting market interested in their products would be a challenge. One of the products for which they needed a great digital campaign was the Mazda2. It is a supermini car that is quite fun to drive. However, they need to ensure they could get customers to be interested. The main concept of the game is to 'Challenge The Night'. The game was made available on digital and mobile platforms. The game starts out as a car ride. However, as players move on, an interactive game phase allows them to explore the car's various features. It is a fun way to ensure that players get to learn more about the car. When a player demonstrates they can maneuver the car with great skill, they stand a chance to win great rewards. The game is available on Mazda's website. A number of statistics indicated that the game was a major success. It received an interaction rate of more than 3%. The normal rate for the automotive industry is 0.5%. In addition, there were over 78% user replays for this game. It a good game ad example that utilises both fun and real world rewards.

McDonalds launched the advertisement in an effort to catch the attention of online gamers. The Filet-O-Fish was among McDonald's first products. The web-based game is an easy way for gamers to interact with McDonald's products through their banner ad games. As a result, next time they visit a McDonalds' joint they would remember to order the product. The advertisement was the brainchild of Moroch, an advertising agency. However, it was only made available in limited markets where McDonalds' Filet-O-fish sell well. The aim is for the player is to last as long as possible without being caught. You are given a Filet-O-Fish sandwich, which you protect from hungry sharks inside a tank. In addition, you must avoid touching the walls of the tanks. A number of codes allow you to unlock higher levels in the game. After each game, you can view how high you rank.

Advergames are more and more getting used as a part of an advertising campaign to sell merchandise and types. Previous studies investigating the quantity to which sport gamers absorb messages in interactive environments has focused on video and more popular online gaming environments. Using a snowball sampling method

Figure 1. Advergaming in Mazda

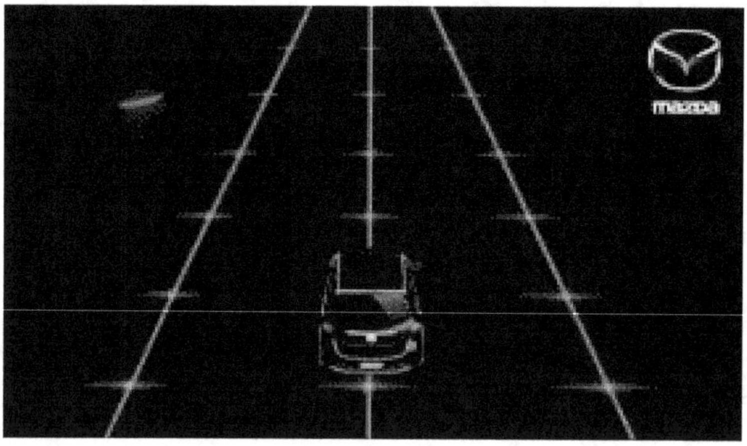

Figure 2. Advergaming on McDonalds

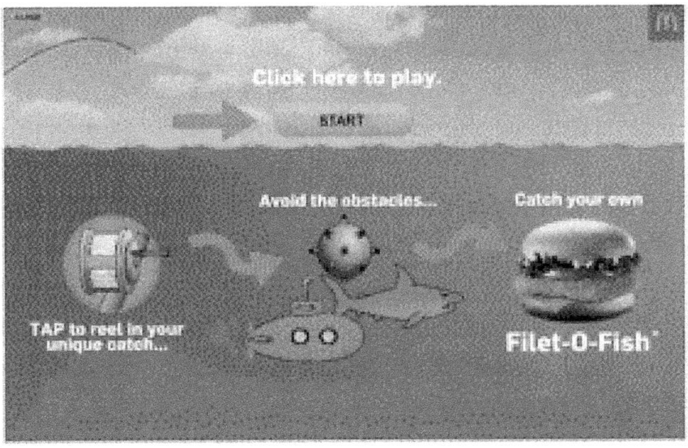

we examined the extent of take into account of products, manufacturers, and organizations in Advergames and whether the acceptability of product placement in Advergames is related to mind-set toward marketing in trendy. Our research indicates don't forget of merchandise and groups is high and that being terrible approximately advertising in well-known has a stronger impact on attitude toward product placement in Advergames than being superb approximately marketing. We conclude that Advergames may work more efficiently for products and types which are already regarded to the sport players and that Advergames may be extra desirable to enhancing and altering emblem impact rather than constructing focus of merchandise which are new to the target audience. (Tina & Buckner,2006). Receptiveness of gamers to embedded emblem messages in Advergames

Campaigns increasingly implement number of Advergames to interact clients with a brand through interactive, enjoyable media content material. However, little research tests the results of precise capabilities of Advergames on favoured advertising outcomes. This article reviews the consequences of a test designed to observe how variation inside the thematic connection between the game related to Advergames and the brand affects the relationship among attitude in the direction of the game (equated with attitude toward the ad) and attitude towards the brand. "The analysis reveals a more potent wonderful courting among attitude toward the Advergames and attitude towards the brand when party play games with a excessive thematic connection to the brand's product. Therefore, designing Advergames that relate thematically to the fabricated from the sponsoring logo ought to boom the participants capability of positive conditioning of brand attitudes evoked with the aid of playing an Advergames (Wise et al, 2008)

The impact of in-game brand exposure strength is explored with the aid of investigating the advertising results of brand prominence and game repetition. Four hundred eighty individuals played an online game two or four times. The outcomes imply a fantastic impact of brand prominence on logo don't forget, without influencing emblem attitude. Repeatedly playing a same game had no impact on brand recall, however had a negative effect on brand attitude, indicating that the wear-out section was reached quickly. Product involvement had a moderating effect for game repetition only, with more negative attitude outcomes of game repetition for a high-involvement product than for an extremely low-involvement product. In a follow-up study in which individuals could play the game as frequently as they desired, the outcomes of repeatedly playing the game have been showed. (Terlutter & Capella, 2013).

Cauberghe and De Pelsmacker (2010) provided framework for the evaluation of advertising and marketing in digital games. They reviewed literature on in-game marketing, Advergames and advertising in social network games. The framework distinguishes between stimulus characteristics of the game as well as of the advertising that result in mental responses in the direction of the game and the logo and to real behaviour in the direction of the game and the brand." It takes into attention individual factors of the player and social elements surrounding the participant. Dham S. O. (2016) have also studied the impact of Advergames on the emotional customer loyalty of the customer and shows that the games lead not only to positive engagement but also higher purchase intention. In addition, theoretical fashions of advertising notion in digital games and troubles regarding regulation are addressed.

Advergames are gaining reputation round the world as brand new, charming, and persuasive surroundings among advertisers. Despite its developing reputation, little or no is understood about the formation of attitudes toward Advergames in rising economies. The targets of their study were the refinement and empirical testing of a version of the reactions generated via exposure to Advergames among Mexicans, Peruvians, and Americans. A series of experiments found out that Hispanics exhibited superb attitudes towards Advergames. Intrusiveness was determined as the factor accounting for most of the poor mind-set toward Advergames. Lack of congruence was determined to be a precursor of intrusiveness. Interestingly, even though ads in video games have been perceived as more intrusive, they have been perceived as much less tense. (Hernandez et.al, 2004)

An and Stern (2011) examined one presently used advertising break for an Advergames to analyse whether its presence helped children apprehend the promotional nature of the Advergame and mitigated the outcomes of marketing within the game. “With the Persuasion Knowledge Model (PKM) because the theoretical frame, the experiment required that 112 youngsters, aged eight to 11, play an Advergame wherein visible and/or audio formats of the ad breakwere present or absent. Results showed that not one of the advert breaks helped kids to genuinely come across the economic nature of the game”. Also, the presence of the advert break no longer relate to children’s correct identification of the persuasive agent. The advert break did mitigate advertising consequences on kids, but, evidenced by reduced choice for and reminiscence of the advertised product”. (An & Stern,2011).

CONCLUSION

Gamification is one of the emerging topics in business today and seems to be on the minds of many of the marketing professionals today. If users have a positive and momentous game-based experience that is well-connected to the fundamental non-game setting, then the organization will benefit in the long run. A recent study by the research group Gartner predicted that 70 percent of the 2,000 biggest organizations will have at least one “gamified” application by 2014. The way these applications have altered over the last few years reflects the change in the way we think about engagement in every aspect of business.

REFERENCES

An, S., & Stern, S. (2011). Mitigating the effects of Advergames on children. *Journal of Advertising*, *40*(1), 43–56. doi:10.2753/JOA0091-3367400103

Bunchball. (2010). *Gamification 101: An Introduction to the Use of Game Dynamics to Influence Behavior*. Retrieved from http://jndglobal.com/wp-content/uploads/2011/05/gamification1011.pdf

de Pelsmacker, P., & Neijens, P. C. (2012). New advertising formats: How persuasion knowledge affects consumer responses. *Journal of Marketing Communications*, *18*(1), 1–4. doi:10.1080/13527266.2011.620762

Deterding, S., Dixon, D., Khaled, R., & Nacke, L. (2011, September). From game design elements to gamefulness: defining gamification. In *Proceedings of the 15th international academic MindTrek conference: Envisioning future media environments* (pp. 9-15). ACM. 10.1145/2181037.2181040

Dham, S. O. (2016). *Study of advergaming as a tool to build emotional customer loyalty and its implication on marketing returns*. Retrieved from ShodhGanga: http://shodhganga.inflibnet.ac.in/handle/10603/176014

Hamari, J., Koivisto, J., & Sarsa, H. (2014, January). Does gamification work?--a literature review of empirical studies on gamification. In *System Sciences (HICSS), 2014 47th Hawaii International Conference on* (pp. 3025-3034). IEEE.

Hernandez, M. D., Chapa, S., Minor, M. S., Maldonado, C., & Barranzuela, F. (2004). Hispanic attitudes toward Advergames: A proposed model of their antecedents. *Journal of Interactive Advertising*, *5*(1), 74–83. doi:10.1080/15252019.2004.10722095

Lee, M., Choi, Y., Quilliam, E. T., & Cole, R. T. (2009). Playing with food: Content analysis of food Advergames. *The Journal of Consumer Affairs*, *43*(1), 129–154. doi:10.1111/j.1745-6606.2008.01130.x

Marczewski, A. (2012). Gamification: A simple introduction & a bit more: Tips. In Advice and Thoughts on Gamification (2nd ed.). Kindle edition.

Moore, E. S., & Rideout, V. J. (2007). The online marketing of food to children: Is it just fun and games? *Journal of Public Policy & Marketing*, *26*(2), 202–220. doi:10.1509/jppm.26.2.202

Nicholson, S. (2012). A user-centered theoretical framework for meaningful gamification. *Games+ Learning+ Society, 8*(1), 223-230.

Ong, M. (2013). *Gamification and its effect on employee engagement and performance in a perceptual diagnosis task*. Academic Press.

Quilliam, E. T., Lee, M., Cole, R. T., & Kim, M. (2011). The impetus for (and limited power of) business self-regulation: The example of Advergames. *The Journal of Consumer Affairs*, *45*(2), 224–247. doi:10.1111/j.1745-6606.2011.01201.x

Redondo, I. (2012). The effectiveness of casual Advergames on adolescents' brand attitudes. *European Journal of Marketing*, *46*(11/12), 1671–1688. doi:10.1108/03090561211260031

Terlutter, R., & Capella, M. L. (2013). The gamification of advertising: Analysis and research directions of in-game advertising, Advergames, and advertising in social network games. *Journal of Advertising*, *42*(2-3), 95–112. doi:10.1080/00913367.2013.774610

Tina, W., & Buckner, K. (2006). Receptiveness of gamers to embedded brand messages in Advergames: Attitudes towards product placement. *Journal of Interactive Advertising*, *7*(1), 3–32. doi:10.1080/15252019.2006.10722123

Van Reijmersdal, E., Neijens, P., & Smit, E. G. (2009). A new branch of advertising. *Journal of Advertising Research*, *49*(4), 429–449. doi:10.2501/S0021849909091065

Wise, K., Bolls, P. D., Kim, H., Venkataraman, A., & Meyer, R. (2008). Enjoyment of Advergames and brand attitudes: The impact of thematic relevance. *Journal of Interactive Advertising*, *9*(1), 27–36. doi:10.1080/15252019.2008.10722145

Wise, K., Bolls, P. D., Kim, H., Venkataraman, A., & Meyer, R. (2008). Enjoyment of Advergames and brand attitudes: The impact of thematic relevance. *Journal of Interactive Advertising*, *9*(1), 27–36. doi:10.1080/15252019.2008.10722145

Wouters, M., & De Pelsmacker, P. (2011). Brand placement in scripted and non-scripted Belgian and US programs on Belgian prime time television. *Journal of Marketing Communications*, *17*(5), 299–318. doi:10.1080/13527261003600421

Chapter 3
Rhetoric of Advergames

Pratibha Kumari Singh
Ansal University, India

ABSTRACT

Advergames bring newness and engage better with customers. However, there is debate among marketers and communication experts as to how this tool could be exploited in the field of advertising and positioning of brands to the best of their advantage. The chapter thus aims to present arresting qualities of advergames under the rubric of rhetoric and claims that a deeper and meaningful understanding of multimodal rhetoric is needed to design and create these games. Further, to understand the working of these games and how they engage with the users, two advergames have been analyzed using multimodal analysis method, and a multimodal rhetorical framework (MRF) has been proposed for the perusal of marketers and communication experts to use as per their need and discretion.

INTRODUCTION

Advergames bring newness and engage better with the customers. However, there is debate among marketers and communication experts as to how these tools could be exploited in field of advertising and positioning of brands to the best of their advantage. The present chapter thus aims to present arresting qualities of advergames under the rubric of rhetoric and claims that a deeper and meaningful understanding of multimodal rhetoric is needed to design and create these games. Further, to understand the working of these games and how do they engage with the users, two advergames have been analyzed using multimodal analysis method and a Multimodal Rhetorical Framework (MRF) has been proposed for the perusal of marketers and communication experts to use as per their need and discretion.

DOI: 10.4018/978-1-5225-6064-7.ch003

Since ancient times, the art of rhetoric, through its means of powerful linguistic devises has enabled the young men to compose and deliver winning arguments. Times have changed now, however. Traditional media such as newspaper, brochure, pamphlets, flyers, etc are still popular, though no more absorbing and engaging as compared to visual medium. With the advent of internet and social media, customers of today have become more aware, brand conscious, ready to pay for the product, but aspire to be well informed to get services worth of the payment made. Amidst such competitive environments, gauging the attention of potential customers comes as one of the biggest challenges for the marketers. What comes as a panacea for them is better engagement through advertisements. Therefore, communication experts and marketers are ever engaged in devising innovative and creative strategies to woo potential customers and convert them into loyal consumers. The art of persuasion thus lies at the heart of marketing.

Can advergames, thus become the new tool to win the customers? The present chapter thus focuses on highlighting those aspects of advergames that present it as one of the most powerful, persuasive communication tools and media devises on the online world of today that pushes it to become a prime choice for advertisers in days to come. Integrated into the game, advergames aim to promote a brand, product or marketing message though an online video game. The popularity is expected to grow in days to come since there is increase in number of people doing online shopping and since advergames are strategic moves by the marketers that are designed with the purpose to increase the brand awareness and sales of the product, they seem to be the most prominent choice for the communication experts of today. If an ad of Bournvita can convince the children that the drink can make them win any competition, what if, they themselves engage through a game and win a competition. However, important for organisations and marketing experts is to design and innovate strong and meaningful games that can engage the customers and convert them into permanent users. Different mediums need to be used and exploited and so is the case with selling techniques.

Historical Overview

The upcoming of new Media platforms have impacted the way people receive and perceive information. Shocked, sometimes as people are, due to pervasiveness and penetration of new technologies in their lives, there is conscious and unconscious selection on their part to accept and make part of these media forms and latest technologies (Adams & Smith; 2015). Social media platforms such as blogs, facebook, Instagram to name a few and video games engage and connect with customers in a much different way as compared to the traditional media. It is the very interactivity and new methodology used to entice the customers that bring forth a kind of new revolution in the way marketing of the products is attempted these days (Miles; 2014). Use of audio-visual applications has deeply impacted the psychology of consumers as compared to traditional media forms. Image is becoming popular and dominant along with the digital devises and 3-D effects in the new media marketing tools, language though is still used (Jewitt 2002).

However, looking at the very root of the persuasive techniques, when we trace the history, we find that the art of rhetoric has used potential linguistic devises to build the persuasive messages arguments. It is imperative at this stage to look at all those elements that were needed to persuade and create the desired impact in the minds of the readers. Now, do communication experts of today still follow those fundamentals? If we know the answer is in affirmation. Then what has changed, how and why, are some of the interrogatives in the present context that need to be answered. It is Aristotle's rhetoric that we look at and try to exhume the answers.

'Enchanting of the soul' as Plato calls it and Aristotle defines it as 'the means of discovering, in any particular case, all the available means of persuasion,' the subject of Rhetoric was formulated to search the philosophical nature of truth that underwent change with the passage of time owning to the very understanding of all the sophists who added to its philosophy and taught this subject in Athens. Out of all the rhetoricians, we however, follow the Aristotle's *Art of Rhetoric*, the book wherein we find a detailed description of prescriptions to build the strong and persuasive arguments based on logic. Aristotle, one of the most celebrated Greek Rhetoricians proposes the five canons that fall under the following categories:

These five canons delineate the process of arrangement of a discourse in the persuasive manner. In the language courses offered such as 'composition', 'academic writing' 'public speaking' and 'business and professional speech' and 'media marketing' this canon is introduced as one of the most important canons for the students. In fact, in the fields of advertisement and marketing also, the invention or the discovery of the very proposition on the basis of which the whole argument would be built and would stand is something very crucial. Once this standpoint or proposition is clear, the next step involved is the collection of relevant material that

Table 1. Five canons of rhetoric

English Term	Meaning
1. Invention	Coming up with materials for arguments
2. Arrangement	Ordering your discourse
3. Style	Saying/writing things and in a persuasive manner
4. Memory	Strategic remembering
5. Delivery	Presenting your ideas

could be in the form of data, facts, figures, statistics, and story to build that entire case or discourse. According to Aristotle, there are two categories of arguments, as mentioned in the *Art of Rhetoric*, the first one refers to the 'internal' that are technical and artistic in nature; the second one refers to the 'external' that are 'non-artistic' and 'non-technical' proofs. Thus, it is at this point, Aristotle elaborates the 'technical' and 'artistic' means of persuasion for the use of speakers, writers or marketers. These means of persuasion demand time, skill and efforts on the part of the maker.

The internal sources of arguments are woven and build around three: 1) Logos (that appeals to ones reason); 2) Pathos (that appeals to ones emotions); 3) Ethos (that has ethical appeal).

Logos that appeal to ones reasons are inductive or deductive, fallacious or non-fallacious, syllogistic or enthymemic. Pathos refers to emotive appeal. As second category of proofs, they engage with the psychology of persuasion and how emotions could be triggered and generated inside the audience by exploitation of language to persuade the audience. One can achieve this appeal by putting the audience/reader/user in a certain frame of mind. It is indubitably the favorite of the writers, poets and novelist along with the market and communication experts because nothing works better than the emotional appeal. Ethos, the third internal source of argument is based on the credibility of the character. Brands with their strong history such as Raymond, Godrej, MDH etc use Ethos in devising their advertising gimmick.

The second canon refers to way contents are organized in any discourse. Every discourse has a beginning, middle and end and how introduction is crafted, statements of facts presented and divided, proofs confirmed and elaborated, points refuted and then summarized to conclude, come under the purview of this canon. Aristotle prescribes, how use of ethos can make the discourse listen credible, rational when logos being used to explain the arguments with the proofs and evidence and could be effectively concluded using pathos so as to emotionally connect with the audience.

Style refers to distinctive manner of expression. It is the third canon. If 'what' is about the content of the discourse, 'how' of the discourse or the form of the discourse refers to style or manner. Rhetoric provides figurative strategies of schemes and tropes that are being employed by the users to make the expression artful and emotionally appealing. Alliteration, assonance, Metaphor, simile, parallelism, personification etc are many such devices that are being exploited by the writes and users to ornate the discourse. It is this section that attracted the attention of writers and marketers the most. However, with the very purpose for which these figures were invented underwent dynamic change. Users reduced this art to chicanery and propaganda and the subject became a guide book to appeal to the emotions, but at the cost of the truth. To understand the right perspective and usage of the devises and strategies proposed become utmost important for the communication experts.

The fourth canon focuses on memory tricks. How a speech could be remembered by a speaker and how it lasts in the memory of the listeners. Mnemonics, elements of repetition, contrast, analogy, story and many such devises were employed by the speakers to make their speech memorable. The listeners and audience must remember the speech even when is over become central work focus in this canon. The fifth canon of rhetoric deals with the delivery and performance wherein visual persuasive tools such as font type and size, layout of the text on the page, typography and its alignment, graphology and use of images etc play a role.

The nature and meaning of the word Rhetoric, however, has changed in all these years. Not confined to debate and persuasion, like old rhetoric, the new rhetoric sees multiplicity in the meaning of words, in the context and for the very purpose for which they are being used. Further, the focus is not only on the very function that is performed by the words, but the way they interact in the linguistic environment of a text (Richards, 1965). According to Campbell (2013), the words that are used to build the argument and reveal the truth, must be understood by the readers first, but then, in order for any argument to be convincing, it must be remembered and engage the user so as to invite the desired action and generate the very interest in the subject. The words of the orator or the user should have power to touch all faculties of mind including memory, passion and imagination.

These canons of rhetoric postulate the prescriptive devises to craft persuasive speeches. The author argues that for advergames, wherein all these elements, along with the multimodal components of visual, auditory, spatial and gestural work are present, the knowledge of the new rhetoric is needed that can lead to better understanding of the rationale and working of these games. It is here that we seek help of analytical approach to investigate working of multimodal levels in discourse of advergames. The analysis of the two advergames presented below reveal how these elements of rhetoric, or persuasion, have been interwoven strategically to engage and connect with the user.

Multimodal Analysis

The art of persuasion has increased manifold since the beginning of the century. While in ancient Greece when Rhetoric was taught, there were set of linguistic devises at the disposal of the sophists to sharpen their point of view and present them in front of their audience. In present times, besides the linguistic strategies deployed by the marketers, there are aural, spatial and visual tools that are at their disposal. There is winning and wooing of the consumer that becomes inspiration behind designing any promotional tool.

To see how these persuasive devises of logos, pathos and ethos have been strategically used by marketers, an analysis would help to understand better. For this very purpose, author uses multimodal analysis method. Multimodal analysis allows looking at different modes present, as shown in figure below, in any media such as texts, videos, TV commercial ads or advergames to examine how they semiotically interact with one another and help in meaning making process. This requires description, analysis and interpretation of various textual, audio, visual, spatial and gestural modes of representation and communication present in the media. The very purpose of the analysis is simply not to enlist the multimodal data present as a decorative and fancy observation, but to find out the very purpose and reason of their presence in the contextual meaning making process. Further, according to Bhatia (1993), more than involving in the thin description of any genre, it is important to understand and focus on the functional and communicative value that those features perform in the ultimate discourse.

Through the analysis process, the purpose is to see how advergames work in alignment with the concept of defamiliarization and have made their niche in the market in recent decades because of their unique and subtle technique in creation. The concept of defamiliarization, literary 'making strange' refers to the way in which the world is shown in an unusual and unexpected manner. The element of uniqueness breaks the monotony and arrests the attention of the reader, viewer or user and brings an element of surprise that makes the world look afresh and from a new perspective.

Figure 1. Elements of multimodality present in any media discourse

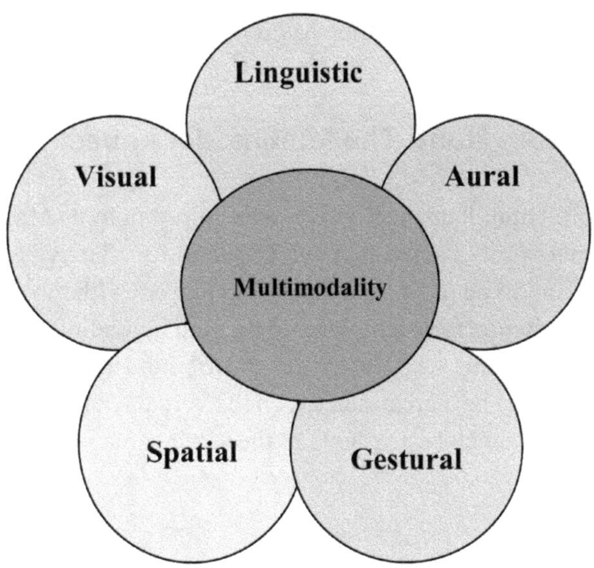

The term was coined by Viktor Shklovsky in his famous essay 'Art as Technique'. According to him, every art form -linguistic or visual- defamiliarizes the world that it creates. When we look at any aesthetic piece of language, art, literature or media, we find that this concept of defamiliarization has been exquisitely woven to make the art strange. Further, various techniques such as: parallelism, repetition, rhyme and rhythm in linguistics; Colour contrast and complementary colour schemes in visuals; rhythm and harmony with slow and faster nodes in music are all exploited in creative ways to defamiliarize the reader/audience/user to seize their attention. Novelists, poets, writers, designers, marketers and communication experts use this concept to engage and persuade the readers, in a novel way (Douthwaite 2000). Advergames too, like any other art form, make use of this concept along with the elements of rhetoric to persuade the customers.

If, as per the understanding of the audience, such games are created, that are absorbing, thrilling, exciting, generate awareness, educate and inform the customers, then, this technique and strategy would be worth because such games would connect meaningfully with the audiences.

The rhetoric of advergames thus refers to the way in which persuasive devises of logos, pathos and ethos are employed by the marketers to engage the user through the concept of defamiliarization at multiple levels where they experience their involvement and participation in the imaginary or virtual world created through the gaming method. While they enjoy the game, they also get to know the product, brand and its purpose or usage to an extent. The entire experience leaves a more lasting impression since the time spent in playing the game is more than few minutes and the thrill of participation leaves them think more about game and indirectly about the product. A multiple modal analysis would help to unfold these intricate blending of various concepts. Thus two advergames have been selected for the analysis, Magnum Pleasure Hunt and Wingo Flies.

Magnum Pleasure Hunt: The Multimodal Aspect

Magnum Pleasure Hunt, launched by Unilever to promote its Magnum ice-cream products, has been highly lauded by experts due to its effective engagement with players that turns out to be more than 7.000.000 players with the approximate time engagement of 5 minutes for each player. The viral spread of the game due to its posting on social networking sites also led to its distribution to wider audience. Further, its hashtag turned out to be a great success on the very day of its launch, convincing the Unilever to soon launch two sequels of the same game in the following years.

Figure 2. Google image credits

Designed and created by Lowe Brindfors, the game allows the players to take a girl on a journey wherein she runs on the road collecting chocolates and bonbons. The game allows the players to control the movements of the girl as she runs and jumps as shown in other video game that provides a sense of power to the players that they can win if they play well. The environment of the game shows different websites and brands, making the visuals appealing and engaging for the players. Some might find the streets distracting though, if they want to focus too much on the run of the girl and miss the hoarding and posters of the brands. It is the journey and run of the girl that makes the most fulfilling and satisfying part for the players. At the end, the girl reaches to the main product-the ice-cream, New Magnum Temptation Hazelnut with Bonbons-and the final scores of the players are displayed on the screen. To further share their scores, players can share the link and scores on Facebook and challenge their friends.

The integration of brand images in the game, music, character and her run through the road to score the points serves to refer to the function of identification with the user, creating a bond between them where they forget the virtual world and form a reality and relish and enjoy being part of the game. A display of the score running somehow keeps their mind engaged, focused and absorbed in winning that result in final satisfaction when the game is over. Once the goal is achieved, score displayed, release of endorphins lead to happiness and satisfaction. In the moment of victory and score gained, user thus feels a compulsiveness to share with others his score board and invite others to experience the game.

Figure 3. Google image credits

Figure 4. Google image credits

The success of the game can be credited to the way entire world of ad and gaming has been created. Once the user enters, the faster description of the game on screen, recognition of the play as the 'self', different movements of running, jumping, flying on the gladiator attributed to the player assure a different experience all together. While in the backdrop, different brands are positioned, entering of the player through them is uniquely displayed. Schemes of colour rhyme with the very brand of Magnum and bring the richness and luxury to the ambience in the game. The music keeps the level of concentration intact wherein no outside distraction allows the user to lose the focus from the game. A user is thus completely absorbed since a loss of concentration means, losing of the bon bon on the way and lower accomplishment of score. While the experience leaves the users thrilled, their scores present encourage them to share their win with the friends and challenge them to beat the score. The very presence of the advergames on the online platform and connect with social media makes it viral. The more the users engaged, the wider the reach of the game spreads. Thus the very key becomes intimate engagement of each player in the game and their overall score where they feel a sense of pride in accomplishment of their high bon bon score. The unique gaming virtual environment, with exposure to brand, where they can run and roam as per their will, leaves the lasting memory in minds of the user.

Wingo Flies: The Game Reviewed From Multimodal Method

Turkish Airlines is one of the first brands to use advergames to position its promotional flights under the name of Wingo flies. The credit of designing this overall campaign and advergame goes to ArnoBrasco, an Istanbul based digital agency. With the coming of 360 video experience, ArnoBrasco exploited this platform to launch #WingoFliest, its first 360 video advergames on YouTube in 2016.

Named after the Greylag character in the game Wingo, the mobile app and the advergames announces all the promotional flights with the help of this leading character. Since, airlines provide experience of the flight, so, it is no wonder that this Greylag symbolizes that flight. The very selection of the Greylag as the leading character is arresting and symbolic both. The users perceive the Greylag giant, with ability to run and fly both. And the very presentation of it with head cap, glares and luggage at the bag make it feel the very air of embarking on an adventurous journey. The wings, like the wings of airplane and that of human imagination make this image apt as the representative of the brand. Further, the real setting of the game shot amidst one of the most exotic places in Turkey, when the Wingoflies takes to the regions of Cappadocia, the user is filled with thrill and adventure to experience the sunrise flying amongst the hundreds of vibrant hot air balloons. These scenes provoke imagination of users. They feel emotional striving to be a part of such flight.

Figure 5. Google image credits

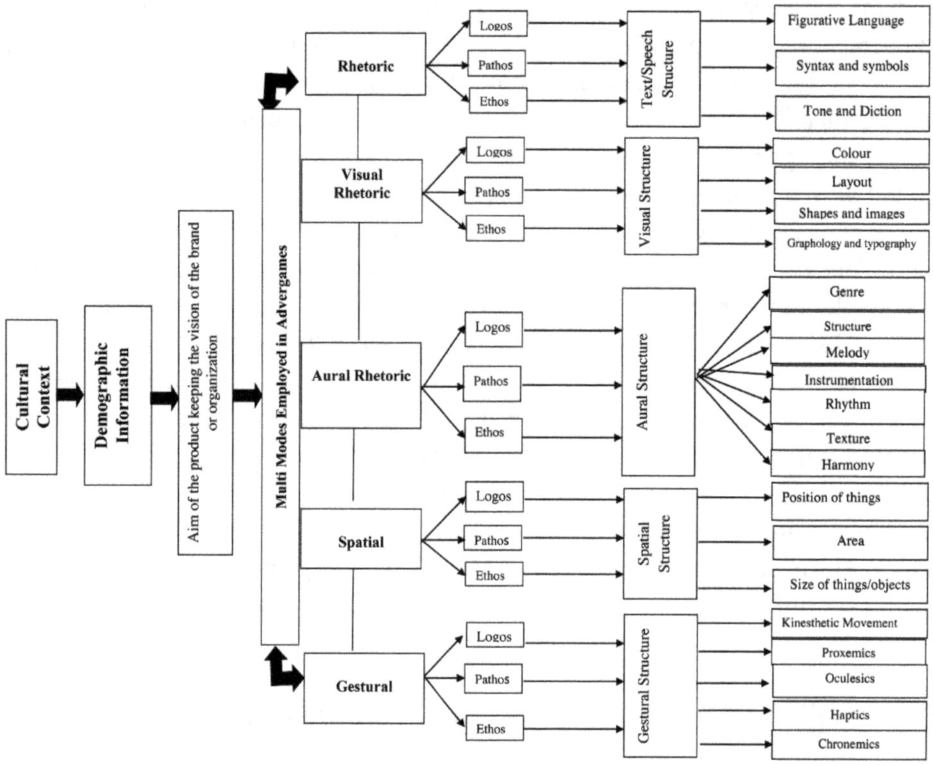

Moreover, to engage them, in the entire flight, users are provided with different clues that disappear, as soon as the user finds them, to make their experience thrilling and absorbing. Shot with one drone and seven GoPros, the game takes the user to a perfect 360 experience of the Wingo driven world.

Critical Issues in Multimodal Analysis of Advergames

While an attempt to analyze an advergame under the rubric of rhetoric with multimodal framework is alluring and informative from academic and marketing point of view since it offers all the details that make an ad game stand, succeed or fail for the very purpose for it is designed, however, it does pose challenges to the analyst as follows. First and foremost, an extensive and full-fledged knowledge of the domain and its nomenclature with a deeper and wider understanding is required on part of the analyst which must be based on theory, knowledge of the culture in which is it framed and the very purpose in lieu of which it might be bring some falsity to the very analysis and interpretation attempted. Since a multimodal analysis is a demanding and extensive exercise, there are two points that an analysis must consider. First, to be unbiased in approach, thereby filtering the personal coloring of dominant ideas to avoid personal projection; and thus making an attempt of the analysis on the basis of fact and proof finding from the very data itself. Second, to ensure that not all the data is important and therefore, use of discretion in selection of the relevant and appropriate data such as textual, typographical, graphological, image, colours, layout, aural, kinesthetics and characters etc that is important for the analysis, which adds in the interpretation and aligns with the very purpose for which the analysis has been attempted, must be selected.

Next, in an analysis such as multimodal, mere identification is not that important as the interpretation that leads to meaning making. Although, the very interpretation is based on the finding of the various modes at different levels and their interaction with one another, however, interpretation of the data gathered is always coloured by the understanding of the analyst, which might differ from culture to culture. It poses a challenge then. Therefore, if needed, an analyst must seek feedback and advice from the experts in various fields of modes and pass on a fair evaluation of the analytical work. For it is almost impossible for an analyst to be a language expert, music expert, image expert, typography expert to attempt a fuller analysis and interpretation of the data gathered from the source. Last but not the least, since multimodality invites multi-layers of analysis, an analyst might find it daunting and may get confused in the line of progress, hence, it is assumed that students, academicians and communication experts would find a single focus at the time of analysis that would enable to draw important conclusion and pass on the recommendations, if any, for better understanding.

Despite these critical issues and challenges, indubitably, students and communication experts would find the very task of analysis and interpretation quite meaningful and informative since that would provide them details of how different modes in any media bring coherence through their association and engage the user through their overall world creation. The better the understanding provided by the analytical practices, the more would be chances on the part of the media experts to innovate and launch new advergames in the market. No, doubt, their success would be attributed to their finer understanding of the multimodality present in the advergames.

Multimodal Rhetorical Framework for Advergames

The new age, new media does proclaim and promise a very bring future of the advergames, however, in no way, that needs to be assumed that it would demarcate the death of the old and traditional media. Rather, this new media offers a new and wide range of options that allow the communication experts to try and launch their products as per the price, policy, brand value, requirement and need of the product. Indubitably, the deviant and arresting quality of advergames provide them a competitive advantage over the other media advertising tools. However, investment in terms of their making and designing poses a challenge to the marketers.

Aristototle's rhetoric extends in linguistic context; however, the new rhetoric claims Visuals and aural sounds to have their own rhetoric and grammar. Thus, for advergames, as we have explored in investigation of two games: The Magnum Treasure Hunt and Wingoflies, require understanding of Multimodal system wherein persuasive strategies could be used at each mode and thus such a framework needs a new term, called Multimodal Rhetorical Framework (MRF) that involves strategies for each mode involved in making and designing of advergames.

The argument of this rhetorical framework is based on this notion that innovation and creativity are the hallmarks of marketing field. To market and launch new products, communication experts and marketers always look for meaningful, engaging and creative ways. Advent of advergames have definitely provided a new tool to them, however, how to use it for optimum advantage where larger goal is fulfilled is an area of concern for marketers.

Here, in the framework that is proposed in paragraphs and Figure 1.2 below, the purpose is to highlight rhetorical strategies and techniques that could be utilized in designing of advergames. First and foremost, important is to place the product in the larger context and analyze its macro and micro aspects that would be enable shaping of the vision for the product.

It is important to understand that a culture and society whose very norms and standards are set the moment ones become more brand conscious and aware. Sometimes, brands also divide and create a world making haves and haves not. Those who use brand are haves and those who do not-haves not. Therefore, a cultural understanding of the place, its people and they way they connect with the product is something worth examination at the first stage. The product should aim to unite and not divide. Inform about the product, rather than simply beguile the users in an enchanting aesthetic world of ads and games. The value system, social norms and sentiments of culture must be understood well at this stage so that chances of acceptability of product through such games are increased manifold.

Since each advergame has a communication function to perform that aims to persuade, entertain, or inform the viewers to become a consumer of the product in the ultimate terms. One of the pre-requisites is to have expertise and deeper understanding of the product and demography for which it needs to designed. A team with proper orientation and equipped with research tools and techniques need to be placed to bring the right data with interpretation and analysis based on customer choices, preferences and values. For example, if for senior Indian citizens a product needs to be launched, it would be better to use a traditional medium of newspaper or visual mode of Television, where they spend more time reading and watching, as compared to spending time on internet. However, this very information, when added, that the product has to be for the IT professionals who are above 60, then definitely option of launching advergames could be thought of. This demographic information would save a lot of time, energy and resources. Since advergames demand considerable amount of money to be invested in their making, decision must be taken as to which product should be launched through advergames, why, what are its advantages and if it would be better than any other media form, then choices must be weighed and examined as shown in case of above example.

The next stage or step demands setting the very purpose or objective of the advergames making and launch. Always, persuasion is at the core, however, at what cost and how, that needs a serious attention. The very ethics these days are put at stake to lure the customer and sometimes, there is no connect seem to be present between the promotion and the product itself. Thus, the very mission, value system of the organization and service or experience that the product offers must play the core element in the designing part. Introduction of elements for the sake of ornamentation should be less; focus must be on revelation of the true nature of the product through the effort.

Further in the framework are the multi modes of rhetoric. The term rhetoric here refers to make use of all the available means to persuade, as Aristotle asserted, and to defamiliarize the content to arrest the attention of the users in context of advergames. The devises of logos, pathos and ethos, as explained in the historical review section are present in all the modes, thus, their understanding and usage should be as per the requirement and need of the ad game. Each of the mode mentioned has a vast field of its own rhetoric and grammar, therefore, a semiotic understanding of their usage in the larger context is what marketers should aim at. As each mode has its structure made of several other micro elements that complete and provides different choices at the disposal of makers, as shown in figure below, some of them are essential and some optional. A deeper, contextual and pragmatic knowledge and understanding of multimodal discourse becomes imperative for designers to attain.

Under the linguistic mode, all the elements of rhetoric including use of figurative language, diction, tone, syntax, symbols and structure are important considerations. Visual rhetoric includes clarity and appropriateness of colour(s), layout, shapes and images, graphology and typography in any game. Aural rhetoric has genre, structure, melody, use of instrumentation to set the mood, rhythm to set the tempo, texture of the music and harmony as essentials. Spatial structure include position of things and objects in a setting in relation with the other objects and elements, overall area selected for the canvass in the gaming and area of white space and textual space or area of white space and coloured elements, along with size of objects and things are important in this rhetoric. Gestural rhetoric has kinesthetic movement of the characters and object making the scene look real in the virtual setting, proxemics reflect the relationship of one object and charater with other in relation to the distance between them and their size shown, oculesics is communication through eyes, haptics is about touch and chronemics is about total time taken in execution of a game. These elements cemented together build the edifice of multimodal rhetorical framework proposed for advergames.

CONCLUSION

Boundaries between the virtual and the real word are diminishing. Online world has its own culture, rules and strategies for survival. In this new online world, customers are more informed and aware today. They know variety of brands, their quality, pricing and availability. Their decisions are emotional and analytical both. How to engage such customers and convert them into loyal customers is what every marketers deals with. While focus on production of quality product is important, however, to always be present and be in the lives of customers is something that every advertiser and marketer must think of. It is here, that advergames come as panacea. Unlike old media methods and tools, which are static, non-interactive and engaging in nature, advergames, offer competitive advantage by being interactive, engaging and involving the customers in real time environment. The subtle inclusion of brand, its tag line and logo through continuous exposure consume a memory unit in mind of the game user and thus unconsciously expose the players to become more aware of the brand. How this persuasive tool could be used more effectively and meaningfully is what this chapter has elaborated and commented upon.

While persuasion is at the heart of marketing, truth has to be at its core. Any Ad or advergames must aim to reveal the truth. It must not extol or exaggerate the experience through falsification as many of the commercial ads do on Television and engage the audience without any logical input. Such ads might be appreciated because of their emotive appeal, aesthetics and connect with the audience, however, what kind of information do they reveal about the product itself is something worth consideration. Thus, critical questioning in terms of deciding what to project on screen is of utmost importance for experts. Timing of the launch, such as festive season for chocolates and sweets, dress and gadgets when maximum shopping is done in Indian context must be kept in mind. Despite competitiveness in the market, organization pressure of marketing and sales team, the onus must be felt and realized by the advertisement agencies before launching of the game. Convincing the potential customers and persuading them to buy the product is important, but phoniness, extreme promises, exalted images must not be depicted to delude the customers. As the saying goes that marketing can only sell the better products, thus the focus must be on the best quality production and then their branding and positioning.

Summary and Future Directions

The present chapter reviewed the available literature on advergames under the focus of rhetoric. Applying method of multimodal analysis to excavate elements of logos, pathos and ethos on two advergames, the author in the preset chapter aimed to highlight various persuasive devises exploited by designers and marketers of these advergames to create a defamilarized world for the users. With the results of the analysis, the author recommends, how full potential of such advergames could be utilized by educators, communication experts and marketers to design and innovate techniques of gaming in alignment with the larger goals of marketing and selling. Better, effective and engaging advergames could be developed for information and education, besides entertainment, when one understands that going beyond the profit is important to engage meaningfully with the customers and convert them into loyal ones for long term relationship building. The multimodal framework proposed offers suggestion and road map to the communication experts where their creativity, value addition and meaningfulness in production of engaging and interactive advergames would prove its full potential and worth.

REFERENCES

Adams, T., & Smith, S. A. (2015). Communication shock: the rhetoric of new technology. Newcastle upon Tyne, UK: Cambridge Scholars Publishing.

Advergaming. (n.d.). Retrieved September 27, 2017, from http://objevit.cz/slovnik-pojmu-co-je-to-advergaming-t169372

Bargiela-Chiappini, F. (2009). *The handbook of business discourse*. Edinburgh, UK: Edinburgh University Press.

Bateman, J. (2008). *Multimodality and genre. A foundation for the systematic analysis of multimodal documents*. Hampshire, UK: Palgrave MacMillan.

Bhatia, V. J. (1993). *Analysing Genre: Language Use in Professional Settings*. London: Longman.

Bogost, I. (2007). *Persuasive games: The expressive power of videogames*. The MIT Press.

Campbell, G. (2013). *The philosophy of rhetoric*. New York: Cambridge University Press.

Corbett, E. P., & Connors, R. J. (1999). *Classical rhetoric for the modern student*. New York: Oxford University Press.

Dixon, P. (2016). *Rhetoric. S.I.* Taylor & Francis.

Douthwaite, J. (2000). *Towards a linguistic theory of foregrounding*. Alessandria: Edizioni dellOrso.

Fairclough, N. (1995). *Media Discourse*. London: Arnold.

Fairclough, N. (1995). *Critical Discourse Analysis: The Critical Study of Language*. London: Longman.

Floch, J. M. (2001). *Semiotics, Marketing and Communication*. Palgrave Macmillan.

Floch, J. M. (2001). *Visual Identities*. London: Bloomsbury.

Gibbons, A. (2012). *Multimodality, cognition, and experimental literature*. London: Routledge.

Hackley, C. E. (2007). *Marketing and social construction: exploring the rhetorics of managed consumption*. London: Routledge.

Halliday, M. A. K. (1975). *Learning How to Mean: Explorations in the development of language*. London: Edward Arnold. doi:10.1016/B978-0-12-443701-2.50025-1

Heinrichs, J. (2013). *Thank you for arguing: what Aristotle, Lincoln, and Homer Simpson can teach us about the art of persuasion*. New York: Three Rivers Press.

Jewitt, C. (2002). The move from page to screen: The multimodal reshaping of school English. *Journal of Visual Communication*, *1*(2), 171–196. doi:10.1177/147035720200100203

Jewitt, C. (2017). *The Routledge handbook of multimodal analysis*. Routledge.

Kress, G. (2010). *Multimodality. A social semiotic approach to contemporary communication*. London: Routledge.

Kress, G., & van Leeuwen, T. (2001). *Multimodal discourse: The modes and media of contemporary communication*. London: Arnold.

Kress, G., & Van Leeuwen, T. (2006). *Reading images: The grammar of visual design*. London: Routledge.

LeVine, P., & Scollon, R. (Eds.). (2004). *Discourse and Technology: Multimodal Discourse Analysis*. Washington, DC: Georgetown University Press.

Machin, D. (2007). *Introduction to multimodal analysis*. London: Hodder Arnold.

Manovich, L. (2001). *The Language of New Media*. Cambridge, MA: The MIT Press.

Melzer, N. (2007). *Advergames: the effects of brand placement and music*. Rotterdam: Erasmus Universiteit.

Miles, C. (2014). *Interactive marketing: revolution or rhetoric?* London: Routledge.

O'Halloran, K. (Ed.). (2004). *Multimodal Discourse Analysis: Systemic-Functional Perspectives*. London: Continuum.

Purswani, G. (2010). Advergames, their use and potential regulation. *Asia Pacific Public Relations Journal, 11*, 7.

Richards, I. A. (1965). *The philosophy of rhetoric*. London: Oxford University Press.

Turkish Airline's #WingoFlies Is The First YouTube 360 Advergame. (2016, May 17). Retrieved September 27, 2017, from https://wersm.com/turkish-airlines-wingoflies-is-the-first-youtube-360-advergame/

van Leeuwen, T. (1999). *Speech, music, sound*. London: Macmillan. doi:10.1007/978-1-349-27700-1

Van Leeuwen, T. (2005). *Introducing social semiotics*. London: Routledge.

van Leeuwen, T., & Jewitt, C. (2001). *Handbook of Visual Analysis*. London: Sage.

ADDITIONAL READING

Adis, A. A. A., & Kim, H. J. (2013). The mediating role of brand recall and brand attitude in influencing purchase intention in advergames. *Asia Marketing Journal*, *15*(3), 117–139.

Burke, M. (2014). *The Routledge handbook of stylistics*. London: Routledge, Taylor & Francis Group.

Konzack, L. (2002). Computer game criticism: A method for computer game analysis. Paper presented at the Computer Games and Digital Culture Conference, Tampere, Finland.

Koster, R. (2005). *A Theory of Fun for Game Design*. Scottsdale, Arizona: Paraglyph Press.

Kress, G. (2003). *Literacy in the new media age*. London: Routledge. doi:10.4324/9780203164754

Lee, M., Choi, Y., Quilliam, E. T., & Cole, R. T. (2009). Playing With Food: Content Analysis of Food Advergames. *The Journal of Consumer Affairs*, *43*(1), 26. doi:10.1111/j.1745-6606.2008.01130.x

Roettl, J., Waiguny, M., & Terlutter, R. (2016). The persuasive power of advergames: A content analysis focusing on persuasive mechanisms in advergames. [AMJ]. *Australasian Marketing Journal*, *24*(4), 275–287. doi:10.1016/j.ausmj.2016.10.001

Salen, K., & Zimmerman, E. (2005). Game Design and Meaningful Play. In J. Raessens & J. Goldstein (Eds.), *Handbook of Computer Game Studies* (pp. 70–75). Cambridge: MIT Press.

Sotirova, V. (2016). *The Bloomsbury Companion to Stylistics*. London: Bloomsbury Academic.

The Forest of Rhetoric (silva rhetoricae) http://rhetoric.byu.edu/

Tuten, T. L., & Solomon, M. R. (2018). *Social media marketing*. Los Angeles: Sage.

KEY TERMS AND DEFINITIONS

Advergames: Etymologically, advergames represent hybrid of advertisement and gaming. Created, used, and promoted by companies, advergames engage the audience through video games with the sole purpose of promotion, positioning, and branding of a company or its products.

Communication Tools: Communication is a dynamic culture- and society-centric process. With the upsurge in available means of persuasion with online marketing, marketers find it challenging to use the perfect blend of communication tools to promote and position their products that can build their loyalty in minds of customers and engage them effectively for longer relationship building. While traditional communication tools such as newspapers, advertisements, and flyers are still used, new tools such as advergames have started creating their own niche in the market.

Multimodal Analysis: The theory of multimodality describes communication process from semiotic understanding; the multimodes include textual, aural, gestural, spatial, or visual.

Persuasion: In terms of internet marketing, the ways contents are designed on the web page that decide how effective they are in luring the customers to purchase the products come under the purview of persuasion.

Rhetoric: Concerned with the content and form of language, the subject of rhetoric exploits the possible choices at each level of language to build the strongest and the most persuasive argument keeping the audience and message in mind. The subject studies the effectiveness of language with focus on *what* and *how* of message.

Social Media: Based on Web 2.0, social media is an interactive and engaging platform that is internet-based and allows sharing of information, interests through virtual communities and networks. Use of social media such as Facebook, blogging, and Instagram are highly exploited by marketers to promote and position their brand these days since they involve low cost and promote viral marketing of the product(s).

Chapter 4
Advergames and Children

Vijita Singh Aggarwal
Guru Gobind Singh Indraprastha University, India

Shefali Khurana
Guru Gobind Singh Indraprastha University, India

ABSTRACT

Online gaming has become a popular form of entertainment which has shifted children's playgrounds to computers, laptops, mobiles, tablets, etc. Children spend their time surfing, playing, and downloading games from the internet. Advergaming is one of the latest digital advertising techniques used by marketers to interact with the children for longer hours by embedding the brand messages in the game action. Advergaming is a blend of fun and promotion to capture the attention of children towards the advertising message associated with the branded product. The objective of this chapter is to determine how children pay attention and absorb the message given by the companies by considering hierarchy of effects models such as AIDA model and DAGMAR model. The purpose of this work as a whole is to bring more understanding of this innovative technique of promoting by detailing the elements, characteristics, advantages, and disadvantages of advergames to achieve communication goals.

INTRODUCTION

Children digital culture has impacted and became the part of billions of lives worldwide. This type of prevalent digital culture comprises of use of internet, social media, mobile applications, online gaming and various digital communication tools (Montogomery, 1999). Digital marketing is progressing very rapidly, surpassing

DOI: 10.4018/978-1-5225-6064-7.ch004

rest with continuing potential to do much more in future. Digital marketing is one of the biggest revolution of an era which has changed the lives of every age group i.e. child, teenager, adults, older persons etc dramatically. With advancement in technology, digital marketing has targeted the most sensitive segment i.e. of children. This technique has changed the perspectives of purchasing of both the parents and children. Children spend their major time on playing games, using social media, exploring the internet which makes them more vulnerable to the marketers. (Aggarwal & Shefali, 2015)

CONCEPTS IN DIGITAL MARKETING

Digital Marketing is defined as "achieving marketing objectives through applying digital technologies and media" (Chaffey & Chadwick, 2012)

This definition explains the use of different online communication channels such as social media, online advertisements mail marketing, search engine marketing to achieve an organisation goals of customer acquisition, customer satisfaction and customer retention.

Digital marketing, which continues to be integrated with multichannel campaign management, includes addressable branding/advertising, contextual marketing, social marketing and transactional marketing. Digital marketing extends the marketing process through channels such as the Web, video, mobile and social applications, point-of-sale terminals, digital signage and kiosks. (Gartner, 2017)

The benefits of Digital Marketing as above said is more justified by the model of Paul Smith 5's of Internet Marketing i.e. Serving, Selling, Speaking, Saving and Sizzling.

1. **Serving:** Companies serve different types of advantages to customer through internet which adds one additional meaning to the customer such as feedback and comments section.
2. **Selling:** This term is directed towards all types of sales generated by digital marketing tools. An open platform is available for both seller and buyer to interact and communicate with each other. For example option of Live chat are provided by the companies on their website/webpage to solve problems of customers.
3. **Speaking:** It is directly related to the selling which explains about the communication and interaction directly with the customer so as to maintain long term relationship with them such as by chats, forums, questionnaire etc.

Table 1. Benefits of digital marketing (Adbot India, 2017; Oza, 2017; Yasmin, et al., 2015)

Update new products and services	Digital Marketing helps the customer to know about new offerings in the market. For example NARS, a cosmetic company uses Snap chat as a digital marketing strategy to launch their new collection
Information about products and services	Customer can get effective and large amount of information by browsing the internet about their products they want to buy
24*7 shopping/ Instant purchase	Buying and selling of products is available all the time. Customer can purchase the product as per his/her convenience.
Transparent/ low cost pricing	This is very cost efficient and transparent method to cater large audience in a nanosecond(very less time)
Trackable, measurable results	The results of Digital marketing are easily measurable with web analytics and other metric tools to check the effectiveness of promotional campaign.
Personalisation	The more customer purchases on the website, the more marketer get personalise with customer and market effectively to them.
Engagement/ Wider reach at low cost	A wide promotional campaign can reach to millions of audience with smaller investment. For e.g. Forever Diamonds use digital marketing campaign to reach and engage customers for less than $1 per engagement.
Social currency	It helps to gain social currency by engaging campaigns through different types of media. It contains viral messages which transfer from one person to another

4. **Saving:** The cost saving is one of the biggest advantage in internet marketing because it reduces the cost of paper, ink, print advertisements, banners etc to curb environmental pollution.
5. **Sizzling:** It is an offering an attractive and different webpage to create distinctive brand image. This is the strategy of companies to create brand awareness.

Digital marketing is becoming an increasingly integrated part of children's lives globally, and digital marketing in one form or another will be part of their online experience. There are various digital marketing techniques used by companies to attract the children and influence their buying behaviour such as Advergames, social networking websites, Mobile and location based Marketing, Viral Marketing etc. This chapter focuses upon the Advergames which occupies special space in the minds of consumers especially children.

LITERATURE REVIEW

Advergames

Advergames are a form of branded entertainment that feature advertising messages, logos, and trade character in a game format (American Psychological Association, 2004).

Advergames can be defined as "an immersive mix of advertising and entertainment that takes the form of used to enhance the brand value. Games are having at video games" (Obringer, 2007).

Commercial messages embedded within the content of retail-accessible video games, online electronic games or apps (Dahl, et al., 2009)

Electronic games that are used to advertise a product, brand or an organisation, accessible on social media sites, companies' own websites and as downloadable content or apps on mobile devices (Advertising standards Authority, 2012)

Objectives of Advergames

Brand immersion is the major objective of advertisers. Young children are the major target audience for online games especially Advergames because with the advent of technology, commercial marketplace is shifted from Television to websites on which children play games for longer durations. The use of attractive animated spokes characters, brand mascots, cartoons, celebrities, logos, musical messages, silly voices etc all are responsible to draw the attention of children towards the advertising message. As a result of exposure to ad in game, positive brand attitude has formed as playing game is the main focus of attention at that time which ultimately leads to the feeling of association and evaluation in the child. It also influences children's brand preferences towards the product.

Relationship Building

It is the ultimate goal of marketers and the way through which marketers are building and maintaining emotional connection with the children as explained in figure

This figure clearly explains the factors affecting buyer decisions. The strong emotional quotient is an important factor used by marketers to bond with the children. Advergames has strong emotional engagement factor which persuades the children to buy the product because of the lack of proper cognitive skills among them. It engages

Figure 1. Factors used by buyers to make buying decision
Source: Hudson Research and Consulting (2011)

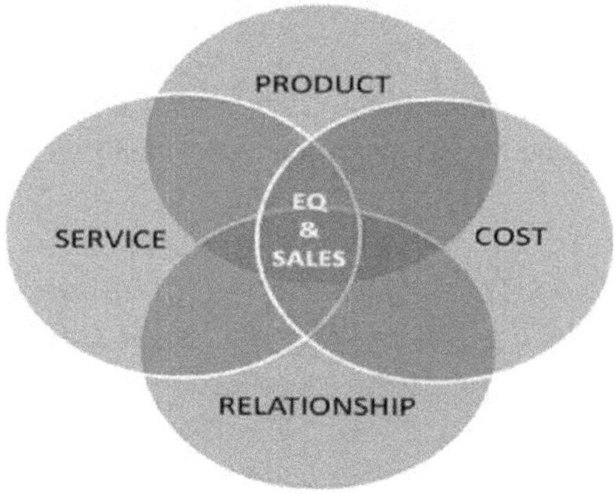

the children whether online or offline and consists of different characters, real or imaginary stories which leads to the positive emotional connect with the product. This positive connection will easily convert into purchases and emotional loyalty.

Return on Investment

The very important objective of marketers is increase in return on investment. The increase in ROI tells about the effectiveness of Advergames. As this effectiveness is hard to measure in certain period of time, For this various methods such as discounted cash flow, Net present value method, brand valuation, Customer lifetime value (CLV) etc.CLV is a tool with helps to distinguish between profitable(regular and loyal) and non-profitable customers.

Types of Advergames

There are three different ways of Advergames used by marketers to reach at their audience. First one is when games are placed on the website of the company and customers are attracted to visit them and stay there for longer durations. It is not necessary in this way that game is related to the product. The second way is like a traditional commercial video game to be played on the computer/laptops/mobiles and are specifically made with some purpose. For eg.US army sponsored a game known as *America's army* to attract youngsters to join army. The third one is in game advertisements where the shown product in the game is the part of marketing (lee & Obringer, 2007)

Table 2. Past research on Advergames

Montogomery, 1999	Increase in Children Digital culture
Pavlou and Stewart, 2000	Advergames are more persuasive than traditional games
Edwards, 2003	Advergames get attention of children for long duration because of animated imagery of a brand
Neeley & W.Schumann, 2004	Cartoon characters catches child attention which leads to product preference
Cowburn and Boxer, 2007	Australian online website games uses games, competition, prizes etc to attract children
Mediamark Research & Intelligence, 2007	Advergames are successful way of attracting children in US
Moore & Rideout, 2007	Long time exposure of games leads t feeling of association and evaluation in the child
Lee, M. and S. Youn, 2008	Food as an integrated part in Advergames
Henry & Story, 2009	Brand immersion is the main motive of advertisers to cultivate in children by use of Advergames
Bailey, Wise et al., 2009	Advergames provide immersion and fun experience to children
Priya, Baisya, & Sharma, 2010	Animated brand icons in Advergames play an important role in children buying process\
Culp.et.al,2010	Brand identifier present in Advergames promotes brand loyalty among the children.
Cai, X. and X. Zhao, 2010	Use of structural cues in advertising
Purswani, 2010	Advergames is an emotional investment and enhances brand memory
Cain, 2011	product placement and product integration in Advergames
Johnson, 2012	Advergames reinforces brand credibility and persuade children to buy the product
A common sense media research brief, 2014	Online gaming changes tastes and preferences of children
Aggarwal&Shefali,2015	Effectiveness of Advergames on children
Cicchirillo, V., & Mabry, A., 2016	Brand integration in Advergames
Vasishth et al., 2017	High game-product congruence results in low persuasion.

Benefits of Advergames

Advergaming is actually a wider marketing strategy which affects both the cognitive and affective behaviour of children. It plays an important role for the marketers to enhance the brand memory of the children. Following are the benefits of playing an Advergames:

- **Boosting Brand Awareness:** Because of interactive nature of an Advergames, children learn various things about the featured product and brand.
- **Selling Products Via Fun:** Children think Advergames are for their fun and they enjoy in playing them but the real purpose behind is to persuade them to buy the product.
- **High Chance to Reach the Audience:** Brand exposition time is more in advergaming than traditional media.
- **Viral Marketing:** Advergames promises to give reward at the end of the game. For this reward marketers motivates children to spread some message among their friends and relatives. For example: Invitation to friends for playing the game.
- **Longevity:** Children can play Advergames for a long time after its release on the website.
- **Telepresence:** Children feel the virtual world of Advergames because they experience the product or brand in some different manner as featured by marketers in the game.
- **Others:** Cost sharing and Training & education are also some benefits of Advergames.

Examples of Advergames

The successful Advergames of Doritos is Hotel626.It is different from the normal games which is having positive themes because it comprises of horror adventure with interesting storyline along with attractive audios and visuals. This scary game got very good response from children in spite of their negative theme. The more excited thing is game is open to play from 6pm to 6am.The makers of the game thought this time period might will act like a barrier but in reality it enhanced the players interest and excitement to a different level. Player found themselves 100% immersed in the brand environment (3RDSENSE, 2010).

Kinder joy which started a promotion named "SMS for Joy" was immensely successful as shown in Figure 2. This campaign consists of prizes to customers who buy kinder joy promotional packs. The prizes comprised of branded mini games along with other merchandise.

Figure 2. KinderJoy campaign
Source: (games, 2017)

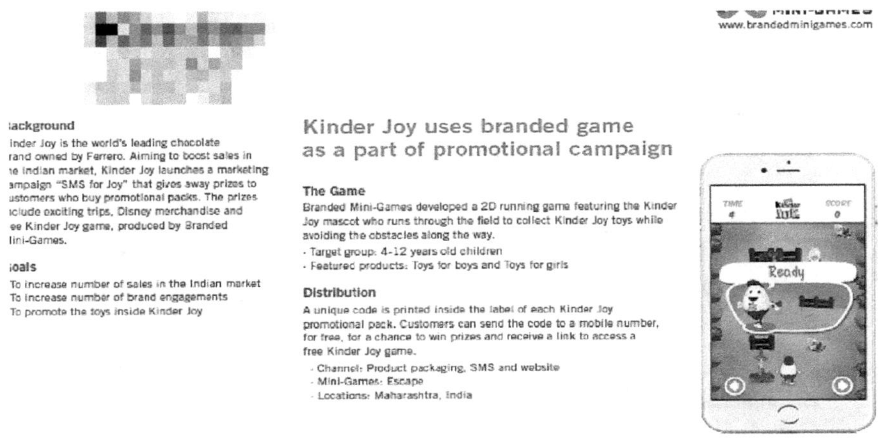

KFC started its promotional campaign known as "Hot Bucket Challenge". In this customers have to finish 5 KFC chicken pieces in lesser time as shown in Figure 3. Those who win will get a chance to play and experience games across multiple devices / screens (games, 2017)

Another example is Sneak King, which is launched by Burger King in 2006 as shown in Figure 4. This is a five week promotional buying campaign of value meals in which Sneak King was used as a promotional tool. It was made for Xbox and Xbox 360 game consoles. This campaign was very successful in terms of profits long with the sale of million units. This project had great financial success, with millions of units sold.

Figure 3. KFC campaign
Source: (games, 2017)

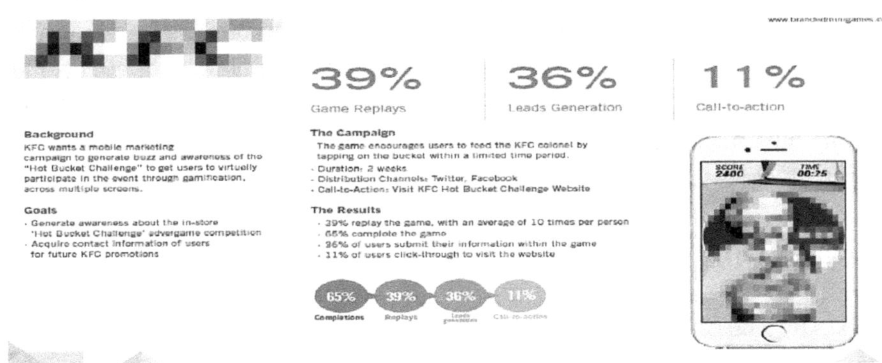

Figure 4. Burger King campaign
Source: (games,2017)

Other are Zool, MarioKart8, Crazy taxi, Chex quest etc. are some Advergames which are breakthrough games in the evolution of Advergames. Advergames are the successful and proven platform for the advertisement of products and services. In recent years, marketers incorporated their products and brands in the videogames itself companies with the partnership with major companies such as with Mario Kart 8 and Mercedes Benz. The crazy car is a very funny game in which very smart work was done by marketers. Children cannot easily recognise that it is Advergames until they go through the logo of KFC. In this game various brands are also present like pizza hut and Levis. This is a very interesting strategy used by marketers to target children by incorporating different brands in one game (Barton, 2017).

HIERARCHY OF EFFECTS MODEL: DAGMAR AND AIDA

The hierarchy of effects model is defined as a multistage process which starts from the unawareness of brand to awareness to preferences to purchase and ultimately to the loyalty for the brand. Although there are different hierarchy of effects model but AIDA (Attention, Interest, Desire & Action) and its descendent DAGMAR(for Defining advertising goals for measured advertising results)are the most popular ones which are discussed in this chapter.

DAGMAR Approach

DAGMAR stands for Defining advertising goals for measured advertising results. This term was first coined by Mr. Russey Colley in 1961 and has got much appreciation.

This approach is still used in setting advertising goals and measuring their results. DAGMAR is a tool of planning and controlling which helps in the creation of an effective advertisements. As per this approach, objectives and goals should be consistent with the tasks in the communication. Then later, the performance and goals are compared to see the effectiveness of communication process.

According to Colley (1961) "Advertisers job, purely and simply is to communicate to a defined audience, information and a frame of mind that stimulates action. Advertising succeeds or fails depends upon how well it communicates the desired information and attitudes to the right people, at the right time and at the right place".

In simple words, it is all about measuring Return on Investment of advertisements. To check the effectiveness of advertisements, Russel proposed two different ways which enhances the ROI of advertising.

- Creation of communication tasks to attain the objectives.
- Defining the communication tasks to measure the output.

Creating a communication task involves the communication between company and consumer to achieve the goals of communication tasks. The purpose of DAGMAR approach is to gain

- **Awareness:** The tasks of communication has the objective to aware the consumer about the product and brand.
- **Comprehension:** The task is to provide the consumer more information about the product, their characteristics, uses and benefits of using the product.
- **Conviction:** In this stage the task is to persuade the consumer that product is meant for them. Consumer evaluate different products and create mental disposition to purchase the product.
- **Action:** The task is about the actual purchase of product by motivating the consumer after conviction.

Defining objectives in the DAGMAR is about how the objectives in the advertisements are understood and incorporated in the communication tasks. Following are the objectives of advertising used to create communication tasks:

- Concrete and measurable
- Defined Target audience
- Degree of change sought (i.e. in Perception, attitude or awareness of consumer)
- Time period (Defined time period to achieve desired results) (Bhasin, 2017) (Kazmi & Batra, 2008)

DAGMAR Approach in Context of Advergames

Awareness

Awareness in the context of Advergames is when children come in the direct contact with the advertisement. Advergames contains subliminal messages, therefore it is not possible for children to extract it because of limited cognitive abilities. But yes, they can do it by playing the games and getting familiar with the product/brand shown in the games. The successful product placement in the game leads to the brand awareness in the children. This can be possible through three different ways i.e. firstly by featuring the brand/product logo of the company in the background so that children can relate logo with brand which is known as associative integration. (Chen &Ringel,2001).The second way is of illustrative integration i.e. Incorporation of product in the game play. For example KFC uses its burgers and other ingredients in its game play. The third one is Demonstrative integration which stands at highest level of brand incorporation. In this type player has an opportunity to take virtual experience of product i.e. selecting the range of products of own choice. For example in car racing game player has a choice to select a car model which helps the company to introduce about their features of product in natural context. The illustrative and associative integration are low cost alternatives for brand awareness which is used to aware potential and existing customers. The demonstrative illustration is much more expensive and difficult to maintain and develop. It comprises of different interactive components which has deep impact on the minds of player. (Winkler & Buckner,2001)

Comprehension

Advertising in Advergames provides positive information about the brand. This changes the children's mental thinking about the brand after being exposed to successful advertising. The core message of the Advergames is transferred to children and brand associations are generally inferred in this stage. Children has the ability to associate themselves with the right character of the brand(Henke,1995). For eg.Bahn,1987 concluded that children of 4 to 5 years old associates themselves with kids cereals which has cartoon characters and is sugary sweet .Rest of them which is not having cartoons is considered unhealthy by the children. Children are capable to associate product logo/music with correct product or brand which is the strongest example of their brand awareness. (Aggarwal &Shefali,2015) also inferred it by asking the children to match the brand or product with their associated characters and 60% of the children have done in the correct way. The use of branded cartoon characters, celebrities, animated spokesperson etc. in Advergames makes the children recognise and associate the promotional intent present in Advergames .This resulted in formation of positive brand attitude and strong brand memory in children(Winkler & Buckner, 2006) (Chen, et al., 2001).

Conviction

In above stages we concluded that children can exhibit high level of awareness/ recognition/association. Now the next step is conviction i.e. evaluation of products and brands by children. This stage requires child's cognitive ability to differentiate one product /brand from other product/brand. Liking, disliking and preferences of the children are generally decided at this stage. Product familiarity is also an important element which is studied in conviction. Children's ability to distinguish between familiar and non-familiar products shapes their preferences and liking and disliking about the product/brand. Repeated exposure of product/brand in the game influence children's preference to purchase the product. When children come in direct exposure to the game for long period, they memorize their major features and other attributes which helps them to recall during the evaluation of that particular product/brand. Strong conviction in the Advergames raises the children's desire to purchase the particular product (Cauberghe & Pelsmacker, 2010).

Action: This is the last stage in which children decides to purchase the product. The brand/product present in the game leaves strong brand impression on the minds of children. The understanding of subliminal message by the children in the game builds positive brand attitude which leads to purchase intentions and choice. If children are not able to infer the embedded message in the game he/she will continue to play the game. However, marketers persuade them to take action and buy the product by offering various discounts, vouchers, contests and promotional schemes. Marketers are also using various strategies such as extended online experiences to retain them online for long time.

AIDA Model in Context of Advergames

AIDA model is an effective method to study consumer behaviour of children. It stands for Attention, Interest, Desire and Action - AIDA model is used to find the possible effects of Advergames on perception and behaviour of children. In the AIDA model there is a sequence of four mental steps that a children gets through from the moment he/she meets a brand for the first time in Advergames and until when, after the virtual experience with the product during the game, ultimately to the purchase of brand. Following are the explanations of effect of Advergames on children on the basis of AIDA model:

Attention

This is the first step of AIDA model and refers to aware the children about the brand i.e. conversion of children's unawareness to awareness. Advertisers use special techniques to attract the consumers. Similarly in case of Advergames, advertisers use different kinds of animated characters, logos, and links to generate children traffic on their websites. This is an important and popular method to draw the attention of children. Invitations, adverts, online promotions etc send by friends, relatives or other players online attract the children. The rest decision of playing the games lies with the children which depend upon various extrinsic factors (Time available, internet connectivity, noise etc). Procedural rhetoric are used by marketers to gain attention of children. Procedural rhetoric is defined as the "way of creating, explaining or understanding processes," and processes as the "methods, techniques and logics that drive the operation of systems" (Bogost,2007). Use of billboards, animated imageries, colourful pictures, certain characteristics help in grabbing the attention of children towards the brand. Brand identifier such as the food item (e.g., Cap'n Crunch cereal in a bowl), a product package, a brand character (if any) and the brand logo draws children attention and helps them to recognise on different times. These strategies will evoke children acceptance towards promotional message and develop positive attitude towards the product. A study done by (Aggarwal&Shefali,2015) concluded that 80% of the experimental children population under their study consistently played KFC games for longer durations. Music, animated characters, silly voices etc helped them in retaining at the website for longer period.

Interest

Children received stimuli after interaction with Advergames arises their interest. After paying attention to the game or any character in the game, he/she starts recognising the product/brand in the game which raises his/her interest level towards the product he/she knows about (Deal 2005). Various elements such as background instructions, isolated messages, bold and colourful texts make children interested towards the product in game. The types of processes which include embedded messages related to the brand needs to be decoded by children in game. Marketer's ultimate objective is to increase sales of product /service related to the game. Therefore, they should differentiate the messages which is understandable and non-understandable by the children. Embedded should be simple enough to be understand by the children while playing the game or during follow up of instructions of game. To retain the interest of children, marketers introduce new stages, complex games and will continue to transform games (Ghirvu, 2013; Gurau, 2008). Personalisation of the game is one way to increase the level of engagement of player. The player is free to choose his own player, opposition player and design the game space as per his/her wish generates interest of player towards the game (Moore, 2006).

Desire

The use of audio, visual and textual elements used in Advergames evoke actual aspiration of children towards particular product, service or brand which is known as desire. The design of characters present in the game, interface design and other game elements creates positive feelings and trigger desire for the product shown in the game. Marketers motive is to position their product in the minds of children by exposing them to such game elements associate with product /brand. Brand preferences are built during this phase as children can easily compare the brand / product which they have seen in game over other brands. The message embedded in the game might not be age appropriate so some children ignore it completely and continues to play. Therefore, marketers purpose will not met in these circumstances (Gurau, 2008; Aggarwal & Shefali, 2015).

Action

This is the final and last step of buying process. As said above if children are not able to capture the message in the game, they will not experience the product and continue to play the game. Marketers use different promotional tools such as price discounts, voucher and create such environment which converts children desire into action. Brand engagement is must in this step where children can change their cognitive processes into final purchase of the product or service or brand. Trial versions, rewards at the end of game by sharing and inviting their friends etc are used by marketers for the actual purchase of the product. This step determine s how effective the embedded message in Advergames is and how successful the Advergames is in transferring the message (Ghirvu, 2013; Gurau, 2008).

LIMITATIONS AND POLICY IMPLICATIONS

Marketers are collecting the personal information about the children from websites on which they play Advergames is against the privacy policies. These pages specifically will target the children and attract them b.3.y placing in game ads on the websites. They collect their potential customers i.e. children, personal information such as about their demographics, tastes & Preferences, attitude and choice via Advergames. This is against their privacy policies. Therefore, special policies should be framed for online marketers so that they will not interfere in the right to privacy of children.

Figure 5. The AIDA model in Advergames context
Source: Realized by the author according to the stages of original AIDA Model (Strong, 1925) (GHIRVU, 2013)

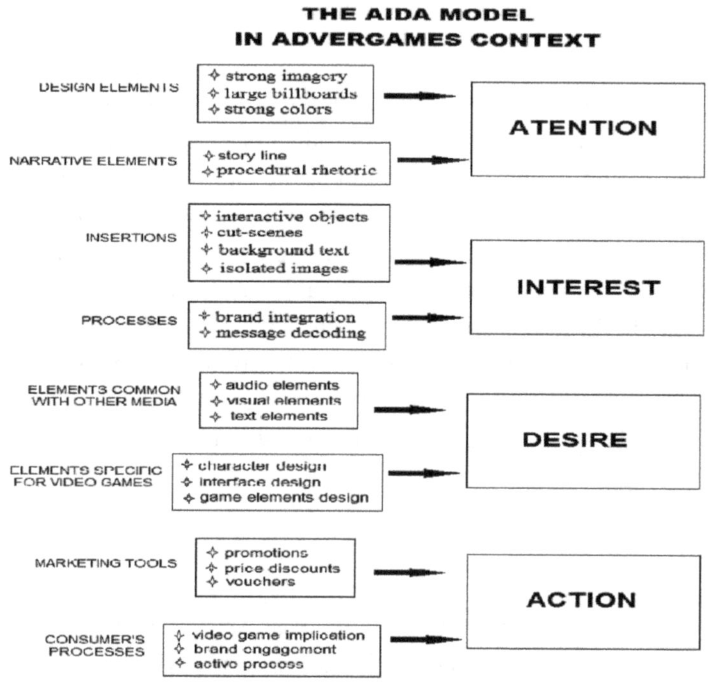

The ads placed on the website are not according to the age group of the children. They do not have the knowledge and ability to judge the advertisements. They cannot differentiate between Advergames and advertisements. Sometimes advertisers use different strategies to cultivate their future consumers by showing them adults related consumption products (Bosman,2006). By doing this they are playing with the interests of children. Through this chapter we are urging to advertisers and marketers along with the legal bodies to carefully screen the advertisements prior to showing it to the children on the websites especially as these kind of ads has a long term impact on the memory of children. As per the report on Advergames by (Nairn & Hang, 2012). It is found that children under the age of 15 are not able to differentiate between advertisements and Advergames. Advergames affect children on their subconscious and emotional level. Most of the ads related to children are of food and drinks. If Advergames affect children at their subconscious level, it poses a huge health concern towards their eating habits. They are consuming excess of fast food, unhealthy snacks, and foods containing high content of salt, sugar and fats. There is a need of responsible and transparent marketing practices which affects children's health and their psychology (Montogomery, 2009). Therefore, it should be mandatory for policy makers to help children by stopping marketers from these kinds of deceptive advertisements. Parents should also come forward and help their children n understanding Advergames(Evans, 2014). As no special guidelines are available tell them how to differentiate between games and commercial messages embedded in games. The Children Advertising Review Unit (CARU) is specifically targeted at the same objectives and issued special guidelines in 2006 to advertisers. As per this unit, advertisers should create any labelling alert, sign, ad break so that children are able recognise that it is an advertisement.

CONCLUSION

This chapter focuses upon advantages and disadvantages of Advergames. Although there are various limitations of Advergaming for children but marketers should take care that Advergames must have uniformity in the message so that it will deliver the whole information correctly, honestly and with good consumer insights to the children. This will help marketers to develop strong emotional connection with children to convert them into loyal customers having sense of affection and love towards their product and brand. The chapter also discussed the application of hierarchy of effects models such as AIDA (Attention, Interest, Desire and Action) and DAGMAR (Defining advertising goals for measured advertising results) on Advergames. The Hierarchy of effects model such as AIDA model and DAGMAR model helps to understand the changing consumer attitudes towards brand communication. These models effectively demonstrate process followed from unawareness to the actual purchase of the product/brand (Wijaya, 2012). However this concept requires thorough research because of faster change in technology, advent of different techniques of media etc globally.

REFERENCES

Aggarwal, V., & Shefali. (2015). A study of effectiveness of Advergames on children. *BVIMSR. Journal of Management Research.*

Aggarwal, V., & Shefali. (2015). A study of effectiveness of Advergames on Children. *BVIMSR's Journal of Management Research.*

An, S., & Stern, S. (2011). Mitigating the Effects of Advergames on Children. *Journal of Advertising*, *40*(1), 43–56. doi:10.2753/JOA0091-3367400103

AuthoriyA. S. (2012). Retrieved from http://www.cap.org.uk/News-reports/Media-Centre/2012/Advergames.aspx

Bahn, K. D. (1987). Do Mothers and Children Share Cereal and Beverage Preferences and Evaluative Criteria? *Advances in Consumer Research. Association for Consumer Research (U. S.)*, 279–282.

Bailey, W., Wise, K., & Bolls, P. (2009). How Avatar Customizability Affects Children's Arousal and Subjective Presence During Junk Food–Sponsored Online Video Games. *Cyberpsychology & Behavior*, *12*(3), 277–283. doi:10.1089/cpb.2008.0292 PMID:19445632

Barton, Z. (2017). *The Evolution of Advergames: Top 3 Examples of Marketing in Gaming*. Retrieved from https://medium.com/@zbbarton0706/the-evolution-of-Advergames-top-3-examples-of-marketing-in-gaming-3e688aad6884

Bhasin, H. (2017). *DAGMAR Approach – Defining advertising goals for measured advertising results.* Retrieved from https://www.marketing91.com/dagmar/

Bogost. (2007). *Persuasive Games: The expressive power of videogames.* Cambridge, MA: MIT Press.

Bosman, J. (2006, June 14). Hey, kid, you want to buy a Toyota Scion? *New York Times.*

Brief, A. C. (2014). *Advertising to children and teens: Current Practices.* Academic Press.

Cai, X., & Zhao, X. (2010). Click here, Kids! *Journal of Children and Media*, *4*(2), 135–154. doi:10.1080/17482791003629610

Cain. (2011). Embedded advertising on television: Disclosure, deception, and free speech rights. *Journal of Public Policy & Marketing*, 226–238.

Cauberghe, V., & Pelsmacker, P. (2010). Advergames: The Impact of Brand Prominence and Game Repetition on Brand Responses. *Journal of Advertising*, *39*(1), 5–18. doi:10.2753/JOA0091-3367390101

Chaffey, D., & Chadwick. (2012). *Digital Marketing: Strategy, Implementation and Practice.* Academic Press.

Chen, J., & Ringel, M. (2001). *Can Advergaming be the Future of Interactive Advertising?* Retrieved from http://www.locz.com.br

Cicchirillo, V., & Mabry, A. (2016). Advergaming and healthy eating involvement: How healthy eating inclinations impact processing of advergame content. *Internet Research, 26*(3), 587–603. doi:10.1108/IntR-04-2014-0091

Cowburn, & Boxer, A. (2007). Magazines for children and young people and the links to Internet food marketing: a review of the extent and type of food advertising. *Public Health Nutrition, 10*, 1024-1031.

Culp, J., & Robert, A. (2010). Characteristics of Food Industry Web Sites and Advergames targeting Children. *Journal of Nutrition Education and Behavior, 42*(3), 197–201. doi:10.1016/j.jneb.2009.07.008 PMID:20434075

Dahl, E., Eagle, L., & Báez, C. (2009). Analysing Advergames: Active diversions or actually deception. An exploratory study of online Advergames content. *Young Consumers, 10*(I), 46–59. doi:10.1108/17473610910940783

Deal. (2005). *The Ability of Branded Online Games to build brand equity.* Retrieved from http://ir.lib.sfu.ca/retrieve/1569/afc2b904c38c1edff4ede5a4bc86.doc (

E, S. (1925). *The Psychology of Selling and Advertising.* New York: McGraw-Hill.

Edwards. (2003). Plug (the Product) and Play. *Washington Post.*

Evans, N. J. (2014). Pinpointing Persuasion in Children's Advergames: Exploring the Relationship Among Parents' Internet Mediation, Marketplace Knowledge, Attitudes, and the Support for Regulation. *Journal of Interactive Advertising, 14*(2), 73–85. doi:10.1080/15252019.2014.943354

Games, B. M. (2017). *Success stories.* Retrieved from http://www.brandedminigames.com/success-stories/page/4/

Gartner. (n.d.). *Digital Marketing.* Retrieved from https://www.gartner.com/it-glossary/digital-marketing

Ghirvu, A. I. (2013). The Aida model for advergames. *The USV Annals of Economics and Public Administration, 13*(1), 90-98.

Gurau, C. (2008). The Influence of Advergames on Players' Behaviour: An Experimental Study. *Electronic Markets, 18*(2), 106–116. doi:10.1080/10196780802044859

Henry, A. E., & Story, M. (2009). Food and Beverage Brands That Market to Children and adolscents on the Internet:A content analysis of branded websites. *Journal of Nutrition Education and Behavior, 41*(5), 353–359. doi:10.1016/j.jneb.2008.08.004

India, A. (2017). *Advantages of Digital marketing.* Retrieved from www.adbot.in: https://www.adbot.in/5-advantages-of-digital-marketing-in-the-present-scenario/

Intelligence, M. R. (2007). *Gaming Is Nearly Ubiquitous with Kids Online.* Retrieved from http://www.gfkmri.com/pdf/ gaming%20is%20nearly%20ubiquitous%20 with%20kids%20online.pdf

Interactive Food and Beverage Marketing: Targeting Adolescents in the Digital Age. (2009). *Journal of Adolescent Health*, 18-29.

Johnson. (2012, June 29). Coca-Cola drives brand awareness via mobile gaming initiative. *Mobile Marketer.*

Kazmi, S., & Batra, S. K. (2008). *Advertising and Sales Promotion.* Academic Press.

Kunkel, D., Wilcox, B. J. C., Palmer, E., Linn, S., & Dowrick. (2004). A Report of the APA Task Force on Advertising and Children. In Psychological Issues in the Increasing Commercialization of Childhood. Washington, DC: American Psychological Association.

Lee, M., & Youn, S. (2008). Leading National Advertisers' Use of Advergames. *Journal of Current Issues in Advertising.*

Lee & Obringer. (2007). *How advergaming works.* Retrieved from https://money.howstuffworks.com/advergaming.htm

Montogomery, K. (2009). *Food marketing in the digital age: A conceptual framework and agenda for research.* Retrieved from Digital ads: how marketers target youth.

Montogomery. (1999). *Digital kids: The new online children's consumer culture.* Academic Press.

Moore, E. S. (2006). *Its child 's play: Advergaming and online marketing of food to children.* A Kaiser Family Foundation Report.

Moore, E. S., & Rideout, V. J. (2007). The Online Marketing of Food to Children: Is It Just Fun and Games? *Journal of Public Policy & Marketing*, *26*(2), 202–220. doi:10.1509/jppm.26.2.202

Nairn, A., & Hang, H. (2012). *Advergames: "It's not an advert – it says play!".* Family and Parenting Institute.

Neeley, S. M., & Schumann, W. (2004). Using animated spokes-characters in advertising to young children: Does Increasing Attention to Advertising Necessarily Lead to Product Preference? *Journal of Advertising*, *33*(3), 7–23. doi:10.1080/009 13367.2004.10639166

Obringe. (2007). *How Advergaming works.* Retrieved from http://money.howstuffworks.com/advergaming.htm/printable

Oza, H. (2017). *0 Advantages Of Digital Marketing Over Traditional Marketing*. Retrieved from https://prowly.com/magazine/2017/10/11/advantages-of-digital-marketing-over-traditional-marketing/

Pavlou & Stewart. (2000). Measuring the Effects and Effectiveness of Interactive Advertising: A Research Agenda. *Journal of Interactive Advertising*.

Priya, P., Baisya, R. K., & Sharma, S. (2010). Television advertisements and children's buying behaviour. *Marketing Intelligence & Planning*, *28*(2), 151–169. doi:10.1108/02634501011029664

Purswani. (2010). Advergames, their use and potential regulation. *Asia Pacific Public Relations Journal*.

3. RDSENSE. (2010). *3Advergames you should be playing*. Retrieved from http://3rdsense.com/blog/2015/9/17/3-Advergames-you-should-be-playing

Vashist, D., & Chauhan, A. (2017). Effect of game-interactivity and congruence on presence and brand attitude. *Marketing Intelligence & Planning*, *35*(6), 789–804. doi:10.1108/MIP-01-2017-0018

Wijaya, B. S. (2012). The Development of Hierarchy of Effects Model in Advertising. *International Research Journal of Business studies, 5*(1), 73-85.

Winkler, T., & Buckner, K. (2006). Receptiveness of Gamers to Embedded Brand Messages in Advergames: Attitudes towards Product Placement. *Journal of Interactive Advertising*, *7*(1).

Yasmin, A., Tasneem, S., & Fatema, K. (2015). Effectiveness of Digital Marketing in the Challenging Age: An Empirical Study. *International Journal of Management Science and Business Administration*, *1*(5), 69–80. doi:10.18775/ijmsba.1849-5664-5419.2014.15.1006

KEY TERMS AND DEFINITIONS

Advergames: The type of games containing commercial messages used to attract and retain their audience for a long duration of time.

Brand Awareness: The extent to which individuals are conscious about the particular product, brand, or service.

Brand Engagement: It is defined as a change in cognitive processes of an individual into final purchase of the product or service or brand.

Digital Marketing: The electronic techniques which are used by marketers to reach to their customers and to sell their products and services.

Hierarchy of Effects Model: It is multistage process which converts brand unawareness to brand loyalty with various stages in between such as brand awareness and brand preference.

Marketing: It stands for identification of the needs of customer and satisfying them with different means.

Relationship Marketing: The use of different marketing strategies to sell their products and services by building and maintaining cordial relationship with the customers.

Chapter 5
Persuasive Advergames:
Boon or Bane for Children

Rupa Rathee
Deenbandhu Chhotu Ram University of Science and Technology, India

Pallavi Rajain
Deenbandhu Chhotu Ram University of Science and Technology, India

ABSTRACT

As the present consumer market is no longer bound to traditional forms of advertising, it has led to several advancements including marketing through online platforms like digital and social media. One such advertising format that appeals most to the youth is advergames. The younger generation spends lot of time on the internet, giving an opportunity to the marketers to make the best use of this medium. Advergames, which consist of online gaming and advertising, are considered a promising form of reaching the youth market. Therefore, this chapter attempts to deal with the concepts related to advergames and a small empirical study showing the impact of advergames on children. The results of the study showed that there existed a relationship between attitude towards advergames and several variables involved. The relationship was most significant between entertainment and attitude towards advergames. The study of demographic variables showed no significant impact of gender, but there was a significant correlation of age with the persuasion knowledge, escape, and attitude towards advergames.

DOI: 10.4018/978-1-5225-6064-7.ch005

INTRODUCTION

Interactive marketing techniques are on a sharp increase since the last decade. These techniques integrate persuasive messages into editorial content or immensely entertaining program which result into faded boundaries between information, entertainment and advertising (Raney *et al.*, 2003). Additionally, these non-traditional types of advertising are often highly interactive and immersive in nature. One promotional method that is, advergaming, is increasingly gaining attention. "Advergaming is the delivery of advertising messages through electronic games" (Hernandez & Chapa, 2010). This technique is a distinctive feature which offers extensive exposure to brands. There is a paucity of literature that assesses consumer memory on advergames despite the possibility of it being used as a promotional tool. Therefore, in the coming sections the researchers will introduce certain concepts related to advergames which have been discussed by previous authors. As early as the 1980s, product placements emerged in video games but still advergames are a matured form of product placement where rather than the brand placed in the game, the game itself is centred around the brand. Such types of marketing tools include advertisements and games which is a good means for brands to target children in a different way (Tóth & Nagy, 2011). There is little knowledge as to how well children discern the commercial nature of advergames despite the increasing prevalence of them and, in particular, the extent to which children can be aided in recognizing the embedded persuasive attempt. Therefore, this chapter attempts to deal with the concepts related to advergames along with a small empirical study which was conducted to show the impact of advergames on children.

BACKGROUND

Affective and Cognitive Responses

There is a concept of advertising literacy which is a part of broad concept of persuasion knowledge (Hudders *et al.*, 2015). Traditionally persuasion knowledge has focussed on cognitive theory developed by psychologists such as Piaget (1929). Therefore, it can be said that advertising literacy comprises of cognitive skills. But recent research has focussed on the affect based nature of advertising content. The affective advertising literacy refers to an automatic affective reaction. In particular, it refers to the innate tendency of individuals to resist persuasion attempts, as they restrict their freedom of choice (van Reijmersdal *et al.*, 2012).

Children's Emotions

The use of emotions has been recognised since a long time by advertisers. In order to magnify the effectiveness of the memorizing process, the use of emotions is crucial (Tóth & Nagy, 2011). Marketers aim to evoke positive appeal in order to evoke an emotional response. The emotional appeal is significant as there is a strong interplay between non-commercial and commercial content. Such mixed messages create confusion among children as they are not able to distinguish between these mixed messages (Verdoodt *et al.*, 2016). This problem is greater among younger children who cannot distinguish among the two types of messages.

Psychological Elements in Advergaming and Memory Development

Psychological elements are used to target children using advergames. These games integrate operant and classical learning theories by associating positive feelings with certain brands. The application of Social Cognition Theory (SCT) to advergames involves identification of game characters by two mechanisms. The characters act as guides during game-playing besides children having control over the characters which assists the identification process. These brand characters are used as models by children (Tóth & Nagy, 2011). Children's memory is affected by gaining positive feelings through such experiences. For studying cognitive development, it is important to study the effects of memory as hinted by many researchers (Piaget & Inhelder, 1973). The incoming information is encoded, stored and retrieved as per normal functions of memory. Memory retrieval is assisted by physical environment corresponding to the instance when the information was being encoded. This fact can be used by advergaming companies by captivating a child's memory through creation of an environment suitable to them on its webpages. A good consumer brand relationship is developed by using advergames because they impact cognitive development process of children (DiClemente & Hantula, 2003). Further it can be added that a positive attitude towards the game helps in forming a positive attitude towards the brands (Wise *et al.*, 2008).

Advergames Persuasion Knowledge

The Persuasion Knowledge model developed by Friestad and Wright in 1994 suggested that people's persuasion knowledge continues developing throughout their life span. This knowledge helps them to identify whenever marketers try to intimidate them. With regard to this, children's understanding of persuasive tactics also develops as they get older. As children grow, they begin to understand the intent of advertisers and use this knowledge while processing commercial messages.

Consequences of Advergaming

This section elaborates on the various consequences of advergames especially for children. The relevance of advergames has come under scrutiny even though advergames give a unique opportunity to marketers for targeting children. Children's food consumption was found to be significantly affected by advergames according to recent experimental studies (Folkvord *et al.*, 2013; Harris *et al.*, 2011; Hernandez & Chapa, 2010; Pempek & Calvert, 2009). Children were more liable to choose foods high in fat and sugar after exposure to advergames that featured unhealthy foods. Children frequently use the games and internet but despite this the phenomenon has only a little while back begun to be researched by public health researchers. Some content analyses published to date have found that food companies rely extensively on a wide array of sophisticated strategies for promotion of products for example using the internet in their efforts to market products. Occasionally these web sites promote food items considered "unhealthful", including fast food, snacks, candy, and high-sugar cereals. As with traditional advertising media like television, similarly with advergames, brand processing is likely to be obvious because the brand is primary to the activity taking place and is integrated strongly into the game. Probing into product integrations and explicit advertising for example in movies suggested that advergames may have a counterproductive effect on purchase intention and brand attitude. It is the general tendency of people to resist communications they assume to be intentionally persuasive (Friestad & Wright, 1994). Nevertheless, advergames research has shown that positive affect transfer can be used to counteract the negative effects associated with explicit branding (Kim *et al.*, 1998). A more favorable attitude toward the brand is shown by players who enjoy playing the game (van Reijmersdal *et al.*, 2010; Wise *et al.*, 2008). Similarly, detachment effect is unlikely to occur due to detection of the persuasive attempt if a child fails to acknowledge the advertising component embedded in advergames (An *et al.*, 2014).

Advergaming in India

Indian businesses are taking a slow approach towards promotion of their products through gaming. This can be seen through the example of Hindustan Unilever Limited that promoted its Surf Excel Matic detergent and its fabric conditioner named Comfort through an online game "Kheloge to Jeetoge". As a reward the customers receive a certain talk time amount in their phones. With the availability of the games on mobile it becomes easier for the target audience i.e. housewives to access it. Brands have been able to successfully position themselves using mobile gaming in western countries. Therefore, Indian marketers also believe that it will be a success among Indian audience as well despite it being a costly investment. This is mainly because it is believed that increase in supply of gaming talent will eventually bring down their costs.

Another example of promotion through games includes film industry wherein movies like Dhoom 3 and Sultan created immersive games for the promotion of their films. Such games became so popular that they beat the traditional online games within 48 hours of their launch. With the rise in the mobile internet there lies a great opportunity for marketers to market their brands through mediums such as advergames (Hanumanthu, 2017). Among advergaming companies, Zapak is the largest online gaming portal with over 250 brands on board. It was the first company in India to provide Advergames on DTH (Direct to Home) platform. This company has launched several advergames targeting particularly the youth of the country (India Infoline News Service, n.d.).

Some of the other popular advergames launched in India include "Circuit Challenge"- a puzzle game developed for Mentos, Paddlepop Gaming League developed for Hindustan Unilever Limited, Mahindra Great Escape developed for automobile company Mahindra & Mahindra (Jayaswal and Malati, 2017). Another advergame that aimed to target particularly young male customers but attracted men of all ages included advergaming campaign by AXE deodorant with the theme of the game focussing on "getting the girlfriend of my choice". Even financial companies like IDBI Fortis and ICICI Prudential Life used Contests2Win for explaining the products in an interactive way which is fun for the customers (Kanth, 2013). One successful partnerships of gaming company with brand is T-mobile with Zynga through a game called "Treasure Isle" (Ojha, 2015).

OBJECTIVES

1. To study the relationship between entertainment, escape, sociability, persuasion knowledge and attitude towards advergames.
2. To study the effect of demographic variables (age and gender) on use of advergames among children.

HYPOTHESIS

Hypothesis One (H_1): Higher entertainment levels of school children will show a positive relationship with favourable attitude toward advergames.

Hypothesis Two (H_2): Higher escapism levels of school children will show a positive relationship with favourable attitude toward advergames.

Hypothesis Three (H_3): Higher sociability levels of school children will show a positive relationship with favourable attitude toward advergames.

Hypothesis Four (H_4): Persuasion knowledge will be positively related to children's attitudes toward advergames.

Figure 1 depicts the several relationships to be verified using the hypothesis as mentioned above.

METHODOLOGY FOR THE STUDY

Sample and Design

The authors conducted extensive literature review covering various dimensions under advergames that influence children which were mentioned in preceding paragraphs. The data was collected through questionnaires. Primary data was collected from children between the age of 10 -17 years regarding attitude towards advergames and the various aspects of advergames like the entertainment factor, sociability, escapism, persuasion knowledge. The study was restricted to the National Capital Region with a sample size of 161 children. The sample consisted of 102 males (63.4 per cent) and 59 females (36.6 per cent). The distribution of children in various age groups was as follows: 5 per cent were ten-year olds, 18 per cent eleven-year olds, 31.1 per cent twelve-year olds, 9.3 per cent thirteen-year olds, 9.9 per cent fourteen-year olds, 18.6 per cent fifteen-year olds, 5 per cent sixteen-year olds and 3.1 per cent seventeen-year olds. The survey helped to analyse the current situation with respect to the use of advergames and to what extent it is useful or harmful for children.

Figure 1. Model of the study

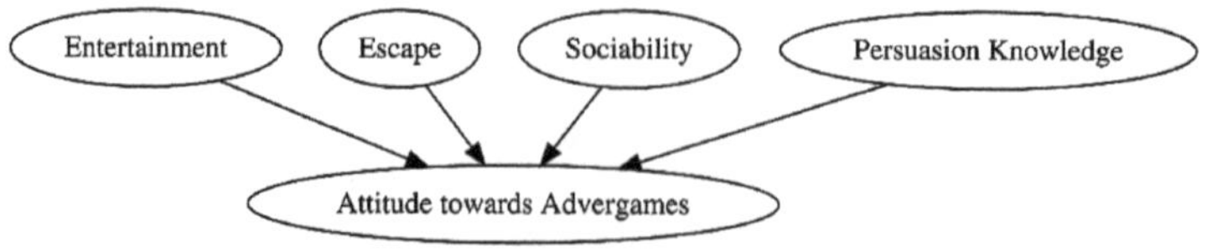

Measures

Attitude Towards Advergames

Seven items were adapted from scale used by Hernandez (2008) and Evans (2014). These items were used to measure the attitude of children towards advergames and demonstrated a strong internal consistency and was measured using five-point Likert scale ranging from strongly disagree to strongly agree.

Entertainment, Escape, Sociability

These three variables were tested through six items for entertainment and four each for escape and sociability. The scale was adapted from study by Hernandez (2008) to measure the entertainment, escape and sociability of advergames using a Likert scale based on five-point ranging from strongly disagree to strongly agree.

Persuasion Knowledge

Persuasion knowledge scale consisting of six items was adapted from Evans (2014) and Rozendaal, Buijzen, and Valkenburg (2010). All items were measured on Likert scale based on five-point ranging from strongly disagree to strongly agree.

DATA ANALYSIS AND INTERPRETATION

Assessment of Reliability

The reliability was assessed using Cronbach's alpha which measures internal consistency of the items. In the current research, the value of alpha coefficient was .786 indicating good consistency among the items of the survey instrument.

Table 1 shows the values of mean for the various variables involved with advergames. The overall value of mean for attitude towards advergames was 3.18. The value of mean for entertainment, sociability and escape was 3.38, 2.98 and 3.23 respectively. The value of overall mean for persuasion knowledge was 3.13.

Regression Analysis

To provide a means of assessing the effect of the direction and magnitude of the dependent variable's relationship with each independent variable, regression analysis was conducted. "Attitude toward advergames" was selected as the dependent variable

Table 1. Descriptive statistics

Statements	Mean	Std. Deviation
Attitude towards Advergames		
I like advergames.	3.317	1.2115
I found advergames boring.	2.683	1.2817
Advergames are artful.	3.416	1.1267
Advergames make children want unnecessary things.	3.404	1.3152
Games like this lead children to make unreasonable purchase demands on their parents.	3.559	1.3174
Games like this treat children fairly.	2.938	1.0349
There are very few advergames directed at children.	2.994	1.2575
Overall mean	**3.187**	**1.2207**
Entertainment		
When I play advergames, I have a good time.	3.329	1.3076
Advergame playing makes me pass the time away when I'm bored.	3.596	1.2368
Advergame playing make me relax.	3.261	1.2017
Advergames are exciting.	3.472	1.1676
Advergame playing offers me companionship when my family and friends are not available.	3.137	1.2723
When I play advergames, I get entertained.	3.509	1.1131
Overall mean	**3.384**	**1.2165**
Escape		
Advergame playing makes me put off something I should be doing.	3.261	1.2375
Advergame playing makes me get away from pressures and responsibilities.	2.894	1.3946
Advergame playing makes me forget about assignments (homework/chores).	2.882	1.3710
Advergame playing makes me get away from what I'm doing.	2.888	1.2845
Overall mean	**2.981**	**1.3219**
Sociability		
Advergame playing offers me something to do with others.	3.168	1.2157
Advergame playing makes me feel less lonely.	2.981	1.2623
Advergame playing allows interaction with people with similar tastes, regardless of location.	3.224	1.1455
Advergame playing promotes competition.	3.571	1.0471
Overall mean	**3.236**	**1.1676**
Persuasion Knowledge		
Advergames provide information about brands.	3.615	1.0843
Advergames make people like brands.	3.373	1.1170
Advergames let people know more about brands.	3.671	1.0593
Advergames are not meant to sell products.	2.497	1.2305
Advergames stimulate the sales of products.	2.950	1.2237
Advergames do not influence opinion about products.	2.720	1.2610
Overall mean	**3.138**	**1.163**

Source: Survey by authors

to test the hypotheses. The "entertainment," "escape", "sociability" and "persuasion knowledge" dimensions were entered as the independent variables.

Table 2 contains the correlations among the four independent variables (Entertainment, Escape, Sociability and Persuasion knowledge) and their correlations with the dependent variable (Attitude towards advergames). Examination of the correlation matrix indicated that all the correlations were significant with ''sociability'' and ''entertainment'' being most closely correlated with the dependent variable.

Tables 3-5 included the multiple regression results, containing the model summary, analysis of variance and the regression coefficients specified.

From Table 5, all the beta coefficients indicated positive relationships with the dependent variable. The beta coefficients also indicated that entertainment (0.418, $p<.001$) was the most important variable followed by persuasion knowledge. Although the beta coefficient for "sociability" and "escape" exhibited the expected positive relationship with the dependent variable, it was not significant. Therefore, H_1, H_2, H_3 and H_4 were all supported.

Table 2. Correlations

Variables		Attitude	Entertainment	Escape	Sociabilty	Persuasion Knowledge
Attitude	Pearson Correlation		.488**	.268**	.355**	.296**
	Sig. (2-tailed)		.000	.001	.000	.000
Entertainment	Pearson Correlation	.488**		.408**	.555**	.162*
	Sig. (2-tailed)	.000		.000	.000	.039
Escape	Pearson Correlation	.268**	.408**		.303**	.230**
	Sig. (2-tailed)	.001	.000		.000	.003
Sociability	Pearson Correlation	.355**	.555**	.303**		.360**
	Sig. (2-tailed)	.000	.000	.000		.000
Persuasion Knowledge	Pearson Correlation	.296**	.162*	.230**	.360**	
	Sig. (2-tailed)	.000	.039	.003	.000	

** Correlation is significant at the 0.01 level (2-tailed).

Source: Survey by authors

Table 3. Model summary

Model	R	R Square	Adjusted R Square	Std. Error of the Estimate
1	.537[a]	.288	.270	.47418

a. Predictors: (Constant), Sociability, Escape, Entertainment, Persuasion Knowledge
Source: Survey by authors

Table 4. ANOVA[a]

Model		Sum of Squares	df	Mean Square	F	Sig.
1	Regression	14.199	4	3.550	15.787	.000[b]
	Residual	35.076	156	.225		
	Total	49.275	160			

a. Dependent Variable: Attitude towards Advergames
b. Predictors: (Constant), Sociability, Escape, Entertainment, Persuasion Knowledge
Source: Survey by authors

Table 5. Coefficients[a]

Model		Unstandardized Coefficients		Standardized Coefficients	t	Sig.
		B	Std. Error	Beta		
1	(Constant)	1.709	.229		7.446	.000
	Entertainment	.248	.051	.418	4.884	.000
	Escape	.024	.046	.039	.512	.609
	Sociability	.028	.065	.037	.426	.670
	Persuasion Knowledge	.182	.065	.206	2.805	.006

a. Dependent Variable: Attitude towards Advergames
Source: Survey by authors

Correlation of Age With Various Variables Associated With Advergames

From Table 6 it can be seen that age of the children is significantly correlated with attitude towards advergames and persuasion knowledge. However, it was not significantly related with entertainment, escape and sociability. All the correlations were positive except the correlation between entertainment and age which suggests that as the age of the children increases the influence of entertainment factor decreases.

Table 6. Correlations of age with various variables associated with advergames

		Attitude	Entertainment	Escape	Sociability	Persuasion Knowledge
Age	Pearson Correlation	.245**	-.064	.201*	.016	.339**
	Sig. (2-tailed)	.002	.419	.011	.844	.000

** Correlation is significant at the 0.01 level (2-tailed).
* Correlation is significant at the 0.05 level (2-tailed).
Source: Survey by authors

T-Test Based on Gender of Respondents

In order to ascertain whether significant difference existed between the male and female respondents' response towards various variables related to advergames t-test was employed. Levene's test checks for equality of variance among various groups. Significance value of Levene's test > 0.05 indicates that equal variance is assumed. In the given table, all groups have equal variances. T-test statistics (significance value) less than level of significance (0.05) indicate that the two categories of independent variables (male and female) differ significantly towards their response to the various statements.

Table 7 showed that in this case no significant difference was observed as all significance values were greater than 0.05 except for persuasion knowledge. Thus, it can be concluded that male and female respondents have no significant difference in their response towards various variables related to advergames. Although previous studies had suggested a potential gender bias in the effectiveness of advergames on attitudes of consumers but such effects were not significant in this study (Kim *et al.*, 1998; Jackson *et al.*, 2008). Table 8 shows the different values of means for males and females.

As it was found through t-test that significant difference existed in opinion of males and females with regard to persuasion knowledge, it can be seen in table 8 that females were more in agreement towards the persuasion knowledge which may be due their higher levels of knowledge of brands.

DISCUSSION

The current research was conducted to empirically test the relationship of different variables with attitude towards advergames. Examination of the correlation matrix indicated that ''entertainment'' and ''sociability'' were the most closely correlated

Table 7. Independent samples test

Variables		Levene's Test for Equality of Variances		t-test for Equality of Means		
		F	Sig.	t	df	Sig. (2-tailed)
Attitude towards Advergames	Equal variances assumed	9.688	0.002	-0.264	159	0.792
	Equal variances not assumed			-0.244	94.071	0.808
Entertainment	Equal variances assumed	0.917	0.34	0.638	159	0.524
	Equal variances not assumed			0.617	109.295	0.538
Escape	Equal variances assumed	12.58	0.001	0.566	159	0.572
	Equal variances not assumed			0.52	93.522	0.604
Sociability	Equal variances assumed	1.136	0.288	0.205	159	0.838
	Equal variances not assumed			0.216	140.939	0.829
Persuasion Knowledge	Equal variances assumed	2.475	0.118	-2.072	159	0.04
	Equal variances not assumed			-1.996	107.937	0.048

Source: Survey by authors

Table 8. Group statistics

Variable	Gender	Mean	Std. Deviation	Std. Error Mean
Attitude towards advergames	Male	3.2689	.48426	.04795
	Female	3.2930	.66395	.08644
Entertainment	Male	3.4199	.89299	.08842
	Female	3.3220	1.01184	.13173
Escape	Male	3.0123	.78851	.07807
	Female	2.9280	1.08978	.14188
Sociability	Male	3.2451	.78742	.07797
	Female	3.2203	.64508	.08398
Persuasion knowledge	Male	3.0605	.58811	.05823
	Female	3.2712	.67658	.08808

Source: Survey by authors

with the dependent variable i.e. attitude towards advergames. Through regression analysis it was found that the beta coefficients indicated entertainment (0.418, $p<.001$) was the most important variable followed by persuasion knowledge. Almost identical outcomes were found in a previous research by Hernandez (2008) who had also found that the beta coefficients signified that "entertainment" (0.486, $p< 0.001$) was the most important variable. A correlation of age with different variables showed that all the correlations were positive except the correlation between entertainment and age which indicates that as the age of the children increases the effect of entertainment factor decreases. It was also concluded that male and female respondents have no significant difference in their response towards various variables related to advergames.

RECOMMENDATIONS

The authors recommend that with the proper use of advergames as a promotional tool, brands can better promote their products. This is mainly because nowadays the masses are connected to the internet. Secondly, it is an entertaining means of attracting customers as customers are lured into playing which is enjoyable and simultaneously the product is promoted. Thirdly, as advergames promote sociability, they can be used as a means of encouraging online competitions with multi-player games. Next, the marketers can make use of the relationship of advergames and the persuasion knowledge which plays a key role in whether the users get manipulated by seeing the brands along with the games. The difference between males and females regarding persuasion knowledge is an important finding in this regard. Lastly, as the age of the respondent is significantly positively correlated with persuasion knowledge it can be understood that with the increase in age of respondents their persuasion knowledge also increases. Hence, marketers can plan their activities accordingly based on the age group of their target audience.

FUTURE RESEARCH DIRECTIONS

The future of advergames is quite promising as interactive technologies are developing at a fast pace and those who do not keep up face the danger of being left behind. These technologies are quite immersive and are require high involvement from the user. Therefore, the brands need to make use of this technology by maintaining a balance because some studies show that when the involvement is too high the consumer may overlook the brand and thus the advergame may fail it's the whole purpose of its creation (Grigorovici & Constantin, 2004). The chapter concludes with a summary, a balanced assessment of the contribution of advergames in persuading children and a roadmap for future directions.

CONCLUSION

More and more companies are adopting advergames to promote their products, therefore an understanding of customers' attitude towards advergames is very important. The present study tries to explain the attitude children have towards advergames. The study was focussed on children as new digital advertising technologies are to a significant extent directed towards a young consumer audience. Children are easily attracted towards fun and interactive content which allows them to be actively involved. Moreover, children are no longer passive buyers but instead they are actively involved in the purchase process. Therefore, targeting them through advergames is quite advantageous. This data for this study was collected from children belonging to the NCR. It was found that there was significant and positive relationship of entertainment with attitude towards advergames. The age of the respondent was also significantly correlated with the different dimensions of advergames. In addition, it was also found that there was no significant difference between males and females regarding the attitude towards advergames.

These findings are useful for marketers promoting different brands who can make best use of advergames particularly for children. But there is also a negative side to the use of advergames as the children are not mature to understand whether the product being promoted is healthy for them or not. There are many countries in the world where obesity is a major problem due last market of junk food. Therefore, it is the ethical responsibility of advertisers to keep in mind the fact that when promoting their products to children they should not take undue advantage and exploit them.

The marketers can make use of the relationship of advergames and the persuasion knowledge which plays a key role in whether the users get manipulated by seeing the brands along with the games. As the age of the respondent is significantly positively correlated with persuasion knowledge it can be understood that with the increase in age of respondents their persuasion knowledge also increases. Hence, marketers can plan their activities accordingly based on the age group of their target audience.

ACKNOWLEDGMENT

This research received no specific grant from any funding agency in the public, commercial, or not-for-profit sectors.

REFERENCES

An, S., Jin, H. S., & Park, E. H. (2014). Children's advertising literacy for advergames: Perception of the game as advertising. *Journal of Advertising*, *43*(1), 63–72. doi:10.1080/00913367.2013.795123

Blades, M., Oates, C., & Blumberg, F. (2014). *Advertising to children: New directions, new media.* Retrieved from http://www.eblib.com

DiClemente, D. F., & Hantula, D. A. (2003). Applied behavioral economics and consumer choice. *Journal of Economic Psychology*, *24*(5), 589–602. doi:10.1016/S0167-4870(03)00003-5

Evans, N. J. (2014). Pinpointing Persuasion in Children's Advergames: Exploring the Relationship Among Parents' Internet Mediation, Marketplace Knowledge, Attitudes, and the Support for Regulation. *Journal of Interactive Advertising*, *14*(2), 73–85. doi:10.1080/15252019.2014.943354

Folkvord, F., Anschütz, D. J., Buijzen, M., & Valkenburg, P. M. (2013). The effect of playing advergames that promote energy-dense snacks or fruit on actual food intake among children. *The American Journal of Clinical Nutrition*, *97*(2), 239–245. doi:10.3945/ajcn.112.047126 PMID:23269821

Friestad, M., & Wright, P. (1994). The persuasion knowledge model: How people cope with persuasion attempts. *The Journal of Consumer Research*, *22*(1), 1–31. doi:10.1086/209380

Grigorovici, D. M., & Constantin, C. D. (2004). Experiencing interactive advertising beyond rich media: Impacts of ad type and presence on brand effectiveness in 3d gaming immersive virtual environments. *Journal of Interactive Advertising*, *6*(1), 30–53.

Hanumanthu, A. (2017). Advergaming in India: An Untapped Business? *Telangana Today*. Retrieved from https://telanganatoday.com/advergaming-india-untapped-business

Harris, J. R. (2011). *The nurture assumption: Why children turn out the way they do*. Simon and Schuster.

Hernandez, M. D., & Chapa, S. (2010). Adolescents, advergames and snack foods: Effects of positive affect and experience on memory and choice. *Journal of Marketing Communications*, *16*(1-2), 59–68. doi:10.1080/13527260903342761

Hofmeister-Tóth, A., & Nagy, P. (2011). The content analysis of advergames in Hungary. *Qualitative Market Research*, *14*(3), 289–303. doi:10.1108/13522751111137514

Hofmeister-Tóth, A., & Nagy, P. (2011). The content analysis of advergames in Hungary. *Qualitative Market Research*, *14*(3), 289–303. doi:10.1108/13522751111137514

Hudders, L., Cauberghe, V., Panic, K., & De Vos, W. (2015). Children's advertising literacy for new advertising formats: The mediating impact of advertising literacy on the (Un)Intended effects of advergames and advertising funded programs. In P. W. J. Verlegh, H. Voorveld, & M. Eisend (Eds.), *Advances in advertising research: The digital, the classic, the subtle and the alternative* (pp. 241–252). Amsterdam: Springer Gabler.

India Infoline News Service. (n.d.). *Zapak launches its first ever AdverGame in India for multiple DTH Players*. Retrieved from https://www.indiainfoline.com/article/news-corporate/zapak-launches-its-first-ever-advergame-in-india-for-multiple-dth-players-113101908813_1.html

Jackson, L. A., Zhao, Y., Kolenic, A. III, Fitzgerald, H. E., Harold, R., & von Eye, A. (2008). Race, gender, and information technology use: The new digital divide. *Cyberpsychology & Behavior*, *11*(4), 437–442. doi:10.1089/cpb.2007.0157 PMID:18721092

Jayaswal, P., & Malati, N. (2017). Impact of Advergames on Children. *International Journal of Innovative Research and Development*, *6*(1), 88–92.

Kanth, K. R. (2013). Catch them young with advergaming. *Business Standard*. Retrieved from http://www.business-standard.com/article/technology/catch-them-young-with-advergaming-110010700030_1.html

Kim, J., Lim, J. S., & Bhargava, M. (1998). The role of affect in attitude formation: A classical conditioning approach. *Journal of the Academy of Marketing Science*, *26*(2), 143–152. doi:10.1177/0092070398262005

Ojha, R. (2015). *Game First, Brand Later: A Strategic Approach to Advergames*. Retrieved from http://trak.in/tags/business/2011/05/23/brand-games-strategic-advergames/

Pempek, T. A., & Calvert, S. L. (2009). Tipping the balance use of advergames to promote consumption of nutritious foods and beverages by low-income African American children. *Archives of Pediatrics & Adolescent Medicine*, *163*(7), 633–637. doi:10.1001/archpediatrics.2009.71 PMID:19581546

Piaget, J. (1929). *The child's conception of the world*. Harcourt, Brace Jovanovich.

Piaget, J., & Inhelder, B. (Eds.). (1973). *Memory and Intelligence*. New York, NY: Basic Books.

Raney, A. A., Arpan, L. M., Pashupati, K., & Brill, D. A. (2003). At the movies, on the web: An investigation of the effects of entertaining and interactive web content on site and brand evaluations. *Journal of Interactive Marketing*, *17*(4), 38–53. doi:10.1002/dir.10064

Rozendaal, E., Buijzen, M., & Valkenburg, P. (2010). Comparing children's and adults' cognitive advertising competences in the Netherlands. *Journal of Children and Media*, *4*(1), 77–89. doi:10.1080/17482790903407333

van Reijmersdal, E. A., Jansz, J., Peters, O., & Van Noort, G. (2010). The effects of interactive brand placements in online games on children's cognitive, affective, and conative brand responses. *Computers in Human Behavior*, *26*(6), 1787–1794. doi:10.1016/j.chb.2010.07.006

van Reijmersdal, E. A., Rozendaal, E., & Buijzen, M. (2012). Effects of Prominence, Involvement, and Persuasion Knowledge on Children's Cognitive and Affective Responses to Advergames. *Journal of Interactive Marketing*, *26*(1), 33–42. doi:10.1016/j.intmar.2011.04.005

Verdoodt, V., Clifford, D., & Lievens, E. (2016). Toying with children's emotions, the new game in town? The legality of advergames in the EU. *Computer Law & Security Review*, *32*(4), 599–614. doi:10.1016/j.clsr.2016.05.007

Wise, K., Bolls, P. D., Kim, H., Venkataraman, A., & Meyer, R. (2008). Enjoyment of advergames and brand attitudes: The impact of thematic relevance. *Journal of Interactive Advertising*, *9*(1), 27–36. doi:10.1080/15252019.2008.10722145

KEY TERMS AND DEFINITIONS

Advergames: Online games that integrate advertisements into the games in order to influence the customers.

Advertising: It is an audio or visual form of marketing communication that employs an openly sponsored, non-personal message to promote or sell a product, service, or idea.

Affective: Relating to, arising from, or influencing feelings or emotions.

Attitude: A settled way of think or feeling about something.

Brand: A brand is a name, term, design, symbol, or other feature that distinguishes an organization or product from its rivals in the eyes of the customer.

Cognitive: Relating to, being, or involving conscious intellectual activity (such as thinking, reasoning, or remembering).

Escape: To get away from what someone is doing.

Persuasion Knowledge: Consumers' beliefs in and knowledge of the marketing system (e.g., production and consumption), a company's goals, marketing strategies, and products.

Sociability: It is a state marked by or conducive to friendliness or pleasant social relations.

Chapter 6 Food Advergames and Children: The Psychodynamics

Tanusree Chakraborty
Presidency University Bangalore, India

Raiswa Saha
SRM University, India

ABSTRACT

Advergames are a very dynamic marketing tool for companies coupled with being interactive, fulfilled, networked, creating positive connection with consumers, provides pleasurable environment marked by two-way communication. Food advergames target children population who without knowing the persuasive content of the games engage in the play. The purpose of this chapter is to highlight the psychodynamics of food advergames, how advergames influences children's eating attitude and behavior, and also discusses about the health hazards that food advergames bring in with itself. Finally, the chapter throws light on the impact and concerns of food advergames on children's eating behavior.

ADVERGAMES: AN OVERVIEW

With the advent of gamification in the world market, advergames have made a different place for itself. In its simple most definition, advergames can be defined as the firmest mounting chunk of the advertising model around the world that has grown in multiplication in recent times; it refers to an online video game that

DOI: 10.4018/978-1-5225-6064-7.ch006

encourages a particular brand, product, or marketing message by assimilating it into the pattern of game. Though the development of advergames has been really in bounds, still the role of advergames in marketing has remained unidentified to the full (Okazaki and Yagüe, 2012). And it is also true; that the question as to how much impact advergames has been able to make on the target audience has been a matter of question. “Advergames”, as a term was first coined in January 2000 by Tony Giallourakis, and immediately mentioned after that by Wired’s “Jargon Watch” column in 2001. Advergames is at present one of the commonly discussed topics and played activity among the young generation, especially children. But there are still many who might not have experienced advergames. Let us define advergames; the way they have been defines by the pioneers in the field. There are different ways how advergames have been defined.

Definitions of Advergames

According to Calin, (2010), advergames are designed by considering the strategic aims of the advertising companies, fitting into the personality of the brand for which the advertisement is intended, the profile of the audience in target, the features of the platform (i.e.,Internet), the strategic goals of the communication drive and of course yes, the corporate image of the company.

Looking at the comprehensive definitions put forth by various authors the following characteristics of advergames can be outlined:

Table 1.

Author	Definition
Culp et al. 2010	The advergames are fun, appealing, and generates a context for associating the brand with positive sentiments.
Culp et al., 2010	Advergame is a brand-rich environment that merges a video game with advertising.
Hernandez et al.,2004	Advergame is internet promotional method containing advertising messages.
Fattah and Paul, 2002	Advergames are interactive advertisements that merge online games with product placement.
Winkler and Buckner, 2006	Advergames are the online games designed for the specific purpose of marketing a single brand or product.
(Kretchmer 2005	Advergames are “computer games specifically created to function as advertisements to promote brands, where the entertainment content mimics traditional game forms”
(Grigorovici and Constantin, 2004; Shrum, 2004	Advergames represent a rapidly evolving sector comprising of embedded commercial messages within the content of retail-accessible video games and on-line electronic games.

1. Has a persuasive messages
2. Carries an embedded commercial messages
3. Brand centric
4. Free to play
5. Played over internet
6. Branded products or services are fundamental in playing them
7. Suitable for viral marketing
8. Promise a longer exposure to brands
9. Offer virtual interaction with a brand name
10. For an advergame, the game is specially made to promote the brand
11. Easily distributed on different platforms

Advergaming: A Snapshot of Literature

See Table 2.

Table 2.

Author and Year	Findings
Bogost 2005, 2007	The content of game influences one's attitudes and further engages in higher learning process.
Cicchirillo, V., & Mabry, A. (2016).	Higher levels of healthy eating involvement showed negative attitudes toward the brand whereas, positive effects is related to lower levels of brand advergames integration.
Lee et al (2009)	Advergames are heavily used by Food marketers in the form of candy and gum.
Hye-Jin Paek (2014)	Children possess higher level of brand integration in terms of Advergames use with ad breaks and number of brand identifiers as two most important food advergames predictor.
An & Kang (2014)	Advergames featuring food are high in calories but, have less nutritional value.
Hofmeister-Tóth, Á.,& Nagy, P. (2011).	Major advergames codes are type, brand, prize, and special features.
Waiguny et al 2013	Advergames with respect to content resulted in less favorable attitudes and Negative associations whereas, the content and explicit attitude toward the brand was mediated by attitude toward the game
Evans et al. (2013)	Parental socialization theory is related to parents' perceptions and attitudes toward advertising of advergames
Vasishth et al. (2017)	Low game-product congruence results in high persuasion than in high game-product congruence.

The (Adver) Gaming Environment

With fun and interactive characteristics to play, lots of child-centric food companies have used the advergames feature on websites for better customer associations and wide exposure to their brand (Harris et al., 2012). Children in their early stages adapt these interactive marketing games for fun and enjoyment, as it creates attractive and popular online activities for children as well as youth (Rideout et al., 2010). Traditional advertisements through television or print media, children are inert in their exposure to brand placement whereas, with the features of Advergames, it creates amusement and focused attention from the player, in which children are active seekers in their interactions with the content (Wise et al., 2008). Brand placements in advergames is a new environment altogether, they are different from games of traditional products, advergames provides an environment for interaction with the brand and the viewer (Kleeberger and Hummel 2002), this interaction plays a major role cognitive involvement of the viewer with the product (Shrum 2004). The Advergaming environment also is characterized by a two way communication between the game player and the game; the content in itself is interactive (Hoffman and Novak 1996. The Advergaming environment also creates a feeling of fun and escapism that is experienced in a gaming environment (Refiana, Mizerski, and Murphy 2005); the target is an active player in a fun-filled environment. The environment is open for all ages and gender, though younger generation is more involved in it. Thus the advergaming environment in a nutshell is dynamic, interactive; full filled, networked, creating positive connection with consumers; pleasurable environment marked by two way communication.

Children Advergames: Advertisements in Disguise

Advergames and Advertising! Are they same or they are different? How much are the child spectators aware of the similarity and difference between the two? And this is of course a matter of concern whether and to what degree children can differentiate between absorbing fun games that are designed to make them buy something and absorbing, fun games that have no ulterior commercial motive. According to Committee of Advertising Practice (CAP) Code Section 2.1 if consumers are unaware that they are being targeted with a commercial message they are unable to critically assess the information, engage uncertainty and make an informed decision as to whether or not to accept or reject the message. Moreover, the companies that create and develop advergames seem to be unaware of CAP Code 2.1. If consumers are not in a position to do this then the advertising is inherently unfair and children are particularly vulnerable in this respect. Children's cognitive processing capability and their interactions with the external world makes them understand messages from a variety of sources. And this information processing will differ among children of various ages, subject to their difference in age and message interpretation ability from an advertisement. For a child to understand the latent meaning of advertising and that they consider not so fair, does not develop until age of four. A few studies have proved the fact that most of the children do not realize that adverts have a latent persuasive commercial message. Children's recognition of the commercial intent of in-game advertising and film product placement is particularly low. The immensely immersive nature of advergames, product placement and in-game advertising added with the fun factor makes it difficult for a child to decipher the commercial persuasive message in the advergames. A few studies have established the fact that children's understanding of advergames objectives is very limited and it should be a good practice for the companies to mention before, during and after they play the game that what they are experiencing is not a pure game but is an attempt by a commercial company to sell them something or to persuade them to develop a positive attitude towards their brand. Lindstrom (2005) suggests computer games generate double the revenue of the film industry.

Drawing from neuroscientific research it can be said that information processing happens at two levels- implicit and explicit - dual-process model of message processing. There is a subconscious information processing too, which is subconscious; beside there is a conscious explicit level also. These systems appear to operate in separate parts of the brain and can lead us to form contradictory attitudes. We may understand that a particular product is not good, but at the same time adore the brand for the liking towards how it is presented. The messages in advergames and other immersive forms of advertising are processed implicitly because the child's cognitive capacity is engaged elsewhere playing the game and there is not enough resource available for them to stop and think about the purpose of the game or to engage any scepticism about the source of the message. Children do not understand that they have been exposed to advertising or do not even recall seeing the brand placed in a game (or a film) but yet their opinions and behaviour are affected. Some argue that advergames may be more effective than television advertising because they blur the distinction between advertising and entertainment content and make it difficult for children to identify the game as advertising (Mallinckrodt &Mizerski, 2007; Moore, 2006)

Table 3. How children interpret adverts

Stage 1	Stage 2	Stage 3	Stage 4
Advertisements have no meaning	Advertisement are fun	Advertisements carry some messages	Advertisements are persuasive

Persuasion Knowledge Model and Advergames

Academic interest and researches in how consumers respond to the persuasive messages in games is growing over years (e.g., Farrar, Krcmar, and Nowak 2006; Yang et al. 2006). To explain the way advergames influence the spectators is very well explained through the Persuasion Knowledge Model (PKM). Persuasion Knowledge Model (PKM) expresses persuasion knowledge as the sureness a user or consumer has in his or her capability to comprehend marketers' motives and strategies (Friestad and Wright's1994). The PKM explains that consumers want cognitive tools (called persuasion knowledge) to "recognize, analyze, interpret, evaluate, and remember persuasion attempts and select and execute coping tactics believed to be effective and appropriate" (Friestad and Wright, 1994). This model also explains the ways how a marketer that people's persuasion knowledge is developmentally contingent; and that this keeps on developing in an individual with time and experience; and it is an acquired learning from outside, learnt from family, friends, environments and gradually it comes from marketers as well; spreading to commentary on advertising and marketing campaigns in the news media and the like. Persuasion knowledge, that the marketers, advertisers, and salespeople hold and disseminate, guides the way they design and deliver their persuasion attempts. According to Vanwesenbeeck, Michel Walrave & Koen Ponnet (2017) a higher level of persuasion knowledge leads to a higher purchase intention to buy the advertised product.Advergames are trying to do the same by exposing the potential consumers with the product.

In case of a child viewer, an underlying universal statement depicts that a child understands level and knowledge adoption essentially mediates the response pattern (Wright, Freistad, and Boush 2005; Robertson and Rossiter 1974; Livingstone 2004; Ward, real, and Levinson 1972). Therefore, a higher knowledge level mediates the persuasive influence of the message to children in a reasoned manner (Adler et al. 1980). Children recurrently come across various commercial content of advergames which are in many ways different from advertisements they see in televisions (Evans,Carlson, and Hoy2013). As consumers gradually understand marketplace experience, their coping becomes smooth; interpretation becomes clearer, inference from memory, reading the persuasion content, understanding advertisement objectives become more effortless and smooth (Wright et al, 2005).

According to Owen et al (2013), children are slightly better than adults in understanding television advertisements. Adults' cognitive ability on the other hand, is higher than children's, so they can infer persuasive knowledge more than children (Freistad and Wright, 1994, John 1999; Wright et al 2005). In a study, Kinard and Hartmen 2013 found that whatever be the advertising formats (traditional or other immersive forms) adults are better in decoding persuasive knowledge. Previous researchers have offered deeper understanding of persuasive knowledge and how it develops over time (Wright, Freistad, & Boush 2005), focused on reasons behind decision making in adults (Freistad & Wright 1994) and children (Moses & Baldwin 2005; Wright, Freistad, & Boush 2005). It has been established by a plethora of researches that consumers' knowledge about persuasion "enables them to recognize, analyze, interpret, evaluate, and remember persuasion attempts and to select and execute coping tactics believed to be effective and appropriate" (Freistad & Wright 1994).

Advergames Influencing Attitude and Behavior Toward Food

Food and beverage companies have taken advantage of the increasing trend of advergames, expanding child-targeted marketing on commercial websites, third-party Internet advertising. Food and beverage websites are estimated to attract forty-nine million child visitors annually, with users spending as much as 1 hour or more on these sites (Moore & Rideout, 2007). Food related advergames incorporate characteristics to reassure that children do return to the website and engage in playing the game several times (Santos, Gonzalo, & Gisbert, 2007). Looking at numbers, there are at least 540 advergames which were found on different food company websites, and a good number of websites contained even as many as sixty-seven games (Moore & Rideout, 2007). As is the case with television advertising, most of the foods and beverages promoted in advergames comprise of higher sugar content, sodium, and/or fat; nearly three-quarters promoted are found to promote candy, some cereals, soft drinks, or salty snacks (Lee et al., 2009). In fact, current researches found significant impact of advergames on children's food consumption (Dias and Agante 2011; Folkvord, Anschütz, Buijzen, and Valkenburg, 2013; Harris et al. 2011; Harnadez and Chapa 2010; Mallinckrodit and Mizerski 2007; Pempek and Calvert 2009). Children who are more exposed to unhealthy food advergames have been found to be more inclined towards food with high sugar content and fat. And this is more evidences after exposing them to such advergames.

The Differential Susceptibility to Media Effects Model (Valkenburg&Preter 2013) predicts that not all children process and react to food cues in advertising to the same extent. Yokum et al. (2014), have shown that neurological responses to food advertisements predicted future weight gain also, thereby supporting the notion of individual differences in neural susceptibility to food advertisements.

According to the *incentive-sensitization theory* given by Gearhardt (2014), in the long run, eating these energy-dense foods may thus result in neurological adaptations and sensitization of these foods.

According to the *Reactivity to Embedded Food Cues in Advertising Model* (REFCAM):

1. Food cues induce physiological and psychological reactivity to food (*advertising effect process*), which
2. Leads to a reciprocal relationship with eating behavior (*incentive-sensitization process).*
3. Individual dispositional factors determine susceptibility to food cues in advertisements.

From latest studies of the effects of interactivity and brand integration in food advergames the impact of advergames on attitude towards food reveals and there is a link between children's food and advergames children play.

1. There is a positive correlation between the level of entertainment the game provides and the brand loyalty towards it (Waiguny et al. 2011). Van Reijmersdal et al. (2012) found that interactivity the game provided was important for brand loyalty.
2. Advergames have a strong impact on children's food preferences, and this impact extends to the older age group as well.
3. Online food game environment guarantees further consideration from policy makers and regulators. Playing with branded food impacts imaginatoion about the food among children, and those imaginations impact their food behavior in real world. The liking for the games influences their liking for the advertised branded food. So attitude towards food is of course encouraged by the advergames children engage in.
4. The birth of advergames and the practice of food marketers using them to target children have stimulated discussions among consumer advocates and policy makers about the potential impact of such a new interactive advertising tactic on children (Mallinckrodt and Mizerski 2007; Moore and Rideout 2007; Weber, Story, and Hamack 2006).
5. Food advergames provide children with new alternative ways to play with the foods. As children do not understand the advergames are advertisements, unknowingly they develop a preference towards the advertised food.
6. Persuasive content of the games impacts food choices. Recent findings of Mallinckrodt and Mizerski's (2007) study demonstrated that impact of integrated branded foods impacted on children's preference for the foods promoted in the game, the study also says that the persuasive potential of playing with foods in advergames in quite strong.

7. The immersive and interactive nature of advergame playing is the actual catalyst; previous research has found that interactivity of a medium leads to a more positive attitude toward the medium and an increased involvement with the medium among adult consumers (Johnson, Bruner, and Kumar 2006; McMillan and Hwang 2002).
8. Impulsivity in children is higher and it plays an important role in susceptibility to food advertisements.

Impact of Advergames on Children's Eating Behaviour

Advertising to children is perceived as one of the triumphant ways to construct a solid customer support, in an attempt to produce an enviable reflection in the wits of the young consumer and hence to make safe lifetime consumer purchasing. Advergames are very important tools for driving brand awareness. Branded entertainment is gaining impetus as the value of traditional advertising formats decays (Lowrey, Shrum, and McCarty 2005). However, researches confirming the effects of advergames on children rather than their understanding of commercial intent corresponds to the findings that older and more experienced children are just equally influence by advergames as younger children are. Children's advertising has both the sides; if it has advantages then it does have negative points too. The American Psychological Association (APA) suggests that interactions with online food promotions endanger children's long-term health by influencing nutritional knowledge and creating poor eating habits (Kunkel et al., 2004). Attempts could be made to disseminate nutritional food value and developing preferences towards nutritional food through advergames. If the impact is felt on attitude built, then target should be made on building positive attitude towards healthy foods. Advergames could also serve as an educational tool to teach children about nutrition, healthy eating, and physical activity in a manner that is fun and engaging (Lee et al., 2009). The impact of these games on food choices is clear. The "several million dollars" in "incremental revenue" represents thousands of unhealthy food choices. But the impact of these games goes far beyond immediate food choices. Bray (2004) stresses that children in particular may be unable to identify or evaluate the material; coupled with their lack of cognitive or critical thinking skills, children may therefore be particularly vulnerable to persuasive communications (Moore, 2004).

Concerns for Children's Food Advergames

One of the main concerns related to food advergames is the perceived misleading nature of rooted advertising materials; the nature may be unclear for identification purposes (Banerjee, 2004; Hertz, 2002; Keaty, John and Henke, 2002; Balasubramanian, 1994). Children generally at their stage lack essential cognitive and mental abilities that can help them to identify or evaluate the advertisement content (Bray 2004) and children may therefore be particularly susceptible to persuasive communications (Moore, 2004). Further, detailed information about players may be required in order to avail the facilities on many interactive sites which can act as positive signals for marketers (Faber et al., 2004; Weingarten, 2002) but, can probably raise issues regarding privacy and protection of vulnerable groups such as children (Fonda, 2004). An additional concern relates to the impact of violent content, ranging from the impact on aggressive or violent behavior as a consequence of violent game use (Walsh, 2001) through to poor social skills and low academic achievement (Chiu et al., 2004), though this may be less with respect to food advergames, but cannot be rules out altogether. Food not only represents one of the product categories most heavily advertised to children, but the food products that are promoted tend to be nutrient poor and calorie dense. Public health researchers have also reported that candy, sweets, and soft drinks lead child-audience food advertising, as children are generally expected to be inclined towards these foods; followed by high-calorie convenience foods, next in the lead are breads and cereals (Harrison and Marske, 2005). Policy makers should be concerned about the prevalence of food advergames that reach children and help prevent children from accessing food advergames by requiring advertisers to include age limit specification in those advergames. Accompanying the rise in childhood obesity and the proliferation of food marketing activities targeted at children the concerns are majorly about the effects of such marketing on children's health. Kellogg Company, for example, has been found to be definite not to advertise low-nutrient food on television and other media that target children below 12 years (Teinowitz 2007). The concerns about the relationship between food advertising and childhood obesity are based on the assumption that children, unlike adults, are unable to comprehend the concept and persuasive objective of advertising. Children are predominantly vulnerable to persuasive messages because of their less understanding about the advertisement component and their underdeveloped skills. Advergames were found to be a powerful medium which influences players' attitudes and behavioural reactions. The concern is about the practice of the marketers to engage children in a exceedingly immersive medium for unrestrained lengths of time to endorse nutrient poor foods is an alarming concern. Advergames thus should be subject to proper regulatory controls

CONCLUSION

The chapter discusses about the nature and features of advergames; and the psychodynamics of child group that marketers target for food advergames. Focusing on the cognitive processing of the advergames and children's susceptibility to get influenced by the food advergames, the chapter draws attention to the persuasive knowledge model, and how it differently impacts adult and children. As advergames have been seen in different ways, a matter for concern for the delicate child group, it is suggested that children advergames should be subject to regulatory controls. Attempts should be made in designing advergames that promote healthy foods. The chapter supports the need for limitations on companies' way of employing advergames to market nutritionally poor foods to children. Editors and creators of advergames and policy makers needs be more conscious of the bearing that branded items have within a gaming environment.

REFERENCES

Adler, R., Lesser, G., Meringoff, L., Robertson, T., Rossiter, J., & Ward, S. (1980). *The Effects of Television Advertising on Children*. Lexington, MA: Lexington Books.

An, S., & Kang, H. (2014). Advertising or games? Advergames on the internet gaming sites targeting children. *International Journal of Advertising*, *33*(3), 509–532. doi:10.2501/IJA-33-3-509-532

Balasubramanian, S. K. (1994). Beyond Advertising and Publicity: Hybrid Messages and Public Policy Issues. *Journal of Advertising*, *23*(4), 29–46. doi:10.1080/0091 3367.1943.10673457

Balasubramanian, S. K. (1994). Beyond advertising and publicity: Hybrid messages and public policy issues. *Journal of Advertising*, *23*(4), 29–46. doi:10.1080/0091 3367.1943.10673457

Banerjee, S. (2004). Playing Games. *Billboard*, *116*(20), 3–4.

Bogost, I. (2005). *Frame and Metaphor in Political Games*. Presented at the Digital Games Research Association (DiGRA) 2005 Conference Changing Views-Worlds in Play, Vancouver, Canada.

Bray, H. (2004). 'Advergames' spark concerns of kids being targeted. *Boston Globe*.

Bray, H. (2004, July 30). "Advergames" Spark Concerns of Kids Being Targeted. *Boston Globe*. Retrieved from http://www.boston.com/

Cicchirillo, V., & Mabry, A. (2016). Advergaming and healthy eating involvement. *Internet Research*, *26*(3), 587–603. doi:10.1108/IntR-04-2014-0091

Culp, J., Bell, R. A., & Cassady, D. (2010). Characteristics of Food Industry Web Sites and 'Advergames' Targeting Children. *Journal of Nutrition Education and Behavior*, *42*(3), 197–201. doi:10.1016/j.jneb.2009.07.008 PMID:20434075

Dias, M., & Aganten, L. (2011). Can Advergames Boost Children's Healthier Eating Habits? A Comparison between Healthy and Non-healthy food. *Journal of Consumer Behaviour*, *10*(3), 152–160. doi:10.1002/cb.359

Evans, N. J., Carlson, L., & Hoy, M. G. (2013). Coddling our kids: Can parenting style affect attitudes toward advergames? *Journal of Advertising*, *42*(2), 228–240. doi:10.1080/00913367.2013.774602

Faber, R. J., Lee, M., & Nan, X. (2004). Advertising and the consumer information environment online. *The American Behavioral Scientist*, *48*(4), 447–466. doi:10.1177/0002764204270281

Farrar, K. M., Krcmar, M., & Nowak, K. L. (2006). Contextual Features of Violent Video Games, Mental Models and Aggression. *Journal of Communication*, *56*(2), 387–405. doi:10.1111/j.1460-2466.2006.00025.x

Fattah, H., & Paul, P. (2002). Gaming gets serious. *American Demographics*, *24*(5), 38–44. Retrieved from http://adage.com/article/americandemographics/gaming/44521/

Folkvord, F., Anschütz, D. J., Buijzen, M., & Valkenburg, P. M. (2012). The Effect of Playing Advergames that Promote Energy-dense Snacks or Fruit on Actual Food Intake among Children. *The American Journal of Clinical Nutrition*, *97*(2), 239–245. doi:10.3945/ajcn.112.047126 PMID:23269821

Fonda, D. (2004). Kill the messenger? *Time Canada*, *163*(26), 57.

Friestad, M., & Wright, P. (1994). Persuasion Knowledge: Lay People's and Researchers' Beliefs About the Psychology of Advertising. *The Journal of Consumer Research*, *22*(June), 62–74.

Friestad, M., & Wright, P. (1994). The Persuasion Knowledge Model: How People Cope with Persuasion Attempts. *The Journal of Consumer Research*, *21*(June), 1–31. doi:10.1086/209380

Gearhardt, A. N., Yokum, S., Stice, E., Harris, J. L., & Brownell, K. D. (2014). Relation of obesity to neural activation in response to food commercials. *Social Cognitive and Affective Neuroscience*, *9*(7), 932–938. doi:10.1093can/nst059 PMID:23576811

Grigorovici, D. M., & Constantin, C. D. (2004). Experiencing Interactive Advertising beyond Rich Media. Impacts of Ad Type and Presence on Brand Effectiveness in 3D Gaming Immersive Virtual Environments. *Journal of Interactive Advertising*, *5*(1), 1–26. doi:10.1080/15252019.2004.10722091

Harnadez, M. D., & Chapa, S. (2010). Adolescents, Advergames and Snack Foods: Effects of Positive Affect and Experience on Memory and Choice. *Journal of Marketing Communications*, *16*(1-2), 59–68. doi:10.1080/13527260903342761

Harris, J., Speers, S., Schwartz, M., & Brownell, K. (2012). US food company branded advergames on the Internet: Children's exposure and effects on snack consumption. *Journal of Children and Media*, *6*(1), 51–68. doi:10.1080/17482798.2011.633405

Harris, J. L., Speers, S. E., Schwartz, M. B., & Brownell, K. D. (2011). US Food Company Branded Advergames on the Internet: Children's Exposure and Effects on 24 Snack Consumption. *Journal of Children and Media*, *6*(1), 51–68. doi:10.1080/17482798.2011.633405

Harrison, K., & Marske, A. L. (2005). Nutritional Content of Foods Advertised during the Television Programs Children Watch Most. *American Journal of Public Health*, *95*(9), 1568–1574. doi:10.2105/AJPH.2004.048058 PMID:16118368

Hernandez, M. D., Chapa, S., Minor, M. S., Maldonado, C., & Barranzuela, F. (2004). Hispanic Attitudes toward Advergames: A Proposed Model of Their Antecedents. *Journal of Interactive Advertising*, *5*(1), 74–83. doi:10.1080/15252019.2004.10722095

Hertz, L. M. (2002). Advertising Regulation on the Internet. *The Computer and Internet Lawyer*, *19*(6), 18–26.

Hertz, L. M. (2002). Advertising regulation on the internet. *The Computer and Internet Lawyer*, *19*(6), 18–26.

Hoffman, D., & Novak, T. P. (1996). Marketing in Hypermedia Computer-Mediated Environments: Conceptual Foundations. *Journal of Marketing*, *60*(3), 50–68. doi:10.2307/1251841

Hofmeister-Tóth, Á., & Nagy, P. (2011). The content analysis of advergames in Hungary. *Qualitative Market Research, 14*(3), 289–303. doi:10.1108/13522751111137514

John, D. R. (1999). Consumer Socialization of Children: A Retrospective Look at Twenty-Five Years of Research. *The Journal of Consumer Research, 26*(3), 183–213. doi:10.1086/209559

Johnson, G. J., Bruner, G. C. II, & Kumar, A. (2006). Interactivity and Its Facets Revisited. *Journal of Advertising, 35*(4), 35–52. doi:10.2753/JOA0091-3367350403

Keaty, A., Johns, R. J., & Henke, L. L. (2002). Can Internet Service Providers and Other Secondary Parties Be Held Liable for Deceptive Online Advertising? *Business Lawyer, 58*(1), 479–511.

Keaty, A., Johns, R. J., & Henke, L. L. (2002). Can internet service providers and other secondary parties be held liable for deceptive online advertising? *Business Lawyer, 58*(1), 479–511.

Kinard, B. R., & Hartman, K. B. (2013). Are You Entertained? The Impact of Brand Integration and Brand Experience in Television-Related Advergames. *Journal of Advertising, 42*(2–3), 196–203. doi:10.1080/00913367.2013.775794

Kleeberger, J., & Hummel, J. (2002). *Online Gaming as Marketing and Sales Catalyst* (Working paper). University of St. Gallen. Available at www.gamasutra.com/ education/theses/20030721/Kleeberger_thesis.pdf

Kretchmer, S. B. (2005). *Changing Views of Commercialization in Digital Games: In-Game Advertising and Advergames as Worlds in Play*. Paper presented at DIGTAR conference, "Changing Views: Worlds in Play," Vancouver, Canada. Retrieved from www.gamesconference.org/digra2005/ overview.php

Lee, M., Choi, Y. H., Quilliam, E. T., & Cole, R. T. (2009). Playing with Food: Content Analysis of Food Advergames. *The Journal of Consumer Affairs, 43*(1), 129–154. doi:10.1111/j.1745-6606.2008.01130.x

Lindstrom, M. (2005). Get a Jump-start on Playing the New Brand Game. *Media Asia, 28*(June), 21.

Livingston, S. (2004). A Commentary on the Research Evidence Regarding the Effects of Food Promotion on Children. In Childhood Obesity—Food Advertising in Context. London: London School of Economics and Political Science, Department of Media and Communications.

Mallinckrodt, V., & Mizerski, D. (2007). The effects of playing an advergame on young children's perceptions, preferences, and requests. *Journal of Advertising*, *36*(2), 87–100. doi:10.2753/JOA0091-3367360206

McCarty, J. A. (2004). Product Placements: The Nature of the Practice and Potential Avenues of Inquiry. In The Psychology of Entertainment Media. Blurring the Lines between Entertainment and Persuasion. Mahwah, NJ: Lawrence Erlbaum.

McMillan, S. J., & Hwang, J.-S. (2002). Measures of Perceived Interactivity: An Exploration of the Role of Direction of Communication, User Control, and Time in Shaping Perceptions of Interactivity. *Journal of Advertising*, *31*(3), 29–42. doi: 10.1080/00913367.2002.10673674

Moore, E. S. (2004). Children and the Changing World of Advertising. *Journal of Business Ethics*, *52*(2), 161–167. doi:10.1023/B:BUSI.0000035907.66617.f5

Moore, E. S. (2004). Children and the changing world of advertising. *Journal of Business Ethics*, *52*(2), 161–167. doi:10.1023/B:BUSI.0000035907.66617.f5

Moore, E. S. (2006). *It's child's play: Advergaming and the online marketing of food to children*. Menlo Park, CA: Henry J. Kaiser Family Foundation.

Moore, E. S., & Rideout, V. J. (2007). The online marketing of food to children: Is it just fun and games? *American Marketing Association, 26*(2), 202–220.

Moses, L. J., & Baldwin, D. (2005). What Can the Study of Cognitive Development Reveal about Children's Ability to Appreciate and Cope with Advertising? *Journal of Public Policy & Marketing*, *24*(Fall), 186–201. doi:10.1509/jppm.2005.24.2.186

Paek, H-J., Elizabeth, T. Q., Kim, S., Weatherspoon, L. J., Rifon, N. J., & Lee, M. (2014). Characteristics of food advergames that reach children and the nutrient quality of the foods they advertise. *Internet Research*, *24*(1), 63–81. doi:10.1108/IntR-02-2013-0018

Pempek, T. A., & Calvert, S. L. (2009). Tipping the Balance: Use of Advergames to Promote Consumption of Nutritious Foods and Beverages by Low-income African American Children. *Archives of Pediatrics & Adolescent Medicine*, *163*(7), 633–637. doi:10.1001/archpediatrics.2009.71 PMID:19581546

Refiana, L., Mizerski, D., & Murphy, J. (2005). Measuring the State of Flow in Playing Online Games. In *Proceedings of ANZMAC 2005 Conference, Marketing Research and Research Methodologies (quantitative)*. Freemantle, Australia: School of Business, University of Western Australia.

Rideout, V., Foehr, U., & Roberts, D. (2010). *Generation M2: media in the lives of 8-to-18 year olds*. Retrieved from www.kff.org/entmedia/upload/8010.pdf

Rip, P. D. (1980). Product Class Advertising Effects on First-Time Buyers' Decision Strategies. *The Journal of Consumer Research*, *7*(September), 176–188.

Robertson, T. S., & Rossiter, J. (1974). Children and Commercial Persuasion: An Attribution Theory Analysis. *The Journal of Consumer Research*, *1*(1), 13–20.

Robertson, T. S., & Rossiter, J. (1976). Short-Run Advertising Effects on Children: A Field Study. *JMR, Journal of Marketing Research*, *13*(1), 68–71. doi:10.2307/3150908

Santos, E., Gonzalo, R., & Gisbert, F. (2007). Advergames: Overview. *Information Technologies and Knowledge*, *1*, 203–208.

Shrum, L. J. (Ed.). (2004). *The Psychology of Entertainment Media: Blurring the Lines Between Entertainment and Persuasion*. Mahwah, NJ: Lawrence Erlbaum.

Teinowitz, I. (2007). Kellogg Move Bodes III for Ads to Kids: More Than a Billion Food Marketing Bucks in Limbo as Companies Try to Satisfy the Critics. *Advertising Age*. Retrieved from http://adage.com/article?article_id=117386

Valkenburg, P. M., & Peter, J. (2013). The differential susceptibility to media effects model. *Journal of Communication*, *63*(2), 221–243. doi:10.1111/jcom.12024

vanReijmersdal, E. A., Rozendaal, E., & Buijzen, M. (2012). Effects of prominence, involvement, and persuasion on children's cognitive and affective responses to advergames. *Journal of Interactive Marketing*, *26*(1), 33–42. doi:10.1016/j.intmar.2011.04.005

Vanwesenbeeck, I., Walrave, M., & Ponnet, K. (2017). Children and advergames: The role of product involvement, prior brand attitude, persuasion knowledge and game attitude in purchase intentions and changing attitudes. *International Journal of Advertising*, *36*(4), 520–541. doi:10.1080/02650487.2016.1176637

Vashisht, D., & S., S. (2017). Effect of nature of the game on ad-persuasion in online gaming context. *Internet Research, 27*(1), 52-73. Retrieved from https://search.proquest.com/docview/1857362515?accountid=177896

Waiguny, M. K. J., Nelson, M. R., & Marko, B. (2013). How advergame content influences explicit and implicit brand attitudes: When violence spills over. *Journal of Advertising*, *42*(2), 155–169. doi:10.1080/00913367.2013.774590

Waiguny, M. K. J., Terlutter, R., & Zaglia, M. E. (2011). The influence of advergames on consumers' attitudes and behavior: An empirical study among young consumers. *International Journal of Entrepreneurial Venturing*, *3*(3), 231–247. doi:10.1504/IJEV.2011.041273

Ward, S., Reale, G., & Levinson, D. (Eds.). (1972). *Children's Perceptions, Explanations, and Judgements of Television Advertising: A Further Exploration.* Washington, DC: U.S. Government Printing Office.

Weber, K., Story, M., & Hamack, L. (2006). Internet Food Marketing Strategies Aimed at Children and Adolescents: A Content Analysis of Food and Beverage Brand Websites. *Journal of the American Dietetic Association*, *106*(9), 1463–1466. doi:10.1016/j.jada.2006.06.014 PMID:16963354

Weingarten, M. (2002). It's an ad! It's a game! It's . . . both! *Business 2.0*, *3*(3), 102.

Winkler, T., & Buckner, T. (2006). Receptiveness of Gamers to Embedded Brand Messages in Advergames: Attitudes towards Product Placement. *Journal of Interactive Advertising*, *7*(1).

Wise, K., Bolls, P., Kim, H., Venkataraman, A., & Meyer, R. (2008). Enjoyment of advergames and brand attitudes: The impact of thematic relevance. *Journal of Interactive Marketing*, *9*(1), 27–36. Retrieved from http://primelab.missouri.edu/pdfs/wbkvm08.pdf

Wright, P., Friestad, M., & Boush, D. M. (2005). The Development of Marketplace Persuasion Knowledge in Children, Adolescents, and Young Adults. *Public Policy and Marketing*, *24*, 222–233.

Wright, P., Friestad, M., & Boush, D. M. (2005). The Development of Marketplace Persuasion Knowledge in Children, Adolescents, and Young Adults. *Journal of Public Policy & Marketing*, *24*(2), 222–233. doi:10.1509/jppm.2005.24.2.222

Yang, M., Roskos-Ewoldsen, D. R., Dinu, L., & Arpen, L. M. (2006). The Effectiveness of 'In-Game' Advertising: Comparing College Students' Explicit and Implicit Memory for Brand Names. *Journal of Advertising*, *35*(4), 143–152. doi:10.2753/JOA0091-3367350410

Yokum, S., Gearhardt, A. N., Harris, J. L., Brownell, K. D., & Stice, E. (2014). Individual differences instriatum activity to food commercials predict weight gain in adolescents. *Obesity (Silver Spring, Md.)*, *12*, 2544–2551. PMID:25155745

Chapter 7
Understanding the Psychology of New Media Audiences From a Marketing Perspective

Amit Nagpal
New Delhi Institute of Management, India

ABSTRACT

Do new media/online audiences have similar psychology and behavior as offline audiences or is it different? If yes, why is the psychology and behavior of new media audience different from traditional media? Why do marketers need to understand new media user psychology to be effective? Let us look at some of the aspects of psychology of new media users and corresponding actions which marketers need to take. For example, in the case of increased tendency for social comparison, consumer behavior-social media has increased the human tendency for social comparison. It is easier to compare lifestyles on Facebook and Instagram, for example, and the users may also seek reassurance from other users. The impact of such comparison on social networking sites is likely to have primary influence of first degree network and secondary influence of second degree network. Marketing actions-advertisements and content can be created keeping in mind the human tendency for social comparison.

OBJECTIVES OF THE CHAPTER

- To understand glasshouse nature of new media
- To understand psychology and behavior of mew media users.
- To understand why online and offline audiences behave differently
- To understand the implications of the above for marketers

DOI: 10.4018/978-1-5225-6064-7.ch007

IMPACT AND VALUE

The chapter will be useful for marketers who wish to develop a deeper understanding of new media and online consumer behavior.

It will also be useful for academicians who wish to gain deeper understanding of new media and digital audiences

Honesty and transparency make you vulnerable. Be honest and transparent anyway.- Mother Teresa

WHAT IS NEW MEDIA?

In simple words, New Media includes means of mass communication using digital technologies such as the Internet (Boiarsky, 1997). New media are native to computers, computational and relying on computers for distribution. Some examples of new media are websites, mobile apps, virtual worlds, multimedia, computer games, human-computer interface, computer animation and interactive computer installations.

New Media can be broadly divided into two types:

1. Content marketing new media- e.g. blogs, social media posts/microblogs
2. Advertising new media- e.g. online advertising (banner ads), online streaming (video streaming), and social media advertising

New media has caught the fancy of consumers and increasing number of customers are searching for information and buying online (Dimmick, Chen, & Li, 2009). For the consumer, new media is easily accessible through different forms of digital media and it empowers businesses (including small and medium enterprises) with the capability to reach both B2B and B2C customers with ease.

Characteristics of New Media and User Psychology

Does the new media audience have similar psychology and behavior as traditional media audience or is it different? If yes, what do marketers need to understand about new media user psychology to be effective?

Mark Schaefer of Rutgers University shared in his blog post, "For a marketing message to go viral, it will need to exhibit the following characteristics: 1) be assimilated by a social media user 2) be retained in that user's memory; 3) be replicated by the user in a way that is observable by other users; 4) be transmitted to other users (who, in turn, assimilate, retain and further replicate the message)" (Shaefer, 2012)

These characteristics of new media compel a marketer to take specific actions under different situations. Let us look at some of these areas and analyze the corresponding actions which marketers need to take.

New Media Encourages Sharing Experiences and Altruism

Consumer Behavior

Social media users readily share information with their friends, connections and followers. (Leinonen, 2010)A combination of altruism and empathy can motivate people to share their experiences. Many travelers selflessly share their experiences so that others can have an equally good or better vacation experience. Sometimes people may share an experience out of empathy that others should not go through similar suffering.

Marketing Actions

As per (Miller, 2016) marketers find it easy to involve customers and prospects when they take up a social cause on new media. When people see an attempt for greater good, they are likely to support the campaign especially causes they emotionally connect with.

New Media Meets Desire for Instant Gratification

Consumer Behavior

Instant gratification is the desire to experience pleasure or fulfillment without delay or deferment. In the recent times, the desire for instant gratification has been increasing and social media is part of the game (Manovich, 2003). Getting a like, positive comment or share meets the desire for instant gratification and also boosts the self-esteem of user. People use social media for two reasons viz. an enjoyable activity (reading humorous content, watching videos, memes etc.) and it provides an opportunity to get pleasure of socializing / meeting people.

Marketing Actions

Marketers can create opportunities for instant gratification like immediate rewards (free eBook, discount coupons etc.)

New Meets Supports Tendency for Social Comparison

Consumer Behavior

Social media has increased the human tendency for social comparison. It is easier to compare lifestyles on Facebook and Instagram for example and the users may also seek reassurance from other users (Shaefer, How Facebook changes our behavior, 2014). The impact of such comparison on social networking sites is likely to have primary influence of first degree network and secondary influence of second degree network.

Marketing Actions

Advertisements and content can be created keeping in mind the human tendency for social comparison (Gorgone, 2017). For e.g. "Your neighbor is perhaps smarter than you and has already bought…"

New Media and Social Closeness

Consumer Behavior

According to a research, Active Facebook users (individuals who posted and contributed to their newsfeed), had a greater sense of social closeness, whereas passive Facebook users, (who only viewed posts and did not contribute to the newsfeed), had a lesser sense of social closeness.

Marketing Actions

The social closeness will also have an impact on the credibility of recommendation / review done by user on his / her network. People trust products which have either been purchased or positively reviewed by members of their social network. It can be highlighted in content and advertisements, "Members of your social network are purchasing it. So don't lag behind"

New Media and Addiction to Social Media

Consumer Behavior

Dopamine or happiness hormone is stimulated by unpredictable nature, small size and possible rewards, which is similar to the context on social media. The pull of dopamine is so strong that studies have shown tweeting is harder for people to resist than cigarettes and alcohol. Human beings are social animals and it is a natural human desire to be a part of something larger and feel connected. Social media satisfies this urge to connect at a time and place of your convenience through few clicks.

According to Mediakix study, an average person will spend more than five years of his or her life using social media (based on current behavior).

Marketing Actions

Marketers can use this addiction for building strong consumer loyalty with their brands. Also marketers need to provide multiple platforms which suit multiple consumer preferences such as Facebook page, Twitter, LinkedIn and so on. Also provide the options to consumers and community members to share their views in text, video, images and other preferred formats.

New Media and Need to Talk About Ourselves

Consumer Behavior

Humans devote about 30–40% of their speech on talking about themselves, and it increases to about 80% in case of social media posts. The reason is that we have more control on self-presentation (how we wish to be perceived) on new media, as we have more time to construct and refine. On the other hand in case of face to face conversations, we may not get time to think and may not have full control on our body language.

New research demonstrates the power of social media further and shows that Facebook (social proof) even contributes to our self-worth and the perceived value of friends.

Marketing Actions

Marketers can provide opportunities for people to talk about themselves for eg post your selfies, post your views and so on on social media pages of the company.

New Media and Emotional Connect With Brands

Consumer Behavior

Brands are a part of who we are and we form emotional connect with brands also. During an experiment, volunteers were shown two types of photos: the logo for a brand they loved and pictures of their partners/ close friends. The physiological response to the logo was as emotional as looking at a picture of family member/ close friend. Brands can form stronger emotional bonds by creating the perception of being more human.

Marketing Actions

Brands can connect with people or prospective customers more easily by being human. Being human means being vulnerable, making mistakes, creating a mess, living with joys, insecurities and anxieties of human life. The human side of brands need to be highlighted in content as well as social media advertisements.

New Media Is Interactive

Consumer Behavior

New media is usually interactive. Even so called social media or sharing sites have also started getting comments e.g. YouTube and SlideShare. Sometimes those who are commenting on the video / presentation also start engaging with each other (replying to each other's comments).

For example in case of advergaming, a company typically provides interactive games on its website in the hope that potential customers will be drawn to the game and spend more time on the website, or simply become more product aware. Products may also be featured prominently in the games.

Marketing Actions

Marketers need to provide opportunities to consumers / prospects for engagement and interaction with brands and social media executives (representatives of organizations and brands)

New Media Creates Communities and Facilitates Relationship Building

Consumer Behavior

When brands build communities, they also need to encourage their community members to interact with each other. The interactive nature of new media can help in building relationships. (Sometimes emotional reactions can damage relationships also).

The marketers also need to keep in mind that the attention span of the online audience is short. For example if the home page of a website is not able to catch sufficient attention within 30 seconds, the traffic bounces or moves to other website.

Marketing Actions

Marketers not only need to build communities of like-minded people with affinity for the brand and its values. It needs to encourage the community members to interact with each other and provide suitable opportunities for the same.

New Media Is Transparent

Consumer Behavior

The comments on our posts are not only visible to us, but to our whole network. While consistent positive comments can enhance brand reputation, consistent criticism can harm the reputation also. On one hand the attention span of the online audience is short but on the other hand, written words (or even podcasts and videos), can become permanent records. While emotions like anger can provoke people to act foolishly, the written word (or recorded video/audio) can become a permanent record of our foolish behavior.

Marketing Actions

The brand's community manager/ social media executive needs to use caution in handling negative comments, complaints etc and also give quick response as far as possible. New media requires new set of actions by marketers as the rules have changed and will continue to change as consumers become more mature and demanding.

New Media Is Dynamic

Consumer Behavior

New Media is dynamic and evolves every day. If one reads popular social media publications like Social Media Examiner, One finds that there are new features being added to Facebook, LinkedIn, Twitter and other social platforms on a weekly or fortnightly basis.

While minor updates are happening on a regular basis, major upgrades also happen once in few months or years. For example Facebook has added profile video feature and LinkedIn has permitted direct uploads of videos as updates.

Marketing Actions

Marketers need to constantly keep a watch on new features and learn how to use them for better engagement with the stakeholders on social and other new media.

New Media Reflects Changing Dynamics of Relationships

Consumer Behavior

The relationship between marketers and audience is constantly changing as the audience evolves. The dynamics between celebrities and fan following is also changing fast. A good example is previously Facebook pages had the 'Fans' feature and now it is called 'Like'. Many people may not feel comfortable in being called the fan of a brand or celebrity but they are comfortable with the like term.

Marketing Actions

The audience is evolving fast and that is changing the negotiation power and the relationship dynamics (Buckingham, 2006). The marketer needs to adjust and adapt to the new dynamic. In fact the marketer needs to modify their approaches to engagement based on the new relationship dynamics.

New Media Creates a More Transparent World

Consumer Behavior

Social Media is a glasshouse and our negative attitudes & biases (and stupidities too) are visible to our network sooner or later (Nakagoshi, 2012). There is a race for online visibility among personal and business brands. Sometimes to gain online visibility, we may be doing things which reduce our credibility. In fact, we must remember that more wisdom & maturity is expected from reputed brands and successful organizations.

Marketing Actions

Marketer needs to be quicker in response for example ads response time for a Facebook comment/ complaint or Twitter complaint is visible to not just the complainant but the public at large (Schaefer, 2012).

Mistakes Can Be Costly to Reputation in the New Media World

Consumer Behavior

Viral videos and viral content has created a new challenge for the marketers as the reputation can be at stake in a matter of few hours as the viral content quickly spreads across the country or world. In 2010, Greenpeace alleged that Nestle was sourcing palm oil from Sinar Mas, an Indonesian company (doing illegal deforestation) encroaching on the habitat of Orangutans. As a mark of protest, Greenpeace released a video with a worker biting an orangutan finger instead of a Kit Kat chocolate unknowingly.

Nestlé's initially used copyright issues to get the video withdrawn from YouTube. But Greenpeace hot it posted on Vimeo and fetched 75,000 plus views in few hours. Ultimately Nestlé realized that legal threats and withdrawals of videos won't work and it began engaging with Greenpeace and other critics to genuinely address their concerns.

Marketing Actions

Don't try to shut up the media and rather genuinely address the concerns of the relevant groups (Thompson, 1995). Create better systems and processes to minimize mistakes at the first place and have a crisis management team ready for online reputation crisis especially.

Marketers Can't Shut Up the New Media

Consumer Behavior

With the rise of the alternate media, marketers or PR agencies or even big money cannot suppress news. As alternate media is mushrooming and social media has empowered the citizens as journalists. Today marketers cannot use big money and PR agencies to shut up the mass media, as even if mass media shuts up alternate media continues the reportage and discussion. And even if an attempt is made to shut up the alternate media, the social media makes sure that the issue catches attention of the public. Thus both mass media and alternate media are under pressure. Alternate media is gaining popularity in both online and offline versions.

Marketing Actions

Don't try to shut up the media and rather genuinely address the concerns of the relevant groups. PR department also needs to be in touch with new media and alternate media and handle their queries and concerns in time. The marketing also needs to have a crisis management team ready especially for online reputation crisis.

Catching and Retaining Attention in an Attention Deficit New Media world

Consumer Behavior

Attention spans are becoming shorter. It is believed that a website home page must catch attention in fifty nine seconds to avoid the bouncing of traffic (Chistian, 2014). According to the Nielsen Norman Group, most website traffic or users stay for less than 59 seconds. This is also called "The 59 Second Rule. "In fact Tony Haile of Chartbeat data says that 55% of visitors spend fewer than 15 seconds on your website.

Marketing Actions

The website marketer has only 15 seconds to catch attention. Catching attention is more difficult and requires more innovative ways. Retaining attention is equally tricky and the message must be conveyed as quickly as possible.

New Media Encourages Authenticity and Spontaneity

Consumer Behavior

Many of the videos which have gone viral emotionally connect with people very well due to their authenticity and spontaneity. Three of the most viral videos of all time viz. Charlie bit my Finger, Kolaveri Di and Will it Blend or not are good examples of being very spontaneous and authentic in their voice. While our workplaces are becoming increasingly formal, being spontaneous and authentic is a value which is admired by online users (Neubaum & Krämer, 2015). A video which goes viral in western part of the world is likely to go viral in rest of the world also. As western cultures evolve and increasingly focus on values like authenticity, digital tools and new media are promoting western values as global values.

Marketing Actions

A global order and global culture is emerging in the cities which is reflecting as well as getting the support of new media. Marketers must keep this fact in mind while creating global strategies for their organizations especially multinationals.

MARKETERS AND THE POWER OF ANALYTICS

Analytics tools create analyzed data from which marketer needs to draw conclusions and insights. Insights are actually deeper conclusions based on data, intuition, observation etc. While each tool has its own analytics (Twitter analytics, LinkedIn page analytics, Facebook insights and so on), (Nesi & Prinstein, 2015) there are multiple paid and free tools for analyzing data. Twitter is an open source site and therefore has hundreds of applications which provide interesting analytics and sometimes insights.

There are sentiment analysis tools also to calculate whether the user postings on social media are positive, negative or neutral. The marketers can understand the tastes and preferences of audiences with reference to content and what makes them share the content. The golden rule of social media is, "Never sell to your market. It makes more sense to engage with them by providing them content which adds value to their lives by suggesting solutions to their pain areas and entertaining them at times. Community building creates brand advocates and engagement creates communities.

CONCLUSION

Marketers must understand the new media characteristics and the psychology of the new media user. While new media may be more effective than traditional media for certain demographics (youth in cities for example), traditional media may be more effective for other segments (youth in interior villages for example).

In many cases it may be wise for the marketer to use a combination of traditional and new media. On one hand traditional media has passed the test of time, on the other hand new media usually delivers better metrics (for measuring results) and has more focused targeting.

So a wise marketer needs to analyze all options and decide what works best for her product and target segment.

REFERENCES

Boiarsky, G. (1997). The Psychology of New Media Technologies Lessons from the Past. *Convergence (London)*, *3*(3), 109–126. doi:10.1177/135485659700300308

Buckingham, D. (2006). Is there a Digital Generation. In D. Buckingum & E. Willett (Eds.), *Digital Generations*. Academic Press. Retrieved Jan 4, 2018, from https://is.muni.cz/el/1423/podzim2013/SOC573/um/Buckingham_-_Is_there_a_digital_generation.pdf

Chistian, G. (2014, Dec 23). *Traditional vs. new media: The balancing effect*. Retrieved from The Absolute Truth: https://www.absolutemg.com/2014/12/23/traditional-media-balancing-effect/

Dimmick, J., Chen, Y., & Li, Z. (2009). Competition Between the Internet and Traditional News Media: The Gratification-Opportunities Niche Dimension. *Journal of Media Economics*, 19–33.

Gorgone, K. (2017, Nov 15). *Social Media Addiction is Real: How to Take Your Life Back*. Retrieved from Mark Schaefer: https://www.businessesgrow.com/2017/11/15/social-media-addiction-2/

Leinonen, T. (2010). Designing Learning Tools. Methodological Insights. *Aalto University School of Art and Design Publication Series*. Retrieved from https://aaltodoc.aalto.fi/handle/123456789/11661

Manovich, L. (2003). New Media from Borges to HTML. In N. Wardrip-Fruin & N. Montfort (Eds.), The New Media Reader (pp. 13-25). Cambridge, MA: MIT Press.

Miller, C. R. (2016, Jun). *The 59 Second Rule: 3 Reasons Why Users Leave a Website*. Retrieved from The Daily Egg: https://www.crazyegg.com/blog/why-users-leave-a-website/

Nakagoshi, K. (2012, Apr 19). *Yes, you can be addicted to social media*. Retrieved from Business Grow: https://www.businessesgrow.com/2012/04/19/yes-you-can-be-addicted-to-social-media/

Nesi, J., & Prinstein, M. (2015). Using Social Media for Social Comparison and Feedback-Seeking: Gender and Popularity Moderate Associations with Depressive Symptoms. *Journal of Abnormal Child Psychology*, *43*(8), 1427–1438. doi:10.100710802-015-0020-0 PMID:25899879

Neubaum, G., & Krämer, N. C. (2015). My Friends Right Next to Me: A Laboratory Investigation on Predictors and Consequences of Experiencing Social Closeness on Social Networking Sites. *Cyberpsychology, Behavior, and Social Networking*, *21*(8), 443–449. doi:10.1089/cyber.2014.0613 PMID:26252929

Schaefer, M. (2012, Feb 21). *The six elements of human behavior that drive social media*. Retrieved from Mark Schaefer: https://www.businessesgrow.com/2012/02/21/the-six-elements-of-human-behavior-that-drive-social-media/

Shaefer, M. (2014, Nov 18). *How Facebook changes our behavior*. Retrieved from Business Grow: https://www.businessesgrow.com/2014/11/18/facebook-changes-our-behavior/

The Media and Modernity A Social Theory of the Media. (1995). Stanford University Press.

Thompson, J. B. (1995). *The Media and Modernity - A Social Theory of the Media*. Stanford University Press.

Chapter 8
Gap Between Mobile and Online Advergames:
The Possible Effects of the Optimal Gaming Experience-Flow

Tugce Ozansoy Çadırcı
Yıldız Technical University, Turkey

Aysegul Sagkaya Gungor
Isik University, Turkey

ABSTRACT

Mobile and online advergames are likely to influence brand associations differently. Regardless of the advergame environment, successful games are capable of taking the player into the flow state. How the experience of flow influences the outcomes of the advergames in different environments is a new and an important subject for the advertisers. In order to understand the outcomes (i.e., brand recall and brand attitude) of the advergames in different mediums (online vs. mobile) with the flow introduced, a lab experiment was conducted. Results of the experiment yielded that brand recall and brand attitude were different in different environments. When the interaction of skill and challenge was introduced to the study, however, hypotheses were partially supported. Furthermore, arousal resulted in better brand recall and more positive brand attitudes in the mobile environment. Lastly, time distortion caused no difference in brand attitude, while supporting mobile in brand recall.

DOI: 10.4018/978-1-5225-6064-7.ch008

INTRODUCTION

Games have always been a way of entertainment and have a great potential to influence the masses. With the latest example of Pokemon Go, it leaves no doubt that the dissemination of digital games will continue (Terlutter & Capella, 2013). When the potential of the digital games to affect masses was noticed, marketers have found a new way to convey their brand messages to the existing and potential customers. It is through the advergames; they try to create brand awareness, persuade potential customers, accelerate purchase, retain customers, and enhance the relationship with them for the lifetime togetherness (HoFacker, De Ruyter, Lurie, Manchande, & Donaldson, 2016). Furthermore; they are creating a positive user experience through entertainment.

With the widespread prevalence of mobile phones, the attention of the marketers turned into the direction of mobile advergames. Marketers are working out to unveil the potential of these games to get the desired results on their target customers (Ollila, 2017). Just before the mobile phone diversity, it was only the online games used as a marketing tool. With the introduction of the mobile to the branded entertainment, the excitement and engagement rules are redefined. Although some remain the same, the perceptions caused by certain elements could be different. Among those, taking the game player into the flow state is one of the necessities for a successfully designed game. It is proved to be a critical determinant of positive online experiences (Hoffman & Novak, 1996).

There is a large amount of research investigating the impact of flow on consumer behavior on online advergames (e.g., Hernandez, 2011; Vanwesenbeeck, Ponnet, & Walrave, 2016; Vermeir, Kazakova, Tessitore, Cauberghe & Slabbinck, 2014; Waiguny, Nelson, & Terlutter, 2012; Waiguny, Nelson, & Marko, 2013). However, mobile advergame context is still a research area needed to be explored further. Besides, there is insufficient research comparing the two environments. As a result, questions remain concerning the potential factors that might affect the yields of mobile advergames compared to online.

The current study aims to fill this gap by investigating the flow experience of the game players on two different environments (online vs. mobile) while focusing on the game player responses in the form of brand recall and brand attitude. To define the differences, three main elements of flow; namely, the interaction of skill and challenge, arousal and time distortion, were taken into consideration. The authors investigated each element separately as their effects on online and mobile advergame players are defined comparatively.

In this paper, at the first section, the authors begin by describing the online and mobile advergames, the concept of flow, and its three antecedents as skill and challenge, arousal and time distortion as well as developing the study hypothesis.

Next, the authors present the study with all the details. The following section is devoted to the solutions and recommendations. At the last section, the authors conclude with research limitations and future research suggestions.

Background

Mobile advergames are rather a new and an undiscovered area in the marketing literature. Although the concept of advergames is in the deployment of the marketers for quite a long time, it is mostly the online advergames under research. Whether being online or mobile, marketers try to find out the best conditions for better affective, conative and cognitive responses. It has been known that positive online experiences are transferred to the associated brand through affect transfer (Fiske & Pavelhack, 1986; Lantos & Craton, 2012; Liu, Hu, & Grimm, 2010). However, depending on the environments that the advergames are presented, outcomes may vary. With the current study, flow is introduced with its three antecedents. The section presented the previous studies on the subject of online advergames, mobile advergames, and flow.

Online vs. Mobile Advergames

Advergames are merging of advertising and entertainment elements to convey the message of the brand to the current and potential customers in a creative way. Stated by Terlutter and Capella (2013, p.96) they are specifically designed to promote a brand, product, service or idea. They are created to enhance the relationship with the brand and customers; meanwhile, they aim to create brand awareness and positive attitudes toward the brand in an entertaining environment (Lee & Youn, 2008; Alina, 2013). Advergames could augment the relationship between the consumers and brand (Wanick, Ranchhod, & Wills, 2014). In an advergame, the message (i.e., brand, logo, value proposition) is embedded into the game. And the game player is in an interactive relationship with the brand while playing the game (Özbük & Ünal, 2017).

Advergames are available on various platforms (Cauberghe & De Pelsmacker, 2010) while online and mobile being the most salient ones. Although the retailers' ultimate aims are no different than each other in different platforms (i.e., to create brand awareness, to facilitate the relationship with the customers, etc.); the platforms differ from each other in their characteristics. Mobile platforms are capable of to be utilized by real-time (Wanick et al., 2014), and location-based marketing through the advergames. Mobile applications, in which the advergames are played on, also include elements of social interaction; game space expansion, and the mobile actions which amplify the impact of the mobile advergames on game player's attitudes and behavior (Sutko & e Silva, 2011). Through the location-based data; pervasive interactions are enabled in the mobile advergames (Bell, Chalmers, Barkhuus, Hall, Sherwood, & Hampshire, 2006). Game players become an element in the game in pervasive mobile advergames (Montola, 2005) leading to the telepresence experience. Along with the others, the intensity of the experience itself would affect the attitudes of the game player in the game and extend the brand message reaches to the game player. Thus it is proposed that;

Hypothesis One (H1): In different gaming environments (mobile vs. online); consumers' a) attitude toward the brand, and b) brand recall are different.

Experience of Flow in Different Gaming Environments

Flow, as defined by Csikszentmihalyi and LeFevre (1989, p.816) broadly, is the *process of optimal experience*. It is an emerging psychological phenomenon which people experience it in various activities such as shopping, dancing, working and game playing (Csikszentmihalyi, 1975; Hoffman & Novak, 1996). Building on Csikszentmihalyi and LeFevre (1989), Hoffman and Novak (1996, p.54) defined online flow as *the state occurring during network navigation which is (1) characterized by a seamless sequence of responses facilitated by machine interactivity, (2) intrinsically enjoyable, (3) accompanied by a loss of self-consciousness, and (4) self-reinforcing*. As the researchers working on the subject, flow is further developed with its antecedents, being the challenge, telepresence, involvement, arousal, time and skill (Nakamura & Csikszentmihalyi, 2009; Refiana, Mizerski, & Murphy, 2005).

When the game player experienced flow in a branded entertainment setting, significant effects on game players' perceptions, attitudes, and the brand memory were observed (Ham, Yoon & Nelson, 2016). A game player experiencing the flow while playing the game will have a more positive attitude toward the game (Waiguny et al., 2012); likewise to the brand(s) in the game, compared to the one not experiencing the flow. It implies that the flow is a state that affects the advertising outcomes (Nelson, Yaros & Keum, 2006; Vermeir et al., 2014). The flow experience in different media (i.e., online vs. mobile) can significantly be different than each other depending on the game environment, gamer players' competence and the game-design elements. If the flow is investigated deeply with its antecedents, there may emerge media-specific findings, which is the purpose of the current study.

Interaction of Skill and Challenge

Weber, Tamborini, Westcott-Baker, and Kantor (2009, p.397) defined flow as "a cognitive synchronization of attentional and reward networks which create a gratifying experience." In the remainder of their definition, they pointed out a condition; a balance between challenge and skill. It implies that people can enjoy themselves and experience flow only when they feel competent enough. And feeling competent requires a balance between challenge and skill (Csikszentmihalyi, 1997; Jin, 2012; Weber et al., 2009).

The flow state is observed when individual's skill and the task challenge meet each other (Berger, Schlager, Sprott, & Herrmann, 2017; Keller & Blomann, 2008). If the task is too easy to accomplish, it resulted in boredom and apathy (Harris, Vine, & Wilson, 2017; Hsu & Wang, 2018). On the other hand, if the task is too difficult for the player, it causes anxiety, stress, and frustration (Haris et al., 2017; Hsu & Wang, 2018). In either case, flow state is hard to observe.

A study by Jin (2012) demonstrated that, in the video games, game players with highly advanced skills experience the flow most under the high challenge condition. On the other hand, low skilled game players experience flow at any challenge condition, regardless of flow (Jin, 2012).

Mobile games are challenging the ways the online games are designed and played (Jin, 2017). They are coming in two types: The ones that induce a high level of challenge, e.g., location-based mobile games, and the others that induce the low level of challenge, e.g., branded app games. When the difficulty level of the game interacts with the player's skill, the boundary condition for flow emerges. Unlike the most mobile game players, online game players are more dedicated. They spare the time to play online games. It is not a not-to-be-bored activity for them, but, for some, a way of life (e.g., the game called Second Life). So the task challenge and, accordingly, required player skills are different in each medium. The optimal level of challenge leads to high concentration. Concentration to the game, combining with the flow, is causing positive attitude which is transferred to the brand through excitation transfer while decreasing the brand recall (Keller & Blomann, 2008; Nelson et al., 2006) because of the players' cognitive occupancy. Therefore;

Hypothesis Two (H2): In online gaming, the interaction between players' skill and challenge leads to a) more positive brand attitude; b) worse brand recall, compared to mobile gaming.

Arousal

Arousal is related to the need for surprising, new and complex stimuli (Berlyne, 1966). It is characterized by the desire to search out fun and pleasurable activities, continuous change and constant variety (Jessor & Jessor, 1977). Arousal is also associated with the motivation toward the game. When the player accomplishes the goals, the feeling comes with fun and pleasure. The next level in the game is a change in the gamer's life.

Arousal level is also dependent on the game elements (Petersen, Thomsen, Mirza-Babaei, & Drachen, 2017). It is proposed that arousal level is the highest when the gamer plays against a human opponent rather than a computer, and the game is perceived more entertaining when it is against a human (Weibel, Wissmath, Habegger, Steiner, & Groner, 2008). It can be inferred that interaction with others is one of the boundary conditions for arousal.

The online and mobile games are designed in a way to raise the level of arousal for the player. When the two are compared for the ability to raise arousal, the online games are expected to create more. Mobile games are more casual, usually played at short periods of time, more convenient and easily accessible (Wei & Lu, 2014), compared to online games. Furthermore, they are usually single-player games. With all those characteristics, it is expected that mobile games are more impotent in raising arousal in a game player.

According to the literature, positive arousal leads to a positive brand attitude (vice versa is also true), since the aroused game player is in a favorable state (Jeong, Bohil, & Biocca, 2011; Jeong, Lee & Wu, 2015; Morris & Boon, 1998; Myers & Sar, 2015). As the affect transfer theory suggests, this positivity is transferred to the brand. When the brand recall is in question, there are contradictory findings in the literature. Yoon and Vargas (2013) suggest that brand memory is better when people experience less arousal (except for unfamiliar brands). On the other hand, others suggest that high arousal increases brand memory (Brave & Nass, 2003; Jeong et al., 2015; Parrot & Spackman, 2000). Building on the limited cognitive capacity theory, in this study the hypothesis is built with the expectation of better recall in low arousal situation.

As a new insight, the authors propose:

Hypothesis Three (H3): In online gaming, feeling of arousal leads to a) more positive brand attitude; b) worse brand recall, compared to mobile gaming.

Time Distortion

Time distortion is losing track of time, and feeling that the time passes very quickly. As the activity that the person is engaged in is pleasing, the time goes by faster (Esteban-Millat, Martínez-López, & Rodríguez-Ardura, 2014). As the person is in the flow state, s/he loses the sense of time, and self-awareness as well (Esteban-Millat et al., 2014; Vanwesenbeeck et al., 2016). Applying it to the context of gaming; if a game player experiences flow, the present activity becomes more pleasing (Waiguny et al., 2013), and it causes the game player's losing track of time (Esteban-Millat et al., 2014).

According to Waiguny et al. (2012), as the flow increases in a game, the attitudes become more positive toward the game and the brand(s) in the game. As the time distortion is a "should have" in a successfully designed game, regardless of being mobile or online, advergames should induce time distortion. When the two different gaming environments are compared, because of the characteristics mentioned above, online games cause more time distortion. Since the player is deeply involved in the virtual environment, time elapses faster, and it does not matter to the game player (Esteban-Millat et al., 2014).

As the time distortion is induced by the flow, it is expected that the player's loss of time track is reflected in the attitudes, making them more positive. On the other hand; the previous researchers pointed out that flow has a negative effect on brand recognition and recall (Nelson & Waiguny, 2012; Waiguny et al., 2012; Vanwesenbeeck et al., 2016). As a construct of flow, time distortion causes all cognitive capacity to be occupied by the game, leaving no spare capacity to process the brand in the game (Cauberghe, Geuens, & De Pelsmacker, 2011). Therefore;

Hypothesis Four (H4): In online gaming, time distortion leads to a) more positive brand attitude; b) worse brand recall, compared to mobile gaming.

MAIN FOCUS OF THE CHAPTER

Issues, Controversies, Problems

As the games become pervasive in the life of the consumers, marketers try to understand the dynamics that lie behind advergaming. It is crucial to provide some certain elements for the success of the game, thus to ensure the widespread play. One of these crucial elements is the player's experience of flow. Flow is a state that takes the game player entirely out of the real world, and an intense engagement with the game (Pelet, Ettis, & Cowart, 2017). Thus, the player loses his/her track of time (Vanwesenbeeck et al., 2016), be in the state of high arousal. It has been known that the flow state influences the attitudes and cognitive state of the game player (some examples; Ham et al., 2016; Vermeir et al., 2014; Waiguny et al., 2012).

Advergames are available both on the mobile and the online platforms. While the aim is the same (to convey the brand message to the target market), they differ in their characteristics. Mobile games are usually more causal, convenient, and designed in a way with easier accomplishments (Wei & Lu, 2014) because the play time is usually shorter than the online games. Furthermore, they are usually played alone. On the other hand, online game players are more dedicated. They take the time to play games and socialize while playing since most of the games are available as the cooperative-competitive games in the online platform. With these noticeable differences, they are expected to cause different outcomes on players' responses, namely brand recall and brand attitude.

To the best of our knowledge, there is no study in the literature comparing online and mobile environments in the context of branded entertainment. The purpose of the study is to fill this gap by investigating whether and how the state of flow affects the game player's brand recall ability and brand attitude while comparing mobile and online advergames. To understand these differences in detail there main elements of flow, i.e., skill and challenge, arousal and time distortion, were used to test the study hypothesis.

The Study

An experiment was conducted to test the hypotheses,. The experiment was designed with two advergames (a mobile and an online game) to create a setting that will enhance validity with the establishment of a realistic experience.

The Method

Experimental Stimuli

Two existing advergames were used. One of them was a mobile advergame, and the other is an online advergame. For the mobile version the Red Bull Air Race 2 (Figure 1) was used, which is available from both Apple and Google Android application stores. The online game chosen for the study was Lego Speed Champions (Figure 2). Both of the games were chosen from the racing genre to control the other possible effects on dependent variables. Both games were easy to play and easy to understand.

Procedure

The experiment was conducted in a computer laboratory. The first group of participants was assigned a computer, and they were informed that the gameplay is part of an interactive class exercise. The other group of participants was asked to download an app from a mobile application provider (either from Google Play or Apple Store) depending on the model of their smartphone. Following the download process, they were asked to play the game as a part of an interactive class exercise. There were

Figure 1. Red Bull air race 2

Figure 2. Lego speed champions

two experimental sessions one with an online advergame (Lego Speed Champions) and the other with a mobile advergame (Red Bull Air Race 2). Participants were assigned to either condition (mobile vs. online) randomly. The game duration in each experimental session was 20 minutes. They were able to play the advergame for the first 15 minutes and after they were asked to complete an online questionnaire. The questionnaire was composed of five sections, including questions concerning their gaming experience, elements of flow (challenge, skills, playfulness), telepresence, brand recall and brand attitudes. The last section of the questionnaire included questions on respondents' demographic profile.

Preliminary Analysis

Sample and Participants

123 students from marketing classes participated to the study for extra course credit. 61 of them were assigned to the online advergame, and the remaining 62 were assigned to the mobile advergame. The sample consisted of 66 males (53.7%) and 57 females (46.3%). The participants' average age was 21.21. Most of the participants stated that they play online and mobile games for more than four years (n=83; 67.5%). Most of the participants' weekly gameplay was between 2-3 hours (n=65; 52.8%).

Since participants' gaming experience can affect brand recall and brand attitudes before analysis, the experiment groups similarities were assessed with the use of two Chi-square analyses. According to the results, both of the experimental groups were similar regarding the duration of the gaming experience (χ^2 =3,610, df=2, p=0.164) and weekly gameplay (χ^2 =1.099, df=2, p=0.604).

Covariate

The use of a covariate is essential when working with experimental data (Howell, 2009: 598). It provides an insight into possible effects that can be created by independent variables. In this study telepresence; which has been proved to be effective on both brand attitude (e.g., Bellman, Kemp, Haddad, & Varan, 2014; Yang & Hung, 2017) and brand recall (e.g., Hernandez, 2011) was used as the covariate. Telepresence creates the feeling of being present in the virtual environment that the game has created (Goh & Ping, 2014). It activates the possible effects of flow in a game setting (Jin, 2012; Gurau, 2009) to generate certain feelings for the players.

Before using the telepresence as the covariate, certain analyses were conducted to understand its suitability. Different experimental groups were compared depending on the feelings of telepresence with the use of a one-way ANOVA. The results of the ANOVA yielded no significant differences between experimental groups (F=0.025, p=0.874). The relationship between the covariate and dependent measures were also tested with the use of correlation coefficients. Correlation results showed significant relationships between telepresence and brand attitude (r=0.369, p=0.000) and brand recall (r=0.333, p=0.000).

Factor Structure and Data Reduction

All of the elements of flow and brand attitude were measured with five-point Likert-items. Before the hypothesis testing to summarize the data a set of factor analyses were employed. The results of the analysis conducted on dimensions on flow including factor scores and reliability statistics are summarized in Table 1.

The Kaiser-Meyer-Olkin (KMO) sampling adequacy measure for the analysis was 0.769, which indicated enough sampling adequacy. The cumulative percentage of variance explained was 79%. As seen in Table 1 all of the factor loadings were between 0.702 and 0.907; and the Cronbach Alpha coefficients for all of the dimensions were higher than the expected level of 0.700.

Table 1. Results of The factor analysis for elements of flow

	Factor Loading	Reliability Statistics
Challenge		
Playing online/mobile games challenges me.	.762	**.782**
Playing online/mobile games challenges me to perform to the best of my ability.	.798	
Playing online/mobile games provides a good test of my skills.	.907	
I find that playing online/mobile games stretches my capabilities to the limits.	.795	
Playing online/mobile games provides many opportunities for action.	.739	
Skills		
I am very skilled at playing online/mobile games.	.859	**.778**
I consider myself knowledgeable about playing online/mobile games.	.862	
I know less about playing online/mobile games than most users.	.859	
Arousal/Playfulness		
I felt excited during gameplay.	.799	**.772**
I felt stimulated during gameplay.	.784	
I felt soothed during gameplay.	.792	
Telepresence		
During gameplay, I felt I was in the world the computer created.	.853	**.872**
During gameplay, my body was in the room, but my mind was inside the world created by the computer.	.874	
The computer-generated video game seemed to me "a game I played" rather than "a game I saw."	.849	
I felt I was more in the "game world" than the "real world" around me when I was going through the exercise.	.864	
I forgot about my immediate surroundings when I was playing the game.	.702	
When the game ended, I felt like I came back to the "real world" after a journey.	.811	
Time Distortion		
When I play good games, I forget about time	.780	**.956**
When I play good games, I lose track of time	.839	

A second-factor analysis was conducted on the items of the brand attitude scale, which also yielded satisfactory results. The KMO measure computed was 0.766, and the factor loadings were between 0.787 and 0.934. The reliability analysis exerted 0.907 as the Cronbach Alpha coefficient.

Hypothesis Testing

The Results for Hypothesis 1

As proposed in Hypothesis 1, it was assumed that in different gaming environments (mobile and online) consumers' attitudes toward the brand (BRa) and their ability to recall the main brand (BRrc) would be different.

The hypothesis was tested with a MANCOVA analysis using BRa and BRrc as dependent, gaming environments as the independent variables. At the same time as stated in the previous section, telepresence was used as the covariate for the analysis. Before MANCOVA, certain assumptions were tested with the use of Levene's test of homogeneity and Box's Test of Equality of Covariance Matrices. Levene's test of homogeneity of variances indicated homogeneity for both BRa (F=0.106; sig=0.746) and BRrc (F=41.534; sig=0.504). Another assumption of MANCOVA is the equality of the covariance matrices of the dependent variables. To test this assumption a Box's M test was deployed, which yielded that the covariance matrices were equal across groups for the dependent variables (F=23.699; sig=0.078).

As expected there was a main effect of gaming environment (GE) on both BRa (BRa in the online environment; M=3.60, sd=0.58 versus BRa in the mobile environment; M=4.23, sd=0.74), and BRrc (BRrc in the online environment; M=1.66, sd=0.48 versus BRrc in the mobile environment; M=1.94, sd=0.23). The detailed findings of the analysis are summarized in Table 2 and Figure 3.

As the results of the MANCOVA yielded a significant difference based on the gaming environment, hypothesis 1 (H1) was supported.

Table 2. Effects of gaming environment on players' attitudes and brand recall

	GE		Between Subjects Effects	
Dependent Variables	**Online (n=61)**	**Mobile (n=62)**	**F-Value**	**Sig.**
Brand Attitude	3.60 (0.58)	4.23 (0.74)	21.354	.000*
Brand Recall	1.66 (0.48)	1.94 (0.23)	14.622	.000*

*p<.01

Figure 3. Effects of gaming environment on players' brand attitudes and brand recall

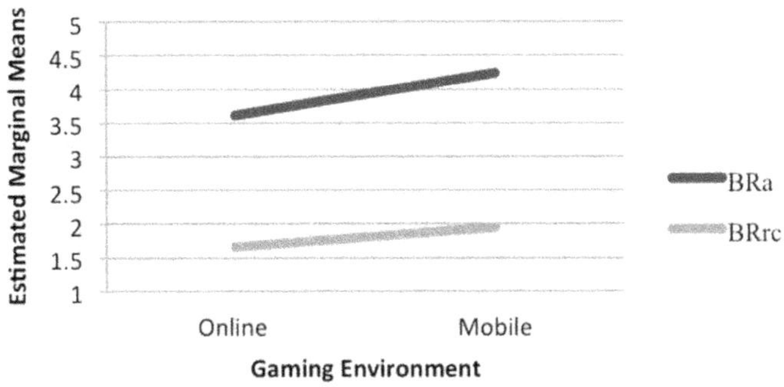

The Results for Hypothesis 2

To test hypothesis 2, a MANCOVA was conducted with BRa and BRrc as dependent and the interaction between skills and challenge and gaming environments as the independent variables. In the test of the second hypothesis, telepresence was used as the covariate again.

The results of Levene's Test of Homogeneity of variances (for BRa: F=23.872; p=0.089; and for BRrc: F=100.656; p=0.067) and Box M's test (F=42.763; p=0.451) proved that the assumption of equality of variances was achieved.

The results of the MANCOVA yielded significant differences for gaming environment (F=9.918; sig.=.002 for BRa and F=25.251; sig.=.000 for BRrc) and challenge (F=5.996; sig.=.016 for BRa and F=10.276; sig.=.002 for BRrc). However, when the effects of skills were not significant for BRa(F=0.195; sig.=.660), yet there were significant differs for BRrc (F=76.661; sig.=.000).The results are summarized in Table 3 and Figures 4 and 5.

To test the second hypothesis, certain interaction effects were also examined. The results of the interaction effects are summarized in Table 4. As seen in Table 4 there were significant effects for overall interaction effects between skills and challenge (F=3.251; sig.=.000 for BRa, and F=2.724; sig.=.000 for BRrc) and gaming environment, skills and challenge (F=6.534; sig.=.000 for BRa, and F=3.571; sig.=.000 for BRrc).

The results were further examined to define the best possible outcomes regarding BRa and BRrc. The best condition for BRa can be created in a mobile environment, with a high level of challenge and low level of skills (M=4.56; sd=0.41). The lowest attitudes toward the main brand are created in an online gaming environment with the low level of challenge and high level of skills (M=3.72; sd=0.67). Overall, high challenge with a high level of skills (M=3.61; sd=1.26) mobile environment creates more positive attitudes than online gaming environment.

Table 3. Effects of gaming environment, skills and challenge on players' attitudes and brand recall

	Levels of Independent Variables			Mean	Between-Subjects Effects		
					F-Value		
	GE	**Challenge**	**Skills**		**GE**	**Challenge**	**Skills**
BRa	**Online**	**High**	**High (n=23)**	4.00 (0.58)	9.918*	5.996**	0.195
			Low (n=24)	4.00 (0.41)			
		Low	**High (n=6)**	3.72 (0.67)			
			Low (n=8)	4.00 (0.55)			
	Mobile	**High**	**High (n=16)**	3.61 (1.26)			
			Low (n=14)	4.56 (0.41)			
		Low	**High (n=9)**	4.15 (0.60)			
			Low (n=23)	4.30 (0.33)			
BRrc	**Online**	**High**	**High (n=23)**	2.11 (0.54)	25.251*	10.276*	76.661**
			Low (n=24)	1.52 (0.47)			
		Low	**High (n=6)**	2.10 (0.63)			
			Low (n=8)	2.18 (0.54)			
	Mobile	**High**	**High (n=16)**	3.01 (0.91)			
			Low (n=14)	2.67 (0.48)			
		Low	**High (n=9)**	2.12 (0.66)			
			Low (n=23)	2.21 (0.47)			

*p<.01; ** p<.05

*Figure 4. Effects of gaming environment*skills*challenge on players' brand attitudes*

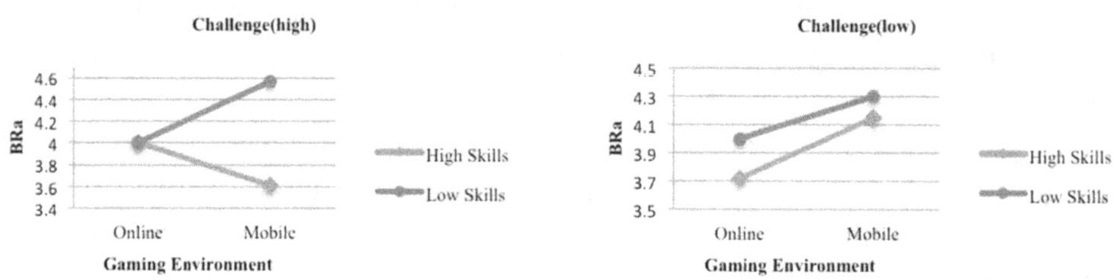

*Figure 5. Effects of gaming environment*skills*challenge on players' brand recall*

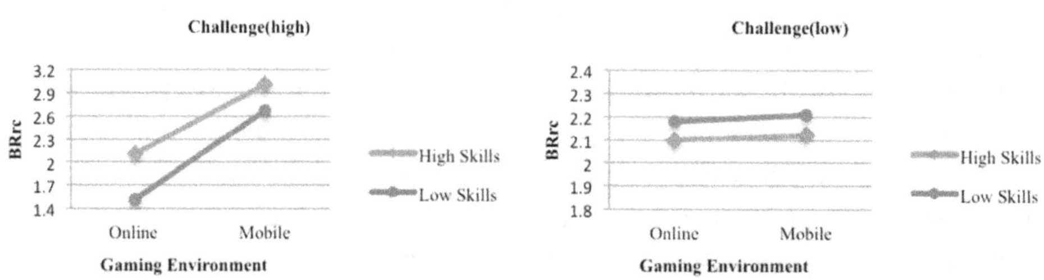

For BRrc the best result is gained in a mobile environment, with the high level of challenge and low level of skills (M=2.67, sd=0.48), and brands are least recalled n an online environment with high level of challenge and low level of skills (M=1.52; sd=0.47). For BRrc gaming environment is the main condition that creates the real difference between subjects. Also in all conditions of mobile gaming environment brands were recognized better than an online gaming environment.

As the results of the MANCOVA did not create a significant effect of skills for BRa, it can be concluded that hypothesis 2 (H2) is partially supported.

The Results for Hypothesis 3

To test hypothesis 3, a MANCOVA was conducted with BRa and BRrc as the dependent, gaming environment and arousal as independent variables and telepresence as the covariate.

Prior to hypothesis testing Levene's Test of Homogeneity of Variances (for BRa: F=1.399; p=0.162; and for BRrc: F=0.275; p=0.073) and Box M's test (F=0.454; p=0.504) were deployed. Both of the analysis showed satisfactory results to carry out a MANCOVA.

MANCOVA yielded significant differences for both gaming environment (F=15.560; p=.000 for BRa and F=57.014; p=.000 for BRrc), and arousal of players (F=11.143; p=.001 for BRa; F=66.138; p=.000 for BRrc). To interpret the differences mean values were examined. The results showed that mobile gaming environment creates more favorable outcomes for both BRa and BRrc. At the same time as the level of arousal increases players' attitudes and brand recall also increase. As a result hypothesis 3 (H3) was supported. Results are summarized in Table 5 and Figure 6.

Table 4. Interaction effects of gaming environment, skills and challenge on players' attitudes and brand recall

	Interaction Effects			
	Skills*Challenge		**GE*Skills*Challenge**	
	F-Value	**Sig.**	**F-Value**	**Sig.**
BRa	3.251	**.000**	6.534	**.000**
BRrc	2.724	**.000**	3.571	**.000**

Table 5. Effects of gaming environment and arousal on players' attitudes and brand recall

	Levels of Independent Variables		Mean	Between-Subjects Effects		Interaction Effects
				F-Value		
	Arousal	Gaming Environment		Arousal	GE	F-Value
BRa	High	Online (n=27) Mobile (n=40)	4.12 (0.45) 4.66 (0.37)	11.143*	15.560*	1.871
	Low	Online (n=34) Mobile (n=22)	3.43 (0.62) 3.62 (0.72)			
BRrc	High	Online (n=27) Mobile (n=40)	0.92 (0.48) 1.93 (0.30)	66.138*	57.014*	59.997*
	Low	Online (n=34) Mobile (n=22)	1.81 (0.73) 2.24 (0.23)			

*p<.01

Figure 6. Effects of gaming environment and arousal on players' brand recall

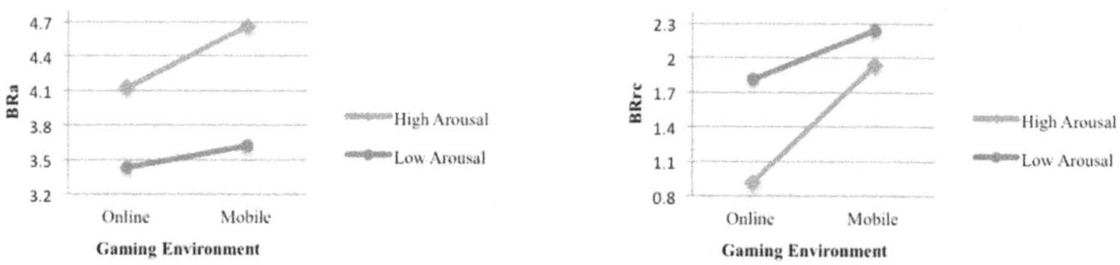

The Results for Hypothesis 4

To test the last hypothesis of the study, another MANCOVA was carried out with BRa and BRrc as the dependent; gaming environments and time distortion as the independent variables. Telepresence was used as the covariate.

Before testing the hypothesis equality of variances were examined with the use of Levene's (F=10,804; p=.069 for BRa; F=22,350; p=.102 for BRrc) and Box's M Test (F=8.987; p=.094), both of which implied the main assumption of equality of variances.

The results of the MANCOVA yielded significant differences for gaming environment (F=24.162; p=.000 for BRa; and F=8.897; p=.000 for BRrc). The results also indicate that time distortion does not create a significant difference regarding BRa (F=0.025; p=.875). But there is a difference in BRrc when time distortion is taken into consideration (F=10.455; p=.002). To investigate the effect of time more thoroughly the interaction effects of the gaming environment and time distortion were also examined. The results yielded significant differences regarding BRrc (F=4.021; p=.040), but there were no significant differences regarding gamers' BRa (F=2.497; p=.117). The results are summarized in Table 6 and Figure 7.

As the results of the MANCOVA yielded no significant differences regarding BRa in both between-subjects and interaction effects, Hypothesis 4 (H4) is partially supported.

Table 6. Effects of gaming environment and time distortion on players' attitudes and brand recall

	Levels of Independent Variables		Mean	Between-Subjects Effects		Interaction Effects
				F-Value		F-Value
	Time Distortion	Gaming Environment		TD	GE	
BRa	High	Online (n=27) Mobile (n=40)	4.01 (0.34) 4.15 (0.86)	.025	24.162*	2.497
	Low	Online (n=34) Mobile (n=22)	2.83 (0.68) 4.41 (0.41)			
BRrc	High	Online (n=27) Mobile (n=40)	1.51 (0.52) 1.91 (0.28)	10.455**	8.987**	4.021***
	Low	Online (n=34) Mobile (n=22)	2.13 (0.49) 2.22 (0.24)			

*p<.01; **p<.05; ***p<.10

Figure 7. Effects of gaming environment and time distortion on players' brand recall

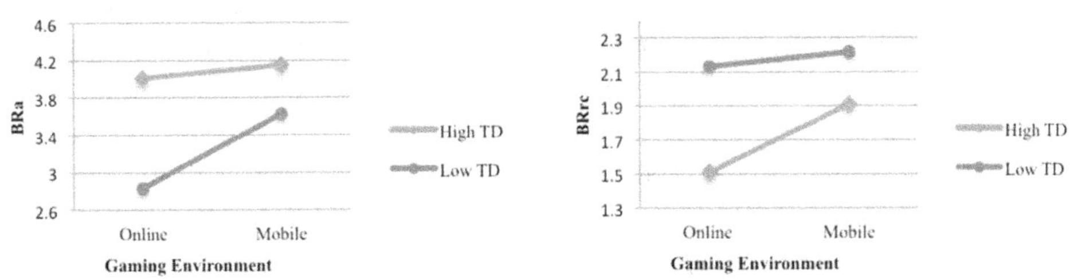

SOLUTIONS AND RECOMMENDATIONS

The Effects of Gaming Environment

This study was an attempt to discover the possible effects of the gaming environment in an advergame setting on consumers' brand attitudes and brand recall. The first analysis of the study was designed to examine the possible effects of the gaming environment with the use of two different advergames (a mobile racing game and an online racing game). The results indicated that gaming environment has significant effects on both BRa and BRrc. When the results were further investigated, mobile gaming environment was found to be creating more positive attitudes and higher brand recall. Using a mobile gaming environment can affect consumers' both cognitive and affective responses toward the main brand.

Introduction of Flow to the Gaming Environment

Flow or the optimal experience as referred by Csikszentmihalyi (1975) is an important antecedent of a persuasive advergame. With the right balance between challenge and the player's skill, the flow experience becomes an important element of compelling advergame settings (Roettl, Waiguny, & Terlutter, 2016). As stated, the balance between challenge and skill can create a difference in gamers' responses. When the desired balance is achieved it becomes easier for players to focus on the task (Pelet & Ettis, 2017). When players' skill exceeds the challenge, both of their cognitive and affective responses are expected to be more positive (Pelet et al., 2017). As a result, as the level of challenge increases and the level of players' skill decrease, it is expected to create both more positive brand attitude and the higher level of brand recall. When the results of the current study are examined, this situation is mostly applicable to mobile gaming environments. In situations of the high challenge with the low level of skills, the gamers' attitudes become more positive. As the second hypothesis of the study suggested, in mobile gaming environments, high level of challenge with a low level of skill is the best condition for brand recall. In online environments, the possible effects of the challenge become less active, yet the level of skill becomes the main reason for changes in both BRa and BRrc. The results also suggested that the interaction effect of skills and challenge together with gaming environment creates different outcomes regarding both BRa and BRrc.

Another important dimension of flow is arousal. Arousal is expected to create negative outcomes regarding BRrc (Scott & Craig-Less, 2010). Arousal is mostly related to the feelings of excitement, fun, enjoyment and even frustration (Boyle, Connoly, Hainey, & Boyle, 2012). Arousal creates a higher level of engagement (Hoffman & Nadelson, 2010) and more positive emotions (Kaye & Bryce, 2012).

As a result, arousal is expected to create more positive brand attitudes (Myers & Sar, 2015). In this study, mobile game environment was found to create more positive results regardless of the level of arousal felt during gameplay. For both level of arousal (high and low) mobile gaming environment created more positive BRa and a higher level of BRrc.

The last dimension of flow used in this study was time distortion. Time distortion is highly related to the enjoyment felt during an activity (Agarwal & Karahanna, 2000). Games are expected to create enjoyment during play; as a result, the players' sense of time becomes distorted during gameplay (Pelet et al., 2017). As the players become absorbed by the flow, they are transported into a new environment, and they tend to lose the sense of time (Scott & Craig-Less, 2010). This situation is expected to create certain results for BRa and BRrc. As stated by the last hypothesis of the study, it was expected time distortion to create more positive results in online environment for BRa. The results did not support this part of the hypothesis. The mobile environment creates a higher level of BRa in any situation created by time distortion (high or low). But when the individual experimental situations are considered; the gaming environment is the actual variable that creates the difference in brand attitudes when time distortion is taken into consideration. Regarding BRrc, the mobile environment creates more positive results at any level of the time distortion. The best situation is created with a low time distortion and mobile games for BRrc. Mobile games have different characteristics than online games as they are mostly played on the go. As the immersion increase, the players' affective and cognitive responses deteriorate.

This study provides important insights to marketers and game developers. When they decide to use a mobile gaming environment to promote their brands with advergaming, they should be careful to create simple, easily played and less destructive gaming environments. Mobile gaming should be simpler and less immersive to create more positive outcomes, compared to online gaming.

FUTURE RESEARCH DIRECTIONS

This study is rather exploratory, and future studies are needed to examine the possible effects of the mobile gaming environment. For example, different consumer responses, especially the conative ones, like purchase intention, recommendations could be researched in upcoming studies. It would also be insightful to study the brand integration process of advergaming. Conducting a study with brand-game congruity in mobile advergaming can provide a more detailed examination. Including the possible effects of consumers' prior brand experience would provide a more exact view of the possible benefits of using advergames as an advertising medium.

CONCLUSION

In summary, the flow experience has an impact on consumers' BRa and BRrc in advergames. With the enhancement of the flow experience consumers' affective and cognitive responses to advergames as an advertising medium can be altered. What is more, the gaming environment (mobile and online) also impacts certain responses. The mobile environment can create more positive affective responses, such as a higher BRa. The mobile environment's ability to create more positive cognitive responses (brand recall and recognition) is changed with the possible effects of the flow experience. It is clear that examining certain differences of mobile environment in gaming would provide valuable insights to both marketers and game developers.

REFERENCES

Agarwal, R., & Karahanna, E. (2000). Time flies when you're having fun: Cognitive absorption and beliefs about information technology usage. *Management Information Systems Quarterly*, *24*(4), 665–694. doi:10.2307/3250951

Alina, G. (2013). Factors responsible for consumer's attitude towards advergames. *Annals of Faculty of Economics*, *1*(1), 1733–1742.

Bell, M., Chalmers, M., Barkhuus, L., Hall, M., Sherwood, S., Tennent, P., & Hampshire, A. (2006, April). Interweaving mobile games with everyday life. In *Proceedings of the SIGCHI conference on Human Factors in computing systems* (pp. 417-426). ACM.

Bellman, S., Kemp, A., Haddad, H., & Varan, D. (2014). The effectiveness of advergames compared to television commercials and interactive commercials featuring advergames. *Computers in Human Behavior*, *32*, 276–283. doi:10.1016/j.chb.2013.12.013

Berlyne, D. E. (1966). Curiosity and exploration. *Science*, *153*(3731), 25–33. doi:10.1126cience.153.3731.25 PMID:5328120

Brave, S., & Nass, C. (2003). Emotion in human-computer interaction. *Human-Computer Interaction*, 53.

Cauberghe, V., & De Pelsmacker, P. (2010). Advergames: The impact of brand prominence and game repetition on brand responses. *Journal of Advertising*, *39*(1), 5–18. doi:10.2753/JOA0091-3367390101

Cauberghe, V., Geuens, M., & De Pelsmacker, P. (2011). Context effects of TV programme-induced interactivity and telepresence on advertising responses. *International Journal of Advertising*, *30*(4), 641–663. doi:10.2501/IJA-30-4-641-663

Csikszentmihalyi, M. (1975). *Beyond Boredom and Anxiety*. San Francisco, CA: Jossey Bass.

Csikszentmihalyi, M. (1997). *Finding flow: The psychology of engagement with everyday life*. New York: Basic Books.

Csikszentmihalyi, M., & LeFevre, J. (1989). Optimal experience in work and leisure. *Journal of Personality and Social Psychology*, *56*(5), 815–822. doi:10.1037/0022-3514.56.5.815 PMID:2724069

Esteban-Millat, I., Martínez-López, F. J., Luna, D., & Rodríguez-Ardura, I. (2014). The concept of flow in online consumer behavior. In *Handbook of strategic e-business management* (pp. 371–402). Springer Berlin Heidelberg. doi:10.1007/978-3-642-39747-9_17

Fiske, S. T., & Pavelchak, M. A. (1986). Category-based versus piecemeal-based affective responses: developments in schema-triggered affect. In R. W. Sorrentino & E. T. Higgines (Eds.), *Handbook of Motivation and Cognition: Foundations of Social Behavior* (pp. 464–473). New York, NY: Guilford Press.

Goh, K. Y., & Ping, J. W. (2014). Engaging consumers with advergames: An experimental evaluation of interactivity, fit and expectancy. *Journal of the Association for Information Systems*, *15*(7), 388–421. doi:10.17705/1jais.00366

Gurau, C. (2009). Characteristics, Limitations, and Potential of Advergames. In *Encyclopedia of Multimedia Technology and Networking* (2nd ed.; pp. 205–211). IGI Global. doi:10.4018/978-1-60566-014-1.ch028

Ham, C. D., Yoon, G., & Nelson, M. R. (2016). The interplay of persuasion inference and flow experience in an entertaining food advergame. *Journal of Consumer Behaviour*, *15*(3), 239–250. doi:10.1002/cb.1564

Harris, D. J., Vine, S. J., & Wilson, M. R. (2017). Flow and quiet eye: The role of attentional control in flow experience. *Cognitive Processing*, 1–5. PMID:28238169

Harris Harris Keller, J., & Blomann, F. (2008). Locus of control and the flow experience: An experimental analysis. *European Journal of Personality*, *22*(7), 589–607. doi:10.1002/per.692

Hernandez, M. D. (2011). A model of flow experience as determinant of positive attitudes toward online advergames. *Journal of Promotion Management*, *17*(3), 315–326. doi:10.1080/10496491.2011.596761

Hofacker, C. F., De Ruyter, K., Lurie, N. H., Manchanda, P., & Donaldson, J. (2016). Gamification and mobile marketing effectiveness. *Journal of Interactive Marketing*, *34*, 25–36. doi:10.1016/j.intmar.2016.03.001

Hoffman, B., & Nadelson, L. (2010). Motivational engagement and video gaming: A mixed methods study. *Educational Technology Research and Development*, *58*(3), 245–270. doi:10.100711423-009-9134-9

Hoffman, D. L., & Novak, T. P. (1996). Marketing in hypermedia computer-mediated environments: Conceptual foundations. *Journal of Marketing*, *60*(3), 50–68. doi:10.2307/1251841

Hsu, H. Y., & Wang, S. K. (2018). Gaming Literacies and Learning. In *Promoting Global Competencies Through Media Literacy* (pp. 79–95). IGI Global. doi:10.4018/978-1-5225-3082-4.ch005

Jeong, E. J., Bohil, C. J., & Biocca, F. A. (2011). Brand logo placements in violent games. *Journal of Advertising*, *40*(3), 59–72. doi:10.2753/JOA0091-3367400305

Jeong, E. J., Lee, H. R., & Woo, J. H. (2015, January). Brand Memory, Attitude, and State Aggression in Violent Games: Focused on the Roles of Arousal, Negative Affect, and Spatial Presence. In *System Sciences (HICSS), 2015 48th Hawaii International Conference on* (pp. 3538-3547). IEEE.

Jessor, R., & Jessor, S. L. (1977). *Problem behavior and psychosocial development: A longitudinal study of youth.* Academic Press.

Jin, D. Y. (2017). The Emergence of Asian Mobile Games: Definitions, Industries, and Trajectories. *Mobile Gaming in Asia: Politics, Culture and Emerging Technologies*, 3-20.

Jin, S. A. A. (2012). "Toward integrative models of flow": Effects of performance, skill, challenge, playfulness, and presence on flow in video games. *Journal of Broadcasting & Electronic Media*, *56*(2), 169–186. doi:10.1080/08838151.2012.678516

Kaye, L. K., & Bryce, J. (2012). Putting the fun factor into gaming: The influence of social contexts on the experiences of playing videogames. *International Journal of Internet Science*, *7*(1), 24–38.

Keller, J., & Blomann, F. (2008). Locus of control and the flow experience: An experimental analysis. *European Journal of Personality*, *22*(7), 589–607. doi:10.1002/per.692

Lantos, G. P., & Craton, L. G. (2012). A model of consumer response to advertising music. *Journal of Consumer Marketing*, *29*(1), 22–42. doi:10.1108/07363761211193028

Lee, C., Yang, C., & Hung, H. (2017). Evaluating Game-Brand Congruity and Flow on Brand Personality by Using Gamifying Learning. *Eurasia Journal of Mathematics Science and Technology Education*, *13*(7), 3083–3097.

Lee, M., & Youn, S. (2008). Leading national advertisers' uses of advergames. *Journal of Current Issues and Research in Advertising*, *30*(2), 1–13. doi:10.1080/10641734.2008.10505243

Liu, X., Hu, M. Y., & Grimm, P. E. (2010). Affect transfer in brand extensions: The role of expectancy and relevancy. *Journal of Product and Brand Management*, *19*(5), 317–326. doi:10.1108/10610421011068559

Montola, M. (2005, December). Exploring the edge of the magic circle: Defining pervasive games. In *Proceedings of DAC* (*Vol. 1966*, pp. 103-106). Academic Press.

Morris, J. D., & Boone, M. A. (1998). *The effects of music on emotional response, brand attitude, and purchase intent in an emotional advertising condition*. ACR North American Advances.

Myers, J., & Sar, S. (2015). The influence of consumer mood state as a contextual factor on imagery-inducing advertisements and brand attitude. *Journal of Marketing Communications*, *21*(4), 284–299. doi:10.1080/13527266.2012.762421

Nakamura, J., & Csikszentmihalyi, M. (2009). Flow theory and research. Handbook of Positive Psychology, 195-206.

Nelson, M. R., & Waiguny, M. K. (2012). Psychological processing of in-game advertising and advergaming: Branded entertainment or entertaining persuasion. *Psychology of entertainment media: Blurring the lines between Entertainment and Persuasion*, 93-146.

Nelson, M. R., Yaros, R. A., & Keum, H. (2006). Examining the influence of telepresence on spectator and player processing of real and fictitious brands in a computer game. *Journal of Advertising*, *35*(4), 87–99. doi:10.2753/JOA0091-3367350406

Ollila, M. (2017). *The game ad-unit: the future of mobile marketing and location-based entertainment after Pokémon GO.* Retrieved from http://www.pocketgamer.biz/comment-and-opinion/65043/the-future-of-mobile-marketing-and-location-based-entertainment/

Özbük, R. M. Y., & Ünal, D. A. (2017). Advergames Aiming Children in Turkey: A Content Analysis of 65 Advergames 1. *Business and Economics Research Journal, 8*(1), 115–130. doi:10.20409/berj.2017126248

Parrot, W. G., & Spackman, M. P. (2000). Emotion and memory. In M. Lewis & J.M. Haviland-Jones (Eds.), Handbook of emotions (2nd ed.; pp. 476-490). The Guilford Press.

Pelet, J. É., Ettis, S., & Cowart, K. (2017). Optimal experience of flow enhanced by telepresence: Evidence from social media use. *Information & Management, 54*(1), 115–128. doi:10.1016/j.im.2016.05.001

Petersen, F. W., Thomsen, L. E., Mirza-Babaei, P., & Drachen, A. (2017, October). Evaluating the Onboarding Phase of Free-to Play Mobile Games: A Mixed-Method Approach. In *Proceedings of the Annual Symposium on Computer-Human Interaction in Play* (pp. 377-388). ACM.

Refiana, L., Mizerski, D., & Murphy, J. (2005, December). Measuring the state of flow in playing online games. In *Proceedings of ANZMAC 2005 Conference, Marketing Research and Research Methodologies (quantitative)* (pp. 108-113). Freemantle, Australia: School of Business, University of Western Australia.

Roettl, J., Waiguny, M., & Terlutter, R. (2016). The persuasive power of advergames: A content analysis focusing on persuasive mechanisms in advergames. *Australasian Marketing Journal, 24*(4), 275–287. doi:10.1016/j.ausmj.2016.10.001

Scott, J., & Craig-Lees, M. (2010). Audience engagement and its effects on product placement recognition. *Journal of Promotion Management, 16*(1-2), 39–58. doi:10.1080/10496490903571803

Sutko, D. M., & de Souza e Silva, A. (2011). Location-aware mobile media and urban sociability. *New Media & Society, 13*(5), 807–823. doi:10.1177/1461444810385202

Terlutter, R., & Capella, M. L. (2013). The gamification of advertising: Analysis and research directions of in-game advertising, advergames, and advertising in social network games. *Journal of Advertising, 42*(2-3), 95–112. doi:10.1080/00913367.2013.774610

Vanwesenbeeck, I., Ponnet, K., & Walrave, M. (2016). Go with the flow: How children's persuasion knowledge is associated with their state of flow and emotions during advergame play. *Journal of Consumer Behaviour, 15*(1), 38–47. doi:10.1002/cb.1529

Vermeir, I., Kazakova, S., Tessitore, T., Cauberghe, V., & Slabbinck, H. (2014). Impact of flow on recognition of and attitudes towards in-game brand placements: Brand congruence and placement prominence as moderators. *International Journal of Advertising, 33*(4), 785–810. doi:10.2501/IJA-33-4-785-810

Waiguny, M. K., Nelson, M. R., & Marko, B. (2013). How advergame content influences explicit and implicit brand attitudes: When violence spills over. *Journal of Advertising, 42*(2-3), 155–169. doi:10.1080/00913367.2013.774590

Waiguny, M. K., Nelson, M. R., & Terlutter, R. (2012). Entertainment matters! The relationship between challenge and persuasiveness of an advergame for children. *Journal of Marketing Communications, 18*(1), 69–89. doi:10.1080/13527266.2011.620766

Wanick, V., Ranchhod, A., & Wills, G. B. (2014). *Effects and opportunities of mobile advergames into brand management and marketing: a content analysis*. At International Conference on Information Society (i-Society 2014).

Weber, R., Tamborini, R., Westcott-Baker, A., & Kantor, B. (2009). Theorizing flow and media enjoyment as cognitive synchronization of attentional and regard networks. *Communication Theory, 19*(4), 397–422. doi:10.1111/j.1468-2885.2009.01352.x

Wei, P. S., & Lu, H. P. (2014). Why do people play mobile social games? An examination of network externalities and of uses and gratifications. *Internet Research, 24*(3), 313–331. doi:10.1108/IntR-04-2013-0082

Weibel, D., Wissmath, B., Habegger, S., Steiner, Y., & Groner, R. (2008). Playing online games against computer-vs. human-controlled opponents: Effects on presence, flow, and enjoyment. *Computers in Human Behavior, 24*(5), 2274–2291. doi:10.1016/j.chb.2007.11.002

Yoon, G., & Vargas, P. T. (2013). Seeing without looking: The effects of hemispheric functioning on memory for brands in computer games. *Journal of Advertising, 42*(2-3), 131–141. doi:10.1080/00913367.2013.774587

KEY TERMS AND DEFINITIONS

Advergame: A game created to promote a certain brand, company, or product.

Arousal: Becoming active, attentive, or excited during gameplay.

Brand Attitude: The positive or negative feelings and opinions of consumers toward a brand.

Brand Recall: A component of brand awareness, which refers to the consumers' ability to remember a certain brand name after being exposed to a communication effort.

Flow: The sense of optimal experience created with the feelings of challenge, telepresence, involvement with the activity, arousal, and time distortion.

Telepresence: The feeling of presence in a virtual environment.

Time Distortion: The loss of track of time with the immersive experience the game creates.

Chapter 9
Nuances of Media Planning in New Media Age

Anandan Pandiyan Pillai
Performics.Resultrix, India

ABSTRACT

This chapter aims to highlight the premises of traditional media planning process, create cognizance about the challenges that media planner today faces. A brief overview of extant literature on media planning, new media, is discussed. The author discusses media planning approach needs to consider marketing funnel and communication plan in consideration while building media plans. Further the chapter suggests a few additional steps that media planners need to consider during their future media planning exercises, given the increasing complexities in media consumption space. The author has mapped each of the media planning stages with the marketing funnel stage to emphasize that media planning is not an independent activity but needs to be closely stitched with the overall marketing strategy. Finally, future research recommendations are suggested.

INTRODUCTION

Today's youth wakes up to a good morning message sent by a close relative / friend. While having breakfast he/she quickly catches up with the news around the world on his/her favorite mobile app. He/she is listening to a Soundcloud or YouTube while on the go the office or college. He/she quickly checks out the updates on Facebook, Twitter, LinkedIn during short breaks or during meetings. While in the late evening he/she probably browses Netflix / Hotstar to stay updated on the TV series that he/she missed watching live, or reads through blogs for one's education.

DOI: 10.4018/978-1-5225-6064-7.ch009

Each one of us could relate to the above scenario. We, new media age consumers have segregated digital platform consumption based on the time frame and the mental state we are present. As a corollary, increasingly media multi-tasking (Chang,2016) or also referred as simultaneous media usage (Pilotta et al, 2004) is observed across the world. With the help of uses and gratification theory and arousal theory, Chang (2016) contributed to literature that media multi-tasking is high amongst high sensation seekers, thereby helping them reach optimal level of arousal. Hence, the media planning exercise is emerging to be more and more complicated (Soberman, 2005) with increased hyper-connected, multi-device media consumption behavior.

In the pre-Internet era, a media planner's primary media vehicles were television, print, radio, outdoor. With the advent of Internet, internet advertising was a new media vehicle that media planner had to think and plan of, along with traditional media vehicles. As time passed by, new technologies evolved, several legs of internet advertising emerged. These included search engine marketing, display advertising, social media advertising, affiliate advertising and mobile advertising etc. In the last decade or so, with the advent and introduction of wearable devices, smart televisions, smartphones, artificial intelligence and virtual reality based devices, the media vehicles that the media planner has at his/her disposal is enormous. Though Internet is the premise of most of these new media vehicles, the human interaction and content consumption pattern of users on these devices vary a lot. Internet / digital advertising empowers marketers to reach and target individual consumer almost at n=1 level, thanks to the targeting parameters that are available in the new media vehicles. This makes it necessary for us to first understand the Internet penetration at a global scale. As of March, 2017 the total number of Internet users worldwide was 3.58 billion, as compared to 3.39 billion in 2016 (Statista, 2017a). The highest number of Internet users, as of June 2017, were in China with 738.54 million, followed by India with 462.12 million and United States at third position with 286.94 million (Statista, 2017b).

Given the fact that almost 50% of the global population is now connected with Internet, it would be a logical sequel to understand the global advertising spends that are made on the digital platforms. The global media advertising outlay in 2017 is expected to be around $583.91 billion (eMarketer, 2017). The global digital advertising outlay is expected to touch $223.74 billion in 2017, approximately 38% of overall media advertising outlay (eMarketer, 2017).

The increasing Internet penetration, staggering digital advertising spends explain just supply side of media industry. The demand side of media industry is equally exciting with increasing media channels, excessive video consumption, e-commerce penetration, mobile device adoption across the world and not to ignore increased social interaction on digital platforms thanks to the connect that Facebook, Twitter, Weibo, LinkedIn have established.

The extant literature on media planning has been approached from the communication planning lens. However, in era of 2018 where devices are seamlessly connected, users are consuming content from multiple channels, media planning needs to be approached more from marketing strategy lens. No more, media strategy can be parked as an end step. The chapter posits how media planning needs to be integrated with the marketing planning along with a marketing funnel-based approach. The takeaway for the chapter readers, researchers and media planners will be on how to simultaneously think about media planning and buying as they start to plan the marketing funnel. Secondly, erstwhile media planning literature has often missed to cover the key success factors of the media planning exercise. Hence, the second key contribution of this chapter to the media planning literature is on key metrics that media planners need to keep an eye on, for each marketing funnel stage. Finally, the chapter concludes with some future recommendations of research and envisages how media planning exercise might get complicated for the media planners with the increasing prominence of latest technologies like Virtual Reality (VR), and Artificial Intelligence (AI) etc.

BACKGROUND

New Media

New media evolution has resulted due to changes in cultural, legal, technological and economic circumstances (Stober, 2004). No one factor can be identified for the institutionalization of new media. The interaction between these factors has resulted into proliferation and acceptance of new media amongst the consumers. In the new media era, communication is driven by algorithms, electronic networks, automated systems (Mulhern, 2009). Logan (2010) referred new media as *those digital media that are interactive, incorporate two-way communication, and involve some form of computing*. The differentiating factors between new and traditional media are – i) two-way communication, ii) continuous learning, iii) alignment and interaction, iv) ease of information access and dissemination, v) community building (Logan, 2010). In the extant literature new media has been equated to digital media / Internet media / Digitization (Mulhern, 2009). This chapter considers new media as any electronic media vehicle that empowers message recipients to react and engage with the communication piece that has been directed to them. The new media channels could include social media, blogs, mobile apps, websites, microblogs, vlogs, etc. As there are number of digital media channels available for attaining various marketing objectives, they could be classified into three major pillars – Paid, Owned, Earned media (Lovett & Staelin, 2016).

Paid media refers to all paid advertisements that are conducted on social media channels, display platforms, mobile apps etc. It substantially helps a brand in attaining incremental reach over the organic reach of each digital channel. Earned media refers to all word of mouth conversations that are shared by users about a brand on social media channels, discussion forums, complaint websites, or blogs. It serves multiple purposes – a) It helps prospective users in making a choice for a brand based on the previous positive experiences of other customers, b) It helps brands in understanding the actual sentiment around the brand and provides brands an opportunity to improvise if there is a scope, c) It helps customers to connect with fellow audience and exchange experiences / learning (especially in case of technical products).

Media Planning

Media planning in the extended literature has mostly been looked upon as an exercise to select most efficient media channels, with the least possible cost and maximum possible reach (Barker, 2015; Schultz, Block & Viswanathan, 2016). The media planners were focused on attaining a certain Reach at a given Frequency (Cannon, 2001). This Reach & Frequency approach (Figure 1) was practiced with the assumption that the brand's communication message can be effectively disseminated with the given reach and frequency. However, in the new media era the challenge is not just to disseminate the message, but also equally challenging to ensure the user understood the message and responded back in the desired manner. As detailed in the earlier section one of the key differentiations between new media and traditional media has been the reciprocity that is available with the new media platforms. Hence, media planners to be cognizant of this fact and need to be prepared for the reciprocity that they would face from the communication receivers.

The media planning process isn't linear and can't end in one iteration. There are multiple iterations on the media planning exercise depending on the interactions with the client team. Barker (2017) proposed an iterative planning cycle, instead of a siloed linear approached as proposed by earlier researchers (Figure 2). This process had two key aspects – i) Inter media decisions (those aimed at comparing various media vehicles, assessing their appropriateness to the client brief and selecting them) and ii) Intra media decisions (once a particular media vehicle is chosen, further decisions are made on when and how the vehicle can be utilized, planning of content schedule etc.). This approach was far more refined and did highlight the refinement of media planning by focusing on each stage of the process.

A parallel set of researchers were still proposing a linear approach where media strategy usually appeared towards end of the planning process (Belch & Belch, 2008).

Figure 1. The frequency value planning process (Cannon, 2001)

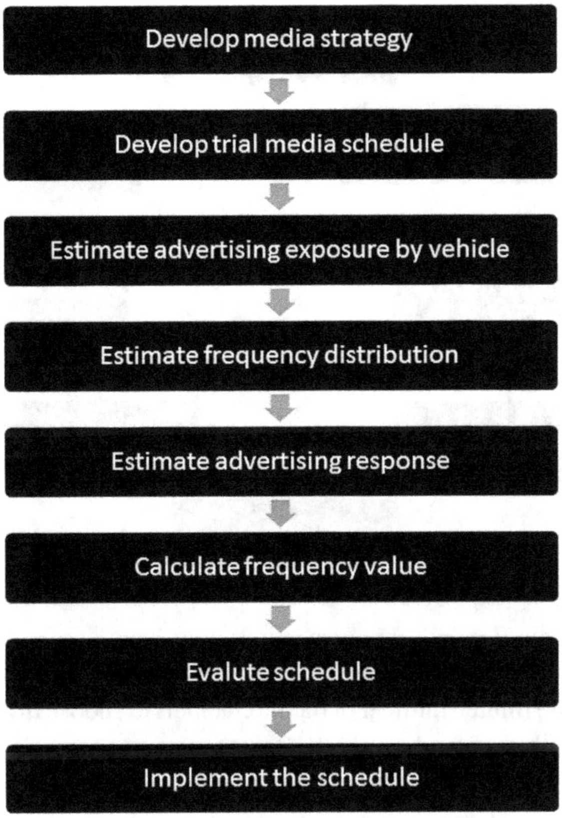

Figure 3 indicates how media strategy found its importance post communication strategy was finalized. This kind of sequential approach was debated and couple of subsequent researchers hypothesized that assuming each media vehicle's input is independent of each other could be a logical fallacy (Schultz, Block & Raman, 2009). In the Internet era and especially after the proliferation of social media channels like Facebook, Twitter etc. users could interact with multiple channels, once they were exposed to a set of communication. For instance, a user once saw a TV commercial, could immediately take help of Google Search on his/her mobile device to further research about the newly launched product. However, this user behavior couldn't be captured in any of the traditional media planning frameworks. It was very evident that in the new media age, consumers were connected to various devices and consumed content on them. Hence, the user journey wasn't as linear as it was proposed to be.

Figure 2. The media planning process (Barker, 2017)

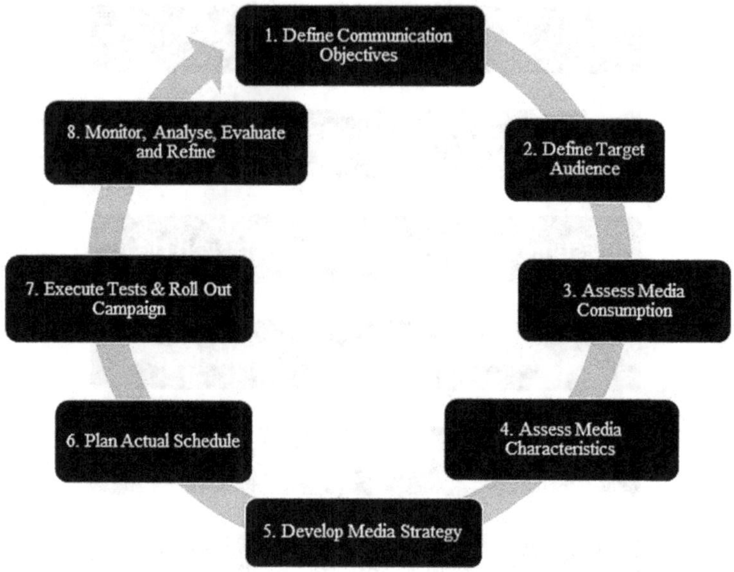

Reach and Frequency could have been an efficient and effective way, while the media planners had limited number of media channels to choose from. However, with the increased number of media vehicles, cross-media communication behavior of users, media planning is not restricted with the objective of finding a cost-effective media mix. The latest media planning literature has focused on programmatic advertising (Gertz and McGlashan, 2016). This involves sophisticated machine-learning driven media planning and buying tools to ensure right set of audiences are identified and message distributed in a most efficient manner (Schultz, Block & Viswanathan, 2016). Still, the researchers focused on effective and efficient message distribution, and the focus on user responses was minimal.

However, now the need of the hour for media planners would be to first understand the marketing problem and solve it through effective media planning exercise (Krajcovic, 2015). There could be various kinds of marketing problems – increase market share, increase sales, launch an upcoming product, drive footfalls to a newly opened retail store, and build superior imagery about after-sales services etc. Krajcovic (2015) also suggests media selection not only depends on the product to be promoted but also on demographic, economic, cultural and social aspects of a particular target audience. Hence, it is advisable that media planning works in tandem with the marketing and communication planning.

Figure 3. Five step planning model (Belch & Belch, 2008)

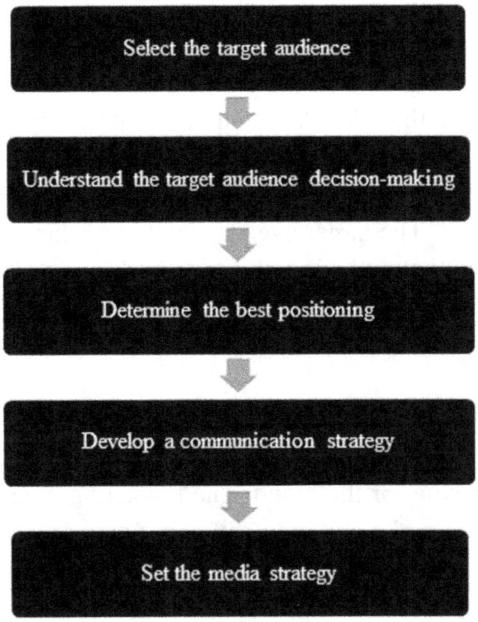

Mulhern (2009) well summarized the shift from traditional media to new media. The media planning process has shifted from being linear to dynamic, targeting has become more contextual than just focused on demographics, primarily news and entertainment channels being primary media partners to all media and digital media emerging as key partners (Mulhern, 2009). The traditional media ecosystem that was primarily led by print, television, radio, outdoor has now become a web of media channels with the introduction of digital platforms and the complex simultaneous media consumption behavior by users.

MAIN FOCUS OF THE CHAPTER

Erstwhile media planning assumed addressing same marketing objective through various media channels. The same brand communication was rendered into media channel specific communication messages. With the increased clutter amongst digital channels, the probability of garnering eyeballs (or Opportunity to See – OTS) has become challenging. Every digital channel transfers messages in a unique manner and each digital channel is consumed by user in a very different manner. The idea of pushing same communication message with a media channel specific tweak might not be yield results in the present and forthcoming multi-device environment.

The research literature has enough proof of debate on whether media planning process should be sequential or cyclical. In today's multi-dimensional world, media planners need to think on multiple dimensions at the same point of time. So, it's much more than deciding on what step should follow next. Hence, based on the industry experience, author details about few aspects that media planners and brand managers should be aware of. Author purposively would like to stay away from the debate on how the process should look like or whether the process should be sequential / cyclical. The larger agenda should be whether the media planning exercise is addressing the marketing objective in the best possible manner or not. Hence, based on this premise author has detailed the key aspects of media planning that one should consider.

1. **Marketing Objective**: The brand managers need to own this at a higher level. Subsequently, it gets passed to the advertising agency that is responsible to plan and buy media for the brand. The marketing objective needs to have a specific direction and magnitude called out precisely. For instance, it could be as clear as, increase sales of North region by 10%. In a scenario where a brand owns large portfolio of products, if the media planning and buying is strategized it should be at a portfolio level. The clarity of marketing objective will help every stakeholder to visualize the marketing problem at hand in an unbiased manner. A sample set of marketing objectives as per each stage of marketing funnel is highlighted in the Table 1 below.
2. **Target Audience**:– The new media technologies has facilitated marketers to choose targeted media vehicles and it has helped them to customers in a better way due to increased qualitative and quantitative data available for customers (Soberman, 2005). This data trend has equipped brand managers and agency media planners to plan it better. Both brand managers and the media agency should agree on the particular target audience that they would like to approach. These could be traditional demographic based target audience measures, first party audience, third party audience, intent-based audience or remarketing audience.

Table 1. Mapping marketing funnel stage with marketing objectives

Marketing funnel stage	Marketing Objective
Upper	Improve aided recall by 20% Improve unaided recall by 10%
Middle	Move consideration / preference for the brand by 10%
Lower	The y-o-y sale for the North region to increase by 15%

a. **Demographic Targeting**: It could include age group, gender targeting (in case of specific gender-oriented products), geographical location (would one want to go all out or specific states or cities), educational background, marital status, etc. The basis of this target audience definition could emerge from brand manager's / media planner's past experience. Alternatively, a research with the help of focus group discussion, in-depth interviews, survey could be organized to identify the needs of the customer. Hence, an appropriate target audience could be arrived at.

b. **First Party Audience**: Thanks to the technological developments now a brand could identify, classify and collect audience who would visit their website. The technology that enables this type of audience mapping is called as Data Management Platform (DMP). A piece of code is placed on all the webpages of the website. This code gets executed as soon as the user visits the webpage. The major DMPs across the globe are Adobe Audience Manager, Oracle BlueKai, Salesforce DMP, MediaMath, and Lotame etc. (G2 Crowd, 2017). The other way of targeting first party audience is by leveraging users' email address or mobile number. When either or both of these contact details are added to the any of the digital platform (Facebook, Twitter, Google) etc. the platform will try to map the users based on match with these email address and/or mobile number. This audience as per advertising parlance is referred to as 'Custom Audience'. So, in cases where repeated / sequential messages are planned to be delivered to the current set of audience who have shown interest in brand (and hence shared their email address or mobile number) or the existing customers, this Custom Audience route could be applied.

c. **Third Party Audience**: In this case an entity asks a publisher to collect audience and share it with them. The data purchasing entity further goes on to build personas of users based on their internet consumption behavior (Marshall, 2014). This data is further sold to the advertisers and media agencies, who would like to target a specific persona. These databases usually are costly and the effectiveness isn't guaranteed. It all depends if the third-party data pool shared to an advertiser delivers or not. Some of the major third-party audience providers across the globe are BlueKai, Lotame, Datalogix, Experian, Acxiom, TruSignal, Alliant, and IXI etc. (Marshall, 2014).

d. **Intent Based Audience**: Online search, the largest chunk of digital advertising can't target users based on demographical criteria. It's an intent driven platform, hence the media serving occurs based on the intent that the user searches for on Google Search, Bing Search or Yahoo Search.

e. **Remarketing Audience:** Remarketing, as the name suggests refers to reaching out the same set of audience for repeated times, who have already once visited the brand website or have interacted with any of their ongoing campaigns (Taylor, 2017). In industries where the customer decision journey (van Bommel, Edelman & Ungerman, 2014) is lengthy and involves multiple stages, it will help advertisers to share sequential communication with the help of remarketing audience and thereby guiding the user to the next stage of marketing funnel.

As suggested earlier each marketing funnel stage could be mapped to the type of audience that the brand should target (Table 2).

3. **Identify Surrogate Targeting Variables**: In the new media era of media planning target audience definition doesn't stop at the previous step. The basic demographical criteria are just the first level of targeting. As discussed earlier in the chapter a modern day consumer is using multiple-devices, is exposed to multiple online destinations and each destination has its own purpose of communication. On some platforms a user visits to just maintain a social connect, while on some the user visits to maintain professional contact, some platforms offer informative knowledge, and hence become a destination for one's research etc. Hence, based on a user's cross-platform consumption of media, every modern platform also provides some additional surrogate variables to fine tune the target audience.

For instance, if a sports brand would like to target youth with interest in soccer, they would like to reach out certain niche youth audience instead of splurging media across the age group of 16 – 20 and pray for soccer enthusiasts to fall in the media trap. The chances of finding the accurate audience with such 'spray and pray' approach (as its commonly referred to in the industry) is very bleak. Let's continue with this example and understand how would a media planner reach out to soccer enthusiast young audience on Facebook. Facebook has classified some users as football enthusiasts based on how users have utilized Facebook for the sport.

Table 2. Mapping marketing funnel stage with various types of target audience

Marketing funnel stage	Target audience
Upper	Demographic targeting, Third party audience
Middle	First party audience, intent based audience
Lower	Remarketing audience

Simplest indicator would be a fan following couple of soccer clubs on Facebook. He/she could have had some discussions about soccer players / matches in the past with friends. The user could have watched some soccer videos on Facebook. Each platform picks up such signals from the user behavior and classifies the user into a certain category. The platforms also allow one to target based on the mobile device a user uses to access the platform, if the user is a frequent traveler or not (signals from each check-in that the user makes), is a parent or not, etc.

The media planners need to be wary about the fact that a particular set of audience could have been classified by a platform (say Facebook) on multiple criteria. A youth might have been classified as a soccer enthusiast, a foodie, a jazz music lover and who loves to go on treks. So, an informed choice of surrogate targeting variables coupled with Boolean operators (AND, OR) etc. need to be used in an efficient manner by the media planner to arrive at an much calculative potential reach, than just the demographical target variables. Most of the social platforms allow such detailed level of targeting. Even programmatic advertising tools like Double Click Bid Manager or Adobe Campaign Manager, fairly allow the media planners to plan for a niche audience. Arriving at the right set of surrogate audience is where the trick lies. This might also become complex in case of certain products. For instance, an energy drink for young students in the age group of 6 – 12. Now, this target audience does watch TV, they would be fairly exposed to newspapers and magazines and they would be definitely active on mobile games or YouTube (watching cartoon series / educational videos). Here the choice of surrogate variables to build an awareness amongst them and their parents would be completely different.

4. **Media Consumption Behavior of Target Audience:** As in the traditional media planning scenario, planners first try to identify if the user is an active TV-viewer or a newspaper reader or a radio listener, it becomes inevitable for media planners to understand the new media consumption behavior. Is the target audience mostly active on a social platform (Facebook / Twitter / Instagram / Snapchat etc.), or are they active on business news websites, or do they spend consuming more of lifestyle content etc. Also, as the media serving can be controlled to a fairly detailed level, it also becomes necessary for media planners to understand and guesstimate if the user is active on online platforms during the early part of the day, or in the late evening. The allocation of budgets and bids could be accordingly optimized to ensure maximum number of relevant audience are reached. Instead of going by macro level estimates from industry, every brand could understand the media consumption behavior with a dip stick research from their end.

5. **Considering the Creative Assets Available**: New media has given various options for marketers to choose from. Every new media platform has different types of creative that a marketer can choose to run. Though the options are enormous, its suggestive for media planners to map these available options with one's marketing funnel and then utilize the best option. Table 3 is a fairly indicative resource of all possible creative assets options that are available at media planner's disposal. The mistake that most media planners make is, going after certain creative asset because it is available on a particular platform or their creative agency has suggested to use them. The trick lies in using right creative asset, for the right marketing funnel stage and with right media optimization technique to achieve the optimum results.
6. **Media Optimization Technique**: Before we get into the details of various media optimization techniques, lets first understand the user journey once he/she is exposed to an advertisement. Once the user views a digital advertisement (banner or video), it is termed as an impression. Subsequently, the user has a choice to click on the banner or the video, and the action is termed as a click. Once the user clicks on the creative asset, the user is directed to a destination on brand's website, which is referred as landing page. Finally, once the user reaches landing page he/she could be asked to share their details for future communication, which is called as a lead. Alternatively, in case of e-commerce website, the user might go ahead with the purchase. So there are four key steps that a user conducts – a) sees a creative asset, b) clicks on the creative asset, c) reaches the landing page, d) shares lead or fulfills purchase.

Table 3. Creative assets mapped against marketing funnel

Marketing Funnel Stage	Facebook	Twitter	YouTube	Programmatic Display	Google Search / GDN	Mobile
Upper	Video, Facebook Live, Cinemagraph	Promoted Trend, Videos	Masthead Truview, Ads	Videos, Rich Media, Expandos, Interstitials	GIFs, Static Banners, Text Ads	Interstitials
Middle	Canvas, Collections, Carousels	GIF	Bumper Ads,	GIF	GIFs, Static Banners, Text Ads	GIF
Lower	Static Banner, Lead Ads	Static Banners	Truview Ads with keyword targeting	Static Banners		Static

Digital media allows media planners to optimize their campaign at each step discussed above. A media planner could either optimize a campaign for an impression, click, lead or sale. The choice of media optimization technique would again depend on the marketing objective and the marketing funnel stage of the campaign. A broad awareness or reach based campaign would be optimized for impressions, which means the media planner is not that concerned about the clicks on the creative asset, but he/she looks to reach maximum possible unique users across the web. In this case the strategy would be a healthy mix of high traffic websites and where the inventory is available at a competitive rate. In case of middle funnel campaigns, where objective could be to drive preference / consideration for the brand, media planners would optimize their campaigns for the clicks. So, the creative asset needs to call out the action that the user needs to take (which is a click). Finally, in case of lower funnel campaigns (driving leads or sales), media planners will optimize the campaign on cost per lead or cost per transaction, depending on the scenario (Table 4).

7. **Ad Viewability**: This aspect is gaining prominence with every dollar being invested in paid media. As paid digital advertising increases, an average encounters more and more ads on digital platforms. This results into a clutter for a user and brand managers have started questioning on the extent to which a human eyeball notices advertisements that are visible on the screen. Viewability or viewable impressions refer to the fact that if a display advertisement or a video advertisement was viewable enough on the screen (on desktop or any mobile device) for the user. There are various viewable standards and they even vary from one platform to another. Though each platform has defined their own viewable standards, we will refer to the standard metrics suggest by Internet Advertising Bureau, UK. Table 5 below details the minimum threshold that each creative unit should meet in order to be qualified as a viewable impression.

As per Facebook, viewable impression is recorded when 50% of creative asset is visible for one second, and as per Twitter a viewable impression is when 100% creative asset is visible for one second (Rowntree, 2017). The classic debate amongst media planners has been on whether the ad effectiveness increased if

Table 4. Mapping marketing funnel stage with media optimization technique

Marketing funnel stage	Media optimization technique
Upper	Optimize for impressions / reach
Middle	Optimize for clicks
Lower	Optimize for leads / sales

Table 5. Threshold requirement for viewable impression (Internet Advertising Bureau, 2017)

Format	Minimum threshold to meet
Desktop standard banner	50% of creative asset area should be visible for a minimum of 1 second
Desktop large canvas creative (Skyscraper, page takeover)	30% of creative assets area should be visible for a minimum of 1 second
Desktop video	50% of creative asset area should be visible for a minimum of 2 seconds

the Viewability of ads was increased (Heine, 2014). The hypothesis doesn't seem to be necessarily true. A study conducted by IPG Media Lab with a sample size of 10,000 respondents concluded that just because the creative asset area is more visible, it doesn't necessarily correlate with ad effectiveness (Barr, 2016). This has resulted into a trend of brands creating their own Viewability standards. HP worked with measurement firm Integral Ad Science (IAS) to create its own viewability standards. So, now as per HP Viewability standards, 100% pixels in display ads should be viewable for five seconds, 100% of video should be viewable for 50% of video length and in case of 30 seconds pre-roll ads, Viewability is defined at 15 seconds play (Johnson, 2017). This indicates that brands are redefining the rules of digital advertising game and are stringent towards every dollar that is spent on it.

8. **Choose Appropriate Media Metrics to Evaluate Campaign:** There exists a long list of metrics that could guide a media planner and brand manager on campaign effectiveness. However, the smartness lies in assessing right set of metrics as per the campaign objective and the marketing funnel stage. Some of the overarching key metrics for each funnel stage are detailed below (Table 6). The equivalent media metrics across various channels could differ to some extent, which media planners need to consider and use the appropriate ones.
9. **Review and Re-Plan During the Campaign Execution**: Unlike in case of traditional media, new media campaign execution could be fairly re-planned and tweaked even after the campaign has gone live. As there are multiple factors that influence the success of campaign, media planners need to continuously keep a track of the campaign. Unfortunately, in many practical situations media planners hop on to another media planning exercise, once they are done with the one media plan. This isn't a good practice. Media planners should diligently focus on the key campaign success metric, whether it is leads, sales or unique users reached and understand how different channels in the media plan are performing. In case some channels aren't performing to the level best,

Table 6. Media metrics vs marketing funnel stage

Marketing funnel stage	Media metrics
Upper	No. of unique people reached ~ Cost Per Unique Reach No. of views ~ Cost Per View
Middle	No. of clicks ~ Click through rate Cost per click No. of website visits ~ Cost per website visit
Lower	No. of leads ~ Cost per lead No. of sales / transactions ~ Cost per transaction / sale No. of app installs No. of registrations

media planners could easily pause the campaign on that particular channel and reallocate the budget to the best performing channels. It is an ongoing, iterative process until the media planners succeed in attaining their goals.

10. **Attribution Modeling:** It's the final, but most important step in the media planning scheme of things. Moffett (2014) defines attribution as, "*the practice of using advanced statistical approaches to allocate proportional credit to marketing communications and media activity across all channels, which ultimately leads to the desired customer action*". The common challenge for marketers or brand manager is to ascertain ROI from various media channels that were used for the campaign (Abhishek, Despotakis, Ravi, 2017). Attribution modeling comes to the rescue of brand managers in such situations. Some of the major attribution models that are prevalent in the industry are Last Interaction, Last Non-Direct Click, Last Adwords Click, First Interaction, Linear and Time Decay, Position Based (Google, 2017). Different media planners opt for the attribution model of their choice, the most prominent in the industry being Last Interaction. Each technique has its own pros and cons, media planners need to evaluate their scheme of things and arrive at a suitable attribution modeling technique that would best fit their business.

As proposed earlier in the section, author believes that it is hard to put media planning into a series of steps. As per Mulhern (2009) media planning doesn't need an incremental change, but an overall mindset needs of media planners needs to go through a change. The mental state of a media planner would inevitably touch upon above discussed ten aspects in multiple stages of the media planning. There would be heavy interaction of these aspects, which enables a media planner to arrive at a comprehensive plan. The final output of a media plan mapped against marketing funnel would like the one shown in the below Table 7.

Table 7. Sample media plan output

Marketing Funnel Stage	Facebook	Google	Twitter	LinkedIn	Mobile Advertising	Display	Affiliate
Upper (Drive Awareness)							
Middle (Build Consideration)							
Lower (Purchase)							

The media planners in this hyper-connected media world need to be cognizant about simultaneous media consumption behavior, marketing funnel oriented communication strategy and accordingly work on media plans. A linear one-time media plan may be a passé now. The media plan might require multiple changes once the campaign begins. The media planners need to be vigilant and dynamic to respond to the situation.

FUTURE RESEARCH DIRECTIONS / OPPORTUNITIES

Media propositions are continuously evolving with the technological advancements. The industry has come a long way from just text advertisements, to banner-based advertisements to video revolution. There are multiple media developments that are evolving and are expected to become mainstream in next few years. Couple of areas where media developments would emerge, that media planners need to keep an eye on are:

1. An in-depth phenomenology oriented study of media planners will help understand how they engage with media planning exercise.
2. Though the budgets for digital marketing are gaining across the world, the presence of traditional media can't be ignored. As refreshed study of convergence between traditional and new media (Lawson-Borders, 2009) with the help of empirical study will help to understand how each of the media is contributing to the marketing objectives in an era, while both are competing for the budgets from brand managers.
3. Augmented reality, virtual reality kind of technologies are enabling users to visualize and experience the product even before they buy (Mangles, 2017). These technologies could be helpful for media planners to consider while they plan for product launch, or creating product experience

4. E-commerce based search especially on Amazon, Flipkart, ebay etc. is expected to spike up. When users have already made up their mind and are in the lower part of marketing funnel, there are chances increasingly users will visit these e-commerce destinations. These e-commerce destinations are themselves expected to compete for a considerable budget from brand managers. Will these channels, emerge from just being a mere channel to a new form of media that media planners need to consider judiciously, needs to be observed.
5. Further new technologies like Voice based search is evolving and with the likes of Google Home, Amazon Alexa in the market, voice search is expected to grow substantially. These technologies are expected to refine and accelerate a customer from intent to purchase stage. It would be interesting to study the impact of these latest technologies on media planner's choices.

REFERENCES

G2 Crowd. (2017). *Best Data Management Platform (DMP) Software*. Retrieved from https://www.g2crowd.com/categories/data-management-platform-dmp

Abhishek, V., Despotakis, S., & Ravi, R. (2017). *Multi-channel attribution: The blind spot of online advertising*. Available at SSRN: https://papers.ssrn.com/soL3/papers.cfm?abstract_id=2959778

Ardley, B. (2011). Marketing theory and critical phenomenology: Exploring the human side of management practice. *Marketing Intelligence & Planning*, *29*(7), 628–642. doi:10.1108/02634501111178668

Barker, B. (2015). *Media planning: Exploration of the media selection decision making process in the digital environment*. Retrieved from http://eprints.bournemouth.ac.uk/22476/1/AM2015%20Media%20planning%20%20Exploration%20of%20the%20media%20decision%20making%20process%20in%20the%20digital%20environment.pdf (2017, December 12).

Barker, B. (2017). Integration – bringing the media plan together – or making it all work – really well! In *IDM Marketing Guide*. Retrieved from https://www.theidm.com/getmedia/ac4b8ea3-0ba8-4309-a2da-11ed27646ece/C-5-11.pdf

Barr, J. (2016). *Are viewable ads actually effective for marketers? 10,000-person study sheds light*. Retrieved from http://www.adageindia.in/media/are-viewable-ads-actually-effective-for-marketers-10000-person-study-sheds-light/articleshow/50858697.cms

Belch, G. E., & Belch, M. A. (2008). *Advertising and Promotion: An Integrated Marketing Communications Perspective* (8th ed.). McGraw-Hill Higher Education.

Cannon, H. M. (2001). Addressing new media with conventional media planning. *Journal of Interactive Advertising*, *1*(2), 28–42. doi:10.1080/15252019.2001.10722049

Chang, Y. (2016). Why do young people multitask with multiple media? Explicating the relationships among sensation seeking, needs, and media multitasking behavior. *Media Psychology*, *20*(4), 685–703. doi:10.1080/15213269.2016.1247717

eMarketer. (2017). *Worldwide ad spending: The eMarketer forecast for 2017*. Retrieved from https://www.emarketer.com/Report/Worldwide-Ad-Spending-eMarketer-Forecast-2017/2002019

Gertz, O., & McGlashan, D. (2016). Consumer-centric programmatic advertising. Programmatic Advertising. Springer.

Google. (2017). *Attribution modeling overview*. Retrieved from https://support.google.com/analytics/answer/1662518?hl=en

Heine, C. (2014). *Trouble brews over the viewability of digital ads*. Retrieved from http://www.adweek.com/brand-marketing/trouble-brews-over-viewability-digital-ads-157305/

Internet Advertising Bureau. (2017). *Viewability status*. Retrieved from https://iabuk.net/viewability-status

Johnson, L. (2017). *Demanding more stringent measurement, some brands are using their own viewability standards*. Retrieved from http://www.adweek.com/digital/demanding-more-stringent-measurement-some-brands-are-using-their-own-viewability-standards/

Krajcovic, P. (2015). Strategies in Media Planning. *Communication Today*, *6*(2), 20–30.

Lawson-Borders, G. (2009). Integrating new media and old media: Seven observations of convergence as a strategy for best practices in media organizations. *International Journal on Media Management*, *5*(2), 91–99. doi:10.1080/14241270309390023

Logan, R. K. (2010). *Understanding new media – Extending Marshall McLuhan*. New York: Peter Lang Publishing.

Lovett, M. J., & Staelin, R. (2016). The role of paid, earned and owned media in building entertaining brands: Reminding, informing and enhancing enjoyment. *Marketing Science*, *35*(1), 142–157. doi:10.1287/mksc.2015.0961

Mangles, C. (2017). *Is marketing ready for VR / AR in 2018?* Retrieved from https://www.smartinsights.com/digital-marketing-platforms/video-marketing/is-marketing-ready-for-vr-ar-in-2018/

Marshall, J. (2014). *WTF is third-party data?* Retrieved from https://digiday.com/media/what-is-third-party-data/

Moffett, T. (2014). *Just published: The Forrester Wave: Cross-Channel Attribution Providers*. Retrieved from https://go.forrester.com/blogs/14-11-07-just_published_the_forrester_wave_cross_channel_attribution_providers/

Mulhern, F. (2009). Integrated marketing communications: From media channels to digital connectivity. *Journal of Marketing Communications*, *15*(2-3), 85–101. doi:10.1080/13527260902757506

Pilotta, J. J., Schultz, D. E., Drenik, G., & Rist, P. (2004). Simultaneous media usage: A critical consumer orientation to media planning. *Journal of Consumer Behaviour*, *3*(3), 285–292. doi:10.1002/cb.141

Rowntree, L. (2017). *Is it worth brands pursuing 100% Viewability*. Retrieved from https://www.exchangewire.com/blog/2017/11/28/worth-brands-pursuing-100-viewability/

Schultz, D. E., Block, M. P., & Raman, K. (2009). Media synergy comes of age – Part 2. *Journal of Direct Data and Digital Marketing Practice*, *11*(2), 88–99. doi:10.1057/dddmp.2009.22

Schultz, D. E., Block, M. P., & Viswanathan, V. (2016). Consumer driven media planning and buying. *Journal of Marketing Communications*. Retrieved from http://www.tandfonline.com/action/showCitFormats?doi=10.1080/13527266.2016.1185833

Soberman, D. (2005). The complexity of media planning today. *Brand Management*, *12*(6), 420–429. doi:10.1057/palgrave.bm.2540237

Statista. (2017a). *Number of internet users worldwide from 2005 to 2007 (in millions)*. Retrieved from https://www.statista.com/statistics/273018/number-of-internet-users-worldwide/

Statista. (2017b). *Countries with the highest number of internet users as of June 2017 (in millions).* Retrieved from https://www.statista.com/statistics/262966/number-of-internet-users-in-selected-countries/

Stober, R. (2004). What media evolution is: A theoretical approach to the history of new media. *European Journal of Communication, 19*(4), 483–505. doi:10.1177/0267323104049461

Taylor, A. (2017). Size, quantity and management capabilities: How Google updates AdWords to increase revenue. *Journal of Digital & Social Media Marketing*, *5*(1), 18–27.

Van Bommel, E., Edelman, D., & Ungerman, K. (2014, June). Digitizing the consumer decision journey. *McKinsey Quarterly,* 1-8. Retrieved from http://kwu-alumni.org/moto/media/5558efe863bec.pdf

Chapter 10
Click to Brick:
Case Study of a Virtual Reality Company

Abhishek Gupta
GreyKernel Technologies India Pvt. Ltd., India

Abhishek Goyal
GreyKernel Technologies India Pvt. Ltd., India

ABSTRACT

In 2017, India witnessed a new technological revolution in new media marketing fueled by the ready availability of high speed data and the emergence of a new generation of advance visualization solutions like virtual reality and augmented reality. Brands today are now focusing on distinguishing themselves from their competitors by redefining the customer experience and engaging them into their brand story. Myntra conceived the idea of creating its own brand of clothing for the travelers called Roadster focused over the needs of new generation of tech-savvy millennial customers. After the initial success of Roadster, it decided to bring Roadster closer to the customers in the form of brick and mortar showroom, opening its first ever store in Bangalore with a revolutionary virtual reality-based gamification experience, Highway 360, for experiential personalized shopping.

INTRODUCTION

In 2017, India is witnessing a new technological revolution in new media marketing; fueled by the readily availability of high speed data and the emergence of new generation of advance visualization solutions like Virtual Reality & Augmented Reality.

DOI: 10.4018/978-1-5225-6064-7.ch010

E-commerce after maturing from the early wave of 2007 which was backed by discounts and cash-burn for customer acquisition, brands today are now focusing on distinguishing themselves from their competitors by redefining the customer experience and engaging them into their brand story.

Myntra, conceived the idea of creating its own brand of clothing for the travelers called "Roadster"; focused over the needs of new generation of tech savvy millennial customers. After the initial success of "Roadster", it decided to bring "Roadster" closer to their customers in the form of brick and mortar showroom; opening its first ever store in Bangalore with a revolutionary Virtual Reality based Gamification experience "Highway 360" for experiential personalized shopping. (Jain, 2017)

ORGANIZATION BACKGROUND

GreyKernel Technologies India Private Limited is India's leading Virtual Reality (VR) & Advance Visualization Company which is continuously re-inventing the experiential content space; disrupting the traditional way of consuming digital content and revolutionizing the new media marketing (Grey Kernal Technologies, 2017). It delivers upon its motto "*Inhabit Your Imagination*" and allows people to live their imagination.

VR teleports people to a world of imagination; a place within their dreams. It allows viewer to be in a story rather than viewing it from an angle thus making every VR experience a personalized experience.

It was incorporated in *2015* and since then it has been creating experiential content to a diverse global client base. Its content has been consumed by *20,000+ global users* with high net promoter score; motivating to continue creating more experiences. It helps its customer to create a lasting impression among their target audience by applying a right mix of state-of-the-art technology with definitive product statement; offering personalized solutions to its clients by designing value driven content and gamification of their brand story/problem statement.

In 2017, India is witnessing a technological revolution fueling the new age entrepreneurs and disrupting the conventional way of doing business. There has been a phenomenal push both from the government and the industry for moving towards digitalization. At the forefront of this revolution are the e-commerce start-ups which were introduced to the Indian Market in 2007 after the initial start-up bubble burst of 2001.

The Indian e-commerce industry has been on an upward growth trajectory and is expected to surpass the US to become the second largest e-commerce market in the world by 2034. India's e-commerce industry is expected to grow at a Compound Annual Growth Rate (CAGR) of 30 per cent to reach US$ 200 billion by 2026.

India's internet economy is expected to double from US$125 billion as of April 2017 to US$ 250 billion by 2020, majorly backed by e-commerce.

Much growth of the industry has been triggered by increasing internet and smartphone penetration. Internet penetration in India grew from just 4 per cent in 2007 to 34.08 per cent in 2016, registering a direct increase of 89 per cent in 2016 over 2007. The number of internet users in India is expected to increase at a CAGR of 15.6 per cent from 450 million as of June 2017 to 700 million by 2020.

The changing consumer lifestyles, internet penetration and better economic performance supported by the younger population base of India, have given a boost to the e-commerce business. More than half of the total 1.3 billion population of India falls under the 'below 25 years of age' bracket. Also, about 65.0 per cent of India's population, representing the working age group of 15 to 64 years, would aid the further growth of e-commerce, driven by their rising disposable income. Notably, discretionary spending in India is expected to jump to 70.0 per cent by 2025. Also, the growing inclination towards purchasing online is reflected in a trend for higher value online transactions. The Government of India's policies and regulatory frameworks such as 100 per cent foreign direct investment (FDI) in B2B e-commerce and 100 per cent FDI under automatic route under the market place model of B2C e-commerce are expected to further propel growth in the sectors.

Initially, all the e-commerce brands started with a 'niche' model on paper and started burning the valuation funds for customer acquisition. And very soon, the 'niche' got blurred and everyone was stepping onto other's toes to acquire the customer. The king customer was pampered like a queen for the eyeballs, customer life cycle, ARPU, etc. among many other parameters.

This sudden flush of e-commerce models into the Indian market with various discounts and inventive has brought some new challenges along with it (United Nations, 2007). The most notable challenge for the marketing people/department was to differentiate their brand from their competitors as every brand was selling at almost same discount price to almost same customer catering to almost same geographies using almost same logistics and almost same payment methods and CRM processes. With loyalty definition getting an overhaul, brands were merely following the traditional decision matrix of 'who has the highest relevant TG community'. Many e-com portals tried various methods to trump this trend, taking a leaf from 'The 7 P concept'. Some branded the packaging, while some boasted home trials before purchase and many such methods, which did help in some loyalty built-up, but nothing notable to establish a 'niche'.

One of the top E-commerce portals (Walia, 2018), Myntra, conceived the idea of creating its own brand of clothing and launching it on its own portal. They hired a team of professionals to create a portfolio, designs, layouts, models, shoots, etc. just like any other popular brand and created their own private label called "Roadster".

Product/Brand: Roadster
Concept/Theme: Wanderlust/Traveler's
SKUs: Casuals including Tees, Shirts, Denims, Jackets, Shoes, Watches etc.

Now, since Myntra controls the supply of merchandise, it also controls the discounts and creates product rivalry among price-sensitive customer base. The new brand quickly started moving up the charts of contribution to overall business. In one interview in March 2017, Mr. Anant Narayanan, the CEO of Myntra said "Our brand has witnessed phenomenal growth at over 80% YoY and is well on its way to achieving a run rate of 1000 crore by FY 19."

This strong statement was supported by the fact that "Roadster Life" contributed 8% of the total revenue of Myntra. With the success, came a pertinent problem, 'I need to be closer to the customer'. Hence, after much internal debate, an idea emerged of expanding from 'Click to Brick' and decided to launch its own retail store. The Retail industry came full circle with this decision as one of the e-commerce giant was embarking into brick-and-motor business.

The first store opened in a 4000 Sq. Ft. space in Bangalore. But along with this retail store, came a major branding issue. 'How Do I connect Myntra with Roadster retail store for my customers'. One of the major issues that the brands always encounter is to convey the brand sentiment to the customers as they wish. A product is always branded/marketed around a theme to appeal to the target audience but the connect needs to be delivered in the most effective to convey the right message.

Consumers today are empowered with an incredible amount of information, allowing them to thoroughly research their purchases before contacting a business. In fact, most people decide to buy before talking to a sales professional. This paradigm shift between buyers and sellers has forced businesses to change their approach to marketing and focus towards more engagement with the customers. The rise of the new media marketing is fueled by the demand for the personalization of the content. More than 2 billion people are active over social media and it forms an important part of one's marketing strategy.

The search for new media marketing solutions started and the objective is to get consumers to interact with the brand, engaging them in a way that increases awareness and correlates to sales. It helps in a number of ways:

- **Customer Data Collection:** New media helps companies to gather far more details about their target customers. By using sophisticated programs like customer relationship management systems, businesses can collect information about their best customers and use it to nurture long-term relationships while collecting data to target new customers;

- **Building Relationships:** Since most of the customers guide themselves through the sales process, companies need to establish a relationship with them before they are ready to buy. Since customers are always looking out to know more about brands, businesses use tools like social media to interact with people on a personal level, sharing information and experiences in a way that humanizes the brand thus establishing a relationship for a more personalized connection of a customer with a brand;
- **Know When to Sell:** With a generation that is always connected and active over social media, people are inundated with advertisements all day long. According to a study by a market research firm SJ Insights, an average person sees 5,000 ads or more every day, resulting in a certain amount of "ad blindness" among users browsing the Internet. Knowing when and how often to send out a sales message is a key component to new media marketing success.

Myntra, started with the conventional standard Audio Visual methods and over the course of experimentation with multiple other newer methods, selected current generation advance visualization and virtual reality solution by a Noida based Virtual Reality firm, GreyKernel.

The VR campaign story-board was developed by team GreyKernel (Abhishek and Pranshul) in collaboration with Myntra and named the solution as Highway360 (BW Online Bureau, 2017).

Virtual Reality (VR) is a computer technology that uses virtual reality headsets, sometimes in combination with physical spaces or multi-projected environments, to generate realistic images, sounds and other sensations that simulate a user's physical presence in a virtual or imaginary environment (Lanier, 2017). Depending upon the nature of experience/content, it could be classified into two types – Immersive and Immersive Plus Interactive.

Within the immersive experience, viewer is teleported to a virtual environment with total immersion; allowing a 360 degree first person view but with limited or no interaction in the virtual environment.

While within the immersive plus interactive experience, viewer can interact in the virtual world thus giving a sense of being totally teleported to that place.

Highway 360 is a gaze based Immersive VR Gamification Experience which is experienced via/by Samsung Gear VR. Every customer walking into the Myntra store is provided with an option to buy and experience the brand "Roadster" in Highway 360.

Highway 360 experience, takes a customers through a virtual road trip through dramatic locales; a video wall with a multi-touch interface that showcases details of Roadster products, provides international trends and communicates the brand story; a 'Selfie Corner' to indulge oneself; multi-touch screens all along the store which provide data on trendy looks and Roadster catalogue; a 'Scan & Go' purchase mechanism that allows shoppers to add their favorites to the shopping cart on the Myntra App; billing anywhere in the store without having to go to the cashier's desk, etc.

Highway 360 helps Myntra increase footfall of Roadster brand store by attracting millennials to try something cool and new, as it uses Virtual Reality based gamification. It established a new level a connect with the customers by redefining the retail experience and making it more personalized.

Ananth Narayanan, CEO of Myntra and Jabong said: "The launch of the first physical store for Roadster is a milestone for Myntra, wherein we are trying to create an unparalleled Roadster brand experience with the innovative use of in-store technology that will engage customers on a different level altogether. Omni-channel has been a buzzword so far; as a leading market player in the fashion, lifestyle and e-commerce business, we believe it is our duty to shape it. This store is an experiment in omni-channel; we will take the learnings from the store over the next 6-12 months to our brand partners."

Thus Myntra is actively working towards taking the customer experience to a whole new level by bringing-in more technological intervention into its way of doing business.

One of the most crucial element of the Highway 360 experience is the gamification. Gamification has emerged as the newest tool in the new media marketing and it has led to a new dimension of engagement with the customers.

Some of the applications/advantages of using gamification in the new media marketing.

A game appeals to a customer on three levels - personal, organizational and societal as it immerses them into its own story and allows them to behave in an independent manner. By integrating games into their brand experiences, it allows brands to know the demographics of gamers as it engages female and other people at home; affecting choice selection of a particular brand even though they not buying directly from the stores.

By developing a game on a brand's business lines and making it accessible to the masses, led to a mass awareness about the brand; connecting with their prospective customers and incentivizing them for playing again and again thus developing a level of connection with their customers and influence their buying pattern. They allow brands to engage its customers in their brand story and provide them with instant feedback regrading perception/adoption of a particular product.

For encouraging customers to play the game again & again; levels are built for posing a challenge and distorting the sense of time as customer subjective experience of time is altered depending upon the game play and the winning/loosing pattern.

Good gamification design seeks to understand and align an organization's objectives with a player's intrinsic motivation. Gifts are one of several types of mechanics used in games to motivate users as the activity in a game is intrinsically rewarding. While some games may utilize real-world gifts in the form of money, gift cards, etc., many games motivate players with virtual gifts; e.g., flowers, badges. Then, through the use of extrinsic rewards and intrinsically satisfying design, move the player through their journey of mastery. This journey requires elements such as desire, incentive, challenge, reward and feedback to create engagement. The essentials of gamified applications and websites is incentivization, where companies incentivize certain activities and then award credits and gifts for desired behaviors thus ensuring continuous dialogue with the customer/user.

Leaderboards is a means by which users can track their performance subjective to others. Leaderboards visually display where a user stands in regards to other users. They are implemented on sites to show which players have unlocked the most achievements. The desire to appear on the Leaderboards drives players to earn more achievements, in turn fueling deep engagement. From the organizational standpoint, games should contribute to an organization's goals; e.g., getting foot traffic into a brick-and-mortar store, demonstrating the personality of your brand and demonstrating your core values.

Designing a game aligning with the organizational goals of a company/brand, makes it a win-win for everyone involved.

A popular example of game mechanics is the profile completeness bar on LinkedIn. By seeing how much more complete the profile needs to be, many people are driven to take steps to 100% completion with the promise of being able to take advantage of LinkedIn's more advanced features thus incentivizing users for adding more information and coming back to LinkedIn again and again.

According to the gamification analytics, brands want to track things such as user participation, daily activities and users by achievement and levels which ultimately will convey upon the brands, whether and to what extent, gamification have impacted the consumer's relationship to its business in a positive way.

Brands market their strategies upon making community a valuable user experience where users will be proud to participate and as a result will be more inclined to value its rewards.

Now traditional companies are building loyalty for their websites using so-called gamification techniques. Tactics such as leaderboards, which encourage users to compete against one another for points, are becoming common across the Web. It panders to the new generation as gamified content gives millennials a form of interaction that they don't often see and it gives this new generation the instant interaction as they demand; giving them a feel as if they are in control of the whole process.

Gamification offers the same rewards and exposure as the conventional form of marketing but without the constant publishing. Based on the user's activity, users are able to unlock achievements, compete with friends, and share their progress over social media platforms which leads to continuous engagement of the user/consumer with the product and the brand.

Gamification also offers unique and endless promotional activities. Whether it's pairing with new products, highlighting old products, or encouraging purchases through discounts and sales, gamification has the potential to increase brand awareness and engagement. Many companies have experimented with point/reward systems to get more products off the shelves. And the strategy is pretty simple. Give customers points for every product they purchase and when they reach a certain amount of points reward them with cash to be used in the store thus increasing sales and ensuring the loyalty of the customer.

Modern Marketing is all about reaching for the roots more than ever before as it all goes back to the fact that the potential consumers want to hear from their friends and other consumers about one's brand and not from the brand itself.

Activating and channelizing the voices of the happy consumers is one of the best things that the brands can do but it's also one of the most difficult activity. Gamification in combination with working real people as influencers weave together in a perfect social strategy as it incorporates fun and an element of competition to a marketing strategy.

It also works with all brand fans and people who want to participate – not just the ones with a ton of followers as it makes an emotional connection with the audience and lead to a longer relationship as opposed to simple brand awareness.

This new technological revolution is bringing a disruption into each and every sector; breaking/reinventing their conventional method of operations. The retail sector is also riding on this new technological wave and undergoing a drastic change in its way of functioning.

Merchants are no longer the driving force for retailers. This is a major change that will be hard to swallow. In the past merchants interacted with customers. They talked to them as a market. Now these same customers are demanding products and services that match their specific needs. In other words, the customer is now in charge.

Myntra is not the first to offer such a brand experience. Van Heusen Style Studio, which unveiled its first digitally immersive store 15 months ago, not far away from the Roadster store, uses technology to address every shopper's pain point of finding the appropriate fit, size and style best suited to his/her personality. A 'Fit Scanner' measures customer in 45 seconds to identify the right fit; a 'Style Bar' digital display helps match shopper's personality to different looks; a 42 inch display offers 'Look of the Day', etc.

In today's world where the physical retail doesn't give customer the personal touch that a one-to-one customized page on your favorite portal can, while buying online still puts customer through the hassle of returns and size mismatches, where the retail industry is divided into Brick-and-mortar and the E-commerce, the future seems to be different with a unified model of brick-and-mortar and e-commerce.

With the advent of technological intervention in the retail industry, the Myntra retail stores provides the glimpses of the future of the retail where unlike today's world, in which retail is split into two distinct categories, there will be a merger of both the categories to give customers a perfect shopping experience incorporating pros of both the brick-and-mortar and e-commerce.

We are living in the age of aggregators where disruption is the word for the innovation. The new smarter tech-savvy consumer looks for value into each and every activity irrespective of the scale. Thus the new age advance visualization solutions along with gamification opens a new door of possibilities for new media marketing of 2017 in which consumer could be completely immersed into brand's story and have a highly personalized experience.

REFERENCES

BW Online Bureau. (2017, March). *Myntra's Lifestyle Brand Roadster's Retail Store Launched in Bengaluru.* Retrieved Dec 4, 2017, from BW Disrupt: http://bwdisrupt.businessworld.in/article/Myntra-s-Lifestyle-Brand-Roadster-s-Retail-Store-Launched-in-Bengaluru/17-03-2017-114509/

Grey Kernal Technologies. (2017, Dec 25). Retrieved from Zauba Corporation: https://www.zaubacorp.com/company/GREYKERNEL-TECHNOLOGIES-INDIA-PRIVATE-LIMITED/U72300UP2015PTC068599

Jain, V. (2017, May 16). *Myntra opens first retail store for Roadster brand in Bengaluru*. Retrieved Dec 12, 2017, from Economic Times: https://retail.economictimes.indiatimes.com/news/e-commerce/e-tailing/myntra-opens-first-retail-store-for-roadster-brand-in-bengaluru/57671838

Lanier, J. (2017). *Dawn of the New Everything: Encounters with Reality and Virtual Reality*. New York: Henry Holt & Company.

United Nations. (2007, August 31). *Growth of E-Business Worldwide*. Retrieved from The American Academy of Project Management: http://www.aapm.info/article4ef9.html?id=12

Walia, T. (2018, Feb 21). *Top 10 E-Commerce Companies in 2018 India*. Retrieved Mar 3, 2018, from Business2Business: http://www.business2business.co.in/article/1345/title/top-10-e-commerce-companies-in-2018-india

Chapter 11
Social Media as a Marketing Tool

Rajeshwari Krishnamurthy
Great Lakes Institute of Management, India

ABSTRACT

This chapter talks about how social media can be used as a marketing tool. Right from describing the various forms of social media, it touches upon the different methods by which social media are engaged with by a marketer. The tasks of creating awareness, generating interest, encouraging action, resulting in purchase, and doing brand advocacy are all covered. There is also a section on how the marketer can evaluate the effectiveness of these social media options both in comparison with traditional media as well as in isolation.

CHAPTER OBJECTIVES

This chapter looks at using social media in the context of it being a marketing technique. In the process, the advantages and disadvantages of this medium versus the traditional media has been discussed. Customer engagement tools for measuring effectiveness (including Return on Investment) along with evaluation methodologies for social media have been highlighted. There is a detailed example of a social medium- mobile application- its uses and challenges. Finally the chapter closes with outlining what maybe the barriers for social media adoption by organizations.

DOI: 10.4018/978-1-5225-6064-7.ch011

INTRODUCTION

Social media is used to refer to those media that use web based and mobile technology to use communication into an interactive dialogue. (Dewing, 2012) Also called 'consumer generated media' the objective here is to combine technology in a social forum to make it user friendly for the public. The biggest advantage here is to offer a two way interactive medium unlike the traditional media which is one way.

The exponential growth of social media in the last few years is indisputable. The medium has altered the way in which people communicate with one another and even do business with each other. Its true value is still being explored and it is growing by leaps and bounds. The mainstream way of doing marketing is undergoing a discontinuous change thanks to this social medium.

The above figure describes the various aspects of social media. Starting from 'Know your customer'- which talks about understanding who is your target profile, moving onto Setting a target for the social media such as reaching so many customers or call to action, then executing a plan that takes into account different platforms and formats and finally monitoring if the results are as per expectations, 'social media' has come a long way.

Compared to this, traditional medium like television or print no longer have the same impact. For decades marketers have been struggling to increase the 'interactivity' factor in communication with the audience i.e. conventional media like Television or Radio talk to consumers in a single direction without taking inputs from them or seeking to even understand if there is adequate comprehension from the other

Figure 1. Social media aspects
Source: (Wasserman, n.d.)

side so that the message can be modified real time. In most cases, feedback used to come in much later that any meaningful change was almost impossible before the campaign finishes. There are also other issues like fixed costs of production that is looming large in traditional medium and takes away a significant portion of the total ad budget. Airing costs in these media is also becoming prohibitive – so much so that companies are looking for cheaper alternatives.

Consumer's comfort with internet and digital medium has also contributed to the growing popularity of the social medium. The broadband penetration in the country has been increasing, thanks to the Government initiatives as well some easy to use hardware that is making this transition easier. From business point of view also, this trend is catching up. Though the shift to making it the solo medium of marketing has not taken place, the spends in this medium is clearly on the rise.

Of course adoption of social media is not easy. There are barriers to be overcome on many fronts. Organizationally, technologically, financially and so on and so forth. There is a lot of learning to do and that is not easy. Some functions take to it more easily than others. And some others have been traditionally more familiar with social media in certain forms. For example, Human Resources department has been using on line tools for personnel selection, psychometric testing etc. But using social media for reaching out to consumers and persuading them to buy products services is a challenge that many companies are struggling with.

SOCIAL MEDIA AS A MARKETING PLATFORM

According to Web 2.0, social media is a pool of information which is designed to be interactive. Social media marketing is an activity where marketing and promotions takes place through various social media platforms. Usually a marketing plan comprise of both traditional and new media.

As is evident from the above Figure 2, social media is becoming the inner core of the Marketing function. Moving onto Digital and then onto online, later to Marketing as a whole, this media has come a long way in making its presence felt. Consumers always lead the way in which marketers have to communicate. The last five years have witnessed discontinuous changes in which media is consumed and technology devices used by consumers. Almost every aspect of the daily life has got disrupted, thanks to technology intervention. Mobile phones, television, air conditioners, laptops- all of them. Which necessarily means that companies need to adopt these in order to reach out to end users. This has an effect in the creative execution, media planning, acquiring media liasioning skills etc. One of the key decisions that advertising industry agency if grappling today is whether they need

Figure 2. Social media as a marketing tool (Nairuthram, 2016)

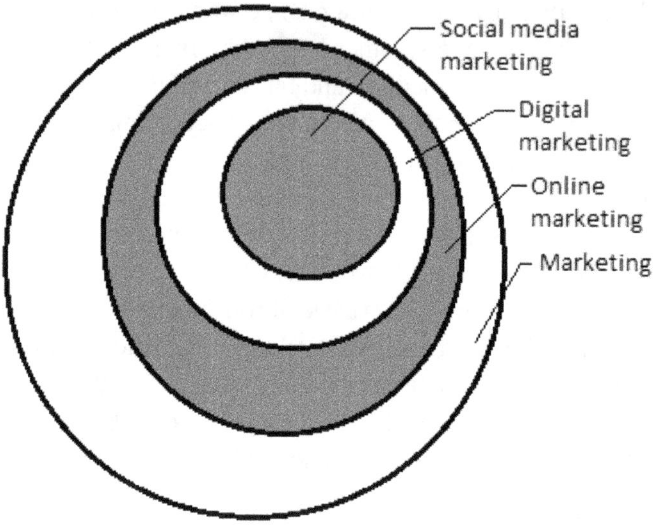

to branch out to become a specialist social media outfit to whether to continue to do the set of traditional agency tasks that they are used to. Always a tough choice.

Social media is an open system that enables two way interaction with consumers and works on building ongoing brand-consumer relationships, unlike in traditional advertising which helps to promote sales.

Some statistics regarding social media importance to business (Nairuthram, 2016):

- There are more than 1.7 billion active Facebook users around the globe!
- Instagram (owned by Facebook) boasts half a billion users;
- Twitter acknowledges one-third of a billion – well, 317 million;
- WeChat has 806 million users.

Fundamentally, social media works because human beings are social creatures who would like to communicate and have social conversations. Social media provides a platform by facilitating discussions and forums for various cause and also helps in collecting reviews and feedbacks on various goods and services. It can also be stated as a platform to share information and develop content which can be viewed by all users. SMM for business helps to increase customer engagement and reach. A seller can track the behavior of potential customers by getting their feedback.

Figure 3. Forms of social media (Davis, 2009)

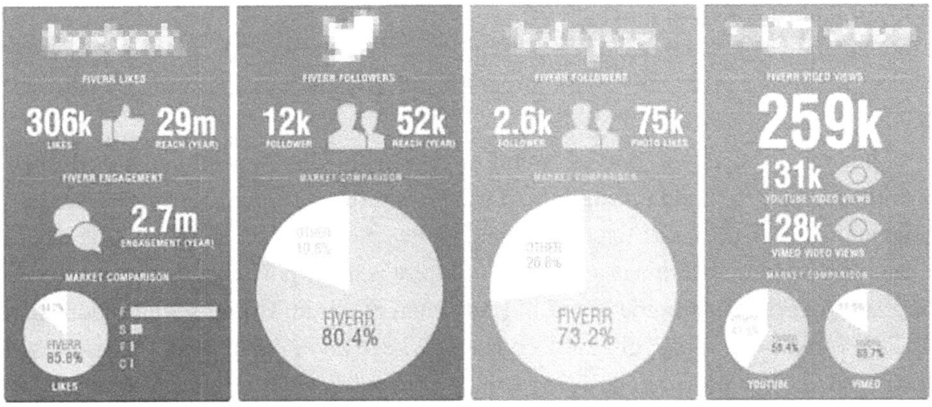

ADVANTAGES AND DISADVANTAGES OVER TRADITIONAL MEDIA

A marketing campaign usually consists of both traditional and social media, which is a part of nontraditional media. Every part of the campaign should be carefully designed to capture as much audience as possible.

The above figure shows comparative aspects between traditional medium and social medium.

First is the point on target audience. Traditional media, though it has well defined target audience, does not customize its messages across the various segments. This

Figure 4. Pros and Cons of social media (Davis, 2009)

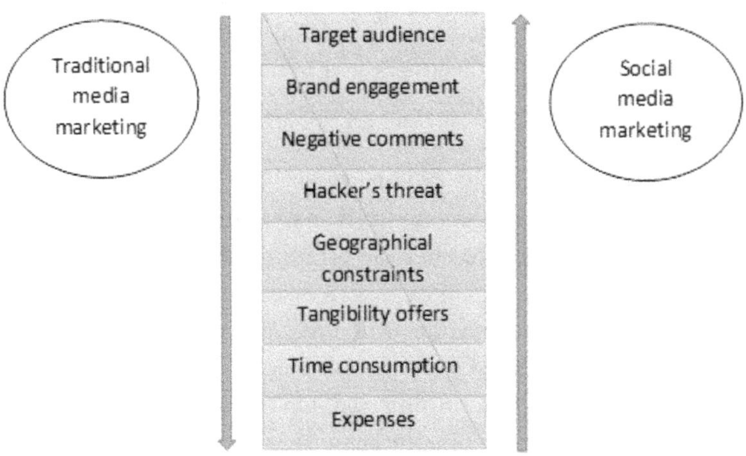

results in a lot of spillage or wastage. Potential customers not intended for this receive communication and in worst cases, this may end up creating displeasure among them. Whereas, social media targets customers in a personal manner and hence has higher relatability with target group. Thus this medium scores better on this aspect of target audience.

The second aspect is that of brand engagement. The capacities of both these media to engage a brand through these media is different. Traditional medium uses television, radio, print etc. to create brand values or personality. Engaging is mostly a one way process and this is a limitation. There is no opportunity for consumers to express their opinion on the brand in traditional medium. But in social media such as Facebook, twitter, blogging etc. consumers have an interactive relationship with the brand. This is useful in building a more robust brand and ends up being a more effective form of brand engagement.

Thirdly, social media allows consumers to own the brand and in the process permits negative comments. This shows the confidence of organizations. By allowing a dialogue, a sense of ownership of the brand among the consumers increases. Whereas in traditional media, there is no window for consumers to allow negative comments. While the positive side of this is that fact that the brand image does not get tarnished publicly, the down side is that the organizations never get to really understand what the consumers think of their brands (Poirier, 2013).

Social media suffers from Hacker's threat. I.e. it has the potential of its image getting modified by hackers as it is in open format. This is a serious issue. But in traditional medium, there is no such problem. The hardware is sealed and delivered tamper proof. This enables far better control of the message being disseminated by traditional media.

The next point is about geographical constraints. This is a big differentiator that results in high amount of cost efficiencies for social media. Due to the globally pervasive nature of internet, social media is able to reach out to audiences worldwide. Compared to this, traditional media has insulated reach. I.e. whether television or radio or print is able to reach consumers within defined geographical boundaries. Given this, the cost per reach of this traditional medium is far higher than social media that covers a much wider canvas.

Tangibility offers refers to the product or service offerings made available by the different media. Social media due to its inherent nature, carries along with it the ability to allow consumers to alter the offerings. Whereas traditional media is unable to do that.

Time consumption for both media is different. The average time of viewing across both these media are different. Given the costs constraints, the traditional format has fixed shorter time slots for consumption. On the other hand, social media has longer duration of consumption of communication.

The last point on expenses has been touched upon before. In terms of both fixed costs of production and media airing costs, social media scores higher over traditional media. To sum up, social media is increasingly becoming a medium of choice for many marketers due to the above list of benefits.

CUSTOMER ENGAGEMENT TOOLS

Customer engagement refers to the ability of a certain medium to be able to engage the customer across various parameters (Klaassen, 2009).

These could range from attracting attention, talk to them captivity, persuade them about a certain offering, nudge them towards a purchase decision etc. The outcome of this customer engagement aspect can therefore be measured in those terms such as conversion rates, amount of traffic etc. Some of these are shown in below Figure 5.

Various tools used by Social Media Marketing are media sharing sites, blogs/ microblogs, social bookmarking sites, virtual/online communities, SNSs, virtual worlds etc.

To do the above, identifying prospective customers is the starting point. Figure 5 above depicts that. Customer engagement is the core of marketing but working on it does not make any sense when we do not have the right customers to follow. So our first priority should be to find our target audience and then plan our activities according to their behavior and interest (By 2016 Why 70% of Small Businesses Will Depend On Social Media Tool To Reach New Customers, 2015).

Figure 5. Customer engagement
Source: (Klaassen, 2009)

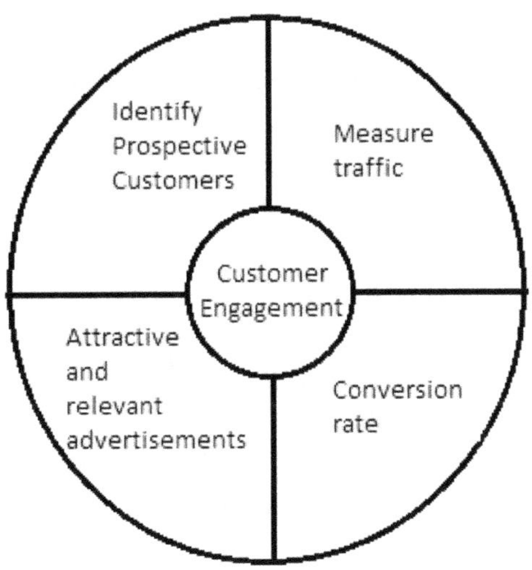

Our task gets easier when we have these customers in our network. Else we have to monitor when they are onboard. To add more value to this network, we should share relevant content and analyze their response. If the response is not favorable, then we need to look for other ways in which we could engage and convert them to prospective customers.

There should be consistent engagement of customers in social media other than posting links and creating advertisements (Media Buying, 2009). Various tools can be used to measure the traffic and also the behavior of customers. Engagement with target audience completely depends on the time spent for interaction. We spend lot of our productive time in answering the queries and getting involved in discussions to make them understand the effectiveness of our product.

Having invested considerable amount of time and monetary requirements, it is obvious that we will measure the returns. Is there any one step solution to measure ROI? To answer this, we need to define our social media goals clearly and also measure them. In this phase, it is easier to know the conversion rate of our customers. If the rate is not as expected, then we can work on changing the current activities and also adding other effective measures to drive traffic and increase the conversion rate.

SETTING GOALS IN SOCIAL MEDIA

Goals in social media can be based on web traffic, customer loyalty, conversion rate etc. Usually, a SMART (Specific Measurable Achievable Realistic Timely) technique is used to set goals in social media. Smaller measurable components are to be arrived at such as - Number of visits, clicks and shares, comments etc.-depending on which goal one is chasing.

The above figure shows the various parameters on measuring social media goals.

At a very basic level, creating brand awareness can be a measure. Just launching a campaign on Facebook or twitter helps do this. Using strong influencers or networks is another way to create brand awareness. This is also done through viral marketing when a particular communication goes viral due to the storytellers in the group. Engagement is yet another way to look at brand awareness since unqualified awareness does not lead to brand recall or equity building but engagement does. Hence awareness has to view in its ability to engage the consumers through its brand communication.

Once this engagement is successful, it may result in 'lead' generation through action/ conversion. If there is a specific call to action by the social medium used, by way of clicks or visit to website etc., then that is measures at this stage. It is classified as potential customer or a prospect or a lead. Once this lead is converted

Figure 6. Goals of social media (Bosomworth & Chaffey, 2012)

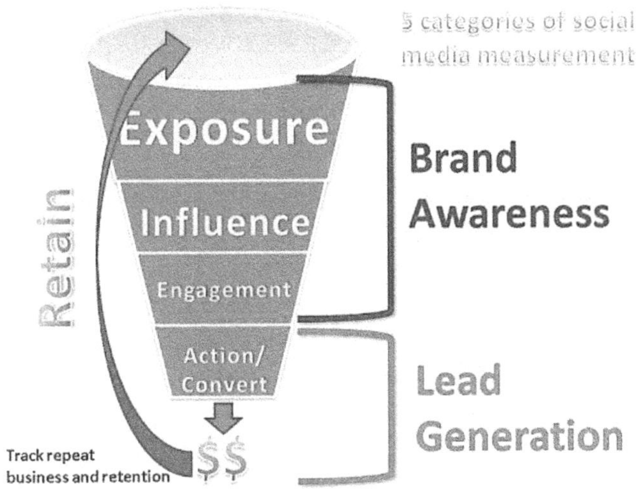

successfully, he/she becomes the customer. Then the organization takes all efforts to 'retain' the customer through various means.

Traditional marketing tools may be successful in acquiring leads but are not cost effective as compared to Social media. Campaigns in Social media are designed with lot of creativity to attract the audience. Whereas in traditional media there are various limitations such as geographical constraints, expense etc. which hinders the overall performance of the campaign and may not reach most of the audience.

MEASURING RETURN ON INVESTMENT ON SOCIAL MEDIA

There are challenges in measuring social media effectiveness. Following are a few of them expressed by organizations- inability to correlate them with business outcomes, insufficient analytics or expertise, inadequate tools for measurement and heavily unreliable data.

However, it is not impossible to measure the ROI of social media. It is more important to identify the RIGHT metrics that will make this possible. Fundamentally, it is critical to understand how much money is going into social media and what is the return one is getting in terms of reach or other media aspects. For most companies, the former is easy but the latter is where organizations get jittery. Specifically, efforts need to go in which part contributes to what part of return on investment for the social media campaign. This will also allow you to understand where to improve your inputs so that the output is more efficient.

If a person ran Google AdWords campaigns and never checked how much they were paying per click, what kind of click-through-rate would they be getting or whether any of the people who clicked on the ads were actually converting, it would be a completely wasted investment. Hence it is essential to measure your ROI.

There are three steps in this:

1. Defining social media goals that require some kind of behavioral change from the point of view of the user and hence are important to be tracked. Metrics like social shares and followers are nice to track too, but they shouldn't be the main goals;
2. The second aspect is that of linking goals to specific campaigns. Each campaign has a specific objective and that has to be taken into account. Unless this context is made clear, marketers can come to wrong conclusions regarding the same;
3. Some tools that help in tracking visits from sites are Google urn builder and this information will be included in Google analytics reporting.

TRACKING THE GOALS

It is important to track the goals that one has set. This is critical and needs understanding of how to go about choosing the tools needed for various purposes. An illustration for the same has been given discussed below.

If one don't have any goals set up, there would be a prompt to create one.

Figure 8 shows a screenshot that describes the procedure to set up a goal that has been defined earlier. For instance, if the goal was to get newsletter signups, one will have to setup a special thank you page on the site for after someone subscribes. But if the goal is to increase time on site for Twitter users by say X%, or to get traffic from Facebook to watch a video on a landing page, one could choose the appropriate goal type. In the given example, the goal can be set as a destination page.

For this part, one needs to enter the actual destination URL that will trigger a conversion. One needs to ensure that this page is not indexed in Google, so that the only way for someone to land on it is by going through the email signup process.

It is essential now to attach a value to each conversation. The process of adding value to a conversation can be described as below:

1. **Lifetime Value x Conversion Rate:** Calculate the lifetime value of a customer, and multiply that by your conversion rate (average number of email subscribers who become customers) to find out what the potential value of each visit is;

Figure 7.
Source: How to Get Google to Instantly Index Your New Website, 2015

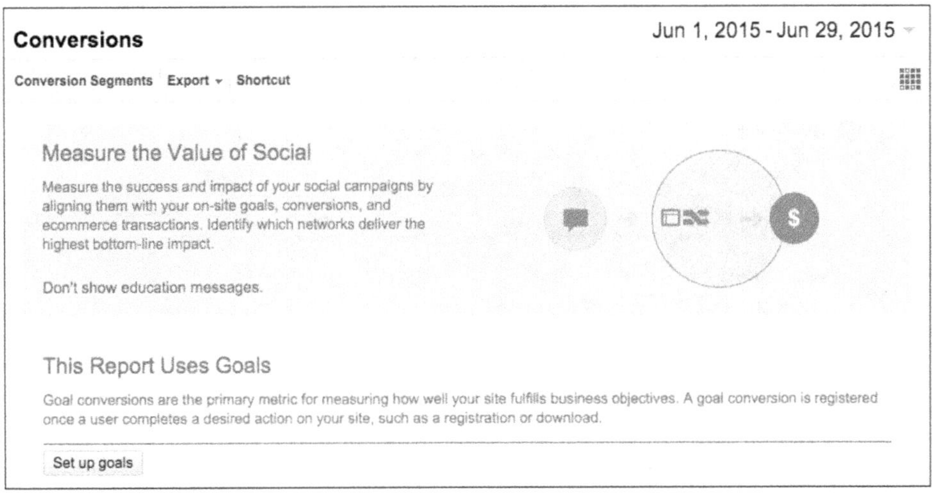

Figure 8.
Source: How to Get Google to Instantly Index Your New Website, 2015

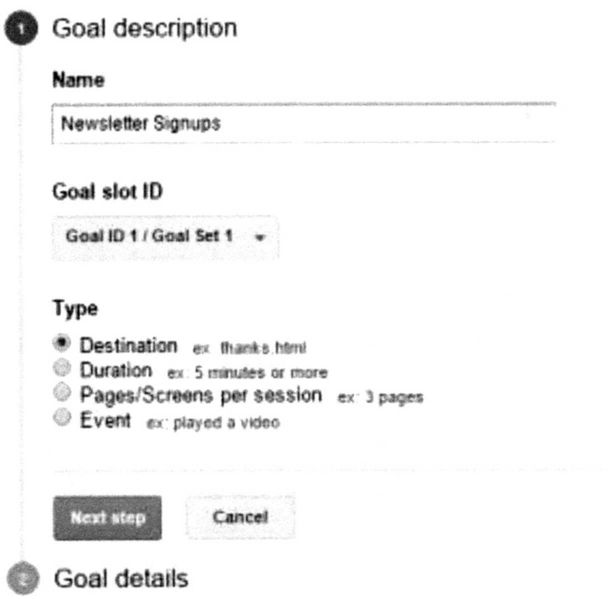

Figure 9. Screenshot depicting goal description
Source: Nizan, 2016

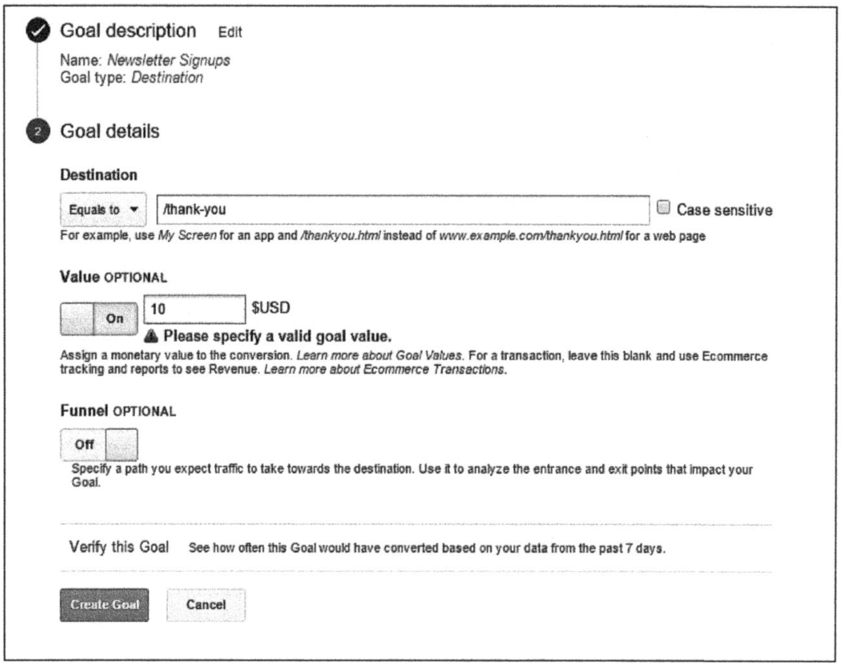

2. **Average Sale:** If the goal of your campaign is to try to get sales, then you'll want to calculate your average sale amount and set that as the value. In this case, your destination page would have to be the page that shows up after a customer completes a purchase.

At the end one would be able to see the conversions and the actual amount earned from those conversions. Figure 6 shows a brief excerpt of the same.

3. **Track Your Social Media Expenses:** In order to figure out whether you're getting a positive or negative ROI for social media campaigns, you'll also have to measure how much you're spending. Here's what should be included in that number:
   a. **Man-hours:** Your time is valuable. Whether you're a solo-preneur, or you have a social media team, add up the man-hours that go into a specific social media marketing campaign over a specified period of time. Don't just use an employee's annual salary, because they're more than likely going to be working on several projects throughout the year. Measure this investment per-campaign;

Figure 10. Screenshot showing status of goals in various social media tools
Source: Nizan, 2016

Social Network	Conversions	Conversion Value
	% of Total: 1.49% ( )	$ % of Total: 1.08% ($)
1. Twitter		
2. Facebook		
3. LinkedIn		

b. **Content:** Did you get a landing page written by a professional copywriter? Or maybe you outsourced status updates. These costs are easy to overlook, but they count.
c. **Social media tools:** Using Facebook and Twitter is free, but if you're using a tool like Sprout Social or other social media management software, you need to add those costs in. Just like with the man-hours, you should calculate this on a per-campaign basis. So if your campaign lasts for one month, only add in the cost of a month of the software, not an entire year;
d. **Ad costs:** If you're running a Promoted Tweet, Facebook Ad or boosting a Facebook post, add in that cost as well.

Once you have your expenses calculated, you'll be able to calculate your social media ROI for every campaign with this simple formula:

(Earnings – Costs) x 100 / Costs

Earnings is based on the value you calculated in the previous section. And your costs are the items listed above (man-hours, content, etc.)

You can figure out the specific ROI for each social network by segmenting your earnings and costs per social channel, and using that same formula above. After looking at the numbers, you'll be able to decide which social platforms are doing the best for your company, and focus in on those. For any social networks or campaigns that are bringing in a negative ROI, you can either try to adjust by spending less, or by making your campaigns more effective.

NON-QUANTITATIVE BENEFITS OF SOCIAL MEDIA

There are innumerable benefits of social media other than just the numbers. Word of mouth or referrals is one such. Getting influenced by peer group on a brand that they just used is a powerful way of marketing a brand. And social media enables that because of the interactive nature.

So while these types of returns are difficult to track, it's important to keep them in mind when you're going over the ROI of social media campaigns. Numbers don't always convey the full picture on what is happening to a brand campaign. Brand building is a key part of social media objective and it has to be viewed in that light.

Social Media Adoption

In recent times, social media spends have gone up across organizations. Of course, the rate of adoption among corporates have not been proportionate to the promise that the medium holds. There are some barriers that need to be unshackled before the medium moves towards it true potential. Let us see some barriers that inhibit the adoption in a corporate setup.

First the unfamiliarity of the medium by Senior Management. Many top management personnel have grown up with traditional medium like television, radio and print. They find it difficult to learn a new medium at a later age. Some of them even consider this' a waste of time'! They'd rather delegate this to the youth in the organizations.

But this approach does more harm than good. Social media has a powerful double edge implication of Ownership versus control. i.e. the more and more brands throw open brand communications and campaigns to the public, making them interactive, shareable and inviting comments, the higher the risk of the management losing control over the brand. A classic example of this would be the social media campaign that the brand Dove undertook. Titled 'real beauty', it encouraged consumers to upload pictures of themselves in candid forms, without make up, making them accept themselves the way they were. In contrast to the huge public admiration of svelte figurines and slim looks, this Dove campaign celebrated the 'inner beauty' in women. The campaign was a smash hit, rapidly increasing market shares over 25% in a few months and the brand imagery scores climbing at a healthy rate. The organization in this case, was willing to give ownership to the consumers and reaped the benefits generously.

The point is this. Social media is risky. But by not embracing it, organizations run a different risk of alienating or not participating in the potential word of mouth opportunity for their brands. Whether the companies have a social media strategy or not, consumers will continue to write/opine about various brands. Hence it is advisable for the senior management to take active interest and immerse themselves to make this happen.

This can take place broadly in two ways- through personal learnings or organizational learnings. The first one recommends that top management starts doing one of the following- blogging, begin social networks, be on twitter/ Facebook themselves, upload/watch YouTube videos etc. All these will make them hands on with social media and make them understand the fine differences between that and traditional media.

The second approach-namely organizational learning- is even more important. Many examples come to mind. Unilever makes its senior management interact/ meet with the top echelons of Facebook/Google/Twitter for some regular periods- to exchanges notes on technology and its possibilities. They also have a reverse mentoring process- wherein the top management is mentored on social media by the younger employees for several weeks. And finally, there is also a 'swapping' arrangement- where employees spend a couple of weeks in the social media organizations and vice versa. In fact one such initiative has resulted in an online campaign for the detergent brand Tide-which went digital and garnered some good reviews for the brand.

The other barrier that impedes social media adoption is the difficulty of efficacy measurement. While there are GRPs, Readership and listenership numbers available for traditional media, social media still focusses on engagement through eyeballs, click throughs etc. that don't reflect spend efficiencies holistically (Stern, 2010). And this becomes a deterrent for organizations.

Overall it can be said that organizations should use Social media not to impress people but to impact people. And work along with it to create great brands.

Purchase Decision Journey

A recent article in New York Times talked about how Amazon has become 'The Shelf Space' for shopping for consumers (Maheshwari, 2017). So much so, that if your product is not present on Amazon, then it is largely invisible to consumers. This radical departure in shopping behavior is reflective of how social media and internet are shaping marketer's strategies across brands.

Increasingly, more than three or four media are used by companies in order to lure customers. And this was referred to as 'Integrated Marketing Communications'. The question that was pertinent was 'how do I therefore allocate monies across the various media". But now the answer to that seems to be found in deciphering what is called the 'Purchase decision journey' of consumers.

Consumers typically go through a series of steps before finalizing to buy a brand. This is referred to as the Purchase decision journey that he/she undertakes (Iblasi, Bader, & Al-Qreini, 2016). Marketers would do well to map this for individual categories and products and this will dictate which medium will be suitable to perform what task. The steps are –Consideration to buy, Evaluating alternatives, decision to buy, forming relationship with the brand and finally becoming an advocate for the brand.

Let us begin with the first one- Consideration to buy. This is the first information seeking step-hence brands will do well to be present through the SEOs. In the Amazon example, it is essential to list your products on the portals to make it visible to consumers. And we need to follow the path that consumers do in order to make that happen. In some categories such as paints, it may still be the dealer network that will proceed information so there is a need to communicate to that network.

The second step is that of evaluating alternatives. This is where product reviews and feedback come in. Given the opinion that gets rapidly formed on social media for brands, companies should have a proactive blog or reviewer team that will engineer this. Amazon reviewers needs to be sensitized about the products and maybe even given a free sample to test them. And companies need to understand competitors' offering very well if they're to give a comparison of that to prospects at this stage.

The third stage is that of buying. This is where transaction ease, price and after sales service factors- all come in. How can social media be helpful here? The website of the company or the products needs to have easy navigation and on-line purchase option. Also there needs to be information on availability in that site. The payment gateways are to be geared such that they facilitate the most common banks' net banking or credit/debit cards. After sales service in terms of warranty or guarantees – need to be built into the product sale visibility. It is also at this stage that one needs emotional gratification for purchasing the brand and hence lean media such an s YouTube advertising will go a a long way in ensuring this. According to survey in the USA, advertising on lean media results in more effective return on investment for any campaign as it is better targeted and the consumers who are watching the shows are more involved unlike watching television where there tends to be more interruption.

The fourth stage of relationship building has been made easy by internet. Again real time feedback, instant consumer complaint handling or changing communication messages if not working- all these help build better messages. Also personal customization goes a long way.

Finally making customers the advocates for the brand. If the first steps are done well among set of consumers very well, the last one falls in place. Word of mouth or viral marketing is the most powerful tool for conversion. Social media through its transparency makes this more convenient.

Increasingly therefore the marketers are allocating monies across how many customers are to be addressed across which stage of the purchase decision journey instead of how much monies are given across various steps.

Social Media and Mobile Applications

One of the biggest impacted area through social media is the mobile application. Apps (aka applications on mobile) have redefined commerce. Since the consumer has become more mobile savvy, companies are scrounging to recruit personnel who are comfortable in this space and are constantly ready to learn and innovate.

The segment that has witnessed radical departure in their job description are the product managers and the marketers. They are learning how to build brands, create marketing campaigns and measure them- all through the usage of mobile applications.

Whether your company is digitally driven or not is irrelevant. Regardless, a product manager will either get busy integrating the front end of product development through apps or the customer transaction step-i.e. sale closure- through apps. Other processes like testing, obtaining customer feedback, tracking customer satisfaction- can also be woven through apps.

All these end up making Apps not just as a tool but a channel for growth itself. It needs to serve as a platform for communication, transactions, time management, ecommerce, etc.

Some things, therefore all product managers need to learn are:

- Doing consumer behavioral research differently;
- Gone are the days when market research was a reactive response from organizations to understand consumer needs. Now the information needs to be real time and interactive. And mobile apps are just the right tool to enable that. This means that the research process of training of researchers, designing questions with simplicity- etc. all need to undergo a change;
- Cross functional effort on product design;

Table 1. Categories of social media

Communication	Collaboration
Blogs-Blogger, Blogspot,Vox	Central desktop
Aggregators-Twine,Netvibes	Social news
Diaspora-Facebook,Hi5, Linkedin	Wikimedia
Microblogs-Twitter	Document Management

Source (Marketing Stack, n.d.)

- Due to the nature of inputs from various stakeholders (customers, vendors, trade, salesforce, R and D), the speedy response needs to get translated into product designs that reflect that superior and holistic understanding. Is your product manager capable of that?
- Aesthetics as important as content.

Today the end user wants it all- form and function, ease and accuracy, instant gratification as well as long term reliability. This means that every interface with the consumer is an opportunity for brand building. The company cannot divorce the role of user interface either through a website or a Facebook page with that of a mobile app that performs a specific function. That puts pressure on the product manager to be familiar with all aspects of social media, as there is very high overlap between users of one medium and others, unlike traditional medium, where apart from the TV viewing, there was not much duplication in reach across other media.

- Evaluating media with new metrics.

The above point on social media savviness means that the product manager should know newer ways of evaluating mobile app effectiveness. What worked yesterday may not be relevant today. Can he look at rapidity of app downloads, time taken for full app navigation, volume of app based transactions, retention of apps by customers etc. as the defining measures for the mobile app performance? These will have to be stitched into his/her media plan evaluation.

These are some ways how a product managers' role is changing. Of course technically there are a lot of challenges that he needs to cope with- starting from synching with the operating system of the mobile to creating an UI for customer engagement and not treat it like a desk top.

The M-Payment

Paying through mobile- 'M Commerce' as it is popularly called, has been growing by leaps and bounds. There are more than 4 billion individuals today, using a mobile phone (Aguilar, n.d.). The mobile payments in the US alone have gone from 14% in 2014 to 39% in 2016 and is expected to reach 70% in 2017-18.All these are making the mobile payments industry and startups in this area transform to meet the growth needs.

While there are many kinds of mobile payments ranging from internet browser led (directing to a shopping cart and then receipts), PIN led (contactless technologies) and mobile wallets (storage of your payment information), it is erroneous to think that the mobile payment transactions will be limited to smartphones or tablets.

In these cases, the technology of Bluetooth plays an active part. The Bluetooth Low Energy (BLE) transfer takes place on either the consumer or merchant's device where data is stored in a mobile payment account. Example PayPal, Apple Pay, Android Pay and Samsung Pay. Here the startups would begin with a text message service, then mobile apps and finally contactless payment systems. Google is also toying with facial recognition to confirm an individual's identity.

The other majors in the customer value chain- namely the banks- such as JPMorgan Chase & Co., Bank of America Corp., Wells Fargo & Co. and U.S. Bancorp, have a created a joint venture called clear change that allows customers to transfer funds instantly to another bank account through their phones. Retailers like Wal-Mart Stores Inc. are rolling out their own products to fuel mobile payments, and also providing additional services like location and customer coupon deals.

Social media and messaging apps have also jumped into the fray. Soon through FB and Whatsapp you will be able to make payments. So these organizations will become all in one- news, entertainment and commerce- formidable giants to deal with. They will also make targeted communication to clients for promotional offers etc. much more effective.

All these will have implications in the Regulations front. This should ensure transparency and standardization of payment mechanisms in the future across the world. The trends indicate that by 2020, 90 percent of smartphone users will have made a mobile payment.

The Marketer needs to learn many things as far as the above trends go. Firstly, the buyer behavior which is an important component of any consumer study is radically shifting. So understanding these patterns across industries is a must. Secondly, brand loyalty is going to move hand in hand with mobile savviness and technology adoption for consumers. This means that brands that are not digital today have no choice but to be so in times to come, if they are to retain their customers. Also a new segment called the 'techno literate' is fast emerging as a basis on which consumers need to be targeted, regardless of other segmentation criteria of age, gender, location etc. Finally, collaboration with stakeholders is expected to reach a new high i.e. to say that to evaluate tie ups with banks on the one hand and social media on the other, as a part of the brand sales and distribution strategy is becoming a need of the hour. Accordingly competencies will need to be drawn up for the marketing team.

CONCLUSION

New age media is synonymous with social media. This is a fast growing medium and has benefited through consumer habit change and their need for instant gratifications (Rajeshwari, n.d.). The audience is getting hooked to scoail media across age, gender, geographies. Social media is tapping on the most basic insitinct of a human being which is of being social and connected. This connectivity is now a boon for the marketers as it helps in increasing the reach of the communication as well as products. It has only made it easier to identify reference groups that are virtually active and create a large contribution to the pocket of the manufacturer. This audience is connected to the social media not just through their systems but also through their mobile apps, which has made them available nearly 24x7. This has further diminished the barriers of time and geography. We are now living in a unified and highly connected society which creates one global market and global communication to the customers. "The future of social media is the future of media itself It is how people access online content *now*" said David Murphy, Founder and Editor of Mobile Marketing Daily. And it is not hard to see why.

REFERENCES

Aguilar, R. (n.d.). *Building an advocacy marketing strategy using the social media funnel*. Retrieved from REmomd: http://remomd.com/social-media/building-advocacy-marketing-strategy-using-social-media-funnel.html

Bosomworth, D., & Chaffey, D. (2012). Creating a Social Media Marketing Plan. *Smart Insights*. Retrieved from http://www.carmichaelcentre.ie/sites/default/files/Need-to-know-social-media-strategy-smart-insights_0.pdf

Buying, M. (2009, Sep 30). *Online's Slice of Ad Spending Grows Worldwide*. Retrieved from eMarketer: https://www.emarketer.com/Article/Onlines-Slice-of-Ad-Spending-Grows-Worldwide/1007298

By 2016 Why 70% of Small Businesses Will Depend On Social Media Tool To Reach New Customers. (2015, Dec 30). Retrieved from SMEJoinup: https://smejoinup.com/blog/by-2016-why-70-of-small-businesses-will-depend-on-social-media-tool-to-reach-new-customers/

Davis, A. (2009, May 13). *Banner ads drive search behaviour: study*. Retrieved from Campaign: Banner ads drive search behaviour: study.

Dewing, M. (2012). *Social Media: An Introduction*. Library of Parliment.

How to Get Google to Instantly Index Your New Website. (2015). Retrieved from Neil Patel Digital: https://neilpatel.com/blog/google-index/

Iblasi, W. N., Bader, D. M., & Al-Qreini, S. A. (2016). The Impact of Social Media as a Marketing Tool on Purchasing Decisions (Case Study on SAMSUNG for Electrical Home Appliances). *International Journal of Managerial Studies and Research*, *4*(1), 14–28.

Klaassen, A. (2009, Nov 2). *The State of Search Marketing: 2009*. Retrieved from AdAge: http://adage.com/article/digital/digital-marketing-state-search-marketing-2009/140083/

Maheshwari, S. (2017, Jul 31). *As Amazon's Influence Grows, Marketers Scramble to Tailor Strategies*. Retrieved from New York Times: https://www.nytimes.com/2017/07/31/business/media/amazon-advertising.html

Marketing Stack. (n.d.). Retrieved Jan 3, 2018, from Alexa: https://try.alexa.com/marketing-stack/

Nairuthram, S. (2016, Jun 15). *Social Media Marketing*. Retrieved from Easy Walkers Digital: http://www.eazywalkers.com/social-media-marketing/

Nizan, Y. (2016, Apr 26). *LTV Calculator – The Naive method*. Retrieved from Soomla Blog: http://blog.soom.la/2016/04/ltv-calculator-naive-method.html

Poirier, S. (2013, Nov 19). *Social Media Building Blocks: The 6 Spheres Of Social Media Marketing*. Retrieved from Business to Community: https://www.business2community.com/social-media/social-media-building-blocks-6-spheres-social-media-marketing-0687662

Rajeshwari, K. (n.d.). *Why is social media adoption low?* Retrieved from BLoC: Business Line On Campus: http://www.bloncampus.com/columns/marketing-moves/why-is-the-adoption-of-social-media-low/article9937231.ece

Stern, A. (2010, Feb 3). *8 Ways to Improve Your Click Through Rate*. Retrieved from iMedia: 8 Ways to Improve Your Click Through Rate.

Wasserman, A. (n.d.). *4 Steps to a Successful Social Media Campaign*. Retrieved from Prescient Digital Media: http://www.prescientdigital.com/articles/web-2.0/4-steps-to-a-successful-social-media-campaign

Chapter 12
Social Media Marketing:
Tools and Techniques

Priyanka Prasad
Institute of Innovation in Technology and Management, India

Pooja Saigal
Institute of Innovation in Technology and Management, India

ABSTRACT

Utilizing internet, particularly social networking websites, for marketing is called social media marketing. It comprises designing a well-structured content that consumers can share with each other to help a company broaden its customer base and increase its brand visibility. However different social media platforms have different target audiences, and therefore, in order to succeed, it is indispensable for marketers to have a thorough understanding of tools and techniques required to attract different clusters of customers.

INTRODUCTION

Marketing is a well structured methodological science, but there is no thumb rule to succeed. Regular upgradation in its pedagogy is required to confront changing consumer's expectations. Every marketing strategy has its life cycle and should be abandoned/ renewed or supplemented at times to guarantee better results. Advertisements on traditional media like Television, Magazines or newspaper are witnessing a huge competition from digital sources. Internet is slowly engulfing traditional media with most of the shows available online at a time and place most comfortable to the customers. In the modern era where customers have limited time

DOI: 10.4018/978-1-5225-6064-7.ch012

slot for entertainment it is a challenge for the marketers to hit them at right time and right place.

Utilizing internet particularly the social networking website for marketing is termed as social media marketing. It comprises of designing a well-structured content that consumers can share with each other to help company broaden their customer base and increase their brand visibility. As per a data published by social Media Examiner (Stelzner Michael, 2015) approximately 92% o of marketers who participated in the study agreed that social media efforts have generated more exposure to their business and they have found it useful. Advertisement on social media is also a WIN-WIN approach for the marketers. For a blog posted on google or for a YouTube advertisement or for a tweet, marketers need not to make heavy reimbursements to the publishers or distributers but can gain a million view overnight. Continuous upgradation or twisting of messages on social media also requires less of effort and cost. The advertisement cost is nominal and the cost incurred per viewer is nil.

Social media comes in many forms. Blogs, microblogs, social networks, media sharing sites, social book making, forum and analysis sites are few of them. Facebook is one of the most popular social networking sites in the present scenario. As per Times of India newspaper report (Shalina Pillai, 2015), India has the largest number of active social network members in the world. It has also been estimated that an active member spends more than 50 minutes in a day scrolling through various social networking sites. Researchers have also indicated that a consumer who follows a brand on social networking sites are mostly a loyal buyer of that brand. The only rocket science that a company needs to learn is to design proper content that can ignite and engage its viewer. Not single strategy is or can be applicable on all the different forms of social media platforms.

Mankind is a social being and, sharing information on their experiences is an important part of its social interactions. Since the inception of business, people ask each other for advices before making any purchase decisions. Recommendation and good word by the original buyer has always been the most authentic information on which a customer can rely. Similarly sharing decision making processes with family and friends is an indispensible part of a consumer shopping behavior. This chapter focuses on different forms of social media and strategies to excel in them. A brief introduction about various strategies dealt in the chapter is as follows.

When and How Much Do Consumers Seek Social Influence?

Multiple factors play role in determining how complex a consumer buying behavior will be. For example, a consumer buying a high involvement product, whether, in terms of money (car, mobile phones, television, etc.), technical aspects (Mutual funds, insurance policy. etc) or status (Jewelry) will be highly dependent on social influence as compared to a person buying a low involvement product like beverages or grocery. Not only consumer's buying behavior but his post purchase behavior also depends on social influence. A consumer seeks social appraisal after his purchase and the products that gains social recognition are likely to increase the satisfaction of the buyers.

What Is Social Media Marketing?

It is about recognizing and tapping the fact that as a customer makes his purchase decision he seeks for suggestions and recommendations from his family, friends or society. Also in this digital era social media platforms are the most preferable place where the consumers meet. Therefore, Social media marketing is a fusion of sociology and technology that helps company build brands by sharing customer's experiences about the product.

Social media marketing is a technique that utilizes internet particularly the social networking website for marketing. It comprises of designing a well-structured content that consumers can share with each other to help company broaden their customer base and increase their brand visibility.

Traditional media like Television, Radio or newspaper no longer share the position of king in information world. Moreover, they are one-way broadcast technologies. In case anyone disagrees with a newspaper article, the maximum one can do is, to draft a letter to the editorial team and wait for their response. In any case his opinions may not reach to the entire readers of that article.

New web technologies facilitate every individual in not only creating but also distributing his own content. Web tools like blogs, posts or YouTube videos provide enough resources to make one creative and expressive and most important one don't have to pay heavy amounts to the distributers or publishers. In other words, one can virtually reach a million of its customer for free.

Who is the customer? In early days of web, it was assumed that the potential customers for any online retail outlets are lonely consumers isolated from their family and friends, self- dependent, late night browsers and needs little suggestions before making his purchase. But, those days are over now and in present scenario that is not how the online buyers profile is. Consumer behavior as well as her sources of information is changing. As per a Nielsen report on social media (Figure 1) an adult spends 22% of his overall media time on social media. The report also says that Generation X (age between 35-49) spends more than 7 hours per week on social media and thirty-nine percent of heavy social users believe one of the important reasons for using social websites is to find information about product and services. In this occupied world where customers have limited time slot it is a challenge for the marketers to hit them at right time and right place.

Figure 1. Nielsen Report on social media
Source: Sean Casey (2016) " Nielson social media report"

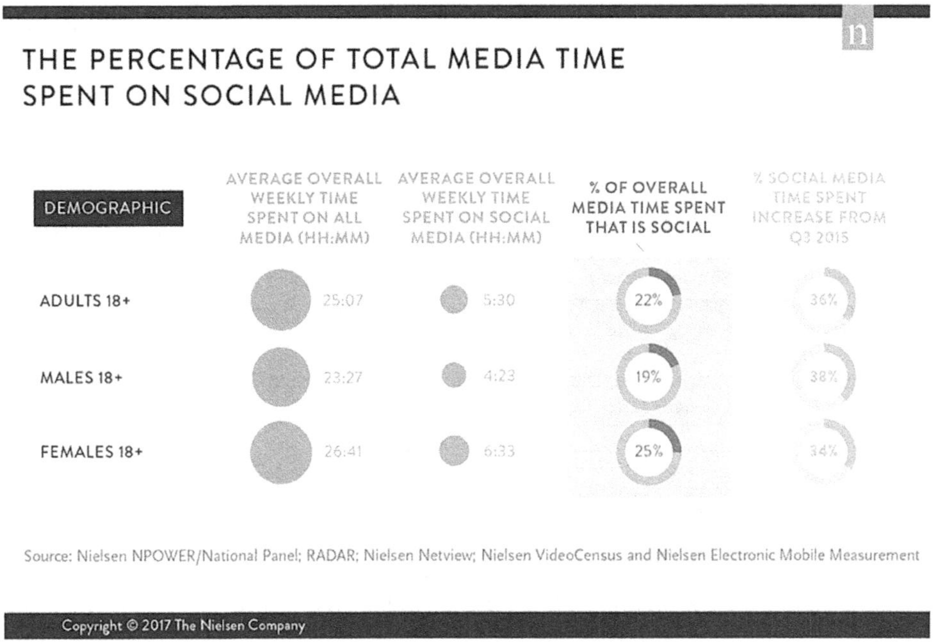

Social Media for Everyone

Whether it be a small business, a giant, a proprietor or a partnership firm, there is no reason for not using social media for the business. Information world has changed and so are the customers. In this competitive era, one can gain advantage and can create an edge above others with the help of various social media tools available and therefore, a marketer need to be more alert and active.

This chapter will provide a brief description about the strategies that one can adopt to flourish his business with minimum investments.

How to Use Social Media for the Business

It is also possible that the Social media may not be suitable for every business. It depends on numerous factors whether social media can act as an effective tool for business or not. It is more important to identify that whether a business is ready for a social media campaign before understanding and implementing strategies for social media marketing. It is also imperative to identify the social media techniques that suits a business and yield good returns. The checklist in table (1) is to be reviewed before ascertaining that a business is ready to sail in the boat of social media.

Table 1. How IBM uses social media to sell

IBM is smartly using social media for their business since four decades. It is astonishing to note that IBM has 17,000 individual blogs, a million daily page views of internal Wikis, 25,000 Twitters and approximately 3,00,000 Linkdin profiles. IBM is transforming the traditional seller concept into "Digital Sellers" . These "Digital Sellers" use Linkdin, Twitter, econtact to engage and collaborate with their clients. Social media is also being used by IBM to generate leads from small and medium businesses. IBM in 2007 launched Lotus Connections, a product that rolled five different social networking sites into one single package. This tool was very helpful in developing a collaborative corporate environment that allowed workers to communicate with each other and also to their existing and potential customers. Recently IBM has announced a partnership with Twitters. This partnership has given IBM access over several accounts to serve different types of customers. This will further help the company to update its customers on new product launches. Software updates, company events and news releases. Adding to it, IBM also manages several YouTube channels and Vine account and even manages collection of Pinterest boards on various topics like Women in Tech, Big Data, and IBM History. *How IBM does it?* No surprise managing all these accounts need lot of hands. IBM has a team dedicated for managing these accounts and each team member is strictly advised to adhere to the company's social computing guidelines.

Table 2. Small brands and social media

While big brands can use social media to excel, small brands can use it to grow big. Blendtec deals in high performance blenders, the time it was struggling for its brand name George Wright, Marketing Director, got a brilliant idea. He designed a series of viral videos picturising blending of everyday objects- I-phones, Television remote control, glow sticks etc. He posted the videos to media sharing sites. Soon the videos were popular and trapped a million viewers. This generated tons of press and buzz about the company. JustBought.it is not only using social media to gain popularity but it has identified its business objective from social recommendation system. JustBought.it inspires its users to tweet about the product whenever they make any purchase. These tweets include pictures of the product purchased and its information and location. The information can be viewed by other users and they can further enquire about the product. This information can even be sorted on the basis of product, location or date. JustBought.it is currently integrated with big brands like Microsoft.net, Magento and more.

One can reap the benefits of social media if his answer is yes to the checklist shown in Table 3.

TECHNIQUES FOR USING SOCIAL MEDIA SITES TO PROMOTE A BUSINESS

Strategy 1: Teach Don't Sell Approach

It is important to understand that social media platform is different from other paid advertising platforms. The information available on social media sites are trusted and relied by customers. The doubting on the credibility of the information might start

Table 3. Checklist to identify readiness towards social media marketing

Is the business suitable for social media marketing
Who are the target audience? Is target audience available online?
What is the business goal? Will social media marketing help in accomplishing those goals?
Does social media marketing support other online and offline marketing strategies.
Do the business has budget for social media marketing? It is a myth that social media comes for free. Social media may not be costly in terms of money but it requires lot of time.

once the sales pitch in the content available on social media platforms is identified. Therefore, it is more important that information should be provided in educating the customers rather than taking a direct sales approach (e.g. Informing about the product). For example- The information should be delivered which build the brand's reputation and facilitate in ameliorating a better customer relationship.

The advertisements might have fed up an average customer. In marketing terms, it is called as "Banner blindness" a phenomenon that leads to conscious or subconscious ignorance by online viewers of anything that looks like an advertisement. The hurdle from passing through these market blockers is done by a content written with the objective to engage and educate customers.

How to sell without letting a customer understand that "HE ARE BEING SOLD".

Some of the tips that might be very helpful in designing a content that will be selling and promoting the product without triggering "It's an advertisement" radar of the customers.

Don't Mention Any Call for Buy

The contents are carefully designed and one needs to be very careful to act as a supporter rather than a businessman. The content should not be containing any call for action to buy or to ask for a demo or to sign in for a catalog or mailing list. The content should have the company logo and URL, however it should not be emphasized much. Every content should direct to the piece of other content or it may have an option for subscription to the channel or newsletter. For example- The blogs on travel and tourism with a logo of the company and URL can be posted for a hotel business. This shall be very helpful in gathering the desired information by the prospective clients and simultaneously help developing awareness about the brand.

Focus on What Audience Wants to Listen to and Not What Business Want to Tell Them

The content should provide information that the customers are looking for and which may provide value addition to their decision-making process. For example- Product comparative table might be prepared that can let a prospective customer knowing all what a specific product provides with respect to the competitors. The thumb rule is again the same- The Product should not be exaggerated. The trusts might also be gained by prospects on a relatively neutral comparison table.

The brand story that can connect customers is created and to keep them engaged throughout the day is another important strategy to gain attention in social media. It is now an important challenge for social media marketeers that the customers must be involved in narrating their own story. Moreover, the content that is designed needs to be improvised on a regular basis to maintain its nobility.

Strategy 2: Research the Platform

The social media are being used by a very large percentage of people and the business can't be afford to miss the opportunity of interacting with the customers through the channels like Facebook, blogs, Twitter etc. It is not mandatory that a business should be on every platform for making use of social media for marketing. The different platforms of social media get varied from each other by goal and target audience. The blasting of similar contents on all the social media platforms may not yield a desired result. It is therefore, important for a company to plan beforehand its goals and target audience for different media platforms. As for example active members of Facebook may be different from that of LinkedIn. Similarly, the objective of using a social platform can also be different. It can be cost saving, competitive, sales or enriching experience. A company needs to co-ordinate its goals with the target audience of the selected media platform. The capabilities of many of these platforms are also overlapping and it is likely to continue as platforms are evolving to improve the involvement of the users. For a marketing campaigns, the best platforms would be where it's buyers are. While selecting the social media platforms, the focus should be on the audience and objectives of business. Some platforms are better suited to meet the objectives at earlier stages of the customer lifecycle, while others, with more advanced targeting options, allows to reach buyers at every stage of the customer lifecycle. As a businessman steer through different social media channels, it is important to have an understanding of the features and capabilities of each platform. This will help one to strategize the course of action.

According to Joe Pulizzi, Founder, Content Marketing Institute, one should only commit to channels that can consistently deliver valuable information; which means that one might only activate content in a few channels and use the others as listening posts. So, it is important for one to invest in the platforms where he is more likely to reach and engage with the target customers. In order to choose the best social media platforms, one need to take time to get acquainted to each platform, understand its operations and demographic distribution of its users. In this section, a brief introduction about few popular social media platforms has been made.

FACEBOOK

How Does Facebook Help in Promoting Any Business?

Facebook is a widely used social media platform that gives an advantage of reaching a huge audience with little investment. According to Pew Research Center (Social media updates, 2016), 71% of American adult internet users are using Facebook and globally, there are more than 1.59 billion active users per month. Adding to it Facebook has approximately 1.44 billion active mobile users. Facebook created a room for brands in 2007 and is evolving continuously to find ways for marketers to engage with their audience.

Facebook not only provides brand visibility but allows customers to monitor business interactions. Facebook allows the entrepreneur to design his own Facebook page which is very much similar to that of Facebook profiles. These Facebook pages will not only allows them to showcase their brand to a large audience but will also make them easily discoverable. This will further help them to interact with their clients individually. This strengthens customers' trust in the business and leads to creation of a strong relationship.

How to Use Facebook for Brand Promotions?

Step 1: Create a Business Page on Facebook

A Facebook profile is much different from a Facebook page. On Facebook profiles are made for individuals while pages are made for business. It should be very clear that a businessman needs to make a page for its business. Facebook has different functionality on pages for promotion of businesses. Theses functionalities are not available on Facebook profiles.

Key Differences Between Facebook Pages and Facebook Profiles

- Unlike profiles Facebook Pages can be managed by multiple administrators. This allows multiple people to manage Facebook content and also allows a smooth flow in management of these pages even when any one of the administrator is leaving the company;
- On Facebook profile acceptance of the administrator is required to become friend and to post or view any content, whereas no acceptance is required to become a fan of these Facebook pages. This allows the business to cover a huge audience;
- These Business pages are by default public and will be ranked on any public search result.

Step 2: Promote the Business Page

To accomplish this, one need to strike the balance by offering content that adds value and is relevant, along with that content that looks interesting to the audience. Business posts should deliver the content and promotional offers in a way that viewers can relate to. This can be done by the use of graphics and multimedia. Applications like discussion board, YouTube videos box etc. can be used to add more interesting and engaging content to the page.

The best part of designing such interesting content is that they become viral and are viewed by many thus accomplishing promotional goal.

Step 3: Create Facebook Advertisements

Facebook ads give an extra push to the business that helps in getting more fans for business pages and therefore generating more prospects for the sales team. Creating and distributing a Facebook ad is very simple. One just need to visit the URL facebook.com/advertising. An option of create ad is there which will then simultaneously instruct to create an ad. Facebook will ask to choose audience for the ad and an ad will succeed and will run uninterruptedly in the world of Facebook only if one can select the right audience. These are the people whom the business is targeting. Facebook offers to select the audience on the basis of their demographic profiles, likes and dislikes, their geographical locations and also on the basis of their social groups.

TWITTER

Twitter started in 2007 as a social media platform, and today, it's power cannot be ignored. It is a *Microblogging* platform, as it limits the size of each post. Twitter has become a stage to discuss industry, politics, and culture and to break news. According to Statista.com (*Social Media usage worldwide, 2018*), the microblogging service averaged at 330 million monthly active users, in the third quarter of 2017. Twitter has become a space where both corporate and personal brands can develop relationships 02 with followers. It requires very little investment in terms of time, and can instantly show results through increased sales, and consumer insight. Twitter is used to announce offers, events, and to keep the readers updated about the important news stories. If the brand is followed by users on Twitter then it is a strong signal of their affinity for business.

How to Use Twitter for Promotions

Step 1. Selecting a proper Twitter handle: While designing Twitter account y need to be very selective In deciding on a username. Username or as it is said in Twitter "handle" is an identity for the outside world. Secondly try to keep the handle around 10-15 characters, so that the customers can easily mention the business without much of trouble. Apart from a proper handle a perfect profile picture and information that one want to offer to its' customers should be mentioned in the bio. The major goal while designing thre profile is to make it easily identifiable by the customers.

Step 2. Find the Right Followers: On Twitter the quality of the content that one can access depends on whom they are following on Twitter. An established business can follow its suppliers, professional friends, local business or competitors. For a new startup the thumb rule is to follow the businesses that are similar and are doing well in their areas. The key reason is to get an idea of how and what to tweet that can gain maximum acceptance.

YOUTUBE

YouTube has reached over one-third of the internet users and is a popular search engine. This suggests the influence of YouTube, particularly as a video search engine for movies, trailers, new songs, do-it-yourself activities and a never-ending list of entertaining and informative videos. YouTube is extensively used for product launch, demos and promotions. Select a title for the video that is customer-centric with relevant keywords, so that viewers can easily search the content. The video should have a description of few sentences that include targeted keywords. One can also take the advantage of tagging feature, which links similar videos and contents together.

INSTAGRAM

Instagram is an application for photo and video sharing, which has become valuable to marketers, post its acquisition by Facebook. Instagram has an active user base. The consumer brands have realized the tremendous success achieved due to Instagram and are using it to showcase their products. The audience is engaged through posts, promotional offers and contests. One should post those images and videos that give their audience an insight into the workings of the business. By acknowledging the audience, one can encourage them to engage and share.

PINTEREST

Pinterest is image-based platform and is seen as one of the best channels to showcase products through images. Pinterest has a quick sharing feature called *re-pinning* which spreads the content quickly. It is perfect platform, if business offers products that can be displayed with high quality photos. One can create boards which display product categories and promote them in an artistic way. To promote product effectively on Pinterest, its images should be visually appealing and attractive.

Strategy 3: Advergames on Social Media Platforms - A New Approach to Improve Marketing

Online videogames available on social media platforms were introduced to entertain social media users. Soon marketers identified the hidden advertisement capabilities and companies started using these videogames to promote their products. Advergames attract the consumer to interact with brand, in a way which they appreciate and at the same time, they value brand ideas. Advergames have various advantages over other traditional marketing ways:

1. The advergames are not forced upon an unwilling viewer; rather they are selected by the player;
2. The player actively interacts with advergames instead of showing passive attitude of the TV audience;
3. It encourages players to share their experience with friends and family.

How to Use Advergaming for Successful Marketing

- **Keep Minimum Entry Barriers:** While designing any advergame for a social media website one should be extra cautious that game should have minimum entry barriers. This means no download for any special software, no complicated registration or such formalities required. The viewer can just click to play the game;
- **Convert Players Into Leads:** The process of registration should be simple and should come once the player has finished playing. Attempt should be made to attract the players for registration by igniting their competitive spirit. Registration will help them to upload and display their scoreboards to their friends and public. This will not only promote business but will also help in generating leads for the business;
- **Encourage for Replay:** Provide incentives to bring players again. The reason is the player should interact with game multiple times so that the brand and it's promotion can also be repeated and the player can feel an association with the brand. One can also announce rewards to the top scorer on leader board ranking;
- **Game Should be Available on Smartphone and Should be Shareable:** Most of the users access social networking websites from their smart phones. Therefore, an extra step should be taken to ensure that game is mobile friendly and will not ask for any software updates if accessed on mobile phones. The games sharable also to ensure better capture of audience.

Strategy 4: Integrate Offline and Online Advertising

In 2012 McDonald introduced a twitter campaign with the hashtag # McDStories with an objective that people will share their happy meal moments. Unfortunately, wrong people got wrong message and the campaign was a big disaster. If they had integrated their Twitter campaign with any other offline marketing platforms, they might have resonated better with their audience, and might have given them the result they expected. IA TV or social media campaign promoting their intention of bringing back nostalgia would have given the food for thought to the audience.

The integration of offline marketing platforms with online channels is beneficial. It acts as a social proof thus inviting potential customers to inspect the business community and develop trust on your business.

Various ways that can help integrate online and offline marketing platforms include:

- **QR Codes:** Quick response codes are a great tool that helps integrate print media advertisements with online platforms. QR leads customer to the websites and helps them gather complete information about the product and to read the tailored content that have been designed for them. With QR readers available on most of the mobile phones, it is easy to access. Companies are now also using QR codes strategically to offer discounts or gift vouchers;
- **Hashtags:** Hashtags are acting as a great tool to know and understand the customers, their expectations and grievances. By initiating a Hashtag event or campaign offline, one can reach it's target audience and can extend its reach by bringing the discussion online. Social media will further help in tracking the discussion and measuring its success rate;
- **Call to Action:** By quoting an URL of the company or a special offer that are available online on the print media ads, a businessman is benefited in two ways. Firstly, he can measure the success of his print advertisement by identifying the increase in the click rates of the websites. Secondly, he can bring prospects to investigate and acquire detailed information about the product.

REFERENCES

Casey, S. (2016). *2016 Nielsen social media report*. Available at http://www.nielsen.com/us/en/insights/reports/2017/2016-nielsen-social-media-report.html

Michael, S. (2015). 2015 Social Media Marketing Industry Report. *Social Media Examiner*. Available at http://www.socialmediaexaminer.com/SocialMediaMarketingIndustryReport2015.pdf

Pillai, S. (2017, December 19). Indians spend 70% of mobile internet time on social media, entertainment. *The Times of India Business*.

Social Media usage worldwide. (2018). Retrieved from: https://www.statista.com/statistics/278414/number-of-worldwide-social-network-users/

Updates, S. M. (2016). *Pew Research Center*. Available at http://www.pewinternet.org/2016/11/11/social-media-update-2016/SS

Chapter 13
Impact of Digital Advertising Post-Demonetization in India

Kamal Singh Rathaur
Kanpur Institute of Management Studies, India

Atul Kumar Agarwal
Ansal University, India

ABSTRACT

Technological changes led to the rise of digital advertising, advertising using internet and other technologies. In India, digital advertising is in the nascent stage with most of the transactions taking place in cash. After demonetization, the surge in the digital advertising was seen. This chapter reviews articles, news reports, journals, and books, and discusses the aftermath of the process on retail and online shopping, how it paves the way for a new trend of digital marketing, and the implications of the same on online shopping and digital payments and implications on the rural consumer. The way we communicate has changed in the past 5 years. A few years back, people were skeptical to buy online, and we never thought we would buy groceries, furniture, cloths online, but now we book our shows, tickets, everything is online and in mobile.

INTRODUCTION

Digital advertising, also called Internet *advertising* ("Internet marketing") is when businesses leverage Internet technologies to deliver promotional advertisements to consumers. Although the government's recent move to demonetize Rs. 500 and Rs. 1000 notes have left a lot of people scrambling for cash, digital payments have

DOI: 10.4018/978-1-5225-6064-7.ch013

been seen an explosion in promotional activity. Brands across sectors have increased their marketing spends by 50-70% to promote digital transactions. E-wallet brands have capitalized on the situation to acquire new consumers and have increased their digital marketing by a staggering 120%. Retail brands, on the other hand, have reduced their digital communications by 20-30% owing to most online orders being made with the cash-on-delivery option. Banking firms have increased their marketing communication by as much as 200-300% to keep people informed about their services and build brand loyalty. Mobile push notifications and SMS have emerged as the most used digital marketing tools by brands in the BFSI and e-wallet segments to engage with their target audience post demonetization. Paytm sees an increase of 435% in the traffic post the announcement. Indian bank announces the digital transaction even while buying vegetables. Future Group makes arrangements to make cashless payments in order to offset the impact of scrapping of rupee notes of 500 and 1000. A temple in Gurugram accepted cashless offerings and invited payments by digital wallets, (Jain, 2016).

Consumers are now using smartphones and tablets to interact with businesses to transact, communicate and obtain information. Companies are accelerating efforts to extend their business offerings and operating models into these growing digital channels, while determining the best way to communicate with customers in a multichannel environment.

Online marketing is becoming a hot topic in every business sector, and gradually plays a truly important role in any company's multi-channel marketing strategy. It uses the Internet to deliver promotional marketing messages to consumers. It includes email marketing, search engine marketing, social media marketing, many types of display advertising (including web banner advertising), and mobile advertising. Like other advertising media, online advertising frequently involves both a publisher, who integrates advertisements into its online content, and an advertiser, who provides the advertisements to be displayed on the publisher's content. Other potential participants include advertising agencies that help generate and place the ad copy, an ad server who technologically delivers the ad and tracks statistics, and advertising affiliates who do independent promotional work for the advertiser.

Tools of Online Marketing, Ronald and Kevin (2015)

- **Display Advertising:** Display advertising conveys its advertising message visually using text, logos, animations, videos, photographs, or other graphics. Display advertisers frequently target users with particular traits to increase the ads' effect.

- **Web Banner Advertising:** Web banners or banner ads typically are graphical ads displayed within a web page. Banner ads can use rich media to incorporate video, audio, animations, buttons, forms, or other interactive elements using Java applets, HTML5, Adobe Flash, and other programs.
- **Frame Ad (Traditional Banner):** Frame ads were the first form of web banners. The colloquial usage of "banner ads" often refers to traditional frame ads. Website publishers incorporate frame ads by setting aside a particular space on the web page.
- **Pop-Ups/Pop-Unders:** A pop-up ad is displayed in a new web browser window that opens above a website visitor's initial browser window. A pop-under ad opens a new browser window under a website visitor's initial browser window.
- **Floating Ad:** A floating ad, or overlay ad, is a type of rich media advertisement that appears superimposed over the requested website's content. Floating ads may disappear or become less obtrusive after a preset time period.
- **Expanding Ad:** An expanding ad is a rich media frame ad that changes dimensions upon a predefined condition, such as a preset amount of time a visitor spends on a webpage, the user's click on the ad, or the user's mouse movement over the ad. Expanding ads allow advertisers to fit more information into a restricted ad space.
- **Interstitial Ad:** An interstitial ad displays before a user can access requested content, sometimes while the user is waiting for the content to load. Interstitial ads are a form of interruption marketing.
- **Text Ads:** A text ad displays text-based hyperlinks. Text-based ads may display separately from a web page's primary content, or they can be embedded by hyperlinking individual words or phrases to advertiser's websites. Text ads may also be delivered through email marketing or text message marketing.
- **Search Engine Marketing (SEM):** Search Engine Marketing, or SEM, is designed to increase a website's visibility in search engine results pages (SERPs). Search engines provide sponsored results and organic (non-sponsored) results based on a web searcher's query. Search engines often employ visual cues to differentiate sponsored results from organic results. Search engine marketing includes all of an advertiser's actions to make a website's listing more prominent for topical keywords.
- **Search Engine Optimization (SEO):** Search Engine Optimization, or SEO, attempts to improve a website's organic search rankings in SERPs by increasing the website content's relevance to search terms. Search engines regularly update their algorithms to penalize poor quality sites that try to game their rankings, making optimization a moving target for advertisers. Many vendors offer SEO services.

- **Sponsored Search:** Sponsored search (also called sponsored links or search ads) allows advertisers to be included in the sponsored results of a search for selected keywords. Search ads are often sold via real-time auctions, where advertisers bid on keywords.
- **Social Media Marketing:** Social media marketing is commercial promotion conducted through social media websites. Many companies promote their products by posting frequent updates and providing special offers through their social media profiles.
- **Mobile Advertising:** Mobile advertising is ad copy delivered through wireless mobile devices such as smartphones, feature phones, or tablet computers. Mobile advertising may take the form of static or rich media display ads, SMS (Short Message Service) or MMS (Multimedia Messaging Service) ads, mobile search ads, advertising within mobile websites, or ads within mobile applications or games (such as interstitial ads, "advergaming," or application sponsorship).
- **Email Advertising:** Email advertising is ad copy comprising an entire email or a portion of an email message. Email marketing may be unsolicited, in which case the sender may give the recipient an option to opt-out of future emails, or it may be sent with the recipient's prior consent (opt-in), Patel (n.d.).

Benefits of Online Marketing

- Internet gives you a wide access of your potential customers. It has been estimated that a couple of billion people around the world use the Internet, and more are becoming aware of Internet with each passing day. So, marketing your business to such a large group of people is only possible through Internet;
- Internet is the only medium that is able to cross geographic and national boundaries;
- The cost of promoting your business on the Internet is cheaper than other mediums of marketing. This makes it easy for small and mid-sized businesses to advertise their products;
- Internet allows the ability to stay connected with customers on a real-time basis. If any discount going on, then it is easier to send an email to customers and they can buy the product instantly. Internet also allows to send multiple messages at the same time, which saves the tedious task of sending a newsletter to every client;
- Internet marketing facilitates an instant feedback from the customers. Customers can share about their experience after using the product;

- Internet marketing saves a lot of time and effort. Instead of having a customer service representative to answer the queries of customers, one can put all the information about the product or service on the Internet so that customers can go through it. The most common way of doing it is to have a section dedicated to frequently asked questions (FAQs) about the product so that customers get all the required information about the product or the service. Internet marketing allows your business to be available 24/7, which means increased sales and profits (Weighing in the Advantages and Disadvantages of Internet Marketing, n.d.).

Limitations of Online Marketing

- Although, Internet marketing allows a wider reach, the start-up costs of a website can be high. This includes the cost of the required software and hardware, and maintenance costs;
- There are still a lot of customers who use the Internet just for having more information about a product and prefer to buy it in person. For example, Internet marketing allows a customer to view how a phone looks like and its technical specifications, but customers prefer having a look at the phone in the store to get a hands-on experience;
- There are a lot of customers who are not proficient in using the Internet and focusing solely on Internet marketing can cause you to lose these customers;
- The rules of the trade change rapidly in Internet marketing, and it requires constant attention and monitoring to ensure that your marketing strategy does not look out-of-date;
- The biggest disadvantage of Internet marketing is its vulnerability to fraudulent activities. There are a lot of illegitimate websites out there which look similar to original websites and rob the customers of their money. Spamming is also one of the biggest challenges for Internet marketing and confidential data can be easily stolen by hackers;
- Internet marketing lacks the human touch that is involved when a customer buys a product from a salesperson. This hampers the prospects of relationship building which plays an important part in repeat sales and word-of mouth publicity;
- Internet marketing depends heavily on technology, which is vulnerable to technical faults. For example, if a customer clicks on your advertisement but due to a technical glitch, is unable to buy the product, he may easily become irate and take his business somewhere else.

Although, there are some challenges involved in Internet marketing, it can be safely said that Internet marketing has led to increased transparency and ease of buying products. The need of the hour is to counter the challenges so that Internet marketing proves to be truly beneficial for all.

LITERATURE REVIEW

Digital Advertising is using technology enabled marketing activities in order to expand customer knowledge by matching their needs and requirements (Chaffey, 2013). Marketing has been around for a long time. Business owners felt the need to spread the word about their products or services through newspapers and word of mouth. Digital marketing on the other end is becoming popular because it utilizes mass media devices like television, radio and the Internet. The most common digital marketing tool used today is Search Engine Optimization (SEO). Its role is to maximize the way search engines like Google find your website. Digital marketing concept originated from the Internet and search engines ranking of websites. The first search engine was started in 1991 with a network protocol called Gopher for query and search. After the launch of Yahoo in 1994 companies started to maximize their ranking on the website (Smyth 2007).

On November 8th, 2016, in what can be said to be the audacious move, Prime Minister Sri.NarendraModi announced the scrapping of 500 and 1000 rupee notes in order to combat the black money and fake currency. As anticipated, the sudden dearth of cash led to the emptiness in the business. Serpentine queues in the ATMs and banks saw the common public frantically exchanging the old notes with the new ones and depositing the old notes in the banks. The shift focused to more of digital, online transactions thus enhancing the payments other than cash. A new 2000 rupee note was brought into circulation as high value currency. New notes of 500 and 1000 rupees were also released in the market in the subsequent days.

Considering the current volume of internet marketing business, it's hard to believe how young the internet marketplace is. While the timeline of internet marketing has been short, the cumulative events leading up to where we are now have impacted the entire globe faster than any marketing revolution in history. In 1994, spending for internet marketing totaled nearly nothing, but increased to over $300 million in 1995. Now, little more than a decade later, marketing spending and internet marketing business has exploded to nearly $200 billion (E-Marketing Strategy of Hamrobazar. Com, 2013). Today, it's hard to believe in having an organization which doesn't have some kind of online presence.

When the internet was first introduced in the early 90s, it wasn't considered to be an advertising medium at all. Instead, the internet was treated as a tool for exchanging emails and digital information, but wasn't yet considered valuable for reaching customers. However, it wasn't long before marketing pioneers began to see the potential for internet marketing business as millions of web surfers logging on each day to find valuable and relevant information. Within just a few years, informative and educational marketing, as well as graphically enticing banner ads began to be show up. It wasn't long before results began to flood in which proved the value of the internet marketplace to even the most skeptical advertisers.

Most importantly, companies which had been spending huge chunks of their marketing budget on offline list building, begin to realize that they could accomplish the same thing via email and for much less. It wasn't long before everyone from industry giants such as Microsoft Corp. to small businesses began to build company sites and spend marketing dollars to attract qualified traffic. Next, search engine companies like Yahoo! began to create significant profits from advertising alone.

Then came the great internet marketing business bust around the year of 2000, which marked the beginning of the end for interruptive marketing such as flashing banner ads. As interactive features were added to web pages, consumers were given the option of turning off marketing messages at will and they did. Then entered the age of education based invitational marketing, which crystallized with the creation of web 2.0 technologies. Suddenly, billions of "voices" began to rise all over the world, as the internet marketplace became as much a global community as it was an advertising medium. This led to a relational based marketing approach which has led to one of the most lucrative opportunities for solo entrepreneurs and small start- ups alike to make a small fortune working from their spare bedroom. Who knows where the internet marketing revolution will lead us, but one this is for sure: Those who understand the principles upon which the thriving internet marketplace is built will most likely never want for opportunities to create internet marketing business success and to earn solid income.

Case Study on 7 Up: Use of Social Media

7 UP Lemon Pattalam Online Championship was an interesting and unique cricket game which was made on the lines of the on-ground version of the championship. The innovative and exciting online cricket tournament, which has 7 players a side, 7 balls per over and 7 overs an innings saw an enthusiastic participation from Facebook fans. With a total number 10015 teams, total number of fans who joined the Facebook page via the game: 61,760 – a growth of 52% in just 45 days (Pawar, A.V., 2014).

7UP Lemon Pattalam was on Facebook in the form of an interactive application based game. Fans can create or join a team and play the game wherein they have to score maximum runs in 7 overs. The winner will get the opportunity to meet the Chennai Super Kings.

The prima objective was to increase the consumer engagement and interaction on the 7 UP Facebook page while acquiring new fans. The on-ground Lemon Pattalam Championship activity gave the perfect chance to leverage on the same through the social media channels.

The strategy was to combine the viral effect of a multiplayer game format with the online version of the Lemon Pattalam championship, an on-ground open format cricket championship. The online version of the project was to extend the exact replica of the format from the offline version giving it to the 7UP's Facebook page. This was to give it an instant connect with an activity the target audience was well aware of.

The entire audience active on the social networking scene was targeted. Lemon Pattalam is a cricket tournament which was happening on-ground. The company wanted to create an online version of the same and promote it on Facebook page of 7UP to increase engagement and also increase the number of fans.

Facebook was the channel of choice in this case as it is the location which houses the maximum number of 7UP fans who are active online.

The 7UP Lemon Pattalam game is an online application which was ported on Facebook. Here, the user needs to install the application and then log on, to play the game. The user can then either create his own team or join any other team (for which he needs to get invited) that's been already formed.

However, if the user creates his own team, he is asked to invite 6 of his friends (from his list) to form a team and then give it a name as per his choice.

The game was designed in such a way that of all the friends who will receive invitations in form of FEEDS on their profile, only the first-six friends who accept the invitation will be part of the team (first come first serve basis). Moreover, the users can also be a part of multiple teams at the same time giving then the opportunity to perform at various places and having their best score acknowledged.

Since the entire campaign was built with the South Indian essence and zest for cricket, company added a tinge of South Indian flavor by having cheerleaders dressed in their regional garb, performing various jigs to cheer the player.

Within the game play there was a 7UP Float designed to hang around the boundary region, which awarded 7 runs to the batsman if he managed to hit it with the ball. In-game branding was carried out by using 7UP Drinks Trolley which would appear at random intervals.

Further, fun bonus factors like "Double Up with 7up" and "Bonus Ball" were added where runs scored in the last delivery would get doubled in the former case and in the later case the user would get a special Lemon Bonus Ball.

The activity got an overwhelming response from the online audience who managed to form over 10015 teams within the span of time. Also, the game drew attention of 61,760 new prospects that joined the fan page through the game. This pronounced a growth of 52% of the fan base in just 45days.

Case Study on HDFC: Use of Social Media Network

Indian banking industry is booming & is on expansion spree. Indian banks contributed 1.7 per cent to the total global brand value at US$ 14.74 billion and grew by 19 per cent in 2011 as per the annual international ranking conducted by UK-based Brand Finance Plc. According to a recent study done by Buzzom.com, Indian banks whether government or private have started using social media to stay in touch with their customers but HDFC stands out as far as leveraging social media is concerned both in terms of number of channels being used as well as engaging with their customers.

As per the graph above HDFC Bank has presence across 8 social media channels out of which the prominent presence is on Facebook, LinkedIn, Twitter, Youtube & their official blog. Important aspect is the engagement which they do on all these channels (Silky, B. 2016).

HDFC's page on Facebook generates admirable feedback from users which serves as a ground for them to understand their fans as well as promote their banking products. They have a money matters section where they provide interesting recent financial news of interest to their fans. Also they keep on engaging the users with interesting puzzles/jigsaws based upon financial terms.

HDFC's twitter approach is built upon again like their Facebook approach on sharing interesting & relevant information with their followers, asking them interesting puzzles, sharing new products & deals from their stable and so on. No wonder that they have a healthy follower count of 1300+ which is growing on the daily basis.

HDFC lacks on its Youtube marketing aspect and needs to learn from other banks like ICICI which is the second most active bank on social media in India. Although HDFC has created some great commercials for their television audience which have found their way on Youtube also and these commercials have large viewership on Youtube too but they need to leverage Youtube by posting such videos regularly on their channel & promoting it further.

HDFC Bank's company page on LinkedIn has more than 13,000 followers. They haven't leveraged this platform to its full potential yet like they can display their products on their page on which they can get recommendation from the users which will serve as a live testimonial but still having a presence on LinkedIn is being helpful to them as the company stats & employees list can be browsed through to get interesting information about them (Digital Vidya, 2011).

RESEARCH METHODOLOGY

This study aims at identifying the importance of digital advertising followed by the effectiveness of online marketing as a part of IMC strategy. Therefore the objective of the research is to understand the massive contribution of Online marketing as a part of Integrated Marketing Communication and to know its splendid efforts towards promotion in practice and also to find out some challenges in using online advertising as a tool of Integrated Marketing Communication. The research objectives are:

1. To know the impact of digital advertising on customers;
2. To know the impact of digital advertising on retailers;
3. To know the impact of digital advertising on business transactions;
4. To know the impact of demonetization on digital advertising.

In order to attain these objectives, the methodology uses descriptive research design. Data is collected from secondary as well as primary sources. Secondary data provides necessary theoretical back up to the study which is collected from published or unpublished sources. Primary data is collected under Survey method using questionnaire as the main research instrument. Since "Customer`s inclination towards Online marketing" is the core focus of the study, a structured & closed ended questionnaire has been prepared for customers only.

The questionnaire incorporated questions related to customers' preference for online marketing and other traditional mediums for getting awareness on various brands and making purchase decision. The questionnaire is then distributed among the sample selected for this study. Convenience sampling is used with sample size as 200 within Kanpur suburbs and sample frame as customers, retailers & corporate offices.

DATA ANALYSIS

- Consumers reckon upon more than one medium to get knowledge of any brand. Due to unlimited brand choices & price sensitivity, they undertake a detailed evaluation of various brands by referring more number of sources of information. So they may be using combination of various mediums such as print ads, television commercials, in-store promotion to know about different aspects of the brand;

- Consumers do refer various mediums to get awareness but highest preference is being given to the online media. Online media incorporates blogs, online PR, Window displays, banner ads etc. And consumers today are more exposed to these forms of online advertising as compared to advertising through other mediums;
- Consumers require more information to take purchase decision but they do not like to spend much of their time for purchasing any commodity;
- Consumers do require plenty of information to take purchase decision. This information may increase their knowledge and assurance on brands' attributes & benefits consumers are likely to gain that will eliminate their confusion in choosing any particular brand. Once they obtain the required information on various brands, they take less time in the purchase of any commodity;
- Consumers are well knowledgeable about various usage, functions and benefits being offered by internet. The analysis reveals that there is high degree of literacy for internet usage;
- Due to its attribute of making life easier by allowing the users to have instant access with every informational, educational, interactive & entertaining material; Internet is heavily used medium today;
- The most important activities to be done through internet are social networking as it connects them with others, online shopping as it offers them convenience of shopping and media sharing site as it allows them to download their favorite enticing material such as songs, video, games etc.;
- Majority of consumers believe that companies should use online activities in their marketing efforts. Since online activities facilitate good access and higher reach to the customers; companies must take this advantage by incorporating online advertising in their marketing strategy;
- Consumers are motivated to use internet as it offers them products at discounted rates, gives access to exclusive content such as specific functional & emotional benefits of the brand, and allows them to give feedback about the brand directly to the company;
- Survey reveals that majority of consumers have stopped preferring television commercials or print ads to get brand awareness. Thus, the popular traditional mediums are no longer remained first preference for the consumers to receive ad messages;
- Consumers like interactive ability of online marketing which is not applied in case of traditional mediums like print ads, television commercials or outdoor media. Consumers like to exchange their views and share their feedback when it comes to evaluating the brand or for taking purchase decision.

Though consumers are convinced with advantages of online activities majority of them still feel that online marketing is not safe as there is more scope of fraudulent activities followed by privacy issues. These may include cheating customers by offering them faulty items, giving wrong demonstrations, taking confidential information from them such as bank details, credit card details and misusing the same.

Impact of Digital Advertising on Customers

Digital advertising in India is forecast to breach the $1 billion milestone in 2016-17. There is a lot of headroom for growth, when you look at the rapidly growing smartphone consumer base over the next five years—projected to rise 4x, up to 820 million. A more compelling indicator for digital spends that can ride this wave is the uptick in data consumption; climbing up at a compounded annual growth rate of 30% and projected to reach 7GB/month (per active user) by 2021 (according to the Ericsson Mobility Report of 2016). So why does digital ad spending in India still stand at just 15% of the total advertising pie, unlike the over 40% share in evolved markets? Where does the problem lie? I believe that the advertising model for digital in India is fundamentally broken. Very little responsible action has been taken by publishers and media agencies and to some extent even clients, rendering a large part of such a potent medium ineffective (Digital advertising in 2017: Elephant in the room?, 2017).

Digital advertising is all about effectiveness—and we all grew up to understand this is the only medium that has the power to deliver the relevant signals from consumers. And yet, in the limited buying exercises we conducted in 2016, we saw publishers turning a blind eye to traffic quality and relevance of audience profile. Unfathomable performance metrics and targeting parameters are spun out as yarns; many clients fall hook, line and sinker for these.

Reliance Jio has 50 mln users who, on average use about 1 GB of data per day. This creates 50 mln GB of traffic per day — increasing the size of the Internet in India by several fold compared to what it was before September.

The impact of this Internet explosion due to Jio is not the same across all genres and categories of online advertising. The biggest difference has been felt in video advertising, since this is where most of the extra data consumption is happening. Many of the people who have got access to free Internet use it for watching videos, primarily on Youtube.

The actual impact on the advertising rate — and consequently the decline in revenue generated per video or per minute — is difficult to get as neither publishers nor platforms like Youtube share their numbers.

Figure 1. Digital Advertising
Source: Experience Commerce

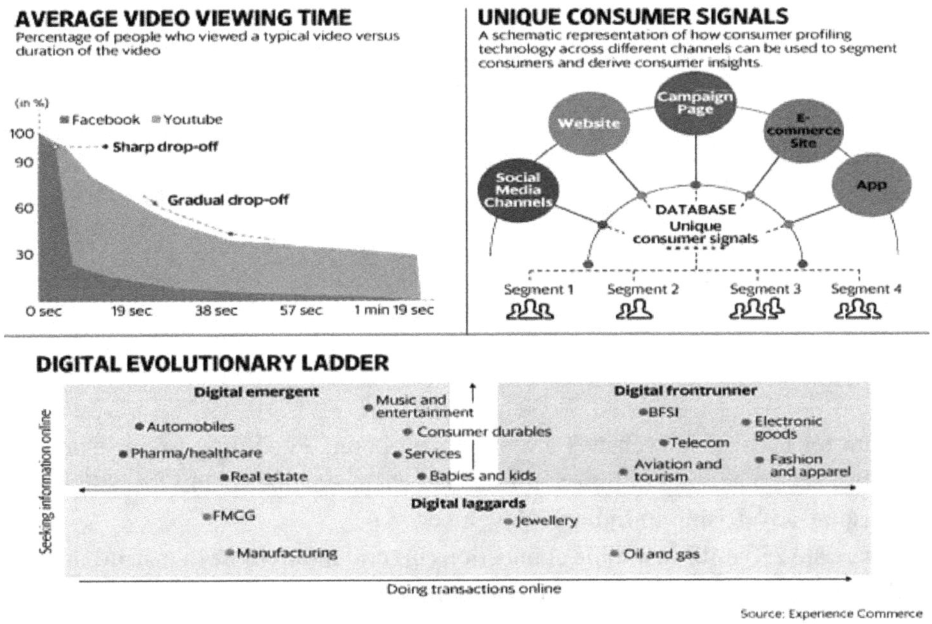

Figure 2. Digital Advertisement Spend
Source: KPMG in India Analysis

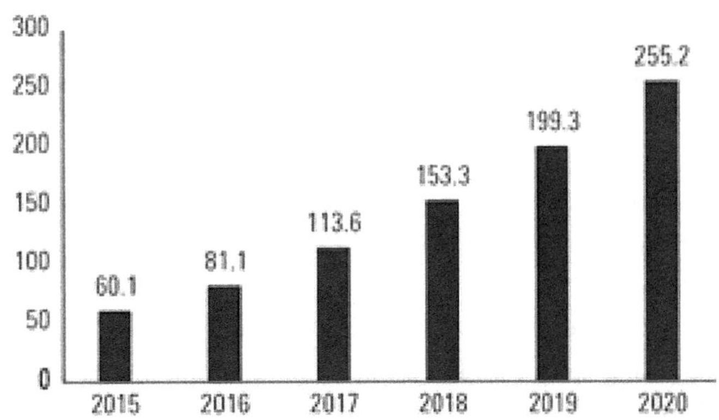

Figure 3. Digital Advertising Spend by Segment, 2015
Source: KPMG in India Analysis

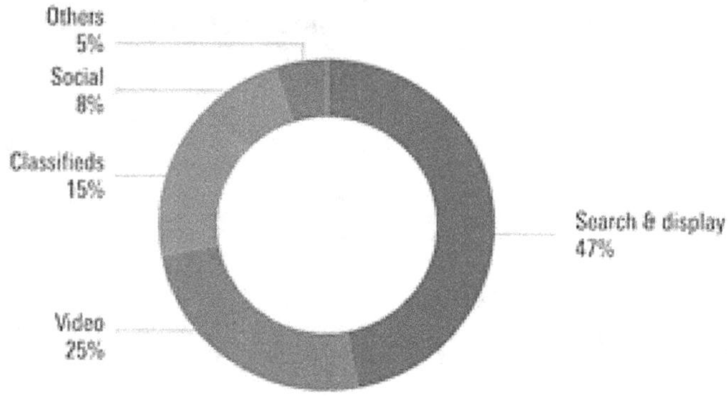

Data for text-based websites are easier to obtain. According to our evidence, there has been a halving of bid rates (also known as cost-per-click) for both search and display advertising in India in November.

There are 250 million mobile connections in rural India (more than in urban parts of the country) representing a huge opportunity to reach consumers on the move.

Impact of Digital Advertising on Retailers

With consumers saving every single penny post the Government's recent decision to *demonetize Rs 500 and Rs 1,000 notes*, offline retailers are extending and encouraging consumers to use digital payment alternatives, in order to counter the short-term loss in consumption emerging from lack of enough liquidity in the economy.

Consider the fact that India is among the most cash-intensive economies in the world, with a cash-to-GDP ratio of 12 per cent. That is almost four times that of countries like Brazil, Mexico and South Africa. The recent decision has led to retail shops and malls wearing a deserted look, albeit even for a short period of time, Pahwa (2016).

As per analysts, sectors with a sizeable magnitude of cash transactions – such as real estate, construction, jewellery, high-end retail and travel and tourism – are expected to be adversely affected. White goods demand, a source of strength for the economy, is also expected to take a hit.

To stay afloat and conquer the challenges demonetization has posed, offline retailers are encouraging consumers to move away from cash and are giving various payments solutions alternatives to avoid purchase hindrances.

In previous years, revenue coming from in-store purchases (even if the consumer has been exposed to online ads) has been solely attributed to direct in-store sales channels. Recently though, Google introduced a new feature allowing advertisers to better estimate revenue generated from their paid search campaigns on AdWords, even if the final purchase was made offline.

This new feature operates quite simply: Google maps out the stores listed in the advertiser's Google My Business account. It then cross references the data with consumers that have location history activated on their mobile phones. When a user clicks on a search ad and visits the store 30 days after interacting with that ad, a "Store Visit" conversion is generated. This process is of course done confidentially.

Impact of Digital Advertising on Business Transactions

Organizations recognize a need to migrate their existing business capabilities to digital channels and to leverage those channels more effectively for customer communications. The speed of deploying strategies to achieve those goals varies greatly and tends to reflect each company's business model, the markets it serves and its customer demographics.

Figure 4. Store Sales lift from Online Search Ads
Source: KPMG in India Analysis

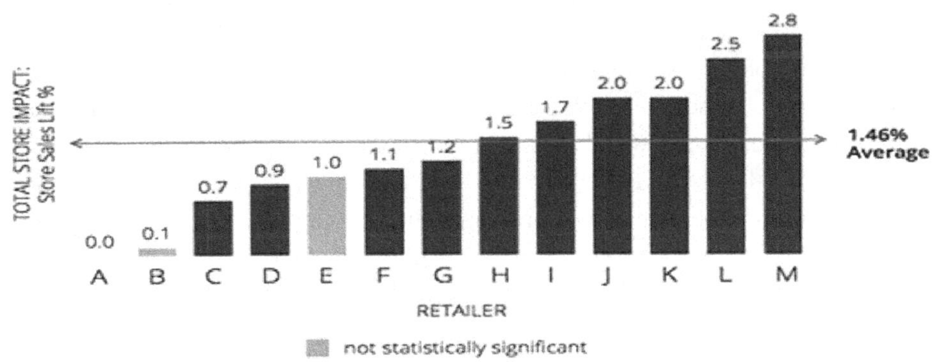

Figure 5. Online Advertising in India
Source: IMRB International, Internet in India 2007

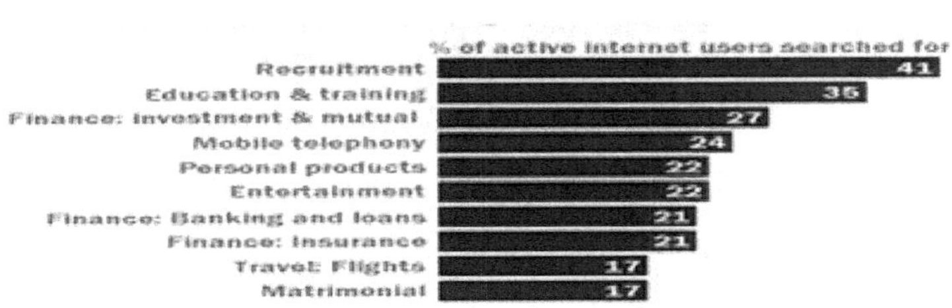

Figure 6. E-Money Gains Currency
Source: Ministry of Electronics and Information Technology

	Transactions/day	Nov 8	Dec 7	% Growth (Dec 7/Nov 8)
RuPay Cards (eComm + POS)	Number (Lakhs)	3.85	16	316
	Value (Cr)	39.17	236	503
e-Wallets	Number(Lakhs)	17	63	271
	Value (Cr)	52	191	267
UPI	Number	3,721	48,238	1,196
	Value (Cr)	1.93	15	677
USSD	Number	97	1,263	1,202
	Value (Lakhs)	1	14	1,300
		Oct Avg	Nov Avg	
PoS	Number(Lakhs)	50.2	98.1	95
	Value (Cr)	1,221	1,751	43
	Value (Lakhs)	1	14	1,300
		Oct Avg	Nov Avg	
PoS	Number(Lakhs)	50.2	98.1	95
	Value (Cr)	1,221	1,751	43

Source: Ministry of Electronics and Information Technology

The organizations are taking four common approaches to digital migration: migrating their banking or biller functionality to all of their digital channels, exploring ways to suppress paper, deploying self-service tools through web portals and through mobile and tablet applications, or simply evaluating how to use and deploy digital channels. Financial institution strategies include enhancing their online banking capabilities and adding mobile banking and remote deposit capture services. For billers, the effort often involves adding the bank channel to their bill payment functionality and improving their web portals to encourage greater participation and more electronic payments. Almost all of the organizations surveyed are simultaneously trying to reduce costs by digitizing transactional documents and encouraging paper suppression.

Many organizations still in the evaluation stage of this initiative, especially when it comes to using digital channels for transactional documents. By contrast, the marketing departments within these organizations often are much further along in adopting digital channels than other functional areas. This suggests that many organizations have a fragmented approach to digital communications. Many respondents experience challenges in getting customers to enroll for electronic services via their websites, to use self-service tools or to suppress paper bills and statements, due to the security and ease-of-use concerns cited earlier.

Among participants in the survey, the rate at which consumers are adopting paper suppression varies widely by industry. The highest rate of paper suppression was found among consumer finance organizations (40 percent), while healthcare organizations reported a much lower rate of 13 percent. The average rate of paper suppression for all survey respondents was 24 percent, average rate of 21 percent paper suppression across all vertical markets.

Most respondents attempt to encourage customers to turn off paper during the account opening or signup process. Other marketing practices commonly used to encourage paper suppression include promotion via website banner ads, statement messages, e-mail, inserts, and call center or branch staff. All respondents require customers to enroll on their websites before they can turn off paper documents.

The survey revealed a fundamental disconnect between what drives consumers to adopt electronic communications and the marketing strategies used by businesses to encourage adoption. According to the survey, the main reasons consumers would be willing to suppress paper documents are financial: They're charged a fee for paper, receive a cash incentive to discontinue paper, or receive loyalty points as a reward for moving to electronic documents. Less common reasons included greater access to more historical data online and delays in mail delivery.

Impact of Demonetization on Digital Advertising

The advertising industry braced for impact on November 8 for a very rough landing as it entered the last quarter of the financial year. According to estimates by industry experts, the move to demonetize high value currency notes in November was expected to impact around 20 per cent of yearly advertising budgets. In fact, FMCG companies, which contribute to nearly 30 per cent of all ad spends, cut advertising spends by large margins soon after the demonetization move was announced. While

Figure 7. Digital Advertising in India: Estimate Spends in Crores
Source GroupM Estimates

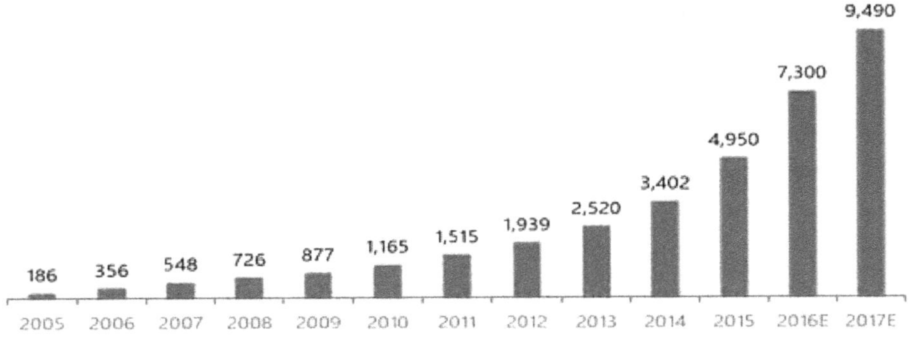

it is true that the industry as a whole bore the brunt of demonetization, the digital advertising sector may have been shielded from the worst of the impact, some experts say Chaturvedi (2016).

Number of industry insiders have observed that ad monies have moved from the more expensive mainline advertising mediums like television to digital in the face of demonetization. Rajiv Dingra, CEO and Founder, WAT Consult, said that the digital marketing sector was not greatly impacted by the demonetization move. He said that if anything, he has noticed a spike in digital advertising post demonetization.

Echoing Dingra's views, Sanjay Mehta, Jt CEO, Mirum, said that he has also not noticed any significant dip in client spends on account of demonetization. He said that some clients, say in the retail sector, who could have been impacted by the cash crunch, and might have even reduced digital spends, did not do so.

A commonly cited obstacle to digital adoption is the fact that customers often view current enrollment methods for electronic bills and statements as cumbersome and not secure. For e-bills, the customer typically must register through the biller's web portal, which requires the creation of a user name and password. For e-statements, customers often must register first for the financial institution's online banking service. Respondents believe these methods create barriers to customer adoption of digital communications and are looking to enhance their web portals to make e-adoption easier and more inviting. They're also adding more self-service tools to drive online payments and reduce costly customer service phone calls. Many organizations are augmenting their paper-based communications by adding digital channels. The most aggressive organizations are working toward migrating all paper-based customer communications to digital channels, using tactics such as pushing PDFs via e-mail and delivering communications through tablets or SMS (text) messaging on smartphones.

CONCLUSION

As we know that Demonetization process is undergoing in INDIA – the currency note of 500 and 1000 are pushed out of the economy. Currency change results into the eminent shift in the paradigm of the INDIAN market. This decision of Honorable Prime Minister wobbled the INDIAN market, Fullmer (n.d.). Many of us fail to decipher the dilemma created in the market after currency ban. A sale of goods or services mainly depends on the following criteria:

1. A need or desire of a customer;
2. Willingness to pay for the good and services to be use or purchase;
3. Ability to pay for the good and services.

Demonetization reduces the cash flow in the economy which directly affects the need, willingness and ability to pay of the customer. Because of lack of cash in hand, customers are not willing to buy any commodity or product. So there is decrease in the sale of the goods and services. If we consider the online marketplaces, most of the cash on delivery orders are cancelled by the customer because of lack of cash resources. It causes heft loss to all the online market places.

But In the era of digitization the customers use the options like online banking or mobile wallet for the payment. There is no issue of cash resources as electronic money is used for transactions. So the revenue generated by it is unaffected. According to survey, sale of apparels, shoes, electronics is not affected at all. So we cannot say that the market is totally collapsed. Many sellers stop promoting and advertising their product at online marketplace under the wrong impression of not getting sale. It is suggested that we should continue all the marketing campaigns as it will help us to improve our market index. This is the start of digital era and gradually the use of electronic money is going to increase to the extent of reducing the use of physical cash to lowest requirements. Our Prime Minister also focuses on the target of making India Digital. The future will be dominated by the trend of "GO CASHLESS". Perception of all these aspects leads to the conclusion that continuing all marketing campaigns will help you to improve your market index. Market index is directly related to the market share for that product category. So this is the right chance for the vendors to gain some ground for them and create brand value.

Overall, companies are using different approaches and moving at different speeds when adopting digital channels. While most are moving quickly to adopt digital channels for business functionality, they are often taking a slower and more measured approach to migrating transactional documents to digital channels. Many businesses and organizations are uncertain about how to best integrate digital channels with their existing communications and are challenged with influencing customers to transact with them online and communicate with them electronically. Their current business practices do not yet align with consumer preferences for digital communications. This creates opportunities to better address consumer preferences to drive greater adoption of electronic transactional documents.

REFERENCES

Chaffey, D. (2013, February 16). Definitions of Emarketing vs Internet vs Digital marketing. *Smart Insight Blog*.

Chaturvedi, O. (2016). *Effects of Demonetization on sales and marketing*. Retrieved from http://www.bmconsulting.in/blog/effect-demonetization-sales-marketing/

Digital advertising in 2017: Elephant in the room? (2017). Retrieved from http://www.livemint.com/Industry/QX0lOVJTUR2Mgn8Cm9fjTP/Digital-advertising-in-2017-Elephant-in-the-room.html

E-Marketing Strategy of Hamrobazar.com. (2013). Retrieved from https://www.bartleby.com/essay/E-Marketing-Strategy-of-Hamrobazar-Com-FKKH8343RYZS

Fullmer, J. (n.d.). More Online Consumers shop Offline [Blog Post]. Retrieved from https://storify.com/VivaKi/more-online-consumers-shop-offline-the-contradicti

Images Retail Bureau. (2016, August 30). *Online shopping trends: facts and figures on Indian e-commerce sector*. Author.

Jain, K. (2016, December 3). Demonetization: A marketing opportunity for digital payment companies [Blog Post]. Retrieved from http://brandequity.economictimes.indiatimes.com/be-blogs/demonetisation-a-marketing-opportunity-for-digital-payment-companies/1971

McGaughey, R. E., & Mason, K. H. (2015). The Internet as a Marketing Tool. *Journal of Marketing Theory and Practice*, *6*(3), 1–11. doi:10.1080/10696679.1998.11501800

Pahwa, N. (2016). *Cash vs Digital Money: why going cashless is going to be tough in India*. Available at: http://www.medianama.com/2016/11/223-cashless-india/

Patel, N. (n.d.). 10 Online Marketing Tools You Need When Starting a Business [Blog Post]. Retrieved from https://neilpatel.com/blog/10-online-marketing-tools-you-need-when-starting-a-business/

Pawar, A. V. (2014). *Study Of The Effectiveness Of Online Marketing On Integrated Marketing Communication* (Master Thesis). D.Y. Patil University, Navi Mumbai, India.

ReportE. M. (2016). Retrieved from https://www.ericsson.com/assets/local/mobility-report/documents/2016/ericsson-mobility-report-june-2016.pdf

Silky, B. (2016). Social Media as a Way for Brand Building. *Academicia. An International Multidisciplinary Research Journal*, *6*(4), 88–94.

Smyth, G. (2007). *The History of Digital Marketing*. Inetasia.

Weighing in the Advantages and Disadvantages of Internet Marketing. (n.d.). Retrieved from https://marketingwit.com/advantages-disadvantages-of-internet-marketing

Why HDFC Is No. 1 Among Indian Banks For Social Media Practice. (2011). [Blog post]. *Digital Marketing Blog*. Retrieved from https://www.digitalvidya.com/blog/why-hdfc-is-no-1-among-indian-banks-for-social-media-practice/

Chapter 14
Gamification in Entertainment Industry:
Glimpses From Indian Film Industry

Savita Sharma
Ansal University, India

Adarsh Somani
New Delhi Institute of Management, India

ABSTRACT

Gamification is a tool used for brand awareness to attract new customers and to make the present customers more loyal towards the product by making them engaged in an enjoyable manner. It has become one of the prominent topics of interest for many academicians and marketing professionals because of the simple reason that it is considered to be the one of effective ways to promote various services and products for many brands and other companies. This chapter explores gamification in the Indian film industry.

INTRODUCTION

Gamification, in most simple words can be defined as "*engaging participants with an activity/task which they perform stress-free and reflects their behaviour*". Gamification is tool used for the brand awareness, to attract new customers, make the present customers more loyal towards the product by making them engaged in an enjoyable manner. It has become one of the prominent topics of interest for many academicians and marketing professionals because of the simple reason that it is

DOI: 10.4018/978-1-5225-6064-7.ch014

considered to be the one of effective ways to promote various services and products for many brands and other companies. In recent years, it has been observed that smartphones and tablets have become essential tools for people irrespective of the age and sexual category. People find these electronic gadgets as important mode to keep them updated, communicated and entertained. One of the most commonly performed activities with the handheld terminal is to interact with different games that can be found at the application market where the consumers spend hours playing them. As the brands become aware of this trend, they include advergaming in their marketing portfolio; video games being used to promote new products, services or ideas that the brand wants to bring to the market. Many companies have launched game apps which can be down loaded in the personal devices to enhance user's participation and their motivation to be participative for maximum time. People get habitual to the games on screen because it makes them joyful and also gives opportunity to win something at the end. According to the FICCI-KPMG Indian Media and Entertainment Industry Report 2013, on an average, Indians spend over two-and-a-half hours on their smartphones every day and less than a quarter of that is spent on voice calls and SMS. The phone, for such users, is becoming a second screen as they spend an average of almost two hours a day browsing, watching videos, playing games and catching up on social networking sites.

Creating an advergame is not suitable for all the brands. But it presents a big opportunity for certain enterprises like sports & sports-related brands or lifestyle brands with positioning which can adapt well to a mobile game. The practice of this idea of advergaming varies from brand to brand. Mobile gaming is boosting growth of the games industry for these reasons: growth of two screens (mobiles and tablets), anytime-anywhere accessibility, free-to-play and freemium models and hardware innovations. Compared to traditional advertising, which is a passive one-way consumption, advergaming scores more in connecting with the consumer when he is completely immersed in a game. Mobiles are extremely personal device that demand fierce and total attention due to its nature. Thus, brands can benefit from this emotional involvement between the consumer and his game. Advertisement through games is becoming very popular in the market as it helps to retain the customers and also attract new customers. Most of the people are tech savvy and prefer to get information instantly and handy. Game apps on mobile phone is the most convenient way to promote services, products and information because it is user friendly and saves the time. It can be played anytime and anywhere, even during commuting from one place to another. In metro cities, people devote a lot of time to travel to the office and vice-versa and utilize their way time through various phone apps, where one of the most interesting and common way for them to get engaged is playing games which further help them to relax and make them fresh when they get down from the transport vehicle. There are instances where people started craving to play the game to reach to the next levels as it was very imaginatively designed to make the player overexcited which makes them play continuously for many hours. These type of games are especially created to popularize a certain product for targeted customers (Sharma, 2016). In present scenario, companies are hiring experts from software background who can create the salient features with systematic mapping of the games with most advanced technology so that people spend good amount of time without feeling tired. Experts strategically keep company's logos, coupons, prizes at various levels so that people would like to clear different levels to complete the targets and get closer to the company's products. There are certain games which are created in such a way that a customer has to even buy the product to reach to the next level of the game and people take pride to buy the product to clear the preceding levels. This happens because game makes the customers spend more time on the game app of the company and compels them to purchase the product.

GAMIFICATION IN BOLLYWOOD

India has one advantage of demographic dividend i.e. roughly 700 million Indians are below 35 years of age and over 550 million are below 25 years. The young population is more adaptive to the advent and percolation of technology and mobile phones and internet are the two mediums that has caught the eyes of the marketing gurus in Bollywood, as they are most popular amongst this age group). Moreover, the internet has become a prime medium of marketing in the recent years (Strauss & Frost, 2008). The number of active internet users is rising and internet enabled games and interfaces are being adapted at a quicker and faster rate.

Gamification is used by various segments like clothing houses, sports brands, coffee shops, eating joints, fast food restaurants, toy shops, health products and even film industry. Gamification in Bollywood industry is not a new concept but making them available on the mobile phone sets is relatively a recent development for the filmstan. Marketing professionals create games similar to the movie names with same characters and release much before with the date of release of the actual movie (AnimationXpress, 2016). As film industry has also made effort to reach to the audience through advergaming which in return given success to the producers and directors, a lot many times. Few directors have even moulded the story line with higher voting count because the audience wanted to see a happy ending. A cleverly supported incentive game app is made available in the market which can be downloaded easily with no cost. Gaming is an addictive act and keeps the participants play for longer hours to get lucrative prizes for movie like 20 percent discount on the tickets, buy one get one ticket free, download the game on phone and get chance to meet the celebrities, participants get points to share the share game with their friends, etc. Basically, games are used as positive marketing tool as a promotional activity. It has been observed that movies with games launching campaign get a fair amount of profitability. There are a number of Indian movies which have launched games like Don, Zindagi na milegi dobara, Ra-one, Singham, Gajini and many more. Following are few movie games to discuss the gaming concept: One of the most successful case in this sense is Sultan. The Game, developed by 99games, which has received excellent reviews from the public. We can also look its review on Google Play and App Store. Also, there is tremendous scope for creativity - be it integrating the brand's promise within the game or creating a game around the brand's promise. In 'Dhoom 3 - The Game', CEAT has been involved and integrated in the game in such a way that consumers has to buy CEAT Nitros from CEAT Shoppes, in order to progress. The game has been seen over 10 million downloads across Indian and other markets.

Sultan Movie: The Game – A Case Study on Gamification

The idea of using a game to engage the target audience for a beneficiary such as a film, may seem odd but is not unheard of. Titular video games being of utmost importance towards the promotion of a film has already become one of the most relevant marketing gimmicks which Bollywood has embraced without a hitch. The biggest name in such a setting is Sultan: The Game, which has beaten the likes of independent games such as Candy Crush and Subway Surfer. The game was developed by 99Games in association with Yash Raj Films and has been the most impactful game released as part of a movie promotion. The idea behind releasing a game with reference to a movie is that while a music launch provides a mellifluous way to promote a movie, video game, especially which is in line with the character of the movie and the story helps in creating a huge amount of interaction among fans and future fans and thus creates a huge fan base for the movie as well.

Games like Sultan create a certain buzz for the movie and acts like a launch pad to bring the fans closer to the movie experience and relate with the theme. Most of the games are based on a freemium model where a large chunk of the game is free to play. Revenue can be brought in two formats one that comes from advertising, then there's partnerships, where a brand is interested to partner and in-app purchase which are almost always shared with the production house. The studio lends support to the game depending on the initial popularity of the film as it helps in more downloads and in turn more revenue through in-app purchases. This is particularly true in case of Sultan which received close to 20,000 pre – registrations prior to the movie launch and over 200,000 installs within 24 hours of release. While gamification helps in increasing the fan base it also helps in discoverability. The game market on handheld devices is an over saturated place. Therefore, having a game that is endorsed by a movie studio or celebrity is the easiest promotional tool which helps the game get the necessary visibility and traction. Also, having a celebrity presence, such as Salman Khan helps in strengthening the shelf life of the game. According to Rohith Bhat, CEO of 99Games, "The success of Sultan: The Game proves that there is a huge demand for high-quality games that appeals to the Indian consumer. The influence of Cinema and Celebrity fan following is notable in India. Despite this, we were more than overwhelmed with how quickly the game rose to #1 on Google Play! The support we've received from YRF on the game trailer & launch post on Facebook and Twitter together with their continuous assistance in promoting the game along with us has been incredible,"

Happy New Year Movie: The Game

If there is any industry that has accepted advergaming with open arms then it is the Hindi entertainment industry (Bollywood). The big brands of the industry like Yash Raj Films, Red Chillies Entertainment and many more have been tying up with gaming application companies to create games based on their movies. The games can be easily downloaded on handheld devices like mobiles and tablets (Menezes, 2016). Such games are usually launched a month or two prior to the release of the movies which makes them a great medium to promote the movies and interact with the potential audience. The 'Badshah of Bollywood' had partnered with Vroovy (a joint venture between South Asia's largest digital media company, Hungama and India's largest game service company Gameshastra) and launched the official mobile game of the film. 'Happy New Year: The Game', is available for download on iOS, Android and Facebook. The game is a side scroller action adventure where a group of six highly trained thieves take on thrilling missions using their unique skill sets and gadgets to pull off the greatest diamond heist of the world. The mobile game encapsulates the essence of the film, which allows gamers to play as Champion Charlie, Marvellous Mohini, Notorious Nandu, Juggernaut Jag, Terrific Tammy or Rowdy Rohan and gear up for an action packed, heart racing adventure where they have to unlock doors, break walls, hack alarm systems, and bash guards. The game has 3D modeled characters of Shahrukh Khan, Deepika Padukone, Abhishek Bachchan, Boman Irani, Sonu Sood and Vivaan Shah (Desk, 2016). The objective of the game is to collect diamonds and discover secret chambers to help you advance in the eight available levels designed to test your mettle at different locations – The Bank, The Dockyard, The Streets of Dubai, to name a few. There are obstacles in the form of watchful guards, lasers, falling cargo, burning barrels to get to the final level: The Magnificent Atlantis Hotel. Along the way one can collect power-ups: With weapons, skill upgrades, invisibility shields, and the much coveted BomankaBatwa! There is also an option for real-time social multiplayer mode: where you can challenge your friends on Facebook/Twitter (Rajani, 2014). Commenting on the same Neeraj Roy, MD & CEO, Hungama Digital Media Entertainment said, “We are delighted to be working with the superstar of Bollywood and creating the magic of his upcoming film – ‘Happy New Year’ – on the mobile devices. The game has eight levels and it allows you to play as the characters of the film, and that I believe is a thrilling experience for the fans. I am certain that the engagement level of the game with its extremely immersive features and gameplay will keep the gamers hooked on to the game. With soaring anticipation for the film and the massive fan following of SRK, we hope the game will be well received by Mobile & Casual gamers across the world”. The game “Happy New Year” has more than a million downloads on Google Play Store and was updated to support virtual reality in 2017.

Dhoom 3 Movie: The Game

Slick graphics, cool cops and superbikes, mean streets and a tenacious anti-hero – Dhoom:3 The Game has it all, and more. Developed by 99Games Online Private Limited in collaboration with Yash Raj Films Private Limited (YRF), Dhoom:3 The Game launched exclusively on Windows Phone. An endless 3D racing game where the player dons the digital avatar of Aamir Khan’s character in the movie, is chased by Abhishek Bachchan and Uday Chopra, who play two cool cops. Soon the game was launched on the Google Play Store and Apple App Store. In Dhoom 3: The Game, the player can don the hat of the villain (or anti-hero) as the lead protagonist (character played by Aamir Khan in Dhoom 3 movie). The game player needs to ride a super bike through the streets of Chicago and try to escape from the cops including ACP Jai Dixit (played by Abhishek Bachan in the movie), Ali (played by Uday Chopra in the movie) and others. It is a 3D racing game in the Arcade & Action category (quite similar to Temple Run or Subway Surfer). The cops chase the player riding the super bike and player is expected to ride as fast as he can tackle traffic and escaping cops on road as well as from air via helicopters. There is a special option “Nitro power-up” (or Nitro boost) that the player can use to make his super bike reach top speed and leave everyone behind. Also, the super bike rider can destroy anything dangerous in its path making use of the “Sonic Pulse” feature. Like in Subway Surfer, the super bike rider can collect points in this game and use them later to buy bikes or racing suits. The player has to handle simple tap and tilt controls while riding the super bike. One can either tap on screen to balance / manage the bike or use accelerometer of the touch device (smartphone) for tilting the super bike towards left or right. The remaining control options for getting boosts, shields, etc. are available at the bottom and top of the game screen. This ensures that the player gets an uncluttered view of the game on screen. The game was such a raging success that 99games and Yash Raj Films came up with a sequel to the game "Dhoom: 3 Jet Speed". The game Dhoom: 3 Jet Speed was launched on the same day of the world television premier of the movie. While both the games has a similar game play Dhoom: 3the game had thrilling bike chase on the road, Dhoom: 3 Jet Speed had the player escaping police on a jet ski on the waters of Chicago. The game's performance was average and was downloaded more than a million times from the Google Play store.

CONCLUSION

Over the recent past years, it has been observed that technology is moving very fast and beating the records of the latest technology in a short span of time. Companies are using gamification as a learning tool to train their employees for launching new products in the market and to attract the customers as well. It has been observed that there are a number of companies from different segment have begun with gamifying processes to promote the products by engaging the customers which leads to increased customer retention. Only challenge for the company is too make the game appealing and interesting so that customers get play for longer hours and get addicted. It should be made strategically so that it is neither first level nor very complex. It has also been found that it is even easy to implement because people are much more tech savvy now days and being handy they can access the games anytime anywhere. Games persuade the customers to buy the promoted product as in return they will be gaining something else also which will be worth for them. Gamification is perfectly suitable for present market state and the customers' perspective but scenario may not be the same when technology takes another turn. Probably the future iterations of gamification may lead to enormous flexibility and configurability which can even allow the participant itself to moderate the game in between to make it interesting and unique. Innovation could be something drastically a new concept. Therefore, companies should start thinking and be ready with the alternative techniques to tackle the market change.

REFERENCES

AnimationXpress. (2016, June 14). *Games*. Retrieved from AnimationXpress.com: http://www.animationxpress.com/index.php/latest-news/sultan-the-game-rises-to-the-top-among-free-games-on-google-play

Desk, E. W. (2016, July 1). *Entertainment*. Retrieved from Indian Express: http://indianexpress.com/article/entertainment/entertainment-others/sultan-the-game-is-out-and-salman-khan-loves-it-too-2845366/

Dhapola, S. (2014, October 31). *Entertainment*. Retrieved from First Post: http://www.firstpost.com/entertainment/happy-new-year-game-review-possibly-even-more-painful-than-the-film-1781035.html

Menezes, R. (2016, July 4). *Digital*. Retrieved from exchange4media: http://www.exchange4media.com/Digital/SultanThe-Game-tops-Google-Play-Store-charts;-celebrity-impact-creativity-spur-gamer-interest_65090.html

Rajani, S. (2014, October 16). *Showbiz*. Retrieved from India.com: http://www.india.com/showbiz/happy-new-year-game-the-official-game-of-shah-rukh-khans-latest-entertainment-saga-is-finally-out-173754/

Sharma, D. (2016, June 10). *Entertainment*. Retrieved from Zee News India: http://zeenews.india.com/entertainment/movies/sultan-the-game-ready-for-download-salman-khan-tweets-the-link_1893764.html

Strauss, J., & Frost, R. (2008). *E-Marketing*. Prentice Hall Press.

Team, A. X. (2014, October 24). *Games*. Retrieved from Animation Xpress.com: http://www.animationxpress.com/index.php/latest-news/shahrukh-khan-and-vroovy-team-up-to-launch-the-official-mobile-game-of-happy-new-year

Chapter 15
Gamification to Promote the Engagement in Healtcare and Wellness of Patients Under Therapeutic Care:
Gamification and Healthcare

Surendra Prasad Mishra
Dr. Ram Manohar Lohia Institute of Medical Sciences, India

Anoop Kumar Srivastava
Dr. Ram Manohar Lohia Institute of Medical Sciences, India

Dinkar Kulshreshtha
Dr. Ram Manohar Lohia Institute of Medical Sciences, India

Ajeet Kumar Gandhi
Dr. Ram Manohar Lohia Institute of Medical Sciences, India

Madhup Rastogi
Dr. Ram Manohar Lohia Institute of Medical Sciences, India

ABSTRACT

The evolution of gaming in healthcare promotion evolved concurrently with the ascendance of computing technology, smart phones, facilitated by video-based 3D technology and virtual reality in the mid-eighties and nineties. Health and wellness in the twenty-first century is interlinked with the wealth of the nation and individuals and its traditional definition of physical, psychological, spiritual, social, and financial optima has seen new paradigms. The gaming technology has found groundbreaking applications in many diagnostic and therapeutic modalities

DOI: 10.4018/978-1-5225-6064-7.ch015

to modulate the behavioral changes, simulation of virtual reality, and passage to recovery through neurologically engaging the cognitive functions with the stimuli produced. Physiological symptoms and life-threatening disorders which may caused be faced by viral inflictions (HIV, Hepatitis C, etc.) and type 2 diabetes could today be significantly managed by gaming technologies for psychosomatic management.

INTRODUCTION

Advent of smartphones have seen the spurt in gaming technology and its utilization by all age groups, genders and classes. It has found more appealing to children and adolescent but youths and elderly too have a liking to it. It is played for entertainment, simulations of adventure, Brooks et al. (2016) and for recreation, Li and Foo (2014). It has been reported by many researchers that over 40% of the United States population is engrossed in computer games for 3 or more hours per week in 2015, Fleming et al. (2014). The games have various designs and have variety of end processes with multiplicity of dimensions, goals, interaction and involved technologies. The variations in gaming have evolved from some very simple key board games inbuilt in computer to sophisticated software based with artificial intelligence. Over the years new spectrums have been added in gaming arena which are designed for variety of applications such as to enhance concentration, (Formagini, 2017), improve memory, enhance information, Fleming et al. (2014) and provide orientations for learning the deeper aspect of the subject, Eagger (1992). Some games are designed to influence the cognitive ability and inculcate innovative methods for problem solving, enhance analytical abilities and modulate behavioral change, Connolly (2012). The past few decades have seen rapid strides in development of gamification industry which has embarked on developing serious games capable of medical interventions. It is generally believed that gaming portals have something new to share about health and educational issues. The gaming interventions have ramifications in societal areas to improve the outcome of a course of medical interventions, Andrews (2011). The reach of *interventional games* have been converted in *gamification* which have been incubated from simple computer key board based games to operate on smartphones with ability to provide counseling and coaching in physiotherapy. However, the various types of games which have reached to market have attempts to influence the thought process in a delicate manner. These are mostly harping on gamification with simulated inputs to make the individual user orient the thought process in a particular direction. Serious games which have potential applications in health care are tuned to utilize gaming as a central and primary medium by providing virtual reality and stimuli of desired quantity and quality, Andrews (2011). In contrast, gamification refers to the addition of game elements to modification of desired thought patterns and creates positive vibrations in non-game contexts, Dondlinger (2007). A gamified intervention may not operate as a full game experience but contains gaming elements, such as the scoring of points, in-game rewards, or engaging in quests and desire to be the best winner. The gamification has found application in healthcare intervention from some time. However, game-based approaches for mental health are in their embryonic stage.The modern gaming technology is one of the most interactive, attractive and entertaining tools by its ability to simulate the virtual reality. These gaming tools are designed to empower a patient with self-promotional ability to behavioral change inducing healthy life style habits. The modern gaming patterns are based on real clinical experiences which have developed with rigorous research and trails in clinics. Hence this can improve self-management and also provide virtual information about progression of both curative and palliative care with improve in the quality of life. It empowers the patient to see for itself the progression of recovery and quality of life thereafter. This adds an element of display of real time recovery and consequences in benefit of medical management. The initial sock of patient on input about fetal diseases are mostly from disbelieve to rejection to *I may not be a victim.* Diagnosis of some of the diseases especially cancer, cardiac, neurological and renal related ailments, HIV, hepatitis and HPV infections have connotations of unpleasant and unbelievable physiological shock. The narration by physician and counseling often leaves an information deficit and patient is keen to learn either *no* or has the fear of the consequences. The gamification not only provide factual information but creates a behavioral acclimatization and introduces the difficult medical procedure and outcome in a virtual reality format for better preparatory response to the shock. It's possible outcome and passage to recovery through virtual environment by neurologically engaging the cognitive ability and stimuli produced by the gaming gives enormous soothing. It is therefore pertinent to mention that the designing of the game could be persuasive which can encourage deeper understanding of physiological pattern of the body and thus can create a virtual reality for assimilation of the scenario to face the challenge upfront. The gaming can introduce the medical events leading to several chronic ailments viz renal failure, cardiac ailments, depression, pediatric sickness and viral manifestation and some very simple and common methods of recovery with high self believe. Evolution in gaming has profound effect on management of these serious ailments, Read (2011). It not only supplements the information given by physician but adds to understanding of patients. It also enables to facilitate the repetitive session in virtual scenario.

Health care is quite a tedious and absorbing subject hence gamification need to be seen in that optics of virtual physician with a real patient and the physician is available with click of a button. The objective of new paradigm in personalized health care is to be more interactive and better monitoring without interfering in routine yet harnesses maximum information about recovery process after any interventions. These new approaches make it possible the physician to have 3D information about the patient even during the periods **there have not been visits.** As a secondary objective some fun and games might be of help both to the patient and their attendance. However, it must be realized that gamification is not a tool to substitute the physician and could not be used at the cost of actual health care needs.

A new paradigm has emerged for improved infiltrations by gamification to motivate behavioral changes of customers and there are inklings to use a specific brand. A competition is ushering in gaming arena where the competitive brands are virtually simulating its superiority. Some are claiming superiority over other in providing better updates and current state of the art information in health care connectivity. In healthcare, it has been found that the games which have shown acclimatization and behavioral alterations have high research and commercials values. Gamification in healthcare should not be confused with patient entertainment. It is not to keep the mind of patient diverted and entertained. The new technology driven gaming has been designed to have a holistic care and are multifocal. It provides patients real time recovery pathways and hope for better outcome and facilitates the physician to monitor and access the desired information for any interventions. This adds to the task of patient critical care and management to treating physician.

PROJECTED BUSINESS POTENTIALS

It is projected that gamification in health care would be a multibillion dollar industry. The gaming industry has been growing in geometric proportion and has been empowered to monitor the walking patterns, cardiac and breathing patterns and even intimate the family physicians any alterations in vital health indicators for timely intervention. It is estimated by published literature that gamification industry has made rapid strides which was estimated to be over 100 billion in 2016 and has grown by an estimated 8.5 percent from 2015 onwards. The larger leap forward in gamification has been feasible due to seamless integration with smart phones. Marketers have projected a revenue share of about 40 billion dollars in the current fiscal year and ascendance of growth by 22 percent. It was also found that these gaming were not limited to children or adolescents alone but has substantial input from adults above 35 years. The integration of gamification with smart phone gives all-round access to current status and search through medical platforms. There are several major players and software giants engaged in healthcare gamification and have developed a deep entrenched clinical team to update the ongoing gaming to be more personalized, realistic, and disease oriented with mindful of societal moorings. These elements would have to be integrated to phones or other electronic devices to provided desired input to patient. The growth of the technology has enormous effect on the empowerment of patent. The patient is in a position to question the physician of a particular choice of treatment. Ironically the gaming industry is attempting to keep pace with clinical literatures but there is lack of evidence and very few clinical trials under way for better assimilation. These updated smart apps softly turn out to be individualistic and the user many times gets emotionally integrated and develop a taste to visualize the full course of action on the path of recovery. It also creates a virtual sense of medical audits and keeps full information of treatment delivered and definitive plan for recovery. The gamification would incorporate an environment where patient and physician are at the same page. The strategies of information through click of a button has easy adoptability and a patient is able to do a self-auditing of ability to adopt the physiotherapeutic, speech therapy procedures and document the progress attained which can be part of medical progress sheet and could be remotely accessed. This is going to totally revolutionaries the gamification and would make deep inroads in patient counselling and management though telemedicine.

Chronic Health Disorders: Diabetic and HIV

Diabetics and HIV are disorders which are mostly lifestyle driven besides and type 2 diabetes having genetic dispositions. Both disorders require lifetime monitoring and advice with the physician. Chronic health care are mostly designed to contain the disease and limit the complications. Diabetes specially has multi factorial component viz food intake exercise, hygiene and periodic monitoring of various parameters and medical remedial interventions accordingly. The smart phones gaming allows to accommodate the full scope of glucose monitoring and precise remedial actions. The other chronic disorders viz. renal, arthritis and hepatic need long term life style and drug managements. Keeping a track of records and access to history of progress of ailments and remedies taken are frequently required. The information could be harnessed through smart app for long term managements. The regulation insulin intake could be addressed and patient also has the confidence of accurate analysis of the situations.

Pediatric Oncology

Pediatric oncology has several difficult areas to medically address besides the emotional challenges. Some of the pediatric cancers viz. lymphoma and leukemia are mostly treatable by high dose chemotherapy. Others childhood cancers viz. retinoblastoma, brain tumours and wilm's tumour are treated by judicious combination of surgery, radiotherapy and chemotherapy. These treatments pose several complexities viz, prolonged duration of treatment, severe toxicity, loss of wait, loss of appetite and general weakness and home sickness. Some of the high end chemotherapy require isolations and barrier nursing. The bone marrow transplant if required poses altogether different issues in nursing and keeping the child motivated. The parents and child both suffer severe mental trauma which has remained a challenge for medical community inspite of large pronounced progress. Some of the pediatric cancer produce very sickening feel specially patients receiving high hose chemotherapy and blood transfusions for treatment of leukemia, retinoblastoma, lymphomas and wilm's tumour. It is to be noted that some of these are not always curable and its management dimension include counseling. Children do not have ability to communicate the quantum of grief and agony with which they are suffering. It is imperative to help such patient to cope with treatment aftermath with care and supportive means in a playful homely environment. Patient empowerment and support to pediatric patients require different ambience as well as a connect to need of growing child, the top priority of the child is to play and be connected to home ambience. The 3D gaming has come as a hope and motivator. These games not only create an illusion of benign in home environments by 3D projections but could also keep the child mentally upbeat and desirous of participation in the gaming activity. Here comes a huge role of gaming industry. The children love video games and many such tools which look real to life experience of home and class room. The long duration treatment maybe of 6-12 month and such engaging games may provide a motivation to child to visit the clinic and may ask for utilization of such tools.

The process of healing in pediatric patients is often complex and time taking. An effort is worth using animation, 3D and other video games to empower the pediatric patients by giving hope to get cure. These gaming have to be focused in physiologically empowering the kids to fight the diseases and have the necessary motivation and zeal to face the treacherous course of chemotherapy and other therapies. These tools could also give instant boost to child to give feedback and visible gleefulness. The pediatric patients pose a very serious problem while undergoing radiotherapy. It is delivered in isolation hence gaming display on roof and colorful radiotherapy immobilization masks have been found to be very handy. The gaming impacts could also be quantified by retrospective study of the observation of the child. The fatigue and toxicity of radiotherapy could be reduced by engaging the child in playful ambience and engaging the mind in overcoming the toxicity. It has also been seen that Pediatric patients in oncology have difficulty and loss of appetite in normal intake. The gaming can provide option to choose from the available food so that their nutritional needs are fulfilled without any difficulty. The gaming has to move on with capability to influence the neurotransmitters for inculcating the positive approach in the mind of child. Children suffering with cancer could be given a hope to cope with treatment process with games which make them feel that they are on path of recovery.

Gaming in Neuropsychiatric Diseases

With the scientific advances in the medical field, computer based technology has been used to diagnose and manage neurological disorders. A fun part of computers is the entertainment from a variety of computer games which apart from recreation also test the individuals' skills and coordination. The wide use of games in computers and now in smart phone devices led to their use in the field of medicine for improving health standards and physical fitness. This aspect of applied games includes serious games and gamification and has been found to improve the mental health and psychological rehabilitation in patients with neuropsychiatric disorders, Read (2011). *Serious games* use applications as a means to educate and motivate patients in learning as enunciated by Dondlinger (2007), Fleming et al. (2014) and have been shown to enhance concentration, improve the skills and learning behavior, Fleming et al., (2016). But their use is limited by the high cost and design complexity. Also, as the target population is a small number of patients with health related issues compared to the general population enjoying the bigger and more entertaining and complex games, the motivation behind their use and development is lacking. Also, serious games require a sophisticated console and a specific space which is not accessible to all in the society, Johnson (2016), Munson (2015). To overcome these hurdles, gamification may be used in an effective way as the response of drug interventions. The mechanism is that the gaming proceeds with an entertainment initially and generates interest which gives endocrine boost in patient to continue. The hormonal surge and feel of winner in gaming indirectly modulated the behavior by helping the cognitive ability and neuron to transmit intelligent gaming engagements. The designing features allow it to use the gaming features for entertainment and as it proceeds it makes the user to modulate the behavior and mode of interactions, Fleming et al. (2016), Johnson et al. (2016).

The gaming business in health commenced around 2008 in moderate scale and since then it has harped in ever evolving mode and more tools have been integrated seamlessly with smart phones. There is healthy competition in various stake holders in conjunction with smart phones to developed more interactive and multi centric games. The idea is that patient remains on the radar of medical monitoring while playing the games.

Gamification is the use of game-like rewards and incentives incorporated in certain tasks that encourages alteration in observational ability and worked towards developing such ability which is part of strategy to motivate and provide orientation to empower in desired directions, Lister et al. (2014). With regards to neuropsychiatry, preventive and social medicine can be largely benefitted from incorporation of new media tools viz e-mental health and smart phone applications, cujipers (2011). In fact, WHO, in its Mental Health Action Plan 2013–2020, suggest *the promotion of self- care with utilization of electronic and mobile health technologies* (16) which will have far reaching ramification in the 21st century. This may help lot many needy and poor patient in developing world who have been left out till now from the ambit of modern medicine.

Gamification can be particularly useful in neuropsychiatric disorders where behavioral modification and motivation is an extremely important aspect apart from therapeutic measures. Mobile apps technology can provide a simple and easy to use tool compared to the conventional practices of extensive counseling and rehabilitative measures to bring about a positive feedback in patients with chronic neurodegenerative disorders. There have been numerous studies on the use of gamification and serious games in the field of both neurology and psychiatry. Stroke rehabilitation, substance abuse, anxiety disorders are some of the examples where gamification has been found to be useful. Following area where gamification is an important rehabilitative tool in neuropsychiatric medicine are:

GAMIFICATION IN PSYCHIATRIC DISORDERS

Gamification and Substance Abuse (Smoking Cessation)

Smoking cessation is an challenge for health care providers and planners. It has very serious health hazards from cancer to heart and affects the functioning of most organs adversely. The utilization of gaming technology to engage the mind to give up smoking or reduce the frequency of smoking would be immense benefit. But this intervention is costly and the bulk of the cost is due to the behavioral support. To look for any better ways to tackle smoking addiction, mobile apps and gamification have been tried in the recent times. There have been studies which have demonstrated that quitting smoking is tedious but gaming has helped many people to quit the smoking easily. It was elucidated by many authors that the gaming induced positive changes in behavior and helped the patients to utilize the self believe as demonstrated in gamification to quit the smoking. The participants found a change in the attitude in the way they looked forward to smoking. Goal tracking in the app helped them keep a note of the progress they made towards smoking cessation. By breaking down the final target of quitting smoking to smaller milestones with rewards and punishments related to these, the participants found this method more interesting compared to the monotonous counseling schedules. Participants using the gamified intervention demonstrated greater levels of motivation and subsequent engagement than the non-gamified groups. Thus, gamification is a low-cost and effective measure in smoking cessation therapies, El-Hilly et al. (2016). The Health Belief Model (HBM) has been postulated to explain the behavioral changes induced by gamification, this model derives its strength from the fact and observations that positives drawn from gaining by the participants believed that facts demonstrated in console is transferable to actual knowledge and could become an strength to forgo the smoking, Carpenter (2010). There are numerous such gamification apps available both in the android and apple version. In the 'kwit' and 'kwit 2' apps, the number of lifetime cigarettes smoked and the money saved since smoking was quit is highlighted. The apps calculate the increase in life expectancy after quitting and savings with graphical representation of health benefits. 'The Hypnomatic' app additionally contains hypnosis sessions, Formagini et al. (2017).

Gamification and Depression

As per WHO, depression was the third largest contributor to global disease burden in 2008. Despite effective pharmacological means available, the prevalence of depression is on the rise, especially in developing countries. Stigma associated with the disease, cost of therapy and limited access to health care facilities hinder in reducing the disease burden. Cognitive behavioral therapy (CBT), the psychological intervention most commonly employed has a response rate around 60%. These factors led to more innovative and easy to use measures to help counter patients with depressive symptoms, DeRubeis et al. (2005). Gamification apps related to this condition measure depressive symptoms, help people with positive thinking, monitor dysfunctional thoughts and altered thinking patterns, Giosan et al (2016). In a systemic review, authors identified nine studies utilizing gaming as a key component in managing depression. Most studies available involve a fantasy world where real life skills are learnt through a virtual world experience, Fleming et al. (2014).

Gamification and Anxiety

Social anxiety disorder has high life time prevalence between 4-6% in Europe. As is the case with depression and other neurotic psychiatric disorders, drugs are only a part of treatment and not all are amenable to much needed CBT, Richards et al. (2016). Gaming based cognitive behavior therapy has been applied in the Cochrane review, the ICBT was not different from face to face interviewing in allaying the anxiety symptoms and improving wellbeing. Smart phone based gamification apps or mobile ICBT has advantages of being cost effective, covering a wider population range and the ease of administration, Olthuis et al. (2015). The challenger app has been developed at the psychology department, Stockholm (Table 1) that uses real-time location awareness, notifications, anonymous social interactions and use of gamification techniques. Psychotherapy is provided and the patients are encouraged to write notes, Miloff et al. (2015).

Similarly, stress which is a precursor for hypertension, diabetes, cardiovascular and neurological catastrophes, is on rise the especially in the developing countries and needs to be tackled at the earliest. Relaxation exercises and acceptance and commitment therapy (ACT), a type of CBT has shown to decrease stress levels at work place. These therapies acts by various modes but contextual theories which have been proposed are acceptance, mindfulness, diffusion, self as context, values and committed action for improvement of the functions using the attributes of gaming, Hayes et al. (2006). In this randomized trial, stress intervention with smart phone app was compared with a wait list control group. The participants were assessed on the basis of generalized health questionnaire at the end of 6-week study period. The game designers have interpolated the technological features of smart phones to piggy back the gaming which induct the modulating in thought by inducing self believe and hope of victory as in gaming in life scenarios. There were modules for each week with audio lectures and few exercises. The authors concluded that participants using the smart phone app had a significant reduction in the stress level compared to the control group, Ly et al. (2014).

The role of gamification and serious games in the field of psychiatry is vast and as a replacement for counseling and therapy, most psychiatric illnesses will get benefit by smart phone apps and gamification maneuvers.

GAMIFICATION IN NEUROLOGICAL DISORDERS

Stroke

IN non communicable diseases besides heart attack and cancer, Stroke or cerebrovascular accident has shown most devastating and major cause of death. It also shows very compelling severe disability to the patients if survived. Problem of stroke related morbidity has grown to epidemic proportions, especially in developing countries. Stroke survivors are left with permanent disabilities in the affected limb and need extensive rehabilitation and physiotherapist has to work hard on habitation, Badachi et al. (2015). Most of the time these exercises or organ specific or site specific depending on which organ has been affected most. Now robotic supported precision exercises has come in place but its high cost and poor accessibility has limited these devices to only a few centers. The gamification of these exercises via smart phone and tablet devices can be an effective way in implementing these at home and can be a cost effective measure. Virtual reality scenarios can be created and can be used to monitor remotely through the period of recovery. The data can be used by a therapist who can then plan any future interventions. A number of smart phone apps are in use for rehabilitation in stroke like Dr Droid, Dr Droid Glove, UBI-Rehab etc., Brewer et al. (2012). Most of these applications are not evidence based but are still favored by the general public. Also, the gamification networks should be such that the care givers can also take active part in the modern rehabilitation process, Jhang et al. (2015). For the same, a stroke support station (S3) has been developed in Singapore for stroke rehabilitation purposes. The program has 3 applications, the S3 stroke survivor, S3 caregiver and S 3 rehabilitation application. Patients can track their international normalised ratio (INR) which has to be frequently monitored in those taking anti-coagulant medications. The associated co-morbidities are also included and a mood tracker and quality of life questionnaires can help in diagnosing depression, a common post stroke manifestation. Care givers are advised on general nursing care and the exercising schedule. In the rehabilitation application, patients can view the exercises and physiotherapy sessions. It has been recommended that stoke patients can put on their smart phone with apps so that the motions, the exercises and limb strengthening exercises could be counted and quantified for monitoring the response. These phone have the inbuilt facility to store the data or transmit to healthcare center for storage which could be analyzed. This way the patients remains in the connect with physicians. Thus, the attending physiotherapist can monitor the progress of the patients' condition, Jhang et al. (2015). The limitation posed by hemiplegia and poor hand functions was assessed by Rinne et al, 2010. In their study they have reported that more than 50% of their patient were able to utilize the console of buttons of smart phone to connect to desired gaming apps. The resultant bonfire were twin fold one the improvement in cognitive ability and second the induction of desired exercise schedules. The direction of movement was inversely proportional to the disability severity. To improve upon this limitation, they used a hand grip controller which improved the cursor control in the hemiplegic subjects, Rinne et al. (2010). As the hand grip functions are relatively well preserved, the improvement in cursor control was but obvious. Such innovations are needed based on the target population especially in stroke where cognitive impairment, aphasia and hemiplegia would always interfere with both the conventional and highly advanced rehabilitative systems.

Cognitive Impairment and Dementia

With medical advances and increased life expectancy, it is not surprising that people with dementia are being increasingly diagnosed. There have been attempts to halt the process of cognitive decline with advancing age, but the pharmacological measures show only a limited effectiveness in controlling progression to Alzheimer's disease (AD), Eagger et al (1992). Dementia per se starts as mild cognitive impairment (MCI) and then progresses to severe decline in memory and executive functions requiring support for activities of daily living. Patients with MCI report mild forgetfulness but are otherwise independent for all daily activities. As with AD, there are no pharmacological measures to halt the progression of MCI to AD. Besides the pharmacological intervention to improve exercises, gaming and gaming related interventions have been reported to be beneficial by MCI, Eagger et al. (1992), Petersen et al. (2005). But cognitive training requires motivation and prolonged therapy sessions. In older individuals with associated neuropsychiatry co-morbidities, there are high dropout rates. To overcome these drawbacks, gamified cognitive training was attempted in patients with MCI using a learning and memory game, the 'game show'. Twenty one patients played eight 1-hour sessions of game show on an iPad. They were awarded gold coins after associating geometrical patterns with spatial locations. They would be encouraged to boost to a higher level in the next session. Their results in terms of cognitive scores, motivation and level of enjoyment were compared with controls who underwent clinical sessions as usual. The authors found that episodic memory robustly improved in the gamified cognitive training group along with visuospatial abilities, Maher et al. Thus, gamification apps can be an effective means to improve motivation and memory training in patients with mild cognitive impairment.

Cerebral Palsy

Cerebral palsy comprises a group of neurological disorders attributable to non-progressive disturbances in developing fetal or infant brain. Cerebral palsy results in limitation of activities caused by motor dysfunction like weakness, dystonia or in co-ordination and is often accompanied by disturbances of perception, cognition, communication, and behavior, Sewell et al. (2014). The only means of ameliorating the symptoms of cerebral palsy is rehabilitation. Persistence with physiotherapy sessions is more problematic as the pediatric population is the one affected and parents are not able to cope up with these sessions and their routine chores. In such cases, gamification through computer based technology can be an effective means in motivating children and parents and can provide active rehabilitation without much effort. Witting Hill et al created a 'Kinect-based' game, 'Burnie' for upper body physiotherapy in pediatric cerebral palsy. In this game, Burnie has to fly through obstacles in search of rewards while avoiding obstacles. The child has to flap his/her arms in order to control burnie's movements. The movements designed are as per the physiotherapy motor training exercises. In this pilot study employing under graduate students, player satisfaction measured along visuo-aesthetics, game control and enjoyment fared better that routine sessions. The authors plan to target individuals with pediatric cerebral palsy for Burnie gamification, Whittinghill and Brown (2014). Replacing physiotherapy sessions with the gamification apps in the future for diseases like cerebral palsy that have no 'cure', should be attempted as the motivation and enjoyment does improve the clinical skills in these patients.

The list of gamification apps in neuropsychiatric diseases is endless and beyond the scope of this chapter. Other diseases where it has been found useful is traumatic brain injury, gait disorders, disorders of co-ordination and thought disorders to name a few.

Gamification in Neuropsychiatric Disorders: The Other Side of the Coin

Gamification apps, despite having numerous advantages, also have some issues that need to be looked into. Foremost is the boredom that seeps once these games with similar patterns are used for prolonged periods of time. Most of the diseases discussed require either long term sessions or similar periods of gamification exercises to make any significant impact. Most studies that find a positive health impact of these apps are analyzed after a brief period of say 5-8 weeks. In such a short period, patients really find it interesting to use a new methodology to train themselves. But these studies lack a follow up data and hence it needs to be seen if the same amount of motivation persists for longer periods or the same becomes a monotonous task and patients then find excuses to carry out the gamification exercises. Maher et al. have elucidated in their published work that the enhancement in intensity of activity does not has long term profound influence on mental cognitive abilities. They have also concluded in their work that patents could not detect any significant benefit in mental ability by using games, Meher et al. The studies till now have small sample sizes, poorly defined control groups and are primarily based on user experience outcomes. There need to be studies that evaluate the long term and sustained effects of gamified products.

Pandher and Bhullar in 2016 examined the salient features of smartphone applications in seizure management. The limitations of gaming industry include the limitations of various apps available in market. It has been observed that only few apps have the ability to induce comprehensive and broad based educational ability. The need is that these gaming should monitor and record the adverse events and keep a video track of the events, Pandher and Bhullar (2016). It is also an important requirements that such events which a health consequences need to be tracked and communicated to treating physicians. The gamification apps studied till date use the two most popular app stores but there are other less popular range of apps available. Thus, it is the patient's choice in selecting the most appropriate tool for health benefits. Thus, the health behaviors targeted are the consumer's choice rather than the health parameters that the health specialists plan to target, Edwards et al. (2016). This appears to be an important drawback and we propose that some guidelines on the content and range of behaviors that the apps target should be set forth before these apps are launched in the market.

Most patients with neuropsychiatric disorders like stroke, dementia, psychosis etc. have severe cognitive disabilities or physical handicaps and are not candidates for gamification intervention. Patients with stroke and language dysfunction have comprehension deficits and in such group of patients, the routine physiotherapy sessions it seems would fare better than the gamification apps requiring self-dependence for rehabilitation. There have been numerous trials on alternate therapies like yoga and relaxation exercises for people with anxiety disorders, Kligler et al. (2016), Ramanathan et al. (2017). The gamification apps to our best knowledge have been compared with the more conservative psychology and counseling sessions. We feel that there should be a side to side comparison of gamification and time tested relaxation therapies and yoga for health benefits.

The gaming has opened a new reach in interventions of health care with added benefit of continuous feedback to physician. However, the old age group patients who are away from modern technology and those groups who have been excluded from development of computer application will always pose a challenged to planner to inculcate them in this stream. Implementation of gaming is both a challenging and opportunity in patients prefer specially in the age old patients and those who are not technical equipped. Thus, gamification in the present scenario can be an additional tool in implementing a healthy lifestyle to people suffering from a wide range of neuropsychiatry diseases.

CONCLUSION

Gamification is a widely acceptable and have fully integrated in one form or the other with every strata of the society. Many use it from diabetic to heart care. some use it for daily running and monitoring the calorie intake and its utilizations. It has

Table 1. The challenger app for anxiety management

1. Guide Get started with the challenger Review off apps key features Helpline number	2. Rewards Add rewards to your game board Type your own reward or be inspired by others	3. Skills Choose which skills you want to work with Set goals for each skill and see how well you master them
4. Challenges Perform challenges and write reflections Write your experiences with facing the challenge tasks	5. Feedback Give and receive feedback anonymously	6. Packages Take in knowledge and tips along the way.

emerged as motivational tool to exercise and follow physiotherapy schedule and being used as more conventional methods of rehabilitation programs. It is note worthy that with such extensive use of smart phones available, the health advantages by introducing effective apps can serve people in remote places and villages for whom to travel for the frequent sessions and consultations to the doctor or a therapist is an expensive and a cumbersome task. The app use is on the discretion of the user and people who are reluctant to go to therapist for the fear of social stigma can be benefitted. The present apps available for implementing motivation and behavioral changes in the patients need to be tested with follow up data on their effectiveness. Also, there is large scope to make it clinically relevant based on long term researches and its systematic evaluations. The gaming has moved from simple computer programming to more interactive input from health planers and health care providers. It is imperative to indulge in randomized trials to evaluate the efficacy of game based health modifications to non-game based conventional method to in large sample to come out with comparative advantages and disadvantages.

BEHAVIORAL MODULATION

Therapeutic Gains Using Behavioral Modulation

Computer games are permeating rapidly and have become all pervasive and can be utilized for serious purposes such as health and education. *Applied games* and gamification (gaming elements used outside of games) have the potential to increase the impact of mental health mainly by *three* processes. First, by extending the reach of online programs to those who might not otherwise use them. Second, by improving engagement through both game-based and *serious* motivational dynamics. Third, by utilizing varied mechanisms for change, including therapeutic processes and gaming features. The potential of gaming has very deep interactive influence on behaviors disorder. The various games which are utilized these days in behavioral modulation are cognitive behavior therapy-based games, entertainment games, biofeedback, and cognitive training games.

The impact of gaming has been elaborated by many works and they have found that gaming and music has worked in providing relief to the symptoms. This cannot be cited as proof that it works in long lasting behavioral alteration. Large sample need to be evaluated which are statistically significant to be conclusive in saying gaming has the ability of modifying the habits. The commercial portal and clinical trials need to study the consequences and establish in which behavioral disorder it is more affective and which it is of peripheral influences. However, in limited fashion it is well argued that it has benefits. The transient changes need to be looked to establish it lasting impacts. there is large potential to developed such apps which works in these areas and would be a huge enterprise and success.

The Intervention of Gaming

The gaming in neurological healthcare is here too stay. It has been widely practiced and has sound footing in its supportive role. Recently evidences have emerged that applied gaming has the deep physiological impact on the neurological stimulating of mental health. The games mostly have the advantage of being likes, relaxing and appealing across the board. Hence this aspect has been exploited to engage the patient for stimulating the neural network and provide a feel good and feel well aspects. It is a fact that many people face mental distress but either do not share because of social trauma it carries but gaming can work as a companion to improve and fill the medical gap is such patients. The other aspect of gaming is that it is quite engaging and user once move the ladders would like to win the episode of game. The wining provides the gleefulness and makes the user to be positive and mentally stimulated for recovery. The user wants to repeat such experiences of winning and devolves a test for the new environment and slowly this positive attitudinal modulation leads to normalcy.

Various Types of Health Care Games

The health care games have widely evolved and have become multi factorial with multiple reach and dimensions. However, it could be categories in six main types based on its modifying and therapeutic applications.

Exergames

The gaming which use a module of sport and movement –based recreations are describes as exergames. These has found utility in older adults who would like to play sporting kind of games and helps in relieving the depressive syndromes. Most of the games developed by commercial and entertainment purposes have found multiple applications and are being utilized for mental health care. There is need to evaluate the therapeutic gains of movement base games and their mechanism of reducing the depressive symptoms on larger samples.

Virtual Reality Games

The advances in computer technology have been phenomenal which includes teleporting, 3/4D virtual reality of visit to a place to altogether another environments.

These virtual reality (VR) or augmented reality (AR) have immense reach through visual, audio and other real kind of sensory stimuli to patients to modulate the behaviour. This has emerged as high impact area of high innovations using modern computing technology and has been exploited commercially

Biofeedback-Based Games

These gaming portals have been designed to provide a two way feedback to patients and health care provider. The patients bears a feedback and stimulating ear plug through which visual and audio feed back is delivered. It was found in a control study that those who received such feed backs recovered faster from depressing and anxiety than those who were kept in waiting in similar environments.

Cognitive Training Games

These games are specially designed for neurological interventions and are programmed to provided stimuli to enhance the cognitive abilities. The gaming engages the subjects in neural exercise and uses numeric, graphic, shapes etc to sharpen the focus and thus modifying the cognitive abilities.

Recreational Computer Games

The entertaining games have direct effect on moods. These have been tested in clinical trails and it was found that subject splaying video games both violent and entertaining after a frustrating task have mood elevation soon after. These entertainment games enhance the mood *via* emotional regulation, stress release, and a pseudo social connect which removes depressive and frustrating environment for the given moments. The computer based gaming in mood elevations have in market from several decades. However, the therapeutic based gaming allows the subject to remember the sequences of events to use it in second stages for winning the episodes. These results into cognitive enhancement and distressing the patients to a large extent. The entertainment has been established long ago in fatigue managements.

Trauma Management Using Surgical Intervention

The medical and surgical management of trauma has various well calibrated steps from resuscitation to surgical corrective procedures. It demand high intensity care and continuous monitoring. In these cases portable and mobile smartphones with appropriate apps can be a good companion and monitoring device of the patients. These apps have been found to be very helpful to clinicians, pharmacist and physiotherapist, Carpenter (2010), L-Hilly et al. (2016), Formagini et al. (2017). There are large number of such devices and apps commercially available for resultant chronic pains, breathing or asthma management and mental strengthening tools, DeRubeis et al. (2005), Fleming et al. (2014), Richards et al. (2016) . Recently FDA has approved a mobile health care platform of Blue Star@ for type-2 diabetes and self-management for behavioral disorders, Hayes et al. (2006), Miloff et al. (2015), Olthuis et al. (2015). The FDA has approved many such devices both for diagnostic and therapeutic purposes which are working for connectivity and reminder for medications etc. Ly et al. (2014). These has been wide utilization of mobile smart phone based application which are being applied for self-management and care in chronic conditions. This has led to exponential growth in new apps which were found to be largely successful as commercial ventures. However, it is pertinent to mention that large scale controlled clinical trial would establish its clinical utility and efficacy in its reproducibility and consistency in performance, Brewer et al. (2012). The video assisted gaming has been found to be affective in monitoring the progress of recovery and patents and relatives could themselves simulate the conditions and feel the path of recovery. This also helps in planning the further course of actions. These apps are like a mobile companion as physiotherapist to patient to help and reproduce the exercise routine and monitor the progress.

Parkinson's Disease, Asthma, Diabetes, Cancer, or Stroke

There are several apps which have been developed for the treatment of depression, anxiety, dementia, pain, attention deficit hyperactivity disorder (ADHD), and cerebral palsy.

The use of video games to modulate the brain neuroplasticity also improved age-related neuronal deficits and enhanced cognitive functions in older adults, Meher et al. The video games does improve the neural cognitive ability by closely following the evolving patterns in the gamification. The observer is so much glued to the screen that patients feels a virtual reality and tries to get in oneness with the process and puts the efforts to be a winner. Many therapeutic innovations have been made in treatment of strokes patients for their programmed recovery. In 2014, the FDA cleared a motion-capture video game, developed by Jintronix as a rehabilitation system for stoke patients. The therapies in brain injuries have utilized music besides the pharmacological treatment with excellent results. The music it is believed triggers the positive neurochemicals in the brain for enhance concurrent affects, Ramanathan et al. (2017), Mallory (2016) . The music therapy in consonance with pharmacological treatment supports the hormones and stimulates the brain. The music therapy and video games have highly engaging stimulants for physiological and moderately mentally unsound patient, Kligler et al. (2016).

A combination of twin mechanism such as gaming and music works at the very fundamental level of endocrine systems by activation of the mesolimbic system and dopaminergic neurotransmission in the brain, Li et al. (2014). The functional study conducted by positron emission tomography and computed tomography (PET CT) using molecular markers identifications, it has been found that well calibrated music and gaming helps in release of fulfilling hormones dopamine D2 receptors which helps in natural help. The functional magnetic resonance imaging (fMRI) which has the capacity to identify the brain centers which are especially responsible for functioning of various organs could be activated by combination of gaming and music. These tools are very handy in quantifying the benefit which could be accrued by new gaming and music video. This is a new direction of research in neurology. The fMRI has demonstrated that influence of gaming and music are profound and has a clear-cut molecular path way. It activates the reward circuitry, as well as parts of prefrontal cortex which provides a feel of wellness. Thus activation of the dopaminergic signaling by therapeutic games or/and tailored music can facilitate behavioral and pharmacological interventions in patients. It has been a subject of many researchers both in clinical and software arena that formation of healthy habits induced by music and gaming may result in unique disease self-management platforms which would be the technology of future with huge commercial opportunity. The concept that non-pharmacological treatments with intervention of specific drugs can improve therapy outcomes for various neurological diseases need to be developed and researched in new formulation and evidences which have emerged based on biochemical and imaging evaluations.

Virtual Connectivity With Patients

Gamification tool is a conglomerate of modern medicine with advance computing. The whole premise is built on a concept that patients is allowed to play and engage with games which is entertaining yet it motivates and stimulates the patient to chart out a path of recovery as medically required. This is growing day by day with advancement in software and interphase with clinical inputs. It is able to impart education about disease recovery process and intelligently modulate the behavioral process. The remote connectivity of the devices with the doctor allows much deeper interaction and computer provides not only the video based narrative but qualitative input such as blood oxygen ratio, pulse rates, ECG, heart and breathing rates and host of parameters which gives free flow. The relatives of patients also feel connected in the virtually and need not feel deprived of disconnect.

For example, the apps developed by *Cohero Health's Asthma Hero app* has an reminder designed based on breathing pattern to inhale the drugs at desired intervals. These apps have a blue tooth connectivity and are online connected to health care providers portals. The comfort level thus attained on intervention of gaming portal is directly visible to patients relative which imbibes confidence in its utility. There are large scale evaluation is going on with more interactive gamification based on clinical trials. The National *Institute for Health Research in the U.K.* is currently conducting large scale trials on the pattern of recovery of patients who underwent surgical procedures for various bony ailments or fractures.

Future Prospective

There are several traditional therapies which are practices in conventional and non-conventional medical therapies for improving the patents over all wellbeing and physiotherapies. There is tremendous scope to convert these traditional therapies in computer gaming and quantifiable gains with inbuilt two way communication systems. There is also a large possibility to explore the impact of some routine games of entertainment of computerization so that it can reach to a large section of society and its beneficial aspect is utilized. However, an independent and larger robust studies on statistically significant sample are needed before using it in health care. Mental stress many times patients do not want to share. Hence if computer games could help in using its standalone part with privacy, it will be a boon to these subsets of patients. The stress management and mood swings which have rooting in frustrations many times could be addressed by gaming on smart phone apps in privacy need to be further explored. There are smart phone based web compatible gaming which has multiple user and multiple episodes could be played and a larger challenges realized by the subject when won gives a feel of participations and containment. There are many areas which need to be researched for further development of interaction between mental health care provider and gaming, software and hardware developers.

Type 2 diabetes can be interphased with quality gaming, these apps should have inbuilt artificial intelligence to help the patient to regulate the It is desired that gaming is further innovated with artificial intelligence and are available on smartphone platform which are more appealing and have the ability to make two way communications with pold Catient and the treating physicians. Figure 1 provides a module where the feedback of a typical glucose intake and drug delivery by a feedback mechanism. Such platform in neurological, trauma, cancer care, cardiology and HIV, diabetes and physiotherapy with new intelligent platform will shape the future researches. Signs and symptoms of mental illness can vary, depending on the disorder, circumstances and other factors. Mental illness symptoms can affect emotions, thoughts and behaviors. Sometimes symptoms of a mental health disorder appear as physical problems, such as stomach pain, back pain, headache,

Figure 1. Management of chronic ailment and gaming apps

or other unexplained aches and pains. It is a challenge for the gaming industry to develop gaming to address these important issues in mental health areas. Innovators, researchers, clinicians and businesses have to pool the resources to augment the subject further in future.

CONCLUSION

The results of the gaming and its ramifications has been profound and it may have large potential to evolve further to support the pharmacological treatment in serious ailments such as neurological treatment, cancer and trauma patients. The gaming through smart apps in health care sector has come long away and it is posed to grow further in more systematic and definite way. More clinical research is required in gaming that how it influences the neurochemicals which work as healing agents. The music therapy and gaming influences the pineal gland to stimulate the hormonal functions in optimizing its function. Smart apps are being developed such as therapeutic music, and video games which are being tested for their ability to improve pharmacotherapy outcomes and medication synergistically. It is now clear that gratification of counseling and smart games helps and functions by way of rewarding mechanism to brain. Some of the areas where music and gaming /video interposes have been established in several disorders such as neurological disorders, neuropathic pain, depression, anxiety, and neurodegenerative disorders, parkinsonism in elderly. It is also required that an innovative method be used by synergy of medical and computer knowledge to combine the conventional treatment with gaming. It will soon be possible for induction of copyright gaming and patented software with artificial intelligence to make its inroads in gaming. The robtonic technology in combinations of artificial intelligence are poised to make large contribution to hitherto unconventional method of healings.

REFERENCES

Andrews, A. (2011). Serious games for psychological health education. In R. Shumaker (Ed.), *Virtual and Mixed Reality – Systems and Applications* (pp. 3–10). Berlin: Springer. doi:10.1007/978-3-642-22024-1_1

Badachi, S., Mathew, T., Prabhu, A., Nadig, R., & Sarma, G. R. (2015). Hurdles in stroke thrombolysis: Experience from 100 consecutive ischemic stroke patients. *Annals of Indian Academy of Neurology*, *18*, 415–418. PMID:26713013

Brewer, L., Horgan, F., Hickey, A., & Williams, D. (2012). Stroke rehabilitation: Recent advances and future therapies. *The Quarterly Journal of Medicine*, *106*(1), 11–25. doi:10.1093/qjmed/hcs174 PMID:23019591

Brooks, F. M., Chester, K. L., Smeeton, N. C., & Spencer, N. H. (2016). Video gaming in adolescence: Factors associated with leisure time use. *Journal of Youth Studies*, *19*(1), 36–54. doi:10.1080/13676261.2015.1048200

Carpenter, C. (2010). A meta-analysis of the effectiveness of health belief model variables in predicting behavior. *Health Communication*, *25*(8), 9. doi:10.1080/10410236.2010.521906 PMID:21153982

Connolly, T. M., Boyle, E. A., MacArthur, E., Hainey, T., & Boyle, J. M. (2012). A systematic literature review of empirical evidence on computer games and serious games. *Comput Educ*, *59*(2), 661–686. doi:10.1016/j.compedu.2012.03.004

Cujipers, P. (2011). The patient perspective in research on major depression. *BMC Psychiatry*, *11*(1), 89. doi:10.1186/1471-244X-11-89 PMID:21592336

DeRubeis, R. J., Hollon, S. D., Amsterdam, J. D., Shelton, R. C., Young, P. R., Salomon, R. M., ... Gallop, R. (2005). Cognitive therapy vs medications in the treatment of moderate to severe depression. *Archives of General Psychiatry*, *62*(4), 409–416. doi:10.1001/archpsyc.62.4.409 PMID:15809408

Dondlinger, M. J. (2007). Educational video game design: A review of the literature. *J ApplEducTechnol*, *4*(1), 21–31.

Eagger, S. A., Levy, R., & Sahakian, B. J. (1992). Tacrine in Alzheimer's disease. *Acta Neurologica Scandinavica. Supplementum*, *139*(S139), 75–80. doi:10.1111/j.1600-0404.1992.tb04459.x PMID:1414271

Edwards, E. A., Lumsden, J., Rivas, C., Steed, L., Edwards, L. A., Thiyagarajan, A., ... Walton, R. T. (2016). Gamification for health promotion: Systematic review of behaviour change techniques in smartphone apps. *BMJ Open*, *6*(10), e012447. doi:10.1136/bmjopen-2016-012447 PMID:27707829

El-Hilly, A. A., Iqbal, S. S., Ahmed, M., Sherwani, Y., Muntasir, M., Siddiqui, S., ... Eisingerich, A. B. (2016, October 24). Muntasir M etal. Game On? Smoking Cessation Through the Gamification of mHealth: A Longitudinal Qualitative Study. *JMIR Serious Games.*, *4*(2), e18. doi:10.2196/games.5678 PMID:27777216

Entertainment Software Association. (2015). *Essential Facts about the Computer and Video Game Industry*. Available from: http://www.theesa.com/ wp-content/uploads/2015/04/ESA-Essential-Facts-2015.pdf

Fleming, T., Cheek, C., Merry, S., Thabrew, H., Bridgman, H., Stasiak, K., & ... . (2014). Serious games for the treatment or prevention of depression: A systematicreview. *Revista de Psicopatología y Psicología Clínica*, *19*(3), 227–242. doi:10.5944/rppc.vol.19.num.3.2014.13904

Fleming, T.M., Bavin, L., Stasiak, K., Hermansson-Webb, E., & Merry, S.N. (n.d.). Serious Games and Gamification for Mental Health: Current Status and Promising Directions. *Front. Psychiatry,* *7*(215). doi: 10.3389/fpsyt.2016.00215

Formagini, T. D. B., Ervilha, R. R., Machado, N. M., & Bottaro de Andrade, B. A. (2017). Gomide HP etal. A review of smartphone apps for smoking cessation available in PortugueseCad. *Saúde Pública*, *33*(2), e00178215. PMID:28300972

Giosan, C., & Mogoase, C. (2016). Using a smartphone app to reduce cognitive vulnerability and mild depressive symptoms: Study protocol of an exploratory randomized controlled trial. *Trials*, *17*(1), 609. doi:10.118613063-016-1740-3 PMID:28031038

Hayes, S. C., Luoma, J. B., Bond, F. W., Masuda, A., & Lillis, J. (2006b). Acceptance and commitment therapy: Model, processes and outcomes. *Behaviour Research and Therapy*, *44*(1), 1–25. doi:10.1016/j.brat.2005.06.006 PMID:16300724

Johnson, D., Deterding, S., Kuhn, K. A., Staneva, A., Stoyanov, S., & Hides, L. (2016). Gamification for health and wellbeing: A systematic review ofthe literature. *Internet Interventions*, *6*, 89–106. doi:10.1016/j.invent.2016.10.002

Kligler, B., Teets, R., & Quick, M. (2016, September 1). Complementary/Integrative Therapies That Work: A Review of the Evidence. *American Family Physician*, *94*(5), 369–374. PMID:27583423

Li, J., Theng, Y. L., & Foo, S. (2014). Game-based digital interventions for depression therapy: A systematic review and meta-analysis. *Cyberpsychology, Behavior, and Social Networking*, *17*(8), 519–527. doi:10.1089/cyber.2013.0481 PMID:24810933

Lister, C., West, J. H., Cannon, B., Sax, T., & Brodegard, D. (2014, August 4). Just a fad? Gamification in health and fitness apps. *JMIR Serious Games.*, *2*(2), e9. doi:10.2196/games.3413 PMID:25654660

Ly, K.H., Asplund, K., & Andersson, G. (2014). Stress management for middle managers via an acceptance and commitment-based smartphone application: A randomized controlled trial. *Internet Interventions,* (1), 95–101.

Maher, C., Ferguson, M., Vandelanotte, C., Plotnikoff, R., De Bourdeaudhuij, I., Thomas, S., ... Olds, T. (2015, July 13). A web-based, social networking physical activity intervention for insufficiently active adults delivered via Facebook app: Randomized controlled trial. *Journal of Medical Internet Research*, *17*(7), e174. doi:10.2196/jmir.4086 PMID:26169067

Miloff, A., Marklund, A., & Carlbring, P. (2015). The challenger app for social anxiety disorder: New advances in mobile psychological treatment. *Internet Interventions*, (2), 382–391.

Munson, S., Poole, E., Perry, D. B., & Peyton, T. (2015). Gamification and health. In S. P. Walz (Ed.), *The Gameful World: Approaches, Issues, Applications* (pp. 597–623). Cambridge, MA: MIT Press.

Olthuis, J. 2015. Therapist-delivered distance cognitive behavioural therapy for anxiety disorders in adults. *Cochrane Libr. Cochrane D,* (3). Available at: http://onlinelibrary.wiley.com

Pandher, P. S., & Bhullar, K. K. (2016, June). Smartphone applications for seizure management. *Health Informatics Journal, 22*(2), 209–220. doi:10.1177/1460458214540906 PMID:25038202

Petersen, R. C., Thomas, R. G., Grundman, M., Bennett, D., Doody, R., Ferris, S., ... Thal, L. J. (2005). Vitamin E and donepezil for the treatment of mild cognitive impairment. *The New England Journal of Medicine, 352*(23), 2379–2388. doi:10.1056/NEJMoa050151 PMID:15829527

Ramanathan, M., Bhavanani, A. B., & Trakroo, M. (2017, January-April). Effect of a 12-week yoga therapy program on mental health status in elderly women inmates of a hospice. *International Journal of Yoga, 10*(1), 24–28. doi:10.4103/0973-6131.186156 PMID:28149064

Read, J. L., & Shortell, S. M. (2011). Interactive games to promote behavior change in pre-vention and treatment. *Journal of the American Medical Association, 305*(16), 1704–1705. doi:10.1001/jama.2011.408 PMID:21447802

Richards, D., Timulak, L., Rashleigh, C., McLoughlin, O., & Colla, A. (2016). Effectiveness of an internet-delivered intervention for generalized anxiety disorder in routine care: A randomised controlled trial in a student population. *Internet Interventions*, (6), 80–88.

Rinne, P., Mace, M., Nakornchai, T., Zimmerman, K., & Fayer, S. (n.d.). Democratizing Neurorehabilitation: How Accessible are Low-Cost Mobile-Gaming Technologies for Self-Rehabilitation of Arm Disability in Stroke? *PLoS ONE, 11*(10). doi:. pone.016341310.1371/journal

Savulich, G., Piercy, T., Fox, C., Suckling, J., Rowe, J. B., O'Brien, J. T., & Sahakian, B. J. (2017). Cognitive Training Using a Novel Memory Game on an iPad in Patients with Amnestic Mild Cognitive Impairment (aMCI). *Int J Neuropsychpharm, 20*(8), 624–633. doi:10.1093/ijnp/pyx040 PMID:28898959

Sewell, M.D., Eastwood, D.M., & Wimalasundera, N. (2014). Managing common symptoms of cerebral palsy in children. *BMJ, 349*.

Whittinghill, D. M., & Brown, J. S. (2014, June). *Gamification of Physical Therapy for the Treatment of Pediatric Cerebral Palsy: A Pilot Study Examining Player Preferences*. Paper presented at 2014 ASEE Annual Conference & Exposition, Indianapolis, IN. Retrieved from https://peer.asee.org/20529

Zhang, M. W., Yeo, L. L., & Ho, R. C. (2015, October). Harnessing smartphone technologies for stroke care, rehabilitation and beyond. *BMJ Innov.*, *1*(4), 145–150. doi:10.1136/bmjinnov-2015-000078 PMID:26692351

Zhang, M. W. B., Ho, C. S. H., Cheok, C. C. S., & Ho, R. C. M. (2015). Bringing Smartphone Technology into undergraduate and postgraduate psychiatry. *BJPsych Advances*, *21*(4), 222–228. doi:10.1192/apt.bp.114.013649

Compilation of References

3. RDSENSE. (2010). *3Advergames you should be playing*. Retrieved from http://3rdsense.com/blog/2015/9/17/3-Advergames-you-should-be-playing

Aarnoutse, F., Peursum, L., & Dalpiaz, F. (2014). The evolution of advergames development: A study in the Netherlands. In *Games Media Entertainment (GEM), 2014* (pp. 1–8). IEEE. doi:10.1109/GEM.2014.7048097

Abhishek, V., Despotakis, S., & Ravi, R. (2017). *Multi-channel attribution: The blind spot of online advertising*. Available at SSRN: https://papers.ssrn.com/soL3/papers.cfm?abstract_id=2959778

Adams, T., & Smith, S. A. (2015). Communication shock: the rhetoric of new technology. Newcastle upon Tyne, UK: Cambridge Scholars Publishing.

Adler, R., Lesser, G., Meringoff, L., Robertson, T., Rossiter, J., & Ward, S. (1980). *The Effects of Television Advertising on Children*. Lexington, MA: Lexington Books.

Advergaming. (n.d.). Retrieved September 27, 2017, from http://objevit.cz/slovnik-pojmu-co-je-to-advergaming-t169372

Agarwal, R., & Karahanna, E. (2000). Time flies when you're having fun: Cognitive absorption and beliefs about information technology usage. *Management Information Systems Quarterly*, *24*(4), 665–694. doi:10.2307/3250951

Aggarwal, V., & Shefali. (2015). A study of effectiveness of Advergames on children. *BVIMSR. Journal of Management Research.*

Aggarwal, V., & Shefali. (2015). A study of effectiveness of Advergames on Children. *BVIMSR's Journal of Management Research.*

Aguilar, R. (n.d.). *Building an advocacy marketing strategy using the social media funnel*. Retrieved from REmomd: http://remomd.com/social-media/building-advocacy-marketing-strategy-using-social-media-funnel.html

Alina, G. (2013). Factors responsible for consumer's attitude towards advergames. *Annals of Faculty of Economics*, *1*(1), 1733–1742.

Andrews, A. (2011). Serious games for psychological health education. In R. Shumaker (Ed.), *Virtual and Mixed Reality – Systems and Applications* (pp. 3–10). Berlin: Springer. doi:10.1007/978-3-642-22024-1_1

AnimationXpress. (2016, June 14). *Games*. Retrieved from AnimationXpress.com: http://www.animationxpress.com/index.php/latest-news/sultan-the-game-rises-to-the-top-among-free-games-on-google-play

An, S., Jin, H. S., & Park, E. H. (2014). Children's advertising literacy for advergames: Perception of the game as advertising. *Journal of Advertising*, *43*(1), 63–72. doi:10.1080/00913367.2013.795123

An, S., & Kang, H. (2014). Advertising or games? Advergames on the internet gaming sites targeting children. *International Journal of Advertising*, *33*(3), 509–532. doi:10.2501/IJA-33-3-509-532

An, S., & Stern, S. (2011). Mitigating the effects of Advergames on children. *Journal of Advertising*, *40*(1), 43–56. doi:10.2753/JOA0091-3367400103

Ardley, B. (2011). Marketing theory and critical phenomenology: Exploring the human side of management practice. *Marketing Intelligence & Planning*, *29*(7), 628–642. doi:10.1108/02634501111178668

Asem, B. (2013). Networked Publics and Identity Construction: Towards an Era of Virtual Socialization. *Media Watch*, *4*(2), 161–174.

AuthoriyA. S. (2012). Retrieved from http://www.cap.org.uk/News-reports/Media-Centre/2012/Advergames.aspx

Badachi, S., Mathew, T., Prabhu, A., Nadig, R., & Sarma, G. R. (2015). Hurdles in stroke thrombolysis: Experience from 100 consecutive ischemic stroke patients. *Annals of Indian Academy of Neurology*, *18*, 415–418. PMID:26713013

Bahn, K. D. (1987). Do Mothers and Children Share Cereal and Beverage Preferences and Evaluative Criteria? *Advances in Consumer Research. Association for Consumer Research (U. S.)*, 279–282.

Bailey, W., Wise, K., & Bolls, P. (2009). How Avatar Customizability Affects Children's Arousal and Subjective Presence During Junk Food–Sponsored Online Video Games. *Cyberpsychology & Behavior*, *12*(3), 277–283. doi:10.1089/cpb.2008.0292 PMID:19445632

Balasubramanian, S. K. (1994). Beyond Advertising and Publicity: Hybrid Messages and Public Policy Issues. *Journal of Advertising*, *23*(4), 29–46. doi:10.1080/00913367.1943.10673457

Balci, K & Salah, A. A. (2014). Automatic analysis and identification of verbal aggression and abusive behaviors for online social games, *Computers in Human Behavior, 53*(2015), 517–526.

Banerjee, S. (2004). Playing Games. *Billboard*, *116*(20), 3–4.

Bargiela-Chiappini, F. (2009). *The handbook of business discourse*. Edinburgh, UK: Edinburgh University Press.

Barker, B. (2015). *Media planning: Exploration of the media selection decision making process in the digital environment*. Retrieved from http://eprints.bournemouth.ac.uk/22476/1/AM2015%20Media%20planning%20%20Exploration%20of%20the%20media%20decision%20making%20process%20in%20the%20digital%20environment.pdf (2017, December 12).

Barker, B. (2017). Integration – bringing the media plan together – or making it all work – really well! In *IDM Marketing Guide*. Retrieved from https://www.theidm.com/getmedia/ac4b8ea3-0ba8-4309-a2da-11ed27646ece/C-5-11.pdf

Barr, J. (2016). *Are viewable ads actually effective for marketers? 10,000-person study sheds light*. Retrieved from http://www.adageindia.in/media/are-viewable-ads-actually-effective-for-marketers-10000-person-study-sheds-light/articleshow/50858697.cms

Barton, Z. (2017). *The Evolution of Advergames: Top 3 Examples of Marketing in Gaming*. Retrieved from https://medium.com/@zbbarton0706/the-evolution-of-Advergames-top-3-examples-of-marketing-in-gaming-3e688aad6884

Bateman, J. (2008). *Multimodality and genre. A foundation for the systematic analysis of multimodal documents*. Hampshire, UK: Palgrave MacMillan.

Belch, G. E., & Belch, M. A. (2008). *Advertising and Promotion: An Integrated Marketing Communications Perspective* (8th ed.). McGraw-Hill Higher Education.

Bell, M., Chalmers, M., Barkhuus, L., Hall, M., Sherwood, S., Tennent, P., & Hampshire, A. (2006, April). Interweaving mobile games with everyday life. In *Proceedings of the SIGCHI conference on Human Factors in computing systems* (pp. 417-426). ACM.

Bellman, S., Kemp, A., Haddad, H., & Varan, D. (2014). The effectiveness of advergames compared to television commercials and interactive commercials featuring advergames. *Computers in Human Behavior*, *32*, 276–283. doi:10.1016/j.chb.2013.12.013

Berlyne, D. E. (1966). Curiosity and exploration. *Science*, *153*(3731), 25–33. doi:10.1126cience.153.3731.25 PMID:5328120

Berthon, P. R., Pitt, L. F., Plangger, K., & Shapiro, D. (2012). Marketing meets Web 2.0, social media, and creative consumers: Implications for International marketing strategy. *Business Horizons*, *55*(3), 261–271. doi:10.1016/j.bushor.2012.01.007

Bhasin, H. (2017). *DAGMAR Approach – Defining advertising goals for measured advertising results*. Retrieved from https://www.marketing91.com/dagmar/

Bhatia, V. J. (1993). *Analysing Genre: Language Use in Professional Settings*. London: Longman.

Bigat, E. C. (2012). Guerrilla advertisement and marketing. *Procedia: Social and Behavioral Sciences*, *51*, 1022–1029. doi:10.1016/j.sbspro.2012.08.281

Blades, M., Oates, C., & Blumberg, F. (2014). *Advertising to children: New directions, new media.* Retrieved from http://www.eblib.com

Bogost, I. (2005). *Frame and Metaphor in Political Games.* Presented at the Digital Games Research Association (DiGRA) 2005 Conference Changing Views-Worlds in Play, Vancouver, Canada.

Bogost. (2007). *Persuasive Games: The expressive power of videogames.* Cambridge, MA: MIT Press.

Bogost, I. (2007). *Persuasive games: The expressive power of videogames.* The MIT Press.

Boiarsky, G. (1997). The Psychology of New Media Technologies Lessons from the Past. *Convergence (London), 3*(3), 109–126. doi:10.1177/135485659700300308

Bosák, P. (2016). *Utilization of advergames in marketing strategies.* Bachelor's Thesis.

Bosman, J. (2006, June 14). Hey, kid, you want to buy a Toyota Scion? *New York Times.*

Bosomworth, D., & Chaffey, D. (2012). Creating a Social Media Marketing Plan. *Smart Insights.* Retrieved from http://www.carmichaelcentre.ie/sites/default/files/Need-to-know-social-media-strategy-smart-insights_0.pdf

Brafton. (2017). *Infographic Marketing.* Retrieved from http://www.brafton.com/glossary/infographics

Brave, S., & Nass, C. (2003). Emotion in human-computer interaction. *Human-Computer Interaction*, 53.

Bray, H. (2004). 'Advergames' spark concerns of kids being targeted. *Boston Globe.*

Bray, H. (2004, July 30). "Advergames" Spark Concerns of Kids Being Targeted. *Boston Globe.* Retrieved from http://www.boston.com/

Brewer, L., Horgan, F., Hickey, A., & Williams, D. (2012). Stroke rehabilitation: Recent advances and future therapies. *The Quarterly Journal of Medicine, 106*(1), 11–25. doi:10.1093/qjmed/hcs174 PMID:23019591

Brief, A. C. (2014). *Advertising to children and teens: Current Practices.* Academic Press.

Brooks, F. M., Chester, K. L., Smeeton, N. C., & Spencer, N. H. (2016). Video gaming in adolescence: Factors associated with leisure time use. *Journal of Youth Studies, 19*(1), 36–54. doi:10.1080/13676261.2015.1048200

Buckingham, D. (2006). Is there a Digital Generation. In D. Buckingum & E. Willett (Eds.), *Digital Generations.* Academic Press. Retrieved Jan 4, 2018, from https://is.muni.cz/el/1423/podzim2013/SOC573/um/Buckingham_-_Is_there_a_digital_generation.pdf

Bunchball. (2010). *Gamification 101: An Introduction to the Use of Game Dynamics to Influence Behavior.* Retrieved from http://jndglobal.com/wp-content/uploads/2011/05/gamification1011.pdf

Buying, M. (2009, Sep 30). *Online's Slice of Ad Spending Grows Worldwide*. Retrieved from eMarketer: https://www.emarketer.com/Article/Onlines-Slice-of-Ad-Spending-Grows-Worldwide/1007298

BW Online Bureau. (2017, March). *Myntra's Lifestyle Brand Roadster's Retail Store Launched in Bengaluru*. Retrieved Dec 4, 2017, from BW Disrupt: http://bwdisrupt.businessworld.in/article/Myntra-s-Lifestyle-Brand-Roadster-s-Retail-Store-Launched-in-Bengaluru/17-03-2017-114509/

By 2016 Why 70% of Small Businesses Will Depend On Social Media Tool To Reach New Customers. (2015, Dec 30). Retrieved from SMEJoinup: https://smejoinup.com/blog/by-2016-why-70-of-small-businesses-will-depend-on-social-media-tool-to-reach-new-customers/

Cain. (2011). Embedded advertising on television: Disclosure, deception, and free speech rights. *Journal of Public Policy & Marketing*, 226–238.

Cai, X., & Zhao, X. (2010). Click here, Kids! *Journal of Children and Media*, *4*(2), 135–154. doi:10.1080/17482791003629610

Campbell, G. (2013). *The philosophy of rhetoric*. New York: Cambridge University Press.

Cannon, H. M. (2001). Addressing new media with conventional media planning. *Journal of Interactive Advertising*, *1*(2), 28–42. doi:10.1080/15252019.2001.10722049

Carpenter, C. (2010). A meta-analysis of the effectiveness of health belief model variables in predicting behavior. *Health Communication*, *25*(8), 9. doi:10.1080/10410236.2010.521906 PMID:21153982

Casey, S. (2016). *2016 Nielsen social media report*. Available at http://www.nielsen.com/us/en/insights/reports/2017/2016-nielsen-social-media-report.html

Cauberghe, V., Geuens, M., & De Pelsmacker, P. (2011). Context effects of TV programme-induced interactivity and telepresence on advertising responses. *International Journal of Advertising*, *30*(4), 641–663. doi:10.2501/IJA-30-4-641-663

Cauberghe, V., & Pelsmacker, P. (2010). Advergames: The Impact of Brand Prominence and Game Repetition on Brand Responses. *Journal of Advertising*, *39*(1), 5–18. doi:10.2753/JOA0091-3367390101

Chaffey, D. (2013, February 16). Definitions of Emarketing vs Internet vs Digital marketing. *Smart Insight Blog*.

Chaffey, D., & Chadwick. (2012). *Digital Marketing: Strategy, Implementation and Practice*. Academic Press.

Chandra, G., Anu, M., Noshir, K., & James, M. (2012). *Online and upcoming: The Internet's impact on India*. Bangalore: McKinsey and Company.

Chang, Y. (2016). Why do young people multitask with multiple media? Explicating the relationships among sensation seeking, needs, and media multitasking behavior. *Media Psychology, 20*(4), 685–703. doi:10.1080/15213269.2016.1247717

Chaturvedi, O. (2016). *Effects of Demonetization on sales and marketing*. Retrieved from http://www.bmconsulting.in/blog/effect-demonetization-sales-marketing/

Chaturvedi, S. & Gupta, S. (2014). Social Media Promotions –Can We Restrict It Under Laws? *International Journal of Research –GRANTHAALAYAH, 1*(1), 43-50.

Chen, J., & Ringel, M. (2001). *Can Advergaming be the Future of Interactive Advertising?* Retrieved from http://www.locz.com.br

Chikhani, R. (2015, Oct 31). *The History of Gaming: An evolving Community*. Retrieved from techcrunch: https://techcrunch.com/2015/10/31/the-history-of-gaming-an-evolving-community/

Chistian, G. (2014, Dec 23). *Traditional vs. new media: The balancing effect*. Retrieved from The Absolute Truth: https://www.absolutemg.com/2014/12/23/traditional-media-balancing-effect/

Christensen, C., Aaron, S., & Clark, W. (2002). Disruption in education. In M. Devlin, R. Larson, & J. Meyerson (Eds.), The internet and the university: forum 2001. Academic Press.

Christensen, C. M. (1997). *The Innovator's Dilemma: When New Technologies Cause Great Firms to Fail*. Boston, MA: Harvard Business School Press.

Cicchirillo, V., & Mabry, A. (2016). Advergaming and healthy eating involvement: How healthy eating inclinations impact processing of advergame content. *Internet Research, 26*(3), 587–603. doi:10.1108/IntR-04-2014-0091

Cleveland, W. S. (1994). *The Elements of Graphing Data* (Revised Edition). Hobart Press.

Connolly, T. M., Boyle, E. A., MacArthur, E., Hainey, T., & Boyle, J. M. (2012). A systematic literature review of empirical evidence on computer games and serious games. *Comput Educ, 59*(2), 661–686. doi:10.1016/j.compedu.2012.03.004

Corbett, E. P., & Connors, R. J. (1999). *Classical rhetoric for the modern student*. New York: Oxford University Press.

Cowburn, & Boxer, A. (2007). Magazines for children and young people and the links to Internet food marketing: a review of the extent and type of food advertising. *Public Health Nutrition, 10*, 1024-1031.

Csikszentmihalyi, M. (1975). *Beyond Boredom and Anxiety*. San Francisco, CA: Jossey Bass.

Csikszentmihalyi, M. (1997). *Finding flow: The psychology of engagement with everyday life*. New York: Basic Books.

Csikszentmihalyi, M., & LeFevre, J. (1989). Optimal experience in work and leisure. *Journal of Personality and Social Psychology, 56*(5), 815–822. doi:10.1037/0022-3514.56.5.815 PMID:2724069

Cujipers, P. (2011). The patient perspective in research on major depression. *BMC Psychiatry*, *11*(1), 89. doi:10.1186/1471-244X-11-89 PMID:21592336

Culp, J., & Robert, A. (2010). Characteristics of Food Industry Web Sites and Advergames targeting Children. *Journal of Nutrition Education and Behavior*, *42*(3), 197–201. doi:10.1016/j.jneb.2009.07.008 PMID:20434075

Cumming, B. S. (1998). Innovation overview and future challenges. *European Journal of Innovation Management*, *1*(1), 21–29. doi:10.1108/14601069810368485

Dahl, E., Eagle, L., & Báez, C. (2009). Analysing Advergames: Active diversions or actually deception. An exploratory study of online Advergames content. *Young Consumers*, *10*(I), 46–59. doi:10.1108/17473610910940783

Davis, A. (2009, May 13). *Banner ads drive search behaviour: study*. Retrieved from Campaign: Banner ads drive search behaviour: study.

de Pelsmacker, P., & Neijens, P. C. (2012). New advertising formats: How persuasion knowledge affects consumer responses. *Journal of Marketing Communications*, *18*(1), 1–4. doi:10.1080/13527266.2011.620762

Deal. (2005). *The Ability of Branded Online Games to build brand equity*. Retrieved from http://ir.lib.sfu.ca/retrieve/1569/afc2b904c38c1edff4ede5a4bc86.doc (

Dehghani, M., Niaki, M. K., Ramezani, I., & Sali, R. (2016). Evaluating the influence of YouTube advertising for attraction of young customers. *Computers in Human Behavior*, *59*, 165–172. doi:10.1016/j.chb.2016.01.037

DeRubeis, R. J., Hollon, S. D., Amsterdam, J. D., Shelton, R. C., Young, P. R., Salomon, R. M., ... Gallop, R. (2005). Cognitive therapy vs medications in the treatment of moderate to severe depression. *Archives of General Psychiatry*, *62*(4), 409–416. doi:10.1001/archpsyc.62.4.409 PMID:15809408

Desk, E. W. (2016, July 1). *Entertainment*. Retrieved from Indian Express: http://indianexpress.com/article/entertainment/entertainment-others/sultan-the-game-is-out-and-salman-khan-loves-it-too-2845366/

Deterding, S., Dixon, D., Khaled, R., & Nacke, L. (2011). From Game Design Elements to Gamefulness:Defining "Gamification". In *Proceedings of the 15th International Academic MindTrek Conference: Envisioning Future Media Environments* (pp. 9-15). New York: ACM.

Deterding, S., Dixon, D., Khaled, R., & Nacke, L. (2011, September). From game design elements to gamefulness: defining gamification. In *Proceedings of the 15th international academic MindTrek conference: Envisioning future media environments* (pp. 9-15). ACM. 10.1145/2181037.2181040

Dewing, M. (2012). *Social Media: An Introduction*. Library of Parliment.

Dham, S. O. (2016). *Study of advergaming as a tool to build emotional customer loyalty and its implication on marketing returns.* Retrieved from ShodhGanga: http://shodhganga.inflibnet.ac.in/handle/10603/176014

Dhapola, S. (2014, October 31). *Entertainment.* Retrieved from First Post: http://www.firstpost.com/entertainment/happy-new-year-game-review-possibly-even-more-painful-than-the-film-1781035.html

Dias, M., & Aganten, L. (2011). Can Advergames Boost Children's Healthier Eating Habits? A Comparison between Healthy and Non-healthy food. *Journal of Consumer Behaviour, 10*(3), 152–160. doi:10.1002/cb.359

DiClemente, D. F., & Hantula, D. A. (2003). Applied behavioral economics and consumer choice. *Journal of Economic Psychology, 24*(5), 589–602. doi:10.1016/S0167-4870(03)00003-5

Digital advertising in 2017: Elephant in the room? (2017). Retrieved from http://www.livemint.com/Industry/QX0lOVJTUR2Mgn8Cm9fjTP/Digital-advertising-in-2017-Elephant-in-the-room.html

Dimmick, J., Chen, Y., & Li, Z. (2009). Competition Between the Internet and Traditional News Media: The Gratification-Opportunities Niche Dimension. *Journal of Media Economics*, 19–33.

Dixon, P. (2016). *Rhetoric. S.I.* Taylor & Francis.

Dobrow, L. (2004, January 15). How to Play Games and Influence People: Advergaming Emerges as New Ad Option. *Media Daily News.*

Dondlinger, M. J. (2007). Educational video game design: A review of the literature. *J ApplEducTechnol, 4*(1), 21–31.

Douthwaite, J. (2000). *Towards a linguistic theory offoregrounding.* Alessandria: Edizioni dellOrso.

E, S. (1925). *The Psychology of Selling and Advertising.* New York: McGraw-Hill.

Eagger, S. A., Levy, R., & Sahakian, B. J. (1992). Tacrine in Alzheimer's disease. *Acta Neurologica Scandinavica. Supplementum, 139*(S139), 75–80. doi:10.1111/j.1600-0404.1992.tb04459.x PMID:1414271

Edwards. (2003). Plug (the Product) and Play. *Washington Post.*

Edwards, E. A., Lumsden, J., Rivas, C., Steed, L., Edwards, L. A., Thiyagarajan, A., ... Walton, R. T. (2016). Gamification for health promotion: Systematic review of behaviour change techniques in smartphone apps. *BMJ Open, 6*(10), e012447. doi:10.1136/bmjopen-2016-012447 PMID:27707829

El-Hilly, A. A., Iqbal, S. S., Ahmed, M., Sherwani, Y., Muntasir, M., Siddiqui, S., ... Eisingerich, A. B. (2016, October 24). Muntasir M etal. Game On? Smoking Cessation Through the Gamification of mHealth: A Longitudinal Qualitative Study. *JMIR Serious Games., 4*(2), e18. doi:10.2196/games.5678 PMID:27777216 eMarketer. (2017). *Worldwide ad spending: The eMarketer forecast for 2017*. Retrieved from https://www.emarketer.com/Report/Worldwide-Ad-Spending-eMarketer-Forecast-2017/2002019

E-Marketing Strategy of Hamrobazar.com. (2013). Retrieved from https://www.bartleby.com/essay/E-Marketing-Strategy-of-Hamrobazar-Com-FKKH8343RYZS

Entertainment Software Association. (2015). *Essential Facts about the Computer and Video Game Industry*. Available from: http://www.theesa.com/ wp-content/uploads/2015/04/ESA-Essential-Facts-2015.pdf

Erragcha, N., & Romdhane, R. (2014). Social networks as marketing tools. *Journal of Internet Banking and Commerce*, *19*(1), 1–12.

Esteban-Millat, I., Martínez-López, F. J., Luna, D., & Rodríguez-Ardura, I. (2014). The concept of flow in online consumer behavior. In *Handbook of strategic e-business management* (pp. 371–402). Springer Berlin Heidelberg. doi:10.1007/978-3-642-39747-9_17

Evans, N. J. (2014). Pinpointing Persuasion in Children's Advergames: Exploring the Relationship Among Parents' Internet Mediation, Marketplace Knowledge, Attitudes, and the Support for Regulation. *Journal of Interactive Advertising*, *14*(2), 73–85. doi:10.1080/15252019.2014.943354

Evans, N. J., Carlson, L., & Hoy, M. G. (2013). Coddling our kids: Can parenting style affect attitudes toward advergames? *Journal of Advertising*, *42*(2), 228–240. doi:10.1080/00913367.2013.774602

Faber, R. J., Lee, M., & Nan, X. (2004). Advertising and the consumer information environment online. *The American Behavioral Scientist*, *48*(4), 447–466. doi:10.1177/0002764204270281

Fairclough, N. (1995). *Critical Discourse Analysis: The Critical Study of Language*. London: Longman.

Fairclough, N. (1995). *Media Discourse*. London: Arnold.

Farrar, K. M., Krcmar, M., & Nowak, K. L. (2006). Contextual Features of Violent Video Games, Mental Models and Aggression. *Journal of Communication*, *56*(2), 387–405. doi:10.1111/j.1460-2466.2006.00025.x

Fattah, H., & Paul, P. (2002). Gaming gets serious. *American Demographics*, *24*(5), 38–44. Retrieved from http://adage.com/article/americandemographics/gaming/44521/

Feld, S., & Carter, W. C. (1998). Foci of activity in changing contexts for friendship. In R. G. Adams & G. Allan (Eds.), *Placing friendship in context* (pp. 136–152). Cambridge, UK: Cambridge University Press.

Fiske, S. T., & Pavelchak, M. A. (1986). Category-based versus piecemeal-based affective responses: developments in schema-triggered affect. In R. W. Sorrentino & E. T. Higgines (Eds.), *Handbook of Motivation and Cognition: Foundations of Social Behavior* (pp. 464–473). New York, NY: Guilford Press.

Fleming, T.M., Bavin, L., Stasiak, K., Hermansson-Webb, E., & Merry, S.N. (n.d.). Serious Games and Gamification for Mental Health: Current Status and Promising Directions. *Front. Psychiatry, 7*(215). doi: 10.3389/fpsyt.2016.00215

Fleming, T., Cheek, C., Merry, S., Thabrew, H., Bridgman, H., Stasiak, K., & .... (2014). Serious games for the treatment or prevention of depression: A systematicreview. *Revista de Psicopatología y Psicología Clínica, 19*(3), 227–242. doi:10.5944/rppc.vol.19.num.3.2014.13904

Floch, J. M. (2001). *Semiotics, Marketing and Communication.* Palgrave Macmillan.

Floch, J. M. (2001). *Visual Identities.* London: Bloomsbury.

Folkvord, F., Anschütz, D. J., Buijzen, M., & Valkenburg, P. M. (2013). The effect of playing advergames that promote energy-dense snacks or fruit on actual food intake among children. *The American Journal of Clinical Nutrition, 97*(2), 239–245. doi:10.3945/ajcn.112.047126 PMID:23269821

Fonda, D. (2004). Kill the messenger? *Time Canada, 163*(26), 57.

Formagini, T. D. B., Ervilha, R. R., Machado, N. M., & Bottaro de Andrade, B. A. (2017). Gomide HP etal. A review of smartphone apps for smoking cessation available in PortugueseCad. *Saúde Pública, 33*(2), e00178215. PMID:28300972

Friestad, M., & Wright, P. (1994). Persuasion Knowledge: Lay People's and Researchers' Beliefs About the Psychology of Advertising. *The Journal of Consumer Research, 22*(June), 62–74.

Friestad, M., & Wright, P. (1994). The persuasion knowledge model: How people cope with persuasion attempts. *The Journal of Consumer Research, 22*(1), 1–31. doi:10.1086/209380

Fullmer, J. (n.d.). More Online Consumers shop Offline [Blog Post]. Retrieved from https://storify.com/VivaKi/more-online-consumers-shop-offline-the-contradicti

G2 Crowd. (2017). *Best Data Management Platform (DMP) Software.* Retrieved from https://www.g2crowd.com/categories/data-management-platform-dmp

Games, B. M. (2017). *Success stories.* Retrieved from http://www.brandedminigames.com/success-stories/page/4/

Gartner. (n.d.). *Digital Marketing.* Retrieved from https://www.gartner.com/it-glossary/digital-marketing

Gearhardt, A. N., Yokum, S., Stice, E., Harris, J. L., & Brownell, K. D. (2014). Relation of obesity to neural activation in response to food commercials. *Social Cognitive and Affective Neuroscience, 9*(7), 932–938. doi:10.1093can/nst059 PMID:23576811

George, S., Saif, N., & Joseph, B. B. (2017). A study on the mobile phone usage pattern and its dependence among medical students of a college in Kerala, India. *International Journal of Research in Medical Sciences, 5*(8), 3615–3619. doi:10.18203/2320-6012.ijrms20173573

Gertz, O., & McGlashan, D. (2016). Consumer-centric programmatic advertising. Programmatic Advertising. Springer.

Ghirvu, A. I. (2013). The Aida model for advergames. *The USV Annals of Economics and Public Administration, 13*(1), 90-98.

Gibbons, A. (2012). *Multimodality, cognition, and experimental literature*. London: Routledge.

Giosan, C., & Mogoase, C. (2016). Using a smartphone app to reduce cognitive vulnerability and mild depressive symptoms: Study protocol of an exploratory randomized controlled trial. *Trials*, *17*(1), 609. doi:10.118613063-016-1740-3 PMID:28031038

Goh, K. Y., & Ping, J. W. (2014). Engaging consumers with advergames: An experimental evaluation of interactivity, fit and expectancy. *Journal of the Association for Information Systems*, *15*(7), 388–421. doi:10.17705/1jais.00366

Google. (2017). *Attribution modeling overview*. Retrieved from https://support.google.com/analytics/answer/1662518?hl=en

Gorgone, K. (2017, Nov 15). *Social Media Addiction is Real: How to Take Your Life Back*. Retrieved from Mark Schaefer: https://www.businessesgrow.com/2017/11/15/social-media-addiction-2/

Grey Kernal Technologies. (2017, Dec 25). Retrieved from Zauba Corporation: https://www.zaubacorp.com/company/GREYKERNEL-TECHNOLOGIES-INDIA-PRIVATE-LIMITED/U72300UP2015PTC068599

Grigorovici, D. M., & Constantin, C. D. (2004). Experiencing Interactive Advertising beyond Rich Media. Impacts of Ad Type and Presence on Brand Effectiveness in 3D Gaming Immersive Virtual Environments. *Journal of Interactive Advertising*, *5*(1), 1–26. doi:10.1080/15252019.2004.10722091

Grigorovici, D. M., & Constantin, C. D. (2004). Experiencing interactive advertising beyond rich media: Impacts of ad type and presence on brand effectiveness in 3d gaming immersive virtual environments. *Journal of Interactive Advertising*, *6*(1), 30–53.

Gupta, H. & Singh, S. (2016). Guerrilla Marketing: An innovative stride. *SMS Journal of Entrepreneurship and Innovation, 3*(1).

Gupta, H., & Singh, S. (2017). Social Media in Contemporary Marketing: YouTube Advertising for the Guerrillas. *Media Watch*, *8*(3), 413–422. doi:10.15655/mw/2017/v8i3/49145

Gupta, H., Singh, S., & Sinha, P. (2016). Multimedia tool as a predictor for social media advertising-A YouTube way. *Multimedia Tools and Applications*, *76*(18), 1–12.

Gurau, C. (2008). The Influence of Advergames on Players' Behaviour: An Experimental Study. *Electronic Markets*, *18*(2), 106–116. doi:10.1080/10196780802044859

Gurau, C. (2009). Characteristics, Limitations, and Potential of Advergames. In *Encyclopedia of Multimedia Technology and Networking* (2nd ed.; pp. 205–211). IGI Global. doi:10.4018/978-1-60566-014-1.ch028

Hackley, C. E. (2007). *Marketing and social construction: exploring the rhetorics of managed consumption*. London: Routledge.

Halliday, M. A. K. (1975). *Learning How to Mean: Explorations in the development of language*. London: Edward Arnold. doi:10.1016/B978-0-12-443701-2.50025-1

Hamari, J., Koivisto, J., & Sarsa, H. (2014, January). Does gamification work?--a literature review of empirical studies on gamification. In *System Sciences (HICSS), 2014 47th Hawaii International Conference on* (pp. 3025-3034). IEEE.

Ham, C. D., Yoon, G., & Nelson, M. R. (2016). The interplay of persuasion inference and flow experience in an entertaining food advergame. *Journal of Consumer Behaviour*, *15*(3), 239–250. doi:10.1002/cb.1564

Hanse'n, S. O., & Wakonen, J. (1997). Innovation, a winning solution*? International Journal of Technology Management*, *13*(4), 345–358. doi:10.1504/IJTM.1997.001668

Hanumanthu, A. (2017). Advergaming in India: An Untapped Business? *Telangana Today*. Retrieved from https://telanganatoday.com/advergaming-india-untapped-business

Harris Harris Keller, J., & Blomann, F. (2008). Locus of control and the flow experience: An experimental analysis. *European Journal of Personality*, *22*(7), 589–607. doi:10.1002/per.692

Harris, D. J., Vine, S. J., & Wilson, M. R. (2017). Flow and quiet eye: The role of attentional control in flow experience. *Cognitive Processing*, 1–5. PMID:28238169

Harris, J. R. (2011). *The nurture assumption: Why children turn out the way they do*. Simon and Schuster.

Harris, J., Speers, S., Schwartz, M., & Brownell, K. (2012). US food company branded advergames on the Internet: Children's exposure and effects on snack consumption. *Journal of Children and Media*, *6*(1), 51–68. doi:10.1080/17482798.2011.633405

Harrison, K., & Marske, A. L. (2005). Nutritional Content of Foods Advertised during the Television Programs Children Watch Most. *American Journal of Public Health*, *95*(9), 1568–1574. doi:10.2105/AJPH.2004.048058 PMID:16118368

Hayes, S. C., Luoma, J. B., Bond, F. W., Masuda, A., & Lillis, J. (2006b). Acceptance and commitment therapy: Model, processes and outcomes. *Behaviour Research and Therapy*, *44*(1), 1–25. doi:10.1016/j.brat.2005.06.006 PMID:16300724

Heine, C. (2014). *Trouble brews over the viewability of digital ads*. Retrieved from http://www.adweek.com/brand-marketing/trouble-brews-over-viewability-digital-ads-157305/

Heinrichs, J. (2013). *Thank you for arguing: what Aristotle, Lincoln, and Homer Simpson can teach us about the art of persuasion*. New York: Three Rivers Press.

Hendricks, D. (2013, May 8). *Complete History of Social Media: Then And Now*. Retrieved Oct 5, 2018, from smallbiztrends.com

Henry, A. E., & Story, M. (2009). Food and Beverage Brands That Market to Children and adolscents on the Internet:A content analysis of branded websites. *Journal of Nutrition Education and Behavior*, *41*(5), 353–359. doi:10.1016/j.jneb.2008.08.004

Hernandez, M. D. (2011). A model of flow experience as determinant of positive attitudes toward online advergames. *Journal of Promotion Management*, *17*(3), 315–326. doi:10.1080/10496491.2011.596761

Hernandez, M. D., & Chapa, S. (2010). Adolescents, advergames and snack foods: Effects of positive affect and experience on memory and choice. *Journal of Marketing Communications*, *16*(1-2), 59–68. doi:10.1080/13527260903342761

Hernandez, M. D., Chapa, S., Minor, M. S., Maldonado, C., & Barranzuela, F. (2004). Hispanic attitudes toward Advergames: A proposed model of their antecedents. *Journal of Interactive Advertising*, *5*(1), 74–83. doi:10.1080/15252019.2004.10722095

Hertz, L. M. (2002). Advertising regulation on the internet. *The Computer and Internet Lawyer*, *19*(6), 18–26.

Hertz, L. M. (2002). Advertising Regulation on the Internet. *The Computer and Internet Lawyer*, *19*(6), 18–26.

Hofacker, C. F., De Ruyter, K., Lurie, N. H., Manchanda, P., & Donaldson, J. (2016). Gamification and mobile marketing effectiveness. *Journal of Interactive Marketing*, *34*, 25–36. doi:10.1016/j.intmar.2016.03.001

Hoffman, B., & Nadelson, L. (2010). Motivational engagement and video gaming: A mixed methods study. *Educational Technology Research and Development*, *58*(3), 245–270. doi:10.100711423-009-9134-9

Hoffman, D., & Novak, T. P. (1996). Marketing in Hypermedia Computer-Mediated Environments: Conceptual Foundations. *Journal of Marketing*, *60*(3), 50–68. doi:10.2307/1251841

Hofmeister-Tóth, A., & Nagy, P. (2011). The content analysis of advergames in Hungary. *Qualitative Market Research*, *14*(3), 289–303. doi:10.1108/13522751111137514

How to Get Google to Instantly Index Your New Website. (2015). Retrieved from Neil Patel Digital: https://neilpatel.com/blog/google-index/

Hsu, H. Y., & Wang, S. K. (2018). Gaming Literacies and Learning. In *Promoting Global Competencies Through Media Literacy* (pp. 79–95). IGI Global. doi:10.4018/978-1-5225-3082-4.ch005

Hudders, L., Cauberghe, V., Panic, K., & De Vos, W. (2015). Children's advertising literacy for new advertising formats: The mediating impact of advertising literacy on the (Un)Intended effects of advergames and advertising funded programs. In P. W. J. Verlegh, H. Voorveld, & M. Eisend (Eds.), *Advances in advertising research: The digital, the classic, the subtle and the alternative* (pp. 241–252). Amsterdam: Springer Gabler.

Iblasi, W. N., Bader, D. M., & Al-Qreini, S. A. (2016). The Impact of Social Media as a Marketing Tool on Purchasing Decisions (Case Study on SAMSUNG for Electrical Home Appliances). *International Journal of Managerial Studies and Research*, *4*(1), 14–28.

Images Retail Bureau. (2016, August 30). *Online shopping trends: facts and figures on Indian e-commerce sector*. Author.

India Infoline News Service. (n.d.). *Zapak launches its first ever AdverGame in India for multiple DTH Players*. Retrieved from https://www.indiainfoline.com/article/news-corporate/zapak-launches-its-first-ever-advergame-in-india-for-multiple-dth-players-113101908813_1.html

India, A. (2017). *Advantages of Digital marketing*. Retrieved from www.adbot.in: https://www.adbot.in/5-advantages-of-digital-marketing-in-the-present-scenario/

Intelligence, M. R. (2007). *Gaming Is Nearly Ubiquitous with Kids Online*. Retrieved from http://www.gfkmri.com/pdf/ gaming%20is%20nearly%20ubiquitous%20 with%20kids%20online.pdf

Interactive Food and Beverage Marketing: Targeting Adolescents in the Digital Age. (2009). *Journal of Adolescent Health*, 18-29.

Internet Advertising Bureau. (2017). *Viewability status*. Retrieved from https://iabuk.net/viewability-status

Isoraite, M. (2010). Guerilla Marketing Strategy Realization Assumptions. *6th International Scientific Conference*.

Jackson, L. A., Zhao, Y., Kolenic, A. III, Fitzgerald, H. E., Harold, R., & von Eye, A. (2008). Race, gender, and information technology use: The new digital divide. *Cyberpsychology & Behavior*, *11*(4), 437–442. doi:10.1089/cpb.2007.0157 PMID:18721092

Jain, K. (2016, December 3). Demonetization: A marketing opportunity for digital payment companies [Blog Post]. Retrieved from http://brandequity.economictimes.indiatimes.com/be-blogs/demonetisation-a-marketing-opportunity-for-digital-payment-companies/1971

Jain, V. (2017, May 16). *Myntra opens first retail store for Roadster brand in Bengaluru*. Retrieved Dec 12, 2017, from Economic Times: https://retail.economictimes.indiatimes.com/news/e-commerce/e-tailing/myntra-opens-first-retail-store-for-roadster-brand-in-bengaluru/57671838

Jayaswal, P., & Malati, N. (2017). Impact of Advergames on Children. *International Journal of Innovative Research and Development*, *6*(1), 88–92.

Jeong, E. J., Lee, H. R., & Woo, J. H. (2015, January). Brand Memory, Attitude, and State Aggression in Violent Games: Focused on the Roles of Arousal, Negative Affect, and Spatial Presence. In *System Sciences (HICSS), 2015 48th Hawaii International Conference on* (pp. 3538-3547). IEEE.

Jeong, E. J., Bohil, C. J., & Biocca, F. A. (2011). Brand logo placements in violent games. *Journal of Advertising*, *40*(3), 59–72. doi:10.2753/JOA0091-3367400305

Jessor, R., & Jessor, S. L. (1977). *Problem behavior and psychosocial development: A longitudinal study of youth*. Academic Press.

Jewitt, C. (2002). The move from page to screen: The multimodal reshaping of school English. *Journal of Visual Communication*, *1*(2), 171–196. doi:10.1177/147035720200100203

Jewitt, C. (2017). *The Routledge handbook of multimodal analysis*. Routledge.

Jin, D. Y. (2017). The Emergence of Asian Mobile Games: Definitions, Industries, and Trajectories. *Mobile Gaming in Asia: Politics, Culture and Emerging Technologies*, 3-20.

Jin, S. A. A. (2012). "Toward integrative models of flow": Effects of performance, skill, challenge, playfulness, and presence on flow in video games. *Journal of Broadcasting & Electronic Media*, *56*(2), 169–186. doi:10.1080/08838151.2012.678516

John, D. R. (1999). Consumer Socialization of Children: A Retrospective Look at Twenty-Five Years of Research. *The Journal of Consumer Research*, *26*(3), 183–213. doi:10.1086/209559

Johnson, L. (2017). *Demanding more stringent measurement, some brands are using their own viewability standards*. Retrieved from http://www.adweek.com/digital/demanding-more-stringent-measurement-some-brands-are-using-their-own-viewability-standards/

Johnson. (2012, June 29). Coca-Cola drives brand awareness via mobile gaming initiative. *Mobile Marketer*.

Johnson, D., Deterding, S., Kuhn, K. A., Staneva, A., Stoyanov, S., & Hides, L. (2016). Gamification for health and wellbeing: A systematic review ofthe literature. *Internet Interventions*, *6*, 89–106. doi:10.1016/j.invent.2016.10.002

Johnson, G. J., Bruner, G. C. II, & Kumar, A. (2006). Interactivity and Its Facets Revisited. *Journal of Advertising*, *35*(4), 35–52. doi:10.2753/JOA0091-3367350403

Kaden, R. J. (2006). *Guerrilla marketing research: Marketing research techniques that can help any business make more money*. Kogan Page Publishers.

Kanth, K. R. (2013). Catch them young with advergaming. *Business Standard*. Retrieved from http://www.business-standard.com/article/technology/catch-them-young-with-advergaming-110010700030_1.html

Kaye, L. K., & Bryce, J. (2012). Putting the fun factor into gaming: The influence of social contexts on the experiences of playing videogames. *International Journal of Internet Science*, *7*(1), 24–38.

Kazmi, S., & Batra, S. K. (2008). *Advertising and Sales Promotion.* Academic Press.

Keaty, A., Johns, R. J., & Henke, L. L. (2002). Can internet service providers and other secondary parties be held liable for deceptive online advertising? *Business Lawyer, 58*(1), 479–511.

Keaty, A., Johns, R. J., & Henke, L. L. (2002). Can Internet Service Providers and Other Secondary Parties Be Held Liable for Deceptive Online Advertising? *Business Lawyer, 58*(1), 479–511.

Kim, J., Lim, J. S., & Bhargava, M. (1998). The role of affect in attitude formation: A classical conditioning approach. *Journal of the Academy of Marketing Science, 26*(2), 143–152. doi:10.1177/0092070398262005

Kinard, B. R., & Hartman, K. B. (2013). Are You Entertained? The Impact of Brand Integration and Brand Experience in Television-Related Advergames. *Journal of Advertising, 42*(2–3), 196–203. doi:10.1080/00913367.2013.775794

Klaassen, A. (2009, Nov 2). *The State of Search Marketing: 2009.* Retrieved from AdAge: http://adage.com/article/digital/digital-marketing-state-search-marketing-2009/140083/

Kleeberger, J., & Hummel, J. (2002). *Online Gaming as Marketing and Sales Catalyst* (Working paper). University of St. Gallen. Available at www.gamasutra.com/ education/theses/20030721/Kleeberger_thesis.pdf

Kligler, B., Teets, R., & Quick, M. (2016, September 1). Complementary/Integrative Therapies That Work: A Review of the Evidence. *American Family Physician, 94*(5), 369–374. PMID:27583423

Kowert, R. & Oldmeadow, J. A. (2014). Playing for social comfort: Online video game play as a social accommodator for the insecurely attached. *Computers in Human Behavior, 53*(2015), 556–566.

Krajcovic, P. (2015). Strategies in Media Planning. *Communication Today, 6*(2), 20–30.

Kress, G. (2010). *Multimodality. A social semiotic approach to contemporary communication.* London: Routledge.

Kress, G., & van Leeuwen, T. (2001). *Multimodal discourse: The modes and media of contemporary communication.* London: Arnold.

Kress, G., & Van Leeuwen, T. (2006). *Reading images: The grammar of visual design.* London: Routledge.

Kretchmer, S. B. (2005). *Changing Views of Commercialization in Digital Games: In-Game Advertising and Advergames as Worlds in Play.* Paper presented at DIGTAR conference, "Changing Views: Worlds in Play," Vancouver, Canada. Retrieved from www.gamesconference.org/digra2005/ overview.php

Krishan, R. (2015). Social Media Challenges and Adoption Patterns among Public Relations Practitioners. *Media Watch, 6*(1), 73–81. doi:10.15655/mw/2015/v6i1/55390

Krishnan, S. G., & Sachdeva, P. (2011). Brand promotion through internet advertising. *Media Watch*, *2*(2), 28–30.

Kumar, N., Scheer, L., & Kotler, P. (2000). From market driven to market driving. *European Management Journal*, *18*(2), 129–142. doi:10.1016/S0263-2373(99)00084-5

Kunkel, D., Wilcox, B. J. C., Palmer, E., Linn, S., & Dowrick. (2004). A Report of the APA Task Force on Advertising and Children. In Psychological Issues in the Increasing Commercialization of Childhood. Washington, DC: American Psychological Association.

Lanier, J. (2017). *Dawn of the New Everything: Encounters with Reality and Virtual Reality.* New York: Henry Holt & Company.

Lantos, G. P., & Craton, L. G. (2012). A model of consumer response to advertising music. *Journal of Consumer Marketing*, *29*(1), 22–42. doi:10.1108/07363761211193028

Lawson-Borders, G. (2009). Integrating new media and old media: Seven observations of convergence as a strategy for best practices in media organizations. *International Journal on Media Management*, *5*(2), 91–99. doi:10.1080/14241270309390023

Lee & Obringer. (2007). *How advergaming works.* Retrieved from https://money.howstuffworks.com/advergaming.htm

Lee, M., & Youn, S. (2008). Leading National Advertisers' Use of Advergames. *Journal of Current Issues in Advertising.*

Lee, C., Yang, C., & Hung, H. (2017). Evaluating Game-Brand Congruity and Flow on Brand Personality by Using Gamifying Learning. *Eurasia Journal of Mathematics Science and Technology Education*, *13*(7), 3083–3097.

Lee, M., Choi, Y., Quilliam, E. T., & Cole, R. T. (2009). Playing with food: Content analysis of food Advergames. *The Journal of Consumer Affairs*, *43*(1), 129–154. doi:10.1111/j.1745-6606.2008.01130.x

Lee, M., & Youn, S. (2008). Leading national advertisers' uses of advergames. *Journal of Current Issues and Research in Advertising*, *30*(2), 1–13. doi:10.1080/10641734.2008.10505243

Leinonen, T. (2010). Designing Learning Tools. Methodological Insights. *Aalto University School of Art and Design Publication Series.* Retrieved from https://aaltodoc.aalto.fi/handle/123456789/11661

Lenhart, A., Jones, S., & Macgill, A. R. (2008). *Adults and video games* (Pew Internet project data memo). Retrieved from http://www.pewinternet.org/Reports/2008/Adults-and-Video-Games.aspx

Lenhart, A., Kahne, J., Middaugh, E., Macgill, A., Evans, C., & Vitak, J. (2007). *Teens, video games and civics* (Pew Internet project data memo). Retrieved from http://www.pewinternet.org/Reports/2008/Teens-Video-Games-and-Civics.aspx

LeVine, P., & Scollon, R. (Eds.). (2004). *Discourse and Technology: Multimodal Discourse Analysis*. Washington, DC: Georgetown University Press.

Li, J., Theng, Y. L., & Foo, S. (2014). Game-based digital interventions for depression therapy: A systematic review and meta-analysis. *Cyberpsychology, Behavior, and Social Networking*, *17*(8), 519–527. doi:10.1089/cyber.2013.0481 PMID:24810933

Lindstrom, M. (2005). Get a Jump-start on Playing the New Brand Game. *Media Asia*, *28*(June), 21.

Lister, C., West, J. H., Cannon, B., Sax, T., & Brodegard, D. (2014, August 4). Just a fad? Gamification in health and fitness apps. *JMIR Serious Games.*, *2*(2), e9. doi:10.2196/games.3413 PMID:25654660

Liu, X., Hu, M. Y., & Grimm, P. E. (2010). Affect transfer in brand extensions: The role of expectancy and relevancy. *Journal of Product and Brand Management*, *19*(5), 317–326. doi:10.1108/10610421011068559

Livingston, S. (2004). A Commentary on the Research Evidence Regarding the Effects of Food Promotion on Children. In Childhood Obesity—Food Advertising in Context. London: London School of Economics and Political Science, Department of Media and Communications.

Logan, R. K. (2010). *Understanding new media – Extending Marshall McLuhan*. New York: Peter Lang Publishing.

Lovett, M. J., & Staelin, R. (2016). The role of paid, earned and owned media in building entertaining brands: Reminding, informing and enhancing enjoyment. *Marketing Science*, *35*(1), 142–157. doi:10.1287/mksc.2015.0961

Ly, K.H., Asplund, K., & Andersson, G. (2014). Stress management for middle managers via an acceptance and commitment-based smartphone application: A randomized controlled trial. *Internet Interventions,* (1), 95–101.

Machin, D. (2007). *Introduction to multimodal analysis*. London: Hodder Arnold.

Mackaya, T., Ewinga, M., Newtona, F., & Windischa, L. (2015). The effect of product placement in computer games on brand attitude and recall. International Journal of Advertising. *The Review of Marketing Communications*, *28*(3), 423–438.

Maher, C., Ferguson, M., Vandelanotte, C., Plotnikoff, R., De Bourdeaudhuij, I., Thomas, S., ... Olds, T. (2015, July 13). A web-based, social networking physical activity intervention for insufficiently active adults delivered via Facebook app: Randomized controlled trial. *Journal of Medical Internet Research*, *17*(7), e174. doi:10.2196/jmir.4086 PMID:26169067

Maheshwari, S. (2017, Jul 31). *As Amazon's Influence Grows, Marketers Scramble to Tailor Strategies*. Retrieved from New York Times: https://www.nytimes.com/2017/07/31/business/media/amazon-advertising.html

Mallinckrodt, V., & Mizerski, D. (2007). The effects of playing an advergame on young children's perceptions, preferences, and requests. *Journal of Advertising*, *36*(2), 87–100. doi:10.2753/JOA0091-3367360206

Mangles, C. (2017). *Is marketing ready for VR / AR in 2018?* Retrieved from https://www.smartinsights.com/digital-marketing-platforms/video-marketing/is-marketing-ready-for-vr-ar-in-2018/

Manovich, L. (2003). New Media from Borges to HTML. In N. Wardrip-Fruin & N. Montfort (Eds.), The New Media Reader (pp. 13-25). Cambridge, MA: MIT Press.

Manovich, L. (2001). *The Language of New Media*. Cambridge, MA: The MIT Press.

Marczewski, A. (2012). Gamification: A simple introduction & a bit more: Tips. In Advice and Thoughts on Gamification (2nd ed.). Kindle edition.

Marketing Stack. (n.d.). Retrieved Jan 3, 2018, from Alexa: https://try.alexa.com/marketing-stack/

Marshall, J. (2014). *WTF is third-party data?* Retrieved from https://digiday.com/media/what-is-third-party-data/

McCarty, J. A. (2004). Product Placements: The Nature of the Practice and Potential Avenues of Inquiry. In The Psychology of Entertainment Media. Blurring the Lines between Entertainment and Persuasion. Mahwah, NJ: Lawrence Erlbaum.

McGaughey, R. E., & Mason, K. H. (2015). The Internet as a Marketing Tool. *Journal of Marketing Theory and Practice*, *6*(3), 1–11. doi:10.1080/10696679.1998.11501800

McGonigal, J. (2012). *Reality is Broken: Why Games Make Us Better and How They Can Change the World*. Penguin Group.

McMillan, S. J., & Hwang, J.-S. (2002). Measures of Perceived Interactivity: An Exploration of the Role of Direction of Communication, User Control, and Time in Shaping Perceptions of Interactivity. *Journal of Advertising*, *31*(3), 29–42. doi:10.1080/00913367.2002.10673674

Medium. (2016a). *Advergaming and Gamification: Funny and Effective Digital Marketing Trends*. Retrieved from: https://medium.com/@ReputationDefender/advergaming-and-gamification-funny-and-effective-digital-marketing-trends-70b0a5b78617

Medium. (2016b). *Mobile Marketing: Why is it important for you?* Retrieved from https://medium.com/@ReputationDefender/mobile-marketing-why-is-it-important-for-you-f085b1c93a62

Melzer, N. (2007). *Advergames: the effects of brand placement and music*. Rotterdam: Erasmus Universiteit.

Menezes, R. (2016, July 4). *Digital*. Retrieved from exchange4media: http://www.exchange4media.com/Digital/SultanThe-Game-tops-Google-Play-Store-charts;-celebrity-impact-creativity-spur-gamer-interest_65090.html

Michael, S. (2015). 2015 Social Media Marketing Industry Report. *Social Media Examiner*. Available at http://www.socialmediaexaminer.com/SocialMediaMarketingIndustryReport2015.pdf

Miles, C. (2014). *Interactive marketing: revolution or rhetoric?* London: Routledge.

Miller, C. R. (2016, Jun). *The 59 Second Rule: 3 Reasons Why Users Leave a Website*. Retrieved from The Daily Egg: https://www.crazyegg.com/blog/why-users-leave-a-website/

Miller, R., & Lammas, N. (2010). Social media and its implications for viral marketing. *Asia Pacific Public Relations Journal*, *11*, 1–9.

Miloff, A., Marklund, A., & Carlbring, P. (2015). The challenger app for social anxiety disorder: New advances in mobile psychological treatment. *Internet Interventions*, (2), 382–391.

Moffett, T. (2014). *Just published: The Forrester Wave: Cross-Channel Attribution Providers*. Retrieved from https://go.forrester.com/blogs/14-11-07-just_published_the_forrester_wave_cross_channel_attribution_providers/

Montogomery, K. (2009). *Food marketing in the digital age: A conceptual framework and agenda for research*. Retrieved from Digital ads: how marketers target youth.

Montogomery. (1999). *Digital kids: The new online children's consumer culture*. Academic Press.

Montola, M. (2005, December). Exploring the edge of the magic circle: Defining pervasive games. In *Proceedings of DAC* (*Vol. 1966*, pp. 103-106). Academic Press.

Moore, E. (2006, July). *It's Child's Play: Advergaming and the Online Marketing of Food to Children*. Kaiser Family Foundation Report.

Moore, E. S. (2006). *Its child 's play: Advergaming and online marketing of food to children*. A Kaiser Family Foundation Report.

Moore, E. S., & Rideout, V. J. (2007). The online marketing of food to children: Is it just fun and games? *American Marketing Association, 26*(2), 202–220.

Moore, E. S. (2004). Children and the Changing World of Advertising. *Journal of Business Ethics*, *52*(2), 161–167. doi:10.1023/B:BUSI.0000035907.66617.f5

Moore, E. S. (2006). *It's child's play: Advergaming and the online marketing of food to children*. Menlo Park, CA: Henry J. Kaiser Family Foundation.

Moore, E. S., & Rideout, V. J. (2007). The online marketing of food to children: Is it just fun and games? *Journal of Public Policy & Marketing*, *26*(2), 202–220. doi:10.1509/jppm.26.2.202

Morris, J. D., & Boone, M. A. (1998). *The effects of music on emotional response, brand attitude, and purchase intent in an emotional advertising condition*. ACR North American Advances.

Morris, S., & Shin, H. (2003). Global Games: Theory and Applications. In *Advances in Economics and Econometrics: Theory and Applications* (pp. 56–114). Cambridge, UK: Cambridge University Press. doi:10.1017/CBO9780511610240.004

Moses, L. J., & Baldwin, D. (2005). What Can the Study of Cognitive Development Reveal about Children's Ability to Appreciate and Cope with Advertising? *Journal of Public Policy & Marketing*, *24*(Fall), 186–201. doi:10.1509/jppm.2005.24.2.186

Mulhern, F. (2009). Integrated marketing communications: From media channels to digital connectivity. *Journal of Marketing Communications*, *15*(2-3), 85–101. doi:10.1080/13527260902757506

Mullins, J. W., & Sutherland, D. J. (1998). New product development in rapidly changing markets: An exploratory study. *Journal of Product Innovation Management*, *15*(3), 224–236. doi:10.1016/S0737-6782(97)00081-7

Munson, S., Poole, E., Perry, D. B., & Peyton, T. (2015). Gamification and health. In S. P. Walz (Ed.), *The Gameful World: Approaches, Issues, Applications* (pp. 597–623). Cambridge, MA: MIT Press.

Myers, J., & Sar, S. (2015). The influence of consumer mood state as a contextual factor on imagery-inducing advertisements and brand attitude. *Journal of Marketing Communications*, *21*(4), 284–299. doi:10.1080/13527266.2012.762421

Nairn, A., & Hang, H. (2012). *Advergames: "It's not an advert – it says play!"*. Family and Parenting Institute.

Nairuthram, S. (2016, Jun 15). *Social Media Marketing*. Retrieved from Easy Walkers Digital: http://www.eazywalkers.com/social-media-marketing/

Nakagoshi, K. (2012, Apr 19). *Yes, you can be addicted to social media*. Retrieved from Business Grow: https://www.businessesgrow.com/2012/04/19/yes-you-can-be-addicted-to-social-media/

Nakamura, J., & Csikszentmihalyi, M. (2009). Flow theory and research. Handbook of Positive Psychology, 195-206.

Nayak, P. R., & Ketteringham, J. M. (1986). *Breakthroughs*. London: Mercury Books.

Neeley, S. M., & Schumann, W. (2004). Using animated spokes-characters in advertising to young children: Does Increasing Attention to Advertising Necessarily Lead to Product Preference? *Journal of Advertising*, *33*(3), 7–23. doi:10.1080/00913367.2004.10639166

Nelson, M. R., & Waiguny, M. K. (2012). Psychological processing of in-game advertising and advergaming: Branded entertainment or entertaining persuasion. *Psychology of entertainment media: Blurring the lines between Entertainment and Persuasion*, 93-146.

Nelson, M. R., Yaros, R. A., & Keum, H. (2006). Examining the influence of telepresence on spectator and player processing of real and fictitious brands in a computer game. *Journal of Advertising*, *35*(4), 87–99. doi:10.2753/JOA0091-3367350406

Nesi, J., & Prinstein, M. (2015). Using Social Media for Social Comparison and Feedback-Seeking: Gender and Popularity Moderate Associations with Depressive Symptoms. *Journal of Abnormal Child Psychology*, *43*(8), 1427–1438. doi:10.100710802-015-0020-0 PMID:25899879

Neti, S. (2011). Social Media and its Role in Marketing. *International Journal of Enterprise Computing and Business Systems*, *1*(2), 1–15.

Neubaum, G., & Krämer, N. C. (2015). My Friends Right Next to Me: A Laboratory Investigation on Predictors and Consequences of Experiencing Social Closeness on Social Networking Sites. *Cyberpsychology, Behavior, and Social Networking*, *21*(8), 443–449. doi:10.1089/cyber.2014.0613 PMID:26252929

Nicholson, S. (2012). A user-centered theoretical framework for meaningful gamification. *Games+ Learning+ Society*, *8*(1), 223-230.

Nizan, Y. (2016, Apr 26). *LTV Calculator – The Naive method*. Retrieved from Soomla Blog: http://blog.soom.la/2016/04/ltv-calculator-naive-method.html

Nouala, M., El Kebir, N. D., & Maitre, I. K. (2016). Social Media as A New Emerging Tool of Marketing: Effect of E-Reputation in Algerian Market. *Maghreb Review of Economic and Management*, *8*(2), 81–95.

O'Halloran, K. (Ed.). (2004). *Multimodal Discourse Analysis: Systemic-Functional Perspectives*. London: Continuum.

Obringe. (2007). *How Advergaming works*. Retrieved from http://money.howstuffworks.com/advergaming.htm/printable

Obringer, L. A. (2007). *How Advergaming works*. Retrieved from http://money.howstuffworks.com/advergaming.htm/printable

Ojha, R. (2015). *Game First, Brand Later: A Strategic Approach to Advergames*. Retrieved from http://trak.in/tags/business/2011/05/23/brand-games-strategic-advergames/

Okazaki, S., & Taylor, C. R. (2013). Social media and international advertising: Theoretical challenges and future directions. *International Marketing Review*, *30*(1), 56–71. doi:10.1108/02651331311298573

Ollila, M. (2017). *The game ad-unit: the future of mobile marketing and location-based entertainment after Pokémon GO*. Retrieved from http://www.pocketgamer.biz/comment-and-opinion/65043/the-future-of-mobile-marketing-and-location-based-entertainment/

Olthuis, J. 2015. Therapist-delivered distance cognitive behavioural therapy for anxiety disorders in adults. *Cochrane Libr. Cochrane D*, (3). Available at: http://onlinelibrary.wiley.com

Ong, M. (2013). *Gamification and its effect on employee engagement and performance in a perceptual diagnosis task*. Academic Press.

Oza, H. (2017). *0 Advantages Of Digital Marketing Over Traditional Marketing*. Retrieved from https://prowly.com/magazine/2017/10/11/advantages-of-digital-marketing-over-traditional-marketing/

Özbük, R. M. Y., & Ünal, D. A. (2017). Advergames Aiming Children in Turkey: A Content Analysis of 65 Advergames 1. *Business and Economics Research Journal*, *8*(1), 115–130. doi:10.20409/berj.2017126248

Paek, H-J., Elizabeth, T. Q., Kim, S., Weatherspoon, L. J., Rifon, N. J., & Lee, M. (2014). Characteristics of food advergames that reach children and the nutrient quality of the foods they advertise. *Internet Research*, *24*(1), 63–81. doi:10.1108/IntR-02-2013-0018

Pahwa, N. (2016). *Cash vs Digital Money: why going cashless is going to be tough in India.* Available at: http://www.medianama.com/2016/11/223-cashless-india/

Pandher, P. S., & Bhullar, K. K. (2016, June). Smartphone applications for seizure management. *Health Informatics Journal*, *22*(2), 209–220. doi:10.1177/1460458214540906 PMID:25038202

Parrot, W. G., & Spackman, M. P. (2000). Emotion and memory. In M. Lewis & J.M. Haviland-Jones (Eds.), Handbook of emotions (2nd ed.; pp. 476-490). The Guilford Press.

Patel, N. (n.d.). 10 Online Marketing Tools You Need When Starting a Business [Blog Post]. Retrieved from https://neilpatel.com/blog/10-online-marketing-tools-you-need-when-starting-a-business/

Pavlou & Stewart. (2000). Measuring the Effects and Effectiveness of Interactive Advertising: A Research Agenda. *Journal of Interactive Advertising*.

Pawar, A. V. (2014). *Study Of The Effectiveness Of Online Marketing On Integrated Marketing Communication* (Master Thesis). D.Y. Patil University, Navi Mumbai, India.

Pelet, J. É., Ettis, S., & Cowart, K. (2017). Optimal experience of flow enhanced by telepresence: Evidence from social media use. *Information & Management*, *54*(1), 115–128. doi:10.1016/j.im.2016.05.001

Pempek, T. A., & Calvert, S. L. (2009). Tipping the balance use of advergames to promote consumption of nutritious foods and beverages by low-income African American children. *Archives of Pediatrics & Adolescent Medicine*, *163*(7), 633–637. doi:10.1001/archpediatrics.2009.71 PMID:19581546

Pertierra, R. (2005). Mobile Phones, Identity and Discursive Intimacy. *An Interdisciplinary Journal on Humans in ICT Environments*, *1*(1), 23–44. doi:10.17011/ht/urn.2005124

Petersen, F. W., Thomsen, L. E., Mirza-Babaei, P., & Drachen, A. (2017, October). Evaluating the Onboarding Phase of Free-to Play Mobile Games: A Mixed-Method Approach. In *Proceedings of the Annual Symposium on Computer-Human Interaction in Play* (pp. 377-388). ACM.

Petersen, R. C., Thomas, R. G., Grundman, M., Bennett, D., Doody, R., Ferris, S., ... Thal, L. J. (2005). Vitamin E and donepezil for the treatment of mild cognitive impairment. *The New England Journal of Medicine*, *352*(23), 2379–2388. doi:10.1056/NEJMoa050151 PMID:15829527

Piaget, J. (1929). *The child's conception of the world.* Harcourt, Brace Jovanovich.

Piaget, J., & Inhelder, B. (Eds.). (1973). *Memory and Intelligence*. New York, NY: Basic Books.

Pillai, S. (2017, December 19). Indians spend 70% of mobile internet time on social media, entertainment. *The Times of India Business*.

Pilotta, J. J., Schultz, D. E., Drenik, G., & Rist, P. (2004). Simultaneous media usage: A critical consumer orientation to media planning. *Journal of Consumer Behaviour*, *3*(3), 285–292. doi:10.1002/cb.141

Pixability. (2013). *The Top 100 Global Brands: Key Lessons for Success on YouTube: The Massive YouTube Ecosystem*. Retrieved from http://concept5.com/how-the-top-100-brands-use-youtube-for-marketing/

Poirier, S. (2013, Nov 19). *Social Media Building Blocks: The 6 Spheres Of Social Media Marketing*. Retrieved from Business to Community: https://www.business2community.com/social-media/social-media-building-blocks-6-spheres-social-media-marketing-0687662

Priya, P., Baisya, R. K., & Sharma, S. (2010). Television advertisements and children's buying behaviour. *Marketing Intelligence & Planning*, *28*(2), 151–169. doi:10.1108/02634501011029664

Purswani. (2010). Advergames, their use and potential regulation. *Asia Pacific Public Relations Journal*.

Purswani, G. (2010). Advergames, their use and potential regulation. *Asia Pacific Public Relations Journal*, *11*, 7.

Quilliam, E. T., Lee, M., Cole, R. T., & Kim, M. (2011). The impetus for (and limited power of) business self-regulation: The example of Advergames. *The Journal of Consumer Affairs*, *45*(2), 224–247. doi:10.1111/j.1745-6606.2011.01201.x

Rajagopal. (2014). *Disruptive Innovations and Technologies. In: Architecting Enterprise*. Palgrave Macmillan.

Rajani, S. (2014, October 16). *Showbiz*. Retrieved from India.com: http://www.india.com/showbiz/happy-new-year-game-the-official-game-of-shah-rukh-khans-latest-entertainment-saga-is-finally-out-173754/

Rajeshwari, K. (n.d.). *Why is social media adoption low?* Retrieved from BLoC: Business Line On Campus: http://www.bloncampus.com/columns/marketing-moves/why-is-the-adoption-of-social-media-low/article9937231.ece

Ramanathan, M., Bhavanani, A. B., & Trakroo, M. (2017, January-April). Effect of a 12-week yoga therapy program on mental health status in elderly women inmates of a hospice. *International Journal of Yoga*, *10*(1), 24–28. doi:10.4103/0973-6131.186156 PMID:28149064

Raney, A. A., Arpan, L. M., Pashupati, K., & Brill, D. A. (2003). At the movies, on the web: An investigation of the effects of entertaining and interactive web content on site and brand evaluations. *Journal of Interactive Marketing*, *17*(4), 38–53. doi:10.1002/dir.10064

Rao, B., & Minakakis, L. (2003). Evolution of Mobile Location Based Services. *Communications of the ACM*, *46*(12), 61–65. doi:10.1145/953460.953490

Read, J. L., & Shortell, S. M. (2011). Interactive games to promote behavior change in pre-vention and treatment. *Journal of the American Medical Association*, *305*(16), 1704–1705. doi:10.1001/jama.2011.408 PMID:21447802

Redondo, I. (2012). The effectiveness of casual Advergames on adolescents' brand attitudes. *European Journal of Marketing*, *46*(11/12), 1671–1688. doi:10.1108/03090561211260031

Reeves, B., & Read, L. (2009). *Total Engagement: Using Games and Virtual Worlds to Change the Way People Work and Businesses Compete*. Boston: Harvard Business School Press.

Refiana, L., Mizerski, D., & Murphy, J. (2005). Measuring the State of Flow in Playing Online Games. In *Proceedings of ANZMAC 2005 Conference, Marketing Research and Research Methodologies (quantitative)*. Freemantle, Australia: School of Business, University of Western Australia.

Refiana, L., Mizerski, D., & Murphy, J. (2005, December). Measuring the state of flow in playing online games. In *Proceedings of ANZMAC 2005 Conference, Marketing Research and Research Methodologies (quantitative)* (pp. 108-113). Freemantle, Australia: School of Business, University of Western Australia.

ReportE. M. (2016). Retrieved from https://www.ericsson.com/assets/local/mobility-report/documents/2016/ericsson-mobility-report-june-2016.pdf

Richards, D., Timulak, L., Rashleigh, C., McLoughlin, O., & Colla, A. (2016). Effectiveness of an internet-delivered intervention for generalized anxiety disorder in routine care: A randomised controlled trial in a student population. *Internet Interventions*, (6), 80–88.

Rideout, V., Foehr, U., & Roberts, D. (2010). *Generation M2: media in the lives of 8-to-18 year olds*. Retrieved from www.kff.org/entmedia/upload/8010.pdf

Rinne, P., Mace, M., Nakornchai, T., Zimmerman, K., & Fayer, S. (n.d.). Democratizing Neurorehabilitation: How Accessible are Low-Cost Mobile-Gaming Technologies for Self-Rehabilitation of Arm Disability in Stroke? *PLoS ONE, 11*(10). doi:.pone.016341310.1371/journal

Rip, P. D. (1980). Product Class Advertising Effects on First-Time Buyers' Decision Strategies. *The Journal of Consumer Research*, *7*(September), 176–188.

Robertson, T. S., & Rossiter, J. (1974). Children and Commercial Persuasion: An Attribution Theory Analysis. *The Journal of Consumer Research*, *1*(1), 13–20.

Robertson, T. S., & Rossiter, J. (1976). Short-Run Advertising Effects on Children: A Field Study. *JMR, Journal of Marketing Research*, *13*(1), 68–71. doi:10.2307/3150908

Roettl, J., Waiguny, M., & Terlutter, R. (2016). The persuasive power of advergames: A content analysis focusing on persuasive mechanisms in advergames. *Australasian Marketing Journal*, *24*(4), 275–287. doi:10.1016/j.ausmj.2016.10.001

Rowntree, L. (2017). *Is it worth brands pursuing 100% Viewability*. Retrieved from https://www.exchangewire.com/blog/2017/11/28/worth-brands-pursuing-100-viewability/

Rozendaal, E., Buijzen, M., & Valkenburg, P. (2010). Comparing children's and adults' cognitive advertising competences in the Netherlands. *Journal of Children and Media*, *4*(1), 77–89. doi:10.1080/17482790903407333

Santos, E., Gonzalo, R., & Gisbert, F. (2007). Advergames: Overview. *Information Technologies and Knowledge*, *1*, 203–208.

Savulich, G., Piercy, T., Fox, C., Suckling, J., Rowe, J. B., O'Brien, J. T., & Sahakian, B. J. (2017). Cognitive Training Using a Novel Memory Game on an iPad in Patients with Amnestic Mild Cognitive Impairment (aMCI). *Int J Neuropsychpharm*, *20*(8), 624–633. doi:10.1093/ijnp/pyx040 PMID:28898959

Scaife, M., & Rogers, Y. (1996). External cognition: How do graphical representations work? *International Journal of Human-Computer Studies*, *45*(2), 185–213. doi:10.1006/ijhc.1996.0048

Schaefer, M. (2012, Feb 21). *The six elements of human behavior that drive social media*. Retrieved from Mark Schaefer: https://www.businessesgrow.com/2012/02/21/the-six-elements-of-human-behavior-that-drive-social-media/

Schultz, D. E., Block, M. P., & Viswanathan, V. (2016). Consumer driven media planning and buying. *Journal of Marketing Communications*. Retrieved from http://www.tandfonline.com/action/showCitFormats?doi=10.1080/13527266.2016.1185833

Schultz, D. E., Block, M. P., & Raman, K. (2009). Media synergy comes of age – Part 2. *Journal of Direct Data and Digital Marketing Practice*, *11*(2), 88–99. doi:10.1057/dddmp.2009.22

Scott, J., & Craig-Lees, M. (2010). Audience engagement and its effects on product placement recognition. *Journal of Promotion Management*, *16*(1-2), 39–58. doi:10.1080/10496490903571803

Sewell, M.D., Eastwood, D.M., & Wimalasundera, N. (2014). Managing common symptoms of cerebral palsy in children. *BMJ, 349*.

Shaefer, M. (2014, Nov 18). *How Facebook changes our behavior*. Retrieved from Business Grow: https://www.businessesgrow.com/2014/11/18/facebook-changes-our-behavior/

Shakeel, M., & Khan, M. M. (2011). Impact of Guerrilla Marketing on Consumer Perception. *Global Journal of Management and Business Research*, *11*(7).

Sharma, D. (2016, June 10). *Entertainment*. Retrieved from Zee News India: http://zeenews.india.com/entertainment/movies/sultan-the-game-ready-for-download-salman-khan-tweets-the-link_1893764.html

Sharma, M. (2014). Advergaming – The Novel Instrument in the Advertising. *Procedia Economics and Finance*, *11*, 247–254. doi:10.1016/S2212-5671(14)00193-2

Sharma, R., & Sharma, S. (2014). *A Review of Guerrilla Marketing & Its Weapons. The international journal Research Publications*. Research Journal of Social Science and Management.

Shrum, L. J. (Ed.). (2004). *The Psychology of Entertainment Media: Blurring the Lines Between Entertainment and Persuasion*. Mahwah, NJ: Lawrence Erlbaum.

Silky, B. (2016). Social Media as a Way for Brand Building. *Academicia. An International Multidisciplinary Research Journal, 6*(4), 88–94.

Siricharoen, W. V. (2013). Infographics: The New Communication Tools in Digital Age. *The International Conference on E-Technologies and Business on the Web (EBW2013),* 169-174. 10.4018/ijeei.2013040104

Smyth, G. (2007). *The History of Digital Marketing*. Inetasia.

Soberman, D. (2005). The complexity of media planning today. *Brand Management, 12*(6), 420–429. doi:10.1057/palgrave.bm.2540237

Social Media usage worldwide. (2018). Retrieved from: https://www.statista.com/statistics/278414/number-of-worldwide-social-network-users/

Sorkin, A. R. (2006). Dot-Com Boom Echoed in Deal to Buy YouTube. *The New York Times*.

Statista. (2017a). *Number of internet users worldwide from 2005 to 2007 (in millions)*. Retrieved from https://www.statista.com/statistics/273018/number-of-internet-users-worldwide/

Statista. (2017b). *Countries with the highest number of internet users as of June 2017 (in millions)*. Retrieved from https://www.statista.com/statistics/262966/number-of-internet-users-in-selected-countries/

Stern, A. (2010, Feb 3). *8 Ways to Improve Your Click Through Rate*. Retrieved from iMedia: 8 Ways to Improve Your Click Through Rate.

Stober, R. (2004). What media evolution is: A theoretical approach to the history of new media. *European Journal of Communication, 19*(4), 483–505. doi:10.1177/0267323104049461

Strauss, J., & Frost, R. (2008). *E-Marketing*. Prentice Hall Press.

Sutko, D. M., & de Souza e Silva, A. (2011). Location-aware mobile media and urban sociability. *New Media & Society, 13*(5), 807–823. doi:10.1177/1461444810385202

Tan, S. (2009). *Predicting the determinants of users' intention in using YouTube to share video*. Institute of Information Management, National Chiao Tung University.

Taylor, A. (2017). Size, quantity and management capabilities: How Google updates AdWords to increase revenue. *Journal of Digital & Social Media Marketing, 5*(1), 18–27.

Team, A. X. (2014, October 24). *Games*. Retrieved from Animation Xpress.com: http://www.animationxpress.com/index.php/latest-news/shahrukh-khan-and-vroovy-team-up-to-launch-the-official-mobile-game-of-happy-new-year

Teinowitz, I. (2007). Kellogg Move Bodes III for Ads to Kids: More Than a Billion Food Marketing Bucks in Limbo as Companies Try to Satisfy the Critics. *Advertising Age*. Retrieved from http://adage.com/article?article_id=117386

Terlutter, R., & Capella, M. L. (2013). The gamification of advertising: Analysis and research directions of in-game advertising, Advergames, and advertising in social network games. *Journal of Advertising*, *42*(2-3), 95–112. doi:10.1080/00913367.2013.774610

The Media and Modernity A Social Theory of the Media. (1995). Stanford University Press.

Thompson, J. B. (1995). *The Media and Modernity - A Social Theory of the Media*. Stanford University Press.

Tina, W., & Buckner, K. (2006). Receptiveness of gamers to embedded brand messages in Advergames: Attitudes towards product placement. *Journal of Interactive Advertising*, *7*(1), 3–32. doi:10.1080/15252019.2006.10722123

Tomas, G., Hult, M., & Ketchen, D. J. Jr. (2017). Disruptive marketing strategy. *Academy of Marketing Science*, *7*, 20–25.

Turkish Airline's #WingoFlies Is The First YouTube 360 Advergame. (2016, May 17). Retrieved September 27, 2017, from https://wersm.com/turkish-airlines-wingoflies-is-the-first-youtube-360-advergame/

United Nations. (2007, August 31). *Growth of E-Business Worldwide*. Retrieved from The American Academy of Project Management: http://www.aapm.info/article4ef9.html?id=12

Updates, S. M. (2016). *Pew Research Center*. Available at http://www.pewinternet.org/2016/11/11/social-media-update-2016/SS

Valkenburg, P. M., & Peter, J. (2013). The differential susceptibility to media effects model. *Journal of Communication*, *63*(2), 221–243. doi:10.1111/jcom.12024

Van Bommel, E., Edelman, D., & Ungerman, K. (2014, June). Digitizing the consumer decision journey. *McKinsey Quarterly*, 1-8. Retrieved from http://kwu-alumni.org/moto/media/5558efe863bec.pdf

van Leeuwen, T. (1999). *Speech, music, sound*. London: Macmillan. doi:10.1007/978-1-349-27700-1

Van Leeuwen, T. (2005). *Introducing social semiotics*. London: Routledge.

van Leeuwen, T., & Jewitt, C. (2001). *Handbook of Visual Analysis*. London: Sage.

van Reijmersdal, E. A., Jansz, J., Peters, O., & Van Noort, G. (2010). The effects of interactive brand placements in online games on children's cognitive, affective, and conative brand responses. *Computers in Human Behavior*, *26*(6), 1787–1794. doi:10.1016/j.chb.2010.07.006

van Reijmersdal, E. A., Rozendaal, E., & Buijzen, M. (2012). Effects of Prominence, Involvement, and Persuasion Knowledge on Children's Cognitive and Affective Responses to Advergames. *Journal of Interactive Marketing*, *26*(1), 33–42. doi:10.1016/j.intmar.2011.04.005

Van Reijmersdal, E., Neijens, P., & Smit, E. G. (2009). A new branch of advertising. *Journal of Advertising Research*, *49*(4), 429–449. doi:10.2501/S0021849909091065

Vanwesenbeeck, I., Ponnet, K., & Walrave, M. (2016). Go with the flow: How children's persuasion knowledge is associated with their state of flow and emotions during advergame play. *Journal of Consumer Behaviour*, *15*(1), 38–47. doi:10.1002/cb.1529

Vanwesenbeeck, I., Walrave, M., & Ponnet, K. (2017). Children and advergames: The role of product involvement, prior brand attitude, persuasion knowledge and game attitude in purchase intentions and changing attitudes. *International Journal of Advertising*, *36*(4), 520–541. doi:10.1080/02650487.2016.1176637

Vashisht, D., & S., S. (2017). Effect of nature of the game on ad-persuasion in online gaming context. *Internet Research, 27*(1), 52-73. Retrieved from https://search.proquest.com/docview/1857362515?accountid=177896

Vashist, D., & Chauhan, A. (2017). Effect of game-interactivity and congruence on presence and brand attitude. *Marketing Intelligence & Planning*, *35*(6), 789–804. doi:10.1108/MIP-01-2017-0018

Verdoodt, V., Clifford, D., & Lievens, E. (2016). Toying with children's emotions, the new game in town? The legality of advergames in the EU. *Computer Law & Security Review*, *32*(4), 599–614. doi:10.1016/j.clsr.2016.05.007

Vermeir, I., Kazakova, S., Tessitore, T., Cauberghe, V., & Slabbinck, H. (2014). Impact of flow on recognition of and attitudes towards in-game brand placements: Brand congruence and placement prominence as moderators. *International Journal of Advertising*, *33*(4), 785–810. doi:10.2501/IJA-33-4-785-810

Veryzer, R. W. (1998). Key factors affecting customer evaluation of discontinuous new products. *Journal of Product Innovation Management*, *15*(2), 136–150. doi:10.1016/S0737-6782(97)00075-1

Waiguny, M. K. J., Nelson, M. R., & Marko, B. (2013). How advergame content influences explicit and implicit brand attitudes: When violence spills over. *Journal of Advertising*, *42*(2), 155–169. doi:10.1080/00913367.2013.774590

Waiguny, M. K. J., Terlutter, R., & Zaglia, M. E. (2011). The influence of advergames on consumers' attitudes and behavior: An empirical study among young consumers. *International Journal of Entrepreneurial Venturing*, *3*(3), 231–247. doi:10.1504/IJEV.2011.041273

Waiguny, M. K., Nelson, M. R., & Terlutter, R. (2012). Entertainment matters! The relationship between challenge and persuasiveness of an advergame for children. *Journal of Marketing Communications*, *18*(1), 69–89. doi:10.1080/13527266.2011.620766

Waiguny, M., & Terlutter, R. (2010). Entertainment in Advergames and its Influence on Brand-Related Outcomes for Children. In R. Terlutter, S. Diehl, & S. Okazaki (Eds.), *Advances in Advertising Research* (Vol. 1). Gabler. doi:10.1007/978-3-8349-6006-1_12

Walia, T. (2018, Feb 21). *Top 10 E-Commerce Companies in 2018 India*. Retrieved Mar 3, 2018, from Business2Business: http://www.business2business.co.in/article/1345/title/top-10-e-commerce-companies-in-2018-india

Wanick, V., Ranchhod, A., & Wills, G. B. (2014). *Effects and opportunities of mobile advergames into brand management and marketing: a content analysis*. At International Conference on Information Society (i-Society 2014).

Ward, S., Reale, G., & Levinson, D. (Eds.). (1972). *Children's Perceptions, Explanations, and Judgements of Television Advertising: A Further Exploration*. Washington, DC: U.S. Government Printing Office.

Wasserman, A. (n.d.). *4 Steps to a Successful Social Media Campaign*. Retrieved from Prescient Digital Media: http://www.prescientdigital.com/articles/web-2.0/4-steps-to-a-successful-social-media-campaign

Weber, K., Story, M., & Hamack, L. (2006). Internet Food Marketing Strategies Aimed at Children and Adolescents: A Content Analysis of Food and Beverage Brand Websites. *Journal of the American Dietetic Association, 106*(9), 1463–1466. doi:10.1016/j.jada.2006.06.014 PMID:16963354

Weber, R., Tamborini, R., Westcott-Baker, A., & Kantor, B. (2009). Theorizing flow and media enjoyment as cognitive synchronization of attentional and regard networks. *Communication Theory, 19*(4), 397–422. doi:10.1111/j.1468-2885.2009.01352.x

Weibel, D., Wissmath, B., Habegger, S., Steiner, Y., & Groner, R. (2008). Playing online games against computer-vs. human-controlled opponents: Effects on presence, flow, and enjoyment. *Computers in Human Behavior, 24*(5), 2274–2291. doi:10.1016/j.chb.2007.11.002

Weighing in the Advantages and Disadvantages of Internet Marketing. (n.d.). Retrieved from https://marketingwit.com/advantages-disadvantages-of-internet-marketing

Weingarten, M. (2002). It's an ad! It's a game! It's . . . both! *Business 2.0, 3*(3), 102.

Wei, P. S., & Lu, H. P. (2014). Why do people play mobile social games? An examination of network externalities and of uses and gratifications. *Internet Research, 24*(3), 313–331. doi:10.1108/IntR-04-2013-0082

Whittinghill, D. M., & Brown, J. S. (2014, June). *Gamification of Physical Therapy for the Treatment of Pediatric Cerebral Palsy: A Pilot Study Examining Player Preferences*. Paper presented at 2014 ASEE Annual Conference & Exposition, Indianapolis, IN. Retrieved from https://peer.asee.org/20529

Why HDFC Is No. 1 Among Indian Banks For Social Media Practice. (2011). [Blog post]. *Digital Marketing Blog*. Retrieved from https://www.digitalvidya.com/blog/why-hdfc-is-no-1-among-indian-banks-for-social-media-practice/

Wijaya, B. S. (2012). The Development of Hierarchy of Effects Model in Advertising. *International Research Journal of Business studies, 5*(1), 73-85.

Winkler, T., & Buckner, K. (2006). Receptiveness of Gamers to Embedded Brand Messages in Advergames: Attitudes Towards Product Placement. *Journal of Interactive Advertising, 7*(1), 37–46.

Winkler, T., & Buckner, K. (2006). Receptiveness of Gamers to Embedded Brand Messages in Advergames: Attitudes towards Product Placement. *Journal of Interactive Advertising, 7*(1).

Winkler, T., & Buckner, T. (2006). Receptiveness of Gamers to Embedded Brand Messages in Advergames: Attitudes towards Product Placement. *Journal of Interactive Advertising, 7*(1).

Wise, K., Bolls, P. D., Kim, H., Venkataraman, A., & Meyer, R. (2008). Enjoyment of Advergames and brand attitudes: The impact of thematic relevance. *Journal of Interactive Advertising, 9*(1), 27–36. doi:10.1080/15252019.2008.10722145

Wise, K., Bolls, P., Kim, H., Venkataraman, A., & Meyer, R. (2008). Enjoyment of advergames and brand attitudes: The impact of thematic relevance. *Journal of Interactive Marketing, 9*(1), 27–36. Retrieved from http://primelab.missouri.edu/pdfs/wbkvm08.pdf

Wouters, M., & De Pelsmacker, P. (2011). Brand placement in scripted and non-scripted Belgian and US programs on Belgian prime time television. *Journal of Marketing Communications, 17*(5), 299–318. doi:10.1080/13527261003600421

Wright, P., Friestad, M., & Boush, D. M. (2005). The Development of Marketplace Persuasion Knowledge in Children, Adolescents, and Young Adults. *Journal of Public Policy & Marketing, 24*(2), 222–233. doi:10.1509/jppm.2005.24.2.222

Wright, P., Friestad, M., & Boush, D. M. (2005). The Development of Marketplace Persuasion Knowledge in Children, Adolescents, and Young Adults. *Public Policy and Marketing, 24*, 222–233.

Yang, M., Roskos-Ewoldsen, D. R., Dinu, L., & Arpen, L. M. (2006). The Effectiveness of 'In-Game' Advertising: Comparing College Students' Explicit and Implicit Memory for Brand Names. *Journal of Advertising, 35*(4), 143–152. doi:10.2753/JOA0091-3367350410

Yasmin, A., Tasneem, S., & Fatema, K. (2015). Effectiveness of Digital Marketing in the Challenging Age: An Empirical Study. *International Journal of Management Science and Business Administration, 1*(5), 69–80. doi:10.18775/ijmsba.1849-5664-5419.2014.15.1006

Yokum, S., Gearhardt, A. N., Harris, J. L., Brownell, K. D., & Stice, E. (2014). Individual differences instriatum activity to food commercials predict weight gain in adolescents. *Obesity (Silver Spring, Md.), 12*, 2544–2551. PMID:25155745

Yoon, G., & Vargas, P. T. (2013). Seeing without looking: The effects of hemispheric functioning on memory for brands in computer games. *Journal of Advertising*, *42*(2-3), 131–141. doi:10.1080/00913367.2013.774587

YouTube. (2008). *YouTube Fact Sheet*. Retrieved from http://youtube.com/t/fact_sheet)

Yüksel, A. B. (2010). Gerilla Sanatı ve Gerilla Reklamcılığı, Marmara Üniversitesi, Güzel Sanatlar Enstitüsü Resim Anasanat Dalı, Yüksek Lisans Tezi, İstanbul, s. 74, 75.

Zhang, M. W. B., Ho, C. S. H., Cheok, C. C. S., & Ho, R. C. M. (2015). Bringing Smartphone Technology into undergraduate and postgraduate psychiatry. *BJPsych Advances*, *21*(4), 222–228. doi:10.1192/apt.bp.114.013649

Zhang, M. W., Yeo, L. L., & Ho, R. C. (2015, October). Harnessing smartphone technologies for stroke care, rehabilitation and beyond. *BMJ Innov.*, *1*(4), 145–150. doi:10.1136/bmjinnov-2015-000078 PMID:26692351

About the Contributors

Pratika Mishra is currently working as Associate Professor at School of Management, Presidency University, Bangalore. She has also worked with G.B. Pant Social Science Institute and Indian Institute of Information Technology, Allahabad. Her Area of Expertise is Strategic Marketing Management including Integrated Marketing Communication and Advertising & Brand Management. She is a Commerce Graduate, from University of Allahabad (Gold Medalist), MBA from IIT-ISM Dhanbad & PhD from prestigious IIIT Allahabad. She has more than 35 research publications and edited books to her credit. She is the founder editor of Management Sapience and Presidency Management Review, Presidency University, NDIM Diorama and has worked as Co-Editor of Review of Professional Management, Bi annual Journal of NDIM. She has also been founder Editor of Newsletter De Facto (Ansal University) founder Editor of International Journal Ansal University Business Review, was Chief Coordinator, Quarterly E Magazine B' Cognizance (IIIT-A). She has also been involved in Content Development of Papers like Research Methodology and Advertising Management for Project under Department of Information Technology, MCIT, GoI. She is considered as great mentor both at PG and PhD level.

Swati Oberoi Dham is the first Ph.D from Ansal University, in the niche area of Advergaming. She is a UGC-NET qualified, an Engineer (ECE) from Galgotia's College of Engineering & Technology and an MBA(Marketing) from IMT-Ghaziabad. Having worked with TATA Consultancy Services, she brings with her, a rich industry and academia experience of nearly 12 years. She has over half a dozen publications in indexed journals of repute. Dr. Swati loves to travel and hence has attended large number of National & International conferences. She was invited as a Session Chair for an International Conference (ICONTES 2017) at Kuala Lumpur. In a quest to upgrade her skills, she has also participated in a short term course on Business Analytics at IIT Roorkee and IIM Bangalore (2017 and 2018). She is actively involved in training young MBA students and making them industry ready by providing them the correct IT exposure. She heads the Marketing Club at School of Management and is also the Coordinator for B.Com(H) students. At

Ansal University, she takes up courses such as Business Intelligence & Analytics, Advanced MS-Excel, Customer Relationship Management, Integrated Marketing Communication and so on.

* * *

Atul Agarwal, an alumnus of the Indian Institute of Technology(IIT) Kanpur with over 21 years of industry and academic experience. He has obtained his MBA (Marketing), M.Phil., M.S.W. and Ph.D. from Central University(HNBU). His teaching interests are in the area of marketing management, Services Marketing, Brand Management, Rural Marketing and entrepreneurship. Prof. Agarwal has conducted many MDPs (Management Development Programs) at Grasim Industries Limited, Ultrapure Technologies Limited. and Ordinance Factory- Deharadun etc., he has authored two books on 'Marketing Management' and 'Data Base Management Systems' . He has published more than dozen research papers in reputed national and international journals. Currently Dr. Agarwal is working with Ansal University as a Professor in School of Management Studies.

Aanchal Aggarwal is currently working as an Assistant Professor at Vivekananda Institute of Professional Studies affiliated to Guru Gobind Singh Indraprastha University. She is a gold medalist in MBA (Insurance) from Amity University. She is currently pursuing her PhD from Ansal University, Gurgaon in the area of marketing and consumer behaviour. She holds fellowship diploma from Insurance Institute of India.

Nupur Arora is currently working as an Assistant Professor at Vivekananda Institute of Professional Studies affiliated to Guru Gobind Singh Indraprastha University. She is a gold medalist in MBA (Insurance) from Amity University. She is currently pursuing her PhD from Ansal University, Gurgaon in the area of marketing and consumer behaviour.

Tanusree Chakraborty is a psychologist and is interested in the area of understanding human behavior. Her area of specialization is Organizational and Environmental Psychology. A Ph.D in Applied Psychology, MA (Applied Psychology),MBA (HR), Dr. Chakraborty is an Associate Professor with Presidency University, Bangalore. An university rank holder throughout, Dr. Chakraborty was the ex-research fellow the Indian Council of Medical Research (ICMR) as Social Scientist for 3 years. She has hands on experience in coaching and counseling too. As a Trainer, Dr. Chakraborty has facilitated many a learning session for organizations both public as well as private from varied sectors. She has a number of publications in leading journals.

Ajeet Gandhi is an Assistant Professor at Department of Radiation Oncology, Dr Ram Manohar Lohia Institute of Medical Sciences, Lucknow, India. He is MD and DNB is Radiation Oncology from prestigious Institutes of India and has been working and Researching to improve medical healthcare and quality of life among cancer patients. He has contributed many research papers in the area of radiation oncology and clinical medicine.

Abhishek Goyal has 17+ years of experience in the space of IT, marketing, Business Management, entrepreneurship, strategic consulting and now Innovation Advisor. He has created a blend of technological innovation and traditional knowledge in the field of Fintech, Insurance, Mutual Fund, Artificial Intelligence, Virtual Reality and Block Chain. He is advisor to many start - ups on competitive edge and strategic growth.

Abhishek Gupta has 10+ years of experience in digital/technology sector leading large scale engineering/product teams in Investment Banking & Gaming Domain before starting up at GreyKernel. He has Setup an Indian upstart in gaming for a German Conglomerate heading/managing 400% growth in 3 years span. He has a rich Global exposure working with brands like Morgan Stanely, Goldman Sachs, Headstrong Capital Markets, Gauselmann AG. He is a Tier 1 Gamer [Rank 40 (Highest)- Global General] in Counter Strike.

Harshita Gupta is a doctoral student in Marketing in the Department of Management Studies, IIT (ISM), Dhanbad. She holds an MBA degree in Marketing and Human Resource Management. She has attended many national and international conferences. Her work consists of articles in journals of both international and national repute and contribution in different newsletters and blogs. She also holds a corporate experience in sales and marketing. Her current research interest is Guerrilla marketing, advertising and other unconventional ways of marketing.

Shefali Khurana is a research scholar at the University School of Management studies, GGS Indraprastha University, Delhi under the guidance of Prof. Vijita S. Aggarwal.

Dinkar Kulshreshtha did his graduation from Chandigarh, India and super specialization in Neurology from NIMHANS, Bengaluru, India. He is currently working as an Associate Professor in Neurology at Dr. RMLIMS, Lucknow, India. Amongst his areas of interest are neuro-muscular disorders and movement disorders. He has more than 20 national and international publications with book chapters and is a co-guide in 2 MD and 5 DM thesis of the residents in pathology/ radiology and neurology.

Surendra Prasad Mishra is M. Sc. (Phy.), Pg.Dip R P (BARC), Ph. D., FICMP, DHHCM MBA (Hosp Admin) Sr. Scientist,"F" Department of Radiation Oncology, Dr. Ram Manohar Lohia Institute Of Medical Sciences, Gomtinagar, Lucknow (UP), India. He is also a Visiting Professor and PhD Guide, University of Mewar, Rajasthan. Before joining his current assignment he has worked as Additional Director Medical and HOD Medical Physics & Radiology, Regional Cancer Centre, Kamala Nehru Memorial Hospital, Allahabad, India. He has published more than 150 papers and 20 chapters in edited books, Guided number of PhD's and have served as technical expert to IAEA, Vienna. Having worked as invited faculty with many institutes he has also worked on government and other reputed agencies funded projects.

Amit Nagpal is Associate Professor (Digital Marketing) at New Delhi Institute of Management, New Delhi. His areas of interest include social media marketing, online branding and digital storytelling. He has a PhD in New Media. He has also authored a book titled Personal Branding, Storytelling And Beyond.

Tuğçe Ozansoy Çadırcı has a PhD degree on marketing. She works as assistant professor of marketing at Yıldız Technical University (YTU), TURKEY. Her main research areas include consumer behavior, digital consumption and fashion marketing. Currently she is lecturing on the subjects of consumption theory, e-commerce, digital marketing, consumer behavior and marketing research at YTU.

Anandan Pillai is an Associate Director (Paid Media) at Performics.Resultrix, a Publicis Media company. He holds Fellow Program in Management degree (equivalent to PhD) from Management Development Institute, Gurugram, India. He has an experience of work a decade in the field of digital marketing, social media marketing, marketing research. He has published extensive management case studies at European Case Clearing House, Richard Ivey School of Business. He has published research papers in peer-reviewed international research journals like Journal of Product & Brand Management, Journal of Brand Management, International Journal of Indian Culture and Business Management, International Journal of E-business Research. His research area interests are community building on digital platforms, digital marketing analytics, media planning and buying, digital strategy, etc.

Priyanka Prasad is a Ph.D in Management (Consumer Behavior) from Indian Institute of Technology (IIT-ISM Dhanbad) and has approximately six years of teaching and research experience. She has a good number of publications in Scopus and SCI indexd Journals (National and International).and has participated in many national and international seminars and conferences.

Pallavi Rajain is pursuing her Ph.D. from DCRUST, Murthal (Haryana). She received her B.Tech. from Kurukshetra University and MBA from DCRUST, Murthal in 2010 and 2012, respectively. She has qualified UGC NET and worked as Project Fellow on a UGC sponsored major research project on Women Entrepreneurship. She has presented papers in 20 national and international conferences. She has received "Second Best Paper Award" in International Conference held at JIMS, Rohini. She has 22 publications in National and International Journals.

K. Rajeshwari is currently an Associate Professor (Marketing) at Great Lakes Institute of Management, Chennai. Prior to this, she completed her Ph.D from IIT Madras and served as a faculty member at XLRI, Jamshedpur. She is also a visiting faculty at various IIMs in the country. Rajeshwari has authored two books (solo) before this- the first one was titled 'My Life My Choice'-published by Macmillan in 2011 and was about mid-life career choices. The second one was a reference text book for B Schools and was titled 'New Product development-a FMCG Perspective', released in 2017. She is a regular columnist in the Hindu Business Line and has published several articles and case studies in International as well as domestic journals. Rajeshwari has won the Women Achiever Award twice in 2011 and 2012 and was recently conferred the title 'Distinguished Woman In Management' in 2017. She is on the academic board of MCC Business School and has been chosen as 'Subject Expert-Marketing' by Tata Consultancy Services, India. She is an Alumnus of IIM Ahmedabad (1994) and worked in the industry for 15 years in top companies like Unilever and Nippon Paint. Her other interests include spending time with her son as well as practicing yoga/listening to music.

Madhup Rastogi is Professor and Head, Department of Radiation Oncology, Dr. Ram Manohar Lohia Institute of Medical Sciences, Lucknow, India. He is a vivid researcher and published more than 70 papers in reputed National and International Journal and Conferences. He is a recipient of many illustrious awards including Frank Neal and CD Joseph fellowship by AROI for the year 2006; AROI-BIOCON Overseas Fellowship, London, UK; AROI- Dr Reddy Overseas Fellowship (40 – 50 yr) for the year 2013-14 at Greenwich Hospital, CT, USA under Prof Ashwatha Narayana. He is a popular doctor, inspiring teacher and a thoughtful researcher in the area of Radiation Oncology.

Rupa Rathee is presently working as Assistant Professor in the Department of Management Studies, DCRUST, Murthal. She has more than sixteen years of teaching experience to her credit. She has attended 21 FDPs at various prestigious institutes like IIM-Bangalore, IIM-Calcutta, IIM-Kozhikode, MDI-Gurgaon, IITM-Gwalior, JNTU-Hyderabad etc. She has contributed papers in 20 international conferences and several national conferences. She has 30 publications to her credit in reputed international and national journals. Her areas of interest are Marketing and HRM.

Ayşegül Sağkaya Güngör has a PhD degree on marketing. Her particular area of interest is new technologies in marketing. Online social networks, advergames, consumer acceptance of technology, and e-commerce are in her particular interests. Currently she is lecturing in various universities on the subjects of e-commerce, e-business, digital marketing and marketing management.

Raiswa Saha is a PhD Research Scholar at SRM University, Sonepat, Haryana. She has earned M.B.A. in Marketing domain from West Bengal State University, with a throughout 1st division. Her current area of research includes CSR, Leadership and Green Marketing, etc. She has published more than 10 articles in different journals.

Pooja Saigal earned her PhD in Computer Science (Machine Learning) from South Asian University, India. She received her MCA degree from GGSIP University in 2004 and BCA degree from Maharishi Dayanand University, in 2001. Her research interests include machine learning, pattern recognition, image retrieval and image segmentation. She is awarded gold medal by the Hon'ble President of India for securing first position in University in MCA, 2004. She has published 10 papers in refereed international journals and international conferences.

Savita Sharma is working as an Assistant Professor at Ansal University and has 14 years of experience. She has done her PhD on the topic "Impact of Corporate Social Responsibility Practices on Employees and Customers of Luxury Chain Hotels in India & its Effect on Corporate Performance". She has done her Masters in Tourism Management and Graduation in Hotel Management. Her areas of interest are customer satisfaction and general management. She is a Certified Hospitality Education (CHE) by AMerican Hotel and Lodging Educational Institute.

Pratibha Kumari Singh is a Gold Medalist in MA English from Banasthali Vidyapith, Rajasthan, is pursuing her PhD in Stylistics from Ansal University, Gurugram. With more than 10 years of experience in the field of teaching, she has to her credit national and international publication in reputed journals and paper presentation in seminars and conferences.

Saumya Singh, a management expert, is presently working as Associate Professor in the Department of Management Studies, IIT (ISM), Dhanbad. Dr. Singh holds a doctorate in Management after completing her MBA. She has several years of academic and industrial experience. As a teacher, trainer and researcher, she has contributed several research and popular articles apart from conducting corporate training for several leading industries. As a prolific writer she has contributed articles to national, international journals and many main line dailies. Her current research interest includes Strategic Management, Corporate Culture, Macroeconomic Issues and Consumer Behaviour.

Vijita Singh Aggarwal is a Professor at the University School of Management studies, GGS Indraprastha University, Delhi. She has pursued the European Masters in Lifelong learning-Policy and Management from the Institute of Education, University of London and University of Deusto Bilbao Spain, and another Master's Programme from London School of Economics on Globalisation Gender and development.

Adarsh Somani is a student at New Delhi Institute of Management and is pursuing his PGDM in Marketing & Finance. He is a brilliant scholar and displays great research and inquisitiveness at this young age.

Anoop Kumar Srivastava after completing Post P.G.Diploma in Radiological Physics, BARC, Mumbai, Joined the field of Medical physics and now with more than 14 years of experience in the field of Clinical Medical Physics and Radiobiology. Presently working as Associate Professor (Medical Physics), Dept. of Radiation Oncology, Dr. Ram Manohar Lohia Institute of Medical Sciences, Lucknow. Before joining the present institution he has contributed to the specialty at HIHT Dehradun and Kamala Nehru Memorial Hospital, Allahabad. Co-guides to Ph.D thesis and having number of publication in indexed journals, he has attended various national and international conferences and has membership of Association of Medical Physicists of India (AMPI).

Index

A

B

C

D

E

F

G

H

I

L

M

N

O

P

R

S

T

V

Y

www.ingramcontent.com/pod-product-compliance
Lightning Source LLC
LaVergne TN
LVHW061547290926
849162LV00004B/935